Edit without Tears with Final Cut Pro

Elevate your video editing skills with
professional workflows and techniques

Bruce G. Macbryde

Edit without Tears with Final Cut Pro

Group Product Manager: Rohit Rajkumar

Publishing Product Manager: Nitin Nainani

Book Project Manager: Sonam Pandey

Senior Editor: Rakhi Patel

Technical Editor: Simran Udasi

Copy Editor: Safis Editing

Language Support Editor: Safis Editing

Proofreader: Safis Editing

Indexer: Subalakshmi Govindhan

Production Designer: Prashant Ghare

DevRel Marketing Coordinators: Anamika Singh and Nivedita Pandey

First published: March 2024

Production reference: 1140224

Published by Packt Publishing Ltd.

Grosvenor House

11 St Paul's Square

Birmingham

B3 1RB, UK.

ISBN 978-1-80461-492-1

www.packtpub.com

This book is dedicated to my wife, Sandra. I also would like to thank all my friends who have been subjected to my incessant chatter about my research for the book. A special thanks to Elizabeth and Mark for the use of their stylish wedding video footage.

– Bruce G. Macbryde

Contributors

About the author

Bruce G. Macbryde is an independent trainer for Final Cut Pro with over 20 years of experience, from the original release of the legacy version of the software in 1999 through to the update to Final Cut Pro X in 2011, and now the current version, 10.7. Bruce gained a marketing certificate from TAFE NSW in 1984. After receiving this qualification, he was employed by TAFE as a tutor of marketing and marketing research courses for several years. He was a contributor to articles in *Australian Computing* magazine while working as an importer of IT at the time of the introduction of the Macintosh to Australia, in 1984. During a seven-year spell in Wellington, New Zealand, he established ECONET, an official Apple reseller, while also teaching courses in Adobe Photoshop, PageMaker, Illustrator, and commercial Microsoft software packages within the New Zealand polytechnic system. On his return to Sydney, he was employed as NSW sales manager for the Australian Authorized Apple distributors, from 1998 to 2004. He was later employed by Apple-authorized resellers as a training manager for Final Cut Pro and other Apple-developed software from 2004 to 2009. In 2004, he established Wedding Media Productions as a wedding video business in Sydney, Australia. He is a YouTube creator on his VideoTutors channel, with over 500 published video tutorials.

About the reviewer

Ravin Apte is a seasoned video editing and post-production trainer with an impressive three decades of experience in educational TV program production. As an Apple-certified trainer for FCP X and a DaVinci Resolve 18-certified trainer, Ravin brings a unique blend of technical expertise and creative insight to his teaching approach. His proficiency extends to training both undergraduate and postgraduate students at leading media training institutes.

Ravin has made significant contributions to the educational field as a cameraman for numerous national and international award-winning educational TV programs. Ravin invented a computer-controllable lighting system for TV studios, a groundbreaking achievement that earned him an Indian patent in 1995.

Table of Contents

Preface   xv

Prologue   xxi

Part 1: Planning

1

It's All about the Media   3

Technical requirements	4	Video formats	19
The Users folder	4	LOG video	22
The definition of a video file	7	The HDR format	25
Aspect ratio	7	RAW video	25
Bit rate	8	Interlaced video	26
Bit depth	8	ProRes	26
Resolution	8	H.264/H.265	27
Where Final Cut Pro libraries are stored	9	Which video format is best for which purpose?	29
Why use an external disk for libraries?	9	Audio formats	30
Camera footage	12	Second monitors	30
Photos/stills	13	Having different windows on each display	32
Music	14	Types of disks	33
The library concept	15	How much storage is enough?	35
The plug-in folders	17	Summary	35

2

Organizing Media   37

Understanding libraries and events   38   Colored lines on browser clips   59
When and why to log clips   42   Analyzing for people   60
Favorites   42   Markers   61
The rating as a favorite method   42   Removing media from categories   63
The adding to favorites method   44   Browser filters   63
How to use Favorites   44   The filters   64

Understanding Keyword Collections   45   Sorting the browser   64
Creating Keyword Collections   45   The Open Clip view   69
Adding shortcuts to Keyword Collections   47   Using the Open Clip function   70

Smart Collections   49   Shortcuts for media actions   71
What is a Smart Collection?   50   Transcoding media   72
Adding a Smart Collection   50
                                            Exploring clip and library
What are folders?   52   information   74
Templates   53   A method of exploring clip information   75
Creating templates   53
                                            Exploring Settings/Preferences   76
Using the Search functionality   54   Summary   81
Filtering method 1   55

3

Planning the Video Story   83

A story is a journey   84   Planning for different types of videos   91
What are the types of stories?   84   Documentary videos   91
Why classify stories?   85   Interviews   91
What are the types of plots?   86   Wedding videos   93
                                            Social media videos   94
What you should remember when   Instructional videos   98
planning a story   87
Knowing your target audience   87   Summary   100
Planning the edit with the target audience
in mind   89
Creating storyboards   90

4

Pre-Editing a Rough Cut   101

**The steps from importing
to rough cut**   102
Steps in video post-production   102
Who does what?   103
The browser or the timeline   103
Initial assembly or rough cut   103

Ingesting the media   104
Setting up media folders in the Finder   104
Importing media directly   107

Logging   108
Categorizing the clips   109
Grading the clips   109

What are projects?   115

Adding clips to the project   116
Connected clips   116
Three-point edits   118

The timeline   118
The skimmer and playhead   120
Timecode   122
The timeline index   123
Roles   123

The initial assembly   127
Assembling audio- or image-focused videos   129
Don't over-edit!   129

The rough cut   130
Adding scratch music   130
Placeholders   131
Alternatives to placeholders   132
Duplicating projects   133

Summary   134

Part 2: Editing

5

Refining the Rough Cut   139

**Understanding the remove, replace,
and add actions**   140
Using the to-do marker   140
Using the audition feature to replace clips 142

**Understanding the timeline
view tools**   145
Ripple edits   146
Roll edits   149

Slip edits   150
Slide edits   150

What is pacing?   151
Consider these conventions   151
Tools that aid pacing   152

**What is the Total Running Time
(TRT)/picture lock?**   156
Summary   156

6

Fixing and Enhancing the Audio   157

Understanding audio in the browser	158	Suggestions for correcting audio	178
Reading the audio meters	161	Settings for the audio meters	178
		Simple methods to increase low volume	179
Audio in the timeline	162	Loop playback	179
Sub-frame audio fine-tuning	163	Removing room noise	180
Audio filters	165	Removing high and low frequencies	180
Expanded audio	166	Sweetening male and female voices	181
		Reducing the music	183
Fixing audio vocal problems	170		
Ambient background noise	171	Using XML files	184
Voices with variable volume levels	172	Exporting with audio-only roles	185
Wind noise	175	Audio tips and tricks	186
Echoes	176	Summary	188
Distorted voices	177		
Ums and ahs, coughs, and sniffs	177		

7

Titles, Effects, and Generators   189

What are titles?	190	Effects categories	201
Animated titles	191	What are transitions?	202
		Two categories of transition	202
Adding text to a title	194		
What are generators?	196	What are Plug-ins?	203
Backgrounds	196	Problems with Plug-ins	203
Elements	197		
Solids and textures	199	Summary	204
What are effects?	199		

8

Setting Up and Editing Multicam   205

What is multicam?	206	How multiple cameras are synchronized	208
What events use multiple cameras?	206		

Suggestions for filming to suit multicam editing — 210

Audio — 211

The two-minute rule — 211

Color balance — 211

Settings before multicam editing — 211

Importing and categorizing media — 211

Creating a new multicam clip — 215

Manual multicam synchronization — 216

Multicam angle timeline adjustments — 217

Fixing audio and video mismatches — 219

Adjusting the angle viewer — 220

Actions in the multicam angle timeline — 224

Audio synchronization — 224

Global adjustments — 225

Audio levels — 225

Color matching — 226

Editing the multicam project — 226

Setting up angles — 228

Switching angles — 230

Correcting the angle — 230

Stabilization — 232

Multicam audio — 234

Simulating a multicam shoot from one camera's footage — 234

Summary — 235

9

Project Workflows – Pace and Structure — 237

Interviews — 238

Pre-editing — 238

Cutting — 241

Restoring removed clips — 243

Hiding jump cuts — 246

Removing fillers — 252

Audio in sync — 255

Conferences and seminars — 257

One long event — 257

Short, independent videos — 258

Weddings — 259

Organizing media — 259

Synchronizing cameras — 263

Full-length movies and documentaries — 264

Pacing — 264

Continuity editing — 265

Parallel editing (cross-cutting) — 266

J and L cuts — 266

Social media videos — 267

Family holiday movies — 268

Cutting to a beat — 272

General techniques — 275

Cutting angles with a green screen — 275

Adding adjustment layers — 279

Storing callouts — 281

Storing titles and corporate intros — 282

Using workspaces — 285

Collapsing clips into connected storylines — 288

Summary — 290

Part 3: Using the Inspector

10

The Inspector Controls   295

The four main tabs of the inspector	296	Effects	320
The Video inspector	299	Audio Configuration	320
Section 1 – Effects	299	Save Audio Effects Preset	321
Section 2 – Transform	301	**The Information inspector**	**323**
Sections 3 and 4 – Crop and Distort	302	Project information	325
Sections 5 and 6 – Stabilization and Rolling Shutter	304	Library information	326
		Export information	327
Section 7 – Spatial Conform	306	**The Titles inspector**	**327**
The Color inspector	307	**The Text inspector**	**329**
Color Board	309	Text division	330
Color Wheels	313	Position division	331
		The Face checkbox	332
The Audio inspector	315	**The Generator inspector**	**333**
Audio Enhancements	316	**The Transition inspector**	**334**
Audio Analysis	317	Summary	336
Pan	319		

11

Using Built-In Plug-Ins   337

An explanation of plug-in terminology	337	Using built-in effects	362
		Using built-in transitions	373
Plug-ins – general knowledge	339	**Creating custom plug-ins from built-in plug-ins**	**377**
Built-in plug-ins	341		
Using built-in titles	341	**Summary**	**377**
Using built-in generators	356		

12

Using Third-Party Plug-Ins   379

Free plug-ins   380   Audio correction plug-ins   400
Andy's plug-ins   380   Eric Lenz   404
BretFX Power Tools Lite   381   Captionator   406

Purchasable plug-ins   383   **Workflow extensions**   407
Lock & Load Stabilize   383   **LUTs**   408
PaintX   386   **Uninstalling plug-ins**   410
Keyper   388   Manually uninstalling plug-ins   410
Neat Video noise reduction   389   **Summary**   411
Titles plug-ins   392

13

Using Keyframes to Animate Objects in Final Cut Pro   413

What is a keyframe?   414   Selecting linear or smooth curves   426
Audio keyframing   416   **Viewer keyframe controls**   428
Keyframing in the inspector   419   **Keyframing video animation**   429
Keyframe conventions   420   **Ken Burns on steroids**   430
Keyframing in the viewer   425   **Summary**   433
Adding new keyframes   425

14

Understanding the Principles of Color   435

Color theory   436   Highlights wheel   450
Color classification   437   **Color harmony**   451
Color values   443   Common color schemes   451
The color wheel   443   Color schemes for non-designers 456
Color wheels in Final Cut Pro   444   Online color calculators   457
Color Board   446   **Monitoring color accuracy**   458
Color wheels   449   Color-accurate monitors   458

Monitor calibration   458

Color correction and grading   461

Adjusting temperature, tint, and hue   461

Subtractive model of color mixing
(CMYK model)   463

Using HSL tuning for color grading   466

Automatic color correction controls in Final
Cut Pro   468

Summary   471

15

Using Color Scopes for Advanced Color Correction   473

Displaying the scopes   474

Waveformmonitor   476

Vectorscope   478

Histogram   479

The Video Scope menu   481

Scopes workflow in Final Cut Pro   482

Step 1 – exposure correction   482

Step 2 – saturation control   485

Step 3 – color balance   487

Color curves   489

Luma curve   489

All color curves – RGB   493

The eyedropper   494

Hue and saturation curves   496

HUE vs HUE   498

HUE vs SAT   499

HUE vs LUMA   500

LUMA vs SAT   500

SAT vs SAT   501

ORANGE vs SAT   501

Color and shape masks   502

Summary   505

Part 4: Outside Final Cut Pro

16

Your Job Role – Collaboration   509

Understanding the job roles in video
production   509

The production team   510

The postproduction editing team   511

Exploring the industries that require
video editors   512

Corporate   512

Social media   512

Movies and TV   513

Documentary   513

Commercials   513

Trailers   514

Should you be a freelancer?   514

How much work from a client   514

Type of work   515

The schedule   515

Balancing time   515

Intensity of work   515

Financial reward   515
The risk/comfort factor   515

**Collaboration between remote
video editors   516**
Sending proxy and XML files   517
Collaborating at the same premises   523

Collaborating on Dropbox   525
Collaborating with LucidLink   528
VPN access to a centralized local server   533
Using SNS EVO with Final Cut Pro   533
Collaboration software   535

Summary   549

17

Supporting Software Applications for Final Cut Pro — 551

**Apple applications that support
Final Cut Pro   552**
Motion 5   552
Compressor   570
QuickTime   578
Preview   582
Keynote   585
iTunes and Photos   586

**Non-Apple applications that
support Final Cut Pro   588**
Final Cut Library Manager   588
CommandPost   589
VLC   590
Handbrake   591
Audacity   591
Pixelmator Pro   593
Miscellaneous applications   594

Summary   594

18

Troubleshooting Final Cut Pro — 597

Updating macOS and Final Cut Pro   598
The spinning beach ball   601

Fixing problems   601
The easy fixes   603
Quitting Final Cut Pro and restarting the
computer   603
Deleting the render files   603
Resetting your Final Cut Pro preferences   606
Copying to a new project   608

The harder fixes   609
Fixing a faulty effect, transition, or title   610

Locating a corruption   612
Clearing export error messages   616
A Final Cut Pro library won't open   623
Trying another user account   624
Trying the library on another computer   625
Reinstalling Final Cut Pro   626
Booting into recovery mode   628

Relinking missing media   629
Consolidating media   633

Final Cut Pro quitting unexpectedly   635
Summary   636

19

Backing Up and Archiving Libraries   637

Working with Final Cut Pro backups 638

Preparing to archive a library 642

Consolidation   642
Motion Content   647
Cache   647
Relinking   647
Deleting render data   651
Further reducing the library size   653

Archiving the library   656
Indexing archives   657
Final Cut Library Manager   657
NeoFinder   658

Maintaining archive devices   658
Summary   659

Index   661

Other Books You May Enjoy   676

Preface

This book is about Apple's Video editing application, Final Cut Pro, and is current for version 10.7 of the software. Final Cut Pro is unique among the leading non-linear editing applications in employing a magnetic timeline that ensures the fastest editing experience. The software is also at the leading edge of collaboration with the Mac operating system, particularly offering the fastest rendering and export times, working together with Apple silicon chips.

Special attention has been paid to ensuring that this book is as up-to-date as possible at the time of publication, including new features that became available with the 10.7 release of Final Cut Pro, such as the scrolling timeline, more efficient **Roles** functionality, and updated object tracking.

The book is broken into four parts to follow the logical order of how an editor will approach the creation of a video. Firstly, by progressing the original idea in the **Planning** process, then the cutting operation in **Editing**. The procedure continues by adjusting **Color**, **Audio**, and **Effects** when using the Inspector. Finally, looking outside Final Cut Pro with the use of supporting software and methods of collaboration with other editors.

Who this book is for

The book is aimed at intermediate-level Final Cut Pro editors who are familiar with Final Cut Pro and are looking to speed up their workflow while gaining more knowledge to produce higher-quality videos more efficiently.

You will be numbered among creative professionals, freelance video editors, YouTube content creators, graphic designers, and especially production houses. You will be looking to produce output for professional-level publications for dramas, documentaries, product commercials, and promo videos, as well as for vlogs for social media. You need to have a macOS operating system to use Final Cut Pro. You should also have an understanding that editing is removing material, leaving just that which is necessary to tell the story.

What this book covers

Chapter 1, *It's All About the Media*, covers media formats where media is stored on a Mac computer so that it can be easily accessed if Final Cut Pro loses connection to the media.

Chapter 2, *Organizing Media*, looks at the paramount importance of knowing where to quickly access media. When an actual edit is progressing, it is important to know how to access extra media quickly without breaking the creative flow of the editing process.

Chapter 3, Planning the Video Story, covers planning – just as you need to plan a journey (otherwise, you won't know where you are going), a video requires similar planning to produce a structure for the clips that tell the story.

Chapter 4, Pre-Editing a Rough Cut, addresses the first step – removing unwanted footage. The pre-edit assembles the media into a coherent list of clips ready for the rough cut.

Chapter 5, Refining the Rough Cut, deals with taking the clips from the pre-edit stage to near final assembly by filling gaps left out of the pre-edit. The length of the clips is adjusted to allow for the pace of the final edit.

Chapter 6, Fixing and Enhancing the Audio, looks into fixing and enhancing audio. Audio is more important than the video itself – your audience will put up with substandard video much longer than bad audio. The ear is much more discerning than the eye.

Chapter 7, Titles, Effects, and Generators, looks at the modification of titles to suit your projects. Some titles are provided with the software and others can be purchased. The use of effects and generators adds extra flair to assembled clips to give them character.

Chapter 8, Setting Up and Editing Multicam, explores multicam, which offers the ability to combine the footage from multiple cameras to be edited as a single video stream.

Chapter 9, Project Workflows – Pace and Structure, delves into how workflows assist with the speed and ease of edits that are of a similar nature. The use of templates, duplication, and compound clips speeds up the editing of similar material.

Chapter 10, The Inspector Controls, looks at how the Inspector is the key to defining the look of the edit. If things can be adjusted, the Inspector is the place to go.

Chapter 11, Using Built-In Plug-Ins, explores the use of the Titles, Effects, and Generator plug-ins supplied with Final Cut Pro.

Chapter 12, Using Third-Party Plug-Ins, looks at third-party plug-ins. There are thousands of plug-ins offered by a multitude of developers. Some are useful, some are important, and some are just fluff.

Chapter 13, Using Keyframes to Animate Objects in Final Cut Pro, tackles the animation of clips with keyframes to move an image within the screen.

Chapter 14, Understanding the Principles of Color, looks at color – integral to how light is seen.

Chapter 15, Using Color Scopes for Advanced Color Correction, explores how to view color as a graph or waveform to match standards, and not just trust your eye to judge what is on your screen.

Chapter 16, Your Job Role – Collaboration, looks at how your job role will define the style of video you create and work with other editors.

Chapter 17, Supporting Software Applications for Final Cut Pro, introduces apps that will assist you with how you use Final Cut Pro.

Chapter 18, Troubleshooting Final Cut Pro, offers a defined workflow to solve issues that can occur when Final Cut Pro encounters problems.

Chapter 19, Backing Up and Archiving Libraries, explores procedures to back up and archive projects and original footage when the edit is completed.

To get the most out of this book

As this book is aimed at intermediate editors, there is a certain amount of basic knowledge of macOS, video editing, and the use of Final Cut Pro that's assumed. If you have not previously used a Mac or Final Cut Pro, you may need to review *Final Cut Pro, Efficient Editing, Second Edition* by *Iain Anderson* first.

Software/hardware covered in the book	Operating system requirements
Final Cut Pro 10.7	macOS Sonoma or later
LucidLink v2.5	
SNS (Studio Network Solutions) EVO	
PostLab 22.1.11	
Motion 5.6.7	
Quicktime 10.5	
Compressor 4.6.6	
Preview 11.0	
Keynote 13.2	
Photos 9.0	
Music (iTunes) 1.4.1.29	
Final Cut Library Manager 3.97	
CommandPost 1.4.22	
VLC 3.0	
HandBrake 1.6.1	
Audacity 3.0	
Pixelmator Pro 3.4.3	

Please refer to the eBook copy of the book for color images.

Conventions used

There are a number of text conventions used throughout this book.

`Code in text`: Indicates code words in text, database table names, folder names, filenames, file extensions, pathnames, dummy URLs, user input, and Twitter handles. Here is an example: "As an example, if you type `clip`, all the media that includes the word `clip` in the name will be filtered and displayed in the browser window."

Bold: Indicates a new term, an important word, or words that you see onscreen. For instance, words in menus or dialog boxes appear in **bold**. Here is an example: "Select the **Event** tab you want to add to, then from the **File** menu, select **New | Smart Collection**."

> **Tips or important notes**
> Appear like this.

Get in touch

Feedback from our readers is always welcome.

General feedback: If you have questions about any aspect of this book, email us at `customercare@packtpub.com` and mention the book title in the subject of your message.

Errata: Although we have taken every care to ensure the accuracy of our content, mistakes do happen. If you have found a mistake in this book, we would be grateful if you would report this to us. Please visit `www.packtpub.com/support/errata` and fill in the form.

Piracy: If you come across any illegal copies of our works in any form on the internet, we would be grateful if you would provide us with the location address or website name. Please contact us at `copyright@packt.com` with a link to the material.

If you are interested in becoming an author: If there is a topic that you have expertise in and you are interested in either writing or contributing to a book, please visit `authors.packtpub.com`

Share Your Thoughts

Once you've read *Edit without Tears with Final Cut Pro*, we'd love to hear your thoughts! Scan the QR code below to go straight to the Amazon review page for this book and share your feedback.

https://packt.link/r/1804614920

Your review is important to us and the tech community and will help us make sure we're delivering excellent quality content.

Download a free PDF copy of this book

Thanks for purchasing this book!

Do you like to read on the go but are unable to carry your print books everywhere?

Is your eBook purchase not compatible with the device of your choice?

Don't worry, now with every Packt book you get a DRM-free PDF version of that book at no cost.

Read anywhere, any place, on any device. Search, copy, and paste code from your favorite technical books directly into your application.

The perks don't stop there, you can get exclusive access to discounts, newsletters, and great free content in your inbox daily

Follow these simple steps to get the benefits:

1. Scan the QR code or visit the link below

https://packt.link/free-ebook/978-1-80461-492-1

2. Submit your proof of purchase
3. That's it! We'll send your free PDF and other benefits to your email directly

Prologue

Film and video editing may be your chosen profession, but more importantly, you could find that it is your passion, and you will be cognizant of this when you can't stay away from the editing suite. Even to the point that you are tempted to miss family gatherings and festive events.

If the above sounds like you, then welcome to the club – this book is truly for you.

No matter what **Non-Linear Editing** (**NLE**) software you use, you will be a die-hard convert to film and video editing. This book is about Final Cut Pro and since you are a professional, you need to be familiar with different NLE software, as work can come from various sources and different editing houses will demand that you are familiar with their preferred NLE software.

So, no matter whether you are an out-and-out Final Cut Pro-only user or work with other NLE software such as Avid, Resolve, or Premiere, you need to know how to edit in Final Cut Pro without tears.

Who this book is for

This book is aimed at intermediate-level Final Cut Pro editors familiar with Final Cut Pro and looking to speed up their workflows while gaining more knowledge to produce higher-quality videos more efficiently.

Numbered among creative professionals, freelance video editors, YouTube content creators, graphic designers, and especially production houses, you will be looking to produce output for professional-level publications, dramas, documentaries, product commercials, and promo videos, as well as for vlogs for social media. You need to have a macOS operating system to use Final Cut Pro, and an understanding that editing is removing material, just leaving that which is necessary to tell the story.

You need to be familiar with the basic concepts of video editing, particularly having an understanding of the principle that editing is removing unwanted material rather than just adding bells and whistles. You should also have an understanding of media formats and how and where macOS stores files.

Editors who have learned Final Cut Pro by self-taught osmosis will be enlightened by the easy-to-understand principles of efficient workflows that this book introduces. This book will help anyone who feels confused by the terminology used by Final Cut Pro and is mostly only using a part of the program's functionality because of a fear of getting it wrong when attempting to use more efficient methods.

You will have the classic tug-of-war between the left-brain demand for logical thinking as opposed to the right-brain desire for creativity and will be looking for practical ways to employ both skills for perfect video production. You will have experienced the normal challenge of knowing where to start. This book provides workflow processes that will provide that leg up.

The book provides unique workflows for a wide range of common procedures, needed to produce a well-paced video.

The communication of efficient workflows is a major objective of this book. It will change how you approach the editing process, from a piecemeal approach to a structured way of working, with the benefit of knowing exactly what is happening and why.

By the end of this book, you will be a more efficient editor, editing faster than you did before reading the book. You will adapt the way you use Final Cut Pro to suit your job role.

What this book covers

This is a list of the chapters in the book and a short explanation of what you will learn in each chapter:

Part 1: Planning

Chapter 1, It's All About the Media

This chapter should be used as a reference to understand the makeup of video files and where they are located on the computer.

Chapter 2, Organizing Media

Knowing where to access media quickly is paramount. In this chapter, you will learn that while the actual edit is progressing, it is important to know how to access extra media quickly without breaking the creative flow of the editing process.

Chapter 3, Planning the Video Story

As an editor, you will need to plan a journey. Otherwise, the outcome is unlikely to be controlled. A video requires planning, as does a literary composition, to produce a structure for the clips to tell the story.

Chapter 4, Pre-Editing a Rough Cut

This chapter shows that removing unwanted media is the first step. The pre-edit assembly gathers the best media into a coherent list of clips ready for the rough cut. It involves labeling scenes, and rating clips.

Part 2: Editing

Chapter 5, Refining the Rough Cut

The rough cut takes the clips from the pre-edit stage to the near-final flow of clips by adjusting the pre-edit for the story to make more sense. The length of the clips is refined to allow for the pace of the final edit.

Chapter 6, Fixing and Enhancing the Audio

This chapter will teach how audio is more important than the video itself. The audience will put up with substandard video much longer than bad audio. The ear is much more discerning than the eye.

Chapter 7, Titles, Effects and Generators

Some titles are provided with the software, others can be purchased. They all can be modified to suit different purposes. The use of plug-ins adds extra flair to the assembled clips to give them a distinctive character.

Chapter 8, Setting Up and Editing a Multicam Edit

In this chapter, you will learn how to manage multicam edits, which offer the ability to combine the footage from multiple cameras so they can be edited as a single video stream and switched for the different camera angles to be added to the edit.

Chapter 9, Project Workflows – Pace and Structure

This chapter shows three examples of workflows that will assist in the speed and ease of edits similar in nature. It will also cover how the use of templates, duplication, and compound clips speeds up the editing process.

Part 3: Using the Inspector

Chapter 10, The Inspector Controls

This chapter demonstrates that the Inspector is the key to defining the look of the edit. If things can be adjusted, the Inspector is the place to go to open the door to a Pandora's box of effects.

Chapter 11, Using Built-In Plug-Ins

This chapter explores the use of the Titles, Effects, and Generator plugins supplied with Final Cut Pro.

Chapter 12, Using Third-Party Plug-Ins

In this chapter, you will learn that there are thousands of plug-ins offered by a multitude of developers. Some are useful, some are important, and some are just fluff. The chapter shows the ones most needed and some that are just nice to have.

Chapter 13, Using Keyframes to Animate Objects

This chapter shows how clips can be animated to pan as background clips to retain a position onscreen as well as being animated to move within the screen. Keyframes are used for animation as well as advanced techniques to improve on the Ken Burns effect.

Chapter 14, Understanding the Principles of Color

This chapter discusses how color is integral to the way that light is seen. Color is made up of three properties: hue, value, and intensity.

Chapter 15, Using the Color Scopes for Advanced Color Correction

In this chapter, you will learn how color scopes allow colors to be visualized with graphs and waveform. This gives you the ability to match standards and not just trust the eye to judge what is on the screen.

Part 4: Outside of Final Cut Pro

Chapter 16, Your Job Role – Collaboration with Others

This chapter looks at the different types of job roles and which style of video is best for you to concentrate on. The chapter also outlines how different methods of collaboration can assist performance by working with other editors.

Chapter 17, Supporting Software Applications for Final Cut Pro

This chapter provides information on applications, both built-in Apple apps and others, available to download for free. There is a list of a number of paid apps that will assist in the usability of Final Cut Pro.

Chapter 18, Troubleshooting Final Cut Pro

This chapter concentrates on solving the main issues that a user will encounter. There is a defined workflow to solve issues that can occur when Final Cut Pro experiences problems. The workflow is a series of steps that need to be actioned in a set order.

Chapter 19, Backing up and Archiving Libraries

The saying "*The Job isn't done until the paperwork is completed*" is rephrased in this chapter to show that when the edit is completed, there are procedures to back up and archive projects along with the original footage.

 In my mind, there is no such thing as an expert when it comes to computer technology. There are those who know a little and those who know quite a bit more, but it's unlikely there is anyone who knows everything. My philosophy when it comes to passing on my knowledge of Final Cut Pro comes down to the way that the information is presented and how it is explained with down-to-earth examples. Hence my motto, borrowed from Albert Einstein: *If you can't explain it to a six-year-old, you don't know it yourself.*

This book is for editors at an intermediate level and explains how to take your Final Cut Pro editing to the next level. The content is not just about Final Cut Pro; as noted above, it will also be of real value to users of other NLE software. An added benefit of this book is upscaling your knowledge of film and video editing in general. Throughout the book, I will refer to and explain editing terminologies and methodologies.

These explanations of methodology will be particularly perceptible in *Chapters 3, 4, 5*, and *6* as these loosely come under the topic of cinematography.

Cinematography is simply visual storytelling. It encompasses all the historical arts of storytelling techniques of songs, plays, and folk tales, developing into books, and in today's world, where images are key, it embraces film and video.

In the broadest terms, cinematography, according to Encyclopedia Britannica, is "the art and technology of motion-picture photography. It involves such techniques as the general composition of a scene; the lighting of the set or location; the choice of cameras, lenses, filters, and film stock; the camera angle and movements; and the integration of any special effects."

The creation of footage is beyond the scope of this book, but it deals with how to combine images created by the camera and relate them to each other.

A video incorporates a succession of still images, and these are called frames. They are played back so quickly that we see them as one continuous moving picture. This group of frames is known as a clip. The speed of the playback is expressed as **frames per second (fps)**. The relationship between the clips is the key to editing. Clips are placed next to each other on purpose so that they shape the story. This is where Final Cut Pro's magnetic timeline achieves distinction.

With the magnetic timeline, the B-roll is connected to the clip in the main timeline, so stays related to the main timeline clip throughout the edit, rather than moving down the timeline as it would in track-based NLE software. I will explain this in detail in *Chapter 5, Refining the Rough Cut.*

A video is not just visual. Audio is an integral part of any video. Audio is more important to retaining an audience's attention than the images themselves. Our ears are more discerning about bad audio than our eyes are about dubious images. We will see more about that in *Chapter 6, Fixing and Enhancing the Audio.*

Editing is a process of removing unwanted clips too. In fact, the definition of "edit" is to cut. Some may think this is easy. That's until you are confronted with some original footage, particularly if you were the cameraperson, who seems just too good to leave out. The real skill is to ruthlessly cut, only leaving the clips that progress the story, no matter how compelling or visual the unnecessary clips are.

A good editor's motto should be *Less is more.*

Once the editor has cut the video to a minimum of clips, it's time to embellish those clips with effects that will color correct, sweeten the audio, or customize the video to give it a unique flavor. *Chapters 10* to *13* will cover these topics.

The most important skill in editing a video is to remain acutely aware of the audience who will be viewing the end result. If you take nothing more away from reading this book, please cement in your mind the personification of who will be viewing the video.

Now that you know what the book is all about, let's get started with the chapters.

Part 1:
Planning

Part 1 covers the initial information needed before the editing process begins, such as video formats and where media is stored on a Mac computer. Part of the planning process is to assemble the media into an organized list, allowing the media to be readily available to the editor in the second part, which focuses on the editing process.

This part has the following chapters:

- *Chapter 1, It's All About the Media*
- *Chapter 2, Organizing Media*
- *Chapter 3, Planning the Video Story*
- *Chapter 4, Pre-Editing a Rough Cut*

1
It's All about the Media

This chapter covers the foundations that Final Cut Pro is built on. In this chapter, we will see how media is stored within libraries and where it can be accessed in the **Finder**. You will be introduced to the library structure, which is the foundation of Final Cut Pro's organizational uniqueness. You will understand the importance of being able to locate and manually install or uninstall plug-ins. Finally, you will gain a thorough understanding of different video formats and how they affect the use of Final Cut Pro. When you have completed this chapter, you will comprehend the individuality of Final Cut Pro's organizational structure and the importance of using the correct video format.

In this chapter, we will cover the following main topics:

- The Users folder
- The definition of a video file
- Where Final Cut Pro libraries are stored
- The library concept
- The plug-in folders
- Video formats
- Audio formats
- Second monitors
- Types of disks

There is no point in knowing all the commands of a software application without knowing how to use them, as well as how they interact with the principles of editing. You will learn about the principles of editing as you progress through this book.

You may feel that this chapter is not essential to get started with your editing in Final Cut Pro, and if that's the case, jump to the next chapter, *Organizing Media*. You can use this chapter as a reference, as you will need the information herein at some time during your editing in Final Cut Pro.

As with any structure, there needs to be foundations to build on.

If you are driving a car, you need to know how it functions. Even just knowing how to fill the fuel tank or open the bonnet is better than not knowing anything about the car's workings, allowing you to be more prepared in an emergency. Even if you don't know the internal workings of a car, you will be a step closer to fixing things in an emergency.

This same principle applies to computer software that you rely on for productivity; just like with a car, there are times in an emergency when you will need to have a basic idea about how it functions.

Technical requirements

The following are the minimum system requirements that you need to be able to run Final Cut Pro 10.6.8:

- macOS 13.4 or later
- 4 GB of RAM (8 GB is recommended for 4K editing, 3D titles, and 360° video editing)
- A Metal-capable graphics card
- 1 GB of VRAM, recommended for 4K editing, 3D titles, and 360° video editing
- 4.5 GB of available disk space

The Users folder

Because Final Cut Pro is produced by Apple, the application files are deeply integrated into macOS, and many parts of the foundations of Final Cut Pro are spread throughout the Mac system.

I'm not suggesting that you need to know completely where everything is, but there are locations that you will need to access on a Mac to make full use of Final Cut Pro.

The Users folder is the most important location for you to know about. It's where most of Final Cut Pro's files are stored – or at least all the files that you need to know about!

Let me give you a little background on how macOS works. All the files that a computer needs are located on the boot disk, which is usually the internal disk – nowadays, that is a **solid-state drive** (SSD).

To find these files, make sure you are looking in the **Finder** window. When **Finder** is selected, the name will appear in the top-left position of the Mac taskbar.

The following screenshot shows the Mac taskbar:

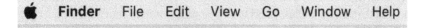

Figure 1.1 – The Mac taskbar

The quickest way to get to **Finder** is to tap the "Happy Mac" icon in the dock:

Figure 1.2 – The Finder logo from the Mac dock

Once you click on **Finder**, select the **GO** menu and then **Computer**.

This will display all of the disks attached to your computer. From these disks, select **Macintosh HD**. There, you will see four folders:

- Applications
- Library
- System
- Users

I would suggest that you treat the Library and System folders as out of bounds. The Applications folder holds all of the applications on the computer. We are only interested in the Users folder, as this is where the Final Cut Pro files are located. As the term implies, this folder contains everything that the computer's users need.

If you open the Users folder, you will find at least two folders. There is one called Shared and one labeled with a *username*. If there are other folders, that means there is more than one user set up on the computer.

When you open the *username* folder, you will find a folder named Movies. The Movies folder is the main folder that is of interest for Final Cut Pro purposes.

Here is the path of the folder for your reference – **Macintosh HD** | Users | YourName | Movies.

When Final Cut Pro is launched for the first time, by default it will create a library named Untitled in the Movies folder. This Untitled library contains an event named after the date it was created. You can rename this Untitled library and the event name in Final Cut Pro.

Among the files and folders, you may see some Final Cut Pro libraries. These libraries have icons, which are four purple squares with a white star in each:

Figure 1.3 – The library icons

By default, Final Cut Pro initially stores its libraries in the Movies folder. However, they don't have to be stored there; they can be moved to other locations. In fact, I strongly suggest that you don't store your Final Cut Pro libraries in this Movies folder. The reason for this will be covered later in this chapter. The convention is to have all Final Cut Pro's libraries located on fast external disks — SSDs by preference – and the Final Cut Pro application on the internal disk – that is, in the Applications folder.

Within the Movies folder, there are two other folders of interest to Final Cut Pro. They are the Final Cut Backups and Motion Templates folders. All the other folders in the Movies folder are not directly related to Final Cut Pro.

The Final Cut Backups folder is where the application automatically backs up all projects at regular intervals. In practice, this is between every five and eight minutes. You don't have any input to the duration, so it's best not to worry about it and let Final Cut Pro look after it for you. You will not notice any system downtime as the backups are processed. Only the editing instructions are backed up, so you always need to have media stored somewhere else. Providing you don't delete the media, Final Cut Pro will keep the project connected to it.

Backups are saved with the time and date in the filename. You can select a backup and restore it to the browser's sidebar in Final Cut Pro by selecting **File** | **Open Library** | **From Backup**.

We will look at how to restore backups in *Chapter 2*.

The Motion Templates folder is where the plug-ins used by Final Cut Pro are located. You will learn more about plug-ins later in the chapter.

As you have seen, the Users folder is where Final Cut Pro locates its support files by default. In the following section, you will be introduced to the different types of files that you will work with in Final Cut Pro.

The definition of a video file

Think of video as being a series of still images with associated audio. Because the images and audio are packaged together, the video file is significantly more complex than a still image or audio file individually.

You will already know the concept of these images moving so fast that they appear to the viewer as moving images. A camera records a set number of **frames per second** (**FPS**) along with masses of metadata.

Since the frame rate is a set number of FPS, when it is increased, the smoothness of the video improves, and any blurriness will likely be removed. The downside is that the file size increases in terms of the storage space on the computer.

Historically, 30 FPS became the norm for analog TV broadcasts in North America, Japan, and South America. Europe and Africa adopted 25 FPS due to the different frequencies in the mains power supply – 60 Hz and 50 Hz, respectively.

There is another important reason that frame rates should be complied with. Because AC power is set at either 60 or 50 Hz, some light bulbs flicker at those rates, which is not noticed by the human eye. The camera will likely see the flicker if you film at 25 FPS in a 60 Hz area. The frame rate is not evenly divided into 60. Conversely, if you filmed at 30 FPS, then it is evenly divided. This is why the general recommendation is to set the camera's shutter speed to match the frame rate.

Cameras are set to record at different frame rates for the following reasons:

- **24 FPS**: This gives a classic cinematic look. This was originally chosen by early movie makers as the best frame rate for sound synchronization while using the least possible amount of film, and it has become the classic standard.
- **25/30 FPS**: This is the frame rate of choice, depending on the NTSC and PAL area.
- **50/60 FPS**: This is better for 4K resolution, as the higher frame rate gives the footage a more detailed and lifelike view and increases the smoothness of the action. Again, this depends on the NTSC and PAL area.
- **120 FPS and above**: This is used where slow motion is required along with fast action.

The following sections will explain the components of a video file.

Aspect ratio

An **aspect ratio** is the size and shape of the outputted video. This is important to consider because it affects how your audience will view the video. The aspect ratio is also critical when you are considering an output for social media, as some platforms prefer vertical or portrait mode videos while others are better suited to square or 16 x 9 aspect ratios.

The aspect ratio is the correlation between the width and the height of the video. An aspect ratio is based on the intended screen size the video will likely be played on. Originally, a video had a ratio of 4:3 – that is, 4 parts wide by 3 parts high, as that was the size of the early TV sets. Now, the frame size is measured in pixels. The principal aspect ratios for video are 16:9, 4:3, 1:1 (square), and 9:16 (vertical portrait mode) for social media. Hollywood films have different aspect ratios, such as 1.85:1 and 2.39:1. Most video projects outside of social media are set at 16:9.

Bit rate

The **bit rate** or data rate is the amount of data transmitted per second, measured in **bits per second** (**bit/s**). The higher the bit rate, the greater the amount of information being transmitted and, generally speaking, the higher the quality of the video signal.

To give an example, the Sony recording format XDCAM EX, in its highest quality mode, has a data rate of 35 **megabits per second** (**mbit/s**), which results in about 50 minutes of video per 16-GB SxS card.

Bit depth

The **bit depth** is the color depth information stored in each pixel of data and determines the number of steps between the minimum and maximum values of a color or grayscale. In an 8-bit RGB image, each pixel has 8 bits of data per color (RGB), so for each color channel, there are 256 possible values. In a 10-bit RGB image, each color channel has 1,024 possible values. A 12-bit video has 4,096 possible values.

ProRes formats, except for ProRes 4444 and 4444 XQ, are 10-bit, with the latter two being 12-bit. AVCHD and H.264 files are 8-bit. HEVC files can be either 8-bit or 10-bit. Low-end cameras tend to shoot in 8-bit images, while professional cameras can shoot at 10-bit or 12-bit.

If a camera has shot in 8-bit, when it's transcoded to a 10-bit codec for editing, the 10-bit file still only has the 8-bit source material. The advantage of transcoding an 8-bit file to a 10-bit one is that the 10-bit codec has more space for any effects that you may want to add to it. Any of the effects or color work that is done within the new 10-bit video will be processed at 10-bit, likely giving a better result to the whole image, even though it's only the color corrections or effects that were processed at 10-bit.

Resolution

Resolution is the number of pixels in a single frame of the video. The higher the resolution, the sharper the image. Resolutions include 480, 720, 1080, and 4K. A low resolution may look good on a small screen, such as a mobile phone, but will be significantly blurred when viewed on a full screen.

Now we know what a video file consists of, it will assist you in recognizing how video files are contained in Final Cut Pro's library structure. It's now time to find out where those libraries are stored.

Where Final Cut Pro libraries are stored

The storage structure that Final Cut Pro uses revolves around a library. To use an analogy, a town's public library contains many books and magazines, DVDs, and other things. The town's library categorizes everything into different sections – for instance, fiction, non-fiction, and sports. Final Cut Pro uses a similar method of categorization to store all of its contents. It uses terms such as **events**, **keywords**, and **smart folders**, which you can give appropriate names so that you have quick access to the contents when you are editing.

A library is a database of all the information required for an edit. It is known as a bundle, which gives you a hint as to its purpose. Libraries contain the media or links to any media stored outside the library. They also store all the metadata and render files, including the projects themselves.

While you are editing, Final Cut Pro libraries keep track of the process of your editing, where the media is categorized, and the rendering of clips.

Think of the library as the top of the hierarchy of everything that's required to edit a video. It simply contains the sum of everything.

You have the choice of where you can store a library when you create a new one. The industry standard is to have Final Cut Pro libraries on external SSDs and not on the computer's internal disk. However, if you don't have any external disk, don't feel that it is inappropriate to have the libraries located on the internal disk.

In the following subsection, we will see the importance of using external disks for libraries.

Why use an external disk for libraries?

The convention to only have a Final Cut Pro application on the drive with the operating system and the Final Cut Pro library with media files and data files on an external disk originates from when hard disks had spinning media, and it was more practical to share the overhead of the physical movements between the drives.

Now, with the commonplace use of SSDs, there is no need to consider the physical limitations of disk heads flying from place to place as they do on spinning disks. SSDs have no moving parts.

The trade-off is that SSDs have a fixed life. Even though they are not susceptible to mechanical failure, other components are vulnerable to malfunctions. The main issue with SSDs is that they have limited read/write cycles. The more reads/writes you make, the quicker the SSD will wear out. The issue here is that every command you make in the Final Cut Pro library will write data to the database, which is the core of Final Cut Pro. This uses the limited read/write cycles on your internal SSD if you have your library on it. You can't replace the internal SSD on an Apple M1 or later computer. It is, however, easy to purchase a new external SSD in the event of a failure.

An important advantage of having your libraries, along with all your data, on an external disk is that you can move from one computer to another and simply connect the external disk to whichever computer you are using at the time. This is ideal if you edit on a MacBook in the field and then come back to the studio and your high-end Mac Studio to complete the edit. It's also a major consideration if you want to move the edit to another editor.

A converse factor to note is the considerably faster speed of the internal SSD in the Apple M series of computers. If you have a Silicon Mac, you may be tempted to take advantage of the internal SSD's speed by storing the Final Cut Pro library on the internal disk. This is tempting indeed but may be not too practical.

The following bullet list shows the differing speeds of common storage devices:

- **Internal SSD on an M-series Mac**: Up to 7,000 Mb/s

- **SSD on Samsung T7**: Approximately 1,050 MB/s

- **SSD on Samsung T5**: Approximately 500 MB/s

- **HDD**: The fastest are up to 140 MB/s

If you do have a Final Cut Pro library on the internal disk, it's not such an issue if you have a 4 TB disk, but you need to be aware that Final Cut Pro libraries can grow substantially with generated media. If your internal disk is 1 TB or less, you will soon fill it when Final Cut Pro is stored on it.

At the end of the day, the speed of a fast SSD will be enough for most purposes, so using the internal SSD to store libraries will not have any real ongoing advantages.

If you collaborate with other editors, shared disks are a practical way of collaboration. With internet speeds improving all the time, shared Final Cut Pro libraries located online in places such as Dropbox are a viable option and will be discussed in detail in *Chapter 19*.

> **Important note**
>
> When connecting an external SSD, make sure you use the Thunderbolt 3-4 port when using Thunderbolt SSDs. Be careful that it's not a USB-C port – the plugs look the same, except the Thunderbolt port has a lightning bolt symbol marked on it.

As mentioned at the beginning of this section, Final Cut Pro puts all of its content into a library by default. The first thing to note is that you can have as many libraries as you like. You have the freedom to decide. However, with freedom comes prudence – don't get too gung-ho, be a bit conservative with the number of libraries, and develop a pattern that suits your workflow. I'll cover this in far more detail with suggestions for different types of editing in *Chapter 2*. Also in *Chapter 2*, we will see how, on creating a new library, you are able to choose what items are contained in the library.

Even if you have already set the storage location and contents for a library, you will be able to view where it is located and modify the settings while you use Final Cut Pro. Follow these steps to modify the library settings:

1. Select the library you want to investigate, and then select the **Inspector** tab at the right of the interface:

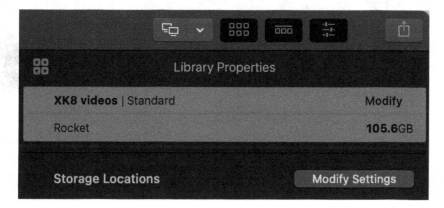

Figure 1.4 – The Inspector window

The library icon looks like this:

Figure 1.5 – The Inspector tab icon

2. Click on the **Modify Settings** option. When you click this option, a pop-up window will appear with a few options. By default, media is stored within the library.

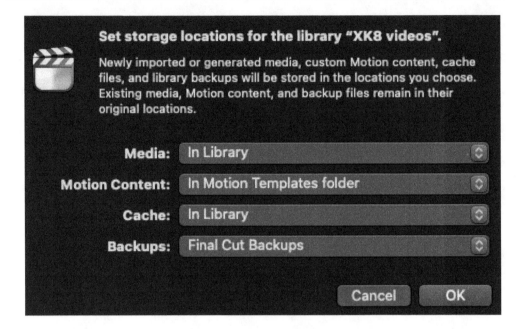

Figure 1.6 – The pop-up window

Cache refers to the render files that Final Cut Pro uses to smooth the editing process.

Incremental backups are stored in the `Final Cut Backups` folder in your `Movies` folder. You can use these options to modify the locations.

3.   To modify where media is stored, click on the blue icon beside the **Media** option and then **Choose**. Then, select a new storage location, and click on **Choose** again.

This is now a perfect place to segue into the following section on how you store and locate your media, including camera footage, music, and photos.

Camera footage

Camera files come in many different formats, and fortunately, most are recognized by Final Cut Pro when they are imported. You will see more details about the different formats and when and where to use them later in this chapter.

When you do proceed to use Final Cut Pro's **Import** window, you can store the camera media in the location of your choice. If you don't use the **Import** window and decide to drag the media into Final Cut Pro, it will use the settings you have entered previously in **Preferences**.

Whether camera files should be part of the Final Cut Pro library or stored independently in different locations outside your library is an important decision. There are implications that can severely affect the amount of storage available on your disks.

Although it's possible to import media from a camera or a camera card, my suggestion is to avoid importing into Final Cut Pro directly from a camera or camera card. Instead, first, copy the camera files directly to your computer by inserting the camera card into an SD card slot on your computer, or by using an external card reader attached to your computer. The first reason for this is that by copying to your computer, you create a backup of the camera files. You are not relying on the card and you are free to reformat it for use in the camera for a different project.

The second reason is that if, for some reason, the files are not fully imported into Final Cut Pro and you then remove the card from your computer, you will see the dreaded red warning message with a camera icon, indicating that the files were not fully imported:

Figure 1.7 – The red warning message

If you do see this message, the only solution is to import the file from scratch again. Even if you insert the card again, Final Cut Pro may not recognize the partially imported file. Just hope you have not reformatted the card!

Once files are on your computer, you can then more speedily import them into Final Cut Pro. At this point, you can decide whether you want the camera media stored as an integral part of the Final Cut Pro library or kept independently on your computer, as mentioned earlier.

Photos/stills

The following screenshot shows options that allow you to select from **photos**, **music**, **titles**, and **generators**:

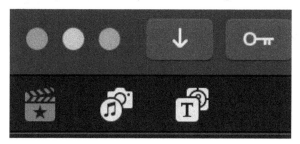

Figure 1.8 – Options to select photos, music, titles, and generators

Because macOS and Final Cut Pro are tightly unified, Final Cut Pro can access the **Photos** app directly if you click on the following icon:

Figure 1.9 – Directly access music and photos

Photos that are not in the Photos app can still be dragged into Final Cut Pro or imported via the **Import** window. Final Cut Pro mostly treats stills as a video clip with just one frame, which can be extended to any length in the timeline. When stills are imported, Final Cut Pro automatically categorizes them in a smart folder called Stills.

The format choice for still images makes a big difference in image quality. If the image is postage stamp size, it is not suitable for video; it can't be resized without pixelization occurring. You need to pass that information to clients when you ask them for their logo. Ask for a PNG of the largest size they can find. Otherwise, a JPG will be OK. Size is what matters, but that said, images can be too large. Final Cut Pro has an upper limit of 4,000 x 4,000 pixels; an image approaching that would slow the whole timeline. If you get an image that is too large, you need to adjust the size. That can simply be done in the default image app on the Mac – **Preview**. You can use any other application too, such as **Photoshop** or **Pixelmator**. It's still always better to ask for the largest size from your client, as you can always reduce the size but you can't increase it.

Something to be aware of is that **dots per inch** (**DPI**) do not matter in video – it's all about the pixels. Still images are usually not at an aspect ratio of 16 x 9 but rather 4 x 3. When a still is added to a project's timeline, Final Cut Pro has a quick solution to fit it into a 16 x 9 window, with the **Fill** option in the **Inspector** window under **Spatial Conform**. It doesn't change the aspect of the still image but fills the screen, hiding content on each side.

PSD (Photoshop) format for images allows layers to be retained and appear in the Final Cut Pro connected tracks. Photoshop and Pixelmator would be the applications of choice for the creation of images with layers in PSD format.

Music

Music is also accessible directly from the **Music** app in the same way as photos from the Photos app. When any audio files are imported, Final Cut Pro automatically categorizes them in a smart folder called Audio.

Music or any audio that is not in the Music app can just be dragged into Final Cut Pro or imported via the **Import** window.

For better playback performance, Final Cut Pro transcodes all MP3 audio files into MOV audio files and retains the original MP3 files for future use. As a general rule, it's best not to use MP3 files with Final Cut Pro. If you have an already compressed audio file, you will compress the audio twice, which leads to lower quality.

Don't be concerned with the issue that MP3 is a smaller file size than WAV. Even in WAV format, audio files are small in comparison to video, so there's no need to worry – just get the best-quality file if you can.

It's best to use `.wav` or `.aiff` for sound effects and music files in your Final Cut Pro projects. This will ensure smooth integration within the application, as well as the highest sound quality. Final Cut Pro prefers audio at a sample rate of 48 kHz, which is within the range of human hearing. There's no need for anything higher than 48 kHz. The higher the sample rate, the bigger the file sizes and the more processing power required.

Now that you understand the importing conventions of Final Cut Pro's media, it is time to discuss the framework of how Final Cut Pro organizes the media, first with the library as the top level and then with an event as the principal subfolder, as you will see in the next section.

The library concept

All Final Cut Pro media, which includes camera footage, music, and stills, is stored in a unique type of folder known as a **library**. Libraries are visible in the Mac's **Finder** window as a purple icon with four white stars, as mentioned earlier in the chapter.

When you double-click on the purple icon, the library opens in Final Cut Pro. It also contains all the files that Final Cut Pro needs to operate, all in one place.

For day-to-day use, there should be no need to access the files contained in the `Library` folder in **Finder**. There are times when you may need to in an emergency; one such occasion would be if you need copies of media files contained in a library.

> **Important note**
> I don't suggest that you access the files contained in the `Library` folder unless you feel confident and know what you are doing.

First, make sure that the library is closed and that you have closed the Final Cut Pro app. Right-click on the *library* icon in **Finder**, which will expose all the files inside when you select **Show Package Contents**:

Figure 1.10 – Show Package Contents

> **A strong word of warning**
>
> Do not move or delete any contents from the Library folder. If you do that, it will cause issues with that library. What you can do is make copies.

When the *library* icon has been clicked, you will see, among other files, a folder named after an event. When you open this event folder, you will see a folder called Original Media. This contains the media being used or an alias to that media located somewhere else. An alias is a signpost to a file that is located elsewhere.

Also inside this event folder, you will find folders named Render Files, Optimized Media, and Proxy Media, provided that they have previously been created for that event. The **Delete Generated Clip Files…** option will empty these folders to save space on your computer.

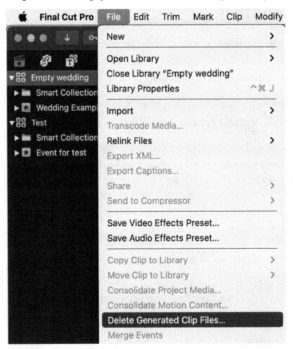

Figure 1.11 – The Delete Generated Clip Files… command

To work successfully in Final Cut Pro, it is essential that you understand the concept of the library and its subfolders, known as Event, Favorites, Keywords, and Smart Collections.

As stated earlier, Final Cut Pro's organizational database revolves around a library. It's a method of categorizing all media into events, keywords, and Smart Collections, to which you can give appropriate names so that you have quick access to the contents when you are editing.

If the library contains all the media, then the event is the sub-directory within the library. It can be confusing as to how to best use events and their own sub-directories – that is, Favorites, Keywords, and Smart Collections. You need to develop an organizational system for your own needs. Perhaps the structure of Library | Event | Keywords can be explained with a further analogy.

Let's take a TV series such as *Grey's Anatomy*. The Final Cut Pro library would represent the whole series, but each weekly episode could be considered an *event*. You can then see that each episode (event) is contained within the series (library). When you add a further set of sub-levels, Favorites, Keywords, and Smart Collections, you start to understand the flexibility that only Final Cut Pro, among all video editing applications, provides to organize and separate your media so that it is quickly available to you when you are editing. This saves an inordinate amount of time and frustration when you are "in the zone" in the middle of an edit.

Now that you have seen how the library in Final Cut Pro is composed, let's look at some other items that are stored in the Users folder, starting with the **plug-ins**.

The plug-in folders

Plug-ins are purchased titles and effects that you will almost certainly be tempted to add to Final Cut Pro. After plug-ins are purchased and downloaded, most of them are supplied with a type of automated installer, but not all. You don't want to be in a situation where a client has specified a particular effect that you can't find out how to add to Final Cut Pro. At times, you may also find yourself in the following situations:

- What will you do when you upgrade macOS and find that an important title used right throughout your project isn't working with the upgrade?

- Where would you look to find a title on the computer's system?

- You may find yourself in a situation where there are some hiccups with Final Cut Pro and you need to access the internal workings on a Saturday night when all your support people are out partying

Don't be stressed about this, as I am exaggerating a little to make a point. This is not something that you will need to do often. However, "be prepared" is a good motto.

At the beginning of this chapter, I showed how to find the Users folder and pointed out the Motion Templates folder – **Macintosh HD** | Users | YourName | Movies | Motion Templates.

This is where Final Cut Pro stores most of the plug-ins that you purchase. The default plug-ins that are supplied with Final Cut Pro are stored in different locations, which are kept from normal view. You can't access the default plug-ins because they are integrated within the application itself.

Some plug-in developers, and CoreMelt and Neat Video are two you may use, tend to store their plug-ins elsewhere. If you can't find a particular plug-in in its usual location, then I suggest you contact the developer should you need to access their plug-ins within **Finder**.

The `Motion Templates` folder has four folders that contain the plug-ins that have been added to Final Cut Pro – `Effects`, `Generators`, `Titles`, and `Transitions`. *Chapter 7* discusses these folders in more detail.

You may be asking why you need to know where the plug-ins are stored. The most common reason will be when you have purchased a new plug-in and you find that the developer did not supply an installer with the purchase.

If there is no installer supplied, these are the steps that will help you to place the new plug-in in the correct location:

1. The plug-in will most likely download to your `Downloads` folder and will more than likely be a ZIP file. When you double-click the ZIP, it will uncompress as a folder with the same name as the ZIP file.

2. The uncompressed folder needs to be inserted into the correct `Motion Templates` folder. If you have purchased a title or a transition, then they are pretty easy to identify. However, effects and generators are not so clear.

There is a foolproof way to check the type of plug-in you have received. When you open a plug-in folder, there will always be a black dog-eared file inside. Select that and press the spacebar. You will see an enlarged version.

The following screenshot shows two images of the dog-eared file icon – inside a plug-in folder and a larger image that appears when the spacebar is pressed.

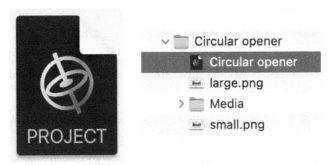

Figure 1.12 – The contents of a plug-in folder

Generators are named *projects*, effects are named *effects*, titles are named *titles*, and transitions are named *transitions*. Drag them into the appropriate folders.

Before you install a plug-in, it is best to quit Final Cut Pro, although it's not necessary if you are in the middle of an important project.

Drag the uncompressed plug-in folder into the appropriate `Motion Templates` folder. If you are working in Final Cut Pro, the new plug-in won't appear immediately, if at all. Try clicking on another folder and then back on the folder where you are expecting the plug-in to appear. You may need to wait, or finally quit and relaunch Final Cut Pro.

Now that you know where plug-ins are located, it's time to look at what formats or codecs can be used by Final Cut Pro.

Video formats

The term **video format** is also loosely interchangeable with **video codec**. There is a difference, but for the sake of simplicity, think of them as the same thing or at least that formats are containers that can hold different codecs.

A container is a package that stores video along with audio data. It is common for a video file format to be referred to as a container. Containers have extensions such as `.mp4`, `.avi`, and `.mov`.

A **codec** is a program or software within the container that encodes and decodes the video signals. It stores the video signals and then processes those signals when a video is played.

A video container can store videos of multiple formats, although not all codecs and containers are perfectly compatible. When a video is recorded or played, a device is configured to choose appropriate codecs and containers by default, so you only need to choose the container/file format.

Uncompressed video files are extremely large, which means they are unwieldy to work with in terms of the amount of space they take up on a storage device, never mind being almost impractical to transfer over the internet. As the term implies, there is no compression applied to the video signal. An uncompressed video that lasts over 20 minutes is enough to fill a 256-GB hard drive.

To overcome the size implications, compression programs were developed, called codecs, to make them easier to store and share. Because of the way these codecs are implemented, it becomes difficult for video editing applications, such as Final Cut Pro, to be able to decipher complex codecs on the fly.

Compression formats fall into two types, **lossy** and **lossless**. As the first term implies, lossy formats remove data from a file, while lossless formats retain all the data so that it can be re-encoded. If you use lossless compression, you do not lose any of the file information. All the information such as color depth, bit depth, pixels, and frame rates is retained. However, in practice, you will not commonly come across true lossless video.

Standard H.264, for instance, is a lossy format, while ProRes 422 and Avid DNxHD are virtually lossless formats. Although not technically lossless, ProRes and Avid DNxHD contain such large amounts of information to manipulate files, making them suitable to even be played on cinema screens.

One of the ways codecs encode data is to compress it, by grouping the parts of each frame that have no change (pixels), ignoring those pixels in the next frame, and then only recording the changes. This technique is called **group of pictures** (**GOP**). A GOP structure usually contains 15 video frames (the length can vary even to one frame). The first image in the group contains all the pixels, and then the following frames only include any variances between the current and surrounding frames. The following group starts with all the pixels and then reiterates the same actions.

The result is that the size of the compressed GOP video is much smaller than the original. Hence, it takes up less storage space and less time to upload/download from the internet. The downside is that compression results in a loss of video quality. This loss of quality varies, depending on the type of compression, the codec used, and the strength that the compression is set at.

Here's a rough example:

- An uncompressed 1-hour 1080p video is about 540 GB
- A compressed 1-hour 1080p H.264 video is about 1.4 GB

The difficulty that Final Cut Pro has with the GOP method is that when a single frame within the group needs to be edited, the GOP needs to be uncompressed into individual iFrames, on the fly, as it is played in the timeline. An iFrames is a single frame of video. The decompressing stresses the processor on your computer, and in cases such as multicam edits, you will see the spinning beach ball or experience dropped frames on playback. Even though Final Cut Pro can edit GOP formats directly, it is better to optimize those files either while importing or manually later, by selecting **Transcode Media…** after import.

Transcoding can be done in Final Cut Pro by transcoding media, on import, to ProRes 422, which is an Apple-developed (lossless) compression that closely resembles the full quality of uncompressed video, but at a much smaller size. More importantly, from Final Cut Pro's point of view, ProRes 422 has single iFrame, so the media does not need to be decoded when an edit is actioned in the timeline.

Even though ProRes 422 is much smaller than uncompressed video, it still results in large file sizes – significantly bigger than H.264, for instance.

The two main forms of compression are GOP and **Intra-frame** (**I-frame**) compression. They are intended for different uses, one for easy editing and the other for smaller file sizes. You can choose the best codec for your purposes. GOP files are smaller and should be optimized for easier editing – we've seen how they are formed. I-frames use a similar principle to that of a physical strip of film; each image is a separate frame of video.

I-frame compression involves a process in which an entire file is scanned, similar or repetitive data is recognized, and then the duplicate data is replaced with a unique code. The code alone is much smaller in size than the original data, thus taking up less space. Even so, I-frame-compressed files are much larger than GOP files but easier to edit, as the individual frames are available for Final Cut Pro to access without having to break up the GOP structure.

It is important to note that some of these compressed formats, usually the I-frame types, don't need to be optimized when imported into Final Cut Pro. The following popular codecs don't require optimization on import: DV and DVCam, AVC-Intra, XDCAM EX, HDCAM HD, all versions of ProRes, DNx, and GoPro Cineform.

These are the popular formats that benefit from optimization: MPEG-2, AVCHD, AVCCAM, AVC-Ultra, XAVC, H.264, and H.265.

However, you don't need to worry about the formats. Once you have set Final Cut Pro to optimize on import, it ignores formats already optimized and doesn't optimize them again.

There is another factor that comes into play when looking at video formats. Up until now, I have mainly compared uncompressed video with compressed formats. In the real world, most of the video media you will work with will come from cameras that use their own compressed codecs, conserving space on their storage cards.

The following page lists the most common digital video formats and their most frequent uses (courtesy of Adobe Australia): `https://www.adobe.com/au/creativecloud/video/discover/best-video-format.html`. Let's go over some video formats:

- MP4

  MPEG-4 Part 14 (MP4) is Apple's preferred format and the most common type of video file format. It will play on most other devices as well.

- MOV

  MOV was developed by Apple for QuickTime Player. MOV plays well on Facebook and YouTube and is suitable for TV viewing.

- WMV

  Windows Media Viewer (WMV) was developed by Microsoft for Windows Media Player.

- AVI

  Audio Video Interleave (AVI) needs to be converted to play on a Mac.

- AVCHD

  Advanced Video Coding High Definition (AVCHD) was created for Panasonic and Sony digital camcorders.

- FLV, F4V, and SWF

  These are also known as Flash formats and have gone out of favor, being mainly replaced by HTML5. Flash will not play on iOS devices.

- MKV

  The **Matroska Multimedia Container** (**MKV**) format is an open source container and supports nearly every codec, but it will not play on Final Cut Pro.

- MPEG-2

  MPEG-2 is specifically for DVD authoring.

It's all well and good knowing about the various video and audio formats and the different types of files that are created, but what type of monitor you will use to display videos needs to be balanced with how easily they can be implemented in your workflow. A color-accurate monitor is a must, but you can work much more efficiently with a second monitor. You will see the advantages in the following section.

Some of these codecs will most commonly be AVCHD, MP4, or MOV. Some recent high-end cameras use ProRes Raw files, which will be natively recognized by the 10.6 version of Final Cut Pro.

LOG video

Before I look at the different video formats that cameras produce, I want to mention LOG video, as this will require color correction before the editing process in Final Cut Pro.

LOG is short for **logarithmic**. Professional cameras have the option to shoot in the LOG format. There are an increasing number of lower-end cameras that shoot in propriety forms of LOG by recording more detail in grayscale, shadows, midtones, and highlights. Cameras that shoot in LOG are able to capture the full dynamic range that the camera's sensor is capable of recording, while still retaining a small container. When a LOG file is imported into Final Cut Pro, a correction process using a preset called a **lookup table** (**LUT**) can be applied to use the extra dynamic range in the LOG file. It is useful to note that LOG files are only created in a camera. A recording can't be converted into a LOG after it is burned to a card by the camera.

LOG footage is specified by each camera brand, and they don't necessarily look the same. S-Log 2 and 3 (Sony), LogC (Arri), Canon Log, V-Log (Panasonic), Red Logfilm, and Blackmagic Log are all made by camera manufacturers, using a proprietary approach to the LOG color space.

Computer monitors can only show a limited range of brightness and grayscale values. This is known as Rec. 709. It compresses shadows and highlights to suit a computer monitor. Cameras can capture at a much higher range, calling the resulting images LOG or HDR. When shown on a computer monitor, these LOG files look washed out in the shadows, with increased midtones.

As a quick way to color grade, Final Cut Pro allows the addition of LUTs. You can still edit LOG files, but the picture will look flat until you color grade either with a LUT or any color correction tool, which will introduce more detail to the highlights and the shadows to show the intended colors. These methods may be a quick fix for color grading, but at least they are a starting point for a full-color grade. To add to the flexibility, a LUT affects a full clip and not just the portion of the clip in the timeline, so they are ideal for creating a themed look to suit a whole edit – for example, a "film noir" effect, a moody red for crime movies, or perhaps an over-saturated look for a Hawaii travel video.

The Rec709 color space produces images that look conventional and realistic, with regular contrast and saturation. While LOG footage looks washed out, Rec709 is close to natural color space. This makes it the "standard" and is why there are so many Rec709 LUTs that return the color of LOG footage to a normal look in post-production. Rec709 footage may have more colors and contrast but has less flexibility in Final Cut Pro, as some colors are baked into the image, so they can't be altered as much as they can when grading the LOG footage.

LOG and LUTs go together like a horse and carriage, and dealing with them requires an understanding of how each suits the other in terms of quality and color. LOGs from different brands of cameras usually need specific LUTs. It helps to know which LUT to use for which camera when you apply them to LOG footage in Final Cut Pro. This will come with experience in working with footage from different cameras.

Usually, a LUT is applied earlier than you would do with conventional color grading. LUTs are applied to a clip in the browser and not in the timeline, by selecting the **Information** tab in the **Inspector** window in the **General** settings.

Figure 1.13 – Choices of LUTs

The drop-down menu next to the **Camera LUT** button shows the default LUTs supplied with Final Cut Pro, suitable for all the major camera brands. Also, there are thousands of LUTs available to download, either for a fee or, in many cases, for free. We will cover this later in *Chapter 12*.

The HDR format

In a similar vein and considering the limitations of some computer monitors, we should look at **High Dynamic Range** (**HDR**), which is also a video format that defines brightness and color and is comparable with **Standard Dynamic Range** (**SDR**). The difference is that HDR, also known as Rec. 2020, expands grayscale values greater than the value of 100 IRE (**IRE** is a scale introduced by the **Institute of Radio Engineers**). It has deeper shadows, brighter highlights, and color values that exceed Rec709. This means that you require an HDR-capable monitor to view HDR footage.

An HDR monitor produces colors and black levels that are much closer to what we see in the real world. An HDR monitor will allow you to see realistic color spaces, such as DCI-P3, without the need to convert HDR to Rec709.

There are a vast number of HDR-capable monitors available to purchase. As you can imagine, they mostly fall into the higher price brackets, but over time, HDR video will become more predominant and prices will reduce.

If you're in the market for a new monitor, or looking at equipping a new editing suite, it would be a good idea to add HDR to the mix.

Not only do you need a monitor that supports HDR to view HDR video but you also need one to create HDR content. Currently, HDR is a requirement for high-end feature films and some streaming services. However, it is not needed for broadcast or cable television, or social media sites.

It is possible to convert HDR footage to use in a Rec709 timeline in Final Cut Pro. You will most likely receive footage in the HDR format that has been recorded on an iPhone (usually recorded in HDR by mistake). You will know it's HDR because the footage looks overexposed when you drag it into the Final Cut Pro timeline. Conversely, it looks normal in the browser, so you won't immediately recognize HDR until the clip is in the timeline.

The simple solution is to reduce the dynamic range of the footage in the Rec709 color space with the **HDR Tools** effect, which is supplied by default in the Final Cut Pro **Effects** browser. You can also use normal color-grading controls or custom LUTs. When you add the **HDR Tools** effect to a timeline clip, you will be able to select the specific type of HDR in the inspector, with the tab selected with the film strip icon.

RAW video

Another form of video that you need to be aware of is **RAW video**. This term is a misnomer, as RAW video is not actually a video format but, rather, its native camera sensor data. Much in the way that old-style film cameras had negatives and the print was processed from that negative, think of RAW as the virtual negative from a digital camera and the digital format that is created from that raw footage as the print.

It is not possible to import RAW video directly into Final Cut Pro; it may need to be converted first, or additional software downloaded. For instance, Canon Cinema RAW Light can be imported with the Canon plug-in installed. Blackmagic RAW can use the BRAW Toolbox. The Color Finale Transcoder plug-in allows you to import BRAW, ARRIRAW, DNG, and CinemaDNG into Final Cut Pro.

A growing number of cameras record natively in **ProRes RAW**. This is a type of hybrid format that allows a camera sensor to create the ProRes RAW file and, in turn, make it available as an editable file for use in Final Cut Pro.

ProRes RAW is different from other RAW formats in the way it converts sensor data into video. It has the added ability to adjust the ISO setting and white point when edited natively.

To access the **ProRes RAW** settings, select a clip in the timeline (not the browser), then go to the **Information** tab in the **Inspector** window, with **Settings** selected. If a **ProRes Raw** file is selected, you will be able to change the ISO from 50 to 25,600. You will be able to change the exposure range from one stop lower to one stop higher. You will be able to adjust the white point to any value from 2,000 K to 15,000 K (according to the Apple ProRes RAW white paper, November 2020, Apple Inc. – www. apple.com/final-cut-pro/docs/Apple_ProRes_RAW.pdf).

Interlaced video

If you receive footage recorded on older cameras, it is possible that it may have been recorded as interlaced video. Without going into too much historical detail, interlaced video was created when TV signals were transmitted as analog signals. Interlacing was added to the video signal so that two halves of the analog TV screen were filled at the same time, due to flickering and the time delay in filling the whole screen with a single image. Today's TV signals are mostly progressive, where the full frame is transmitted. Interlaced video is outdated and not needed for today's TVs.

Early video cameras recorded interlaced video, 480i, 576i, or 1080i. If you put interlaced video into a progressive timeline, you will see artifacts of blurry lines at the edges of the images, particularly hands. You can remove interlacing with a process called **deinterlacing**. This can be done outside of Final Cut Pro before import, or you could, if your whole project uses interlaced footage, set your project at 1080i when you create a new project. Alternatively, you could edit the interlaced project and then deinterlace after export.

> **Warning**
> If you are exporting to social media, it is not a good idea to upload interlaced video.

ProRes

The difference between ProRes 422 and ProRes 4444 codecs is the RGB colors. **RGB** stands for **red, green, and blue**. As you will be aware, this is how digital colors are mixed, as opposed to **Cyan, Magenta, Yellow, and Black (CMYK)**, which is for printed material. Digital video uses *Y* for brightness and *Cr* and *Cb* for the video values of RGB. *Y*, *Cr*, and *Cb* are the recognized characters for brightness and color. *Y* is luma (brightness), *Cb* is blue minus luma (*B-Y*), and *Cr* is red minus luma (*R-Y*). It's all about reducing the file size by removing colors that are least sensitive to the eyes. The eyes are most sensitive to green and brightness, so they are given priority, and other colors are reduced.

All ProRes 4444 versions have full color and brightness; they also have an alpha channel that allows them to have a transparency option as a part of the image. Formats without an alpha channel always show a background if there is no object displayed. ProRes 4444 files are very large in size.

With ProRes 422 versions, the grayscale part of the image has a full resolution, and the color part of the image has a full vertical resolution but only half of the horizontal resolution. There is no alpha channel.

Lower-quality cameras tend to shoot in a 4:2:0 format; the grayscale part of the image still has a full resolution, but both the horizontal and vertical parts have a half resolution.

ProRes is what Final Cut Pro prefers to edit smoothly; however, H.264/H.265 are much more commonly used file types, so you need to understand them and how Final Cut Pro processes them.

H.264/H.265

It's worth mentioning that, even though this is not directly about Final Cut Pro, most Macs have built-in hardware that encodes acceleration for H.264 and H.265. Most Macs since 2016, with a Core i3, i5, i7, or i9, can encode H.264 or H.265 **High-Efficiency Video Coding** (**HEVC**) using Intel's hardware acceleration.

It's always a good idea to keep your macOS updated, but wait until at least a .1 version, allowing for any potential bugs to be ironed out. I will discuss update issues in more detail, particularly with plug-ins in mind, in *Chapter 17*.

Apple silicon Macs will also accelerate H.264, 8-bit HEVC, and 10-bit HEVC encoding, using hardware that speeds the compression of these codecs. Early M1 Macs were slower for hardware encoding than most Intel chips, but as M series processors have improved over time, the encoding speed has increased.

Since the H.264 and H.265 formats are similar, which is the best to use and why? H.265 has the advantage of being a smaller file while having almost exactly the same quality, so why consider H.264 at all? If you want to appeal to all possible audiences, then use H.264, as there is a possibility that some playback devices will not play H.265. If you are sure that the devices that will play your video are H.265-capable, then that will be the better choice to export from Final Cut Pro.

As mentioned before, not all computers will hardware-accelerate H.265, so that in itself is a consideration as well.

If you plan to upload files to social media, then the files will be recompressed anyway, so it is better to have the extra data for the social media site to discard, which will likely result in a better overall outcome for your file.

H.265 should be used if you are considering exporting higher than 4K or HDR files, as H.264 will only support 4K and lower grayscale and color range.

You should know about what formats Final Cut Pro will not import. The common ones that it can't import are AVI, FLV, F4V, MKV, and SWF. If you need to import these formats, it is necessary to convert them before you can import them into Final Cut Pro.

The best solution is to use the free-to-download **HandBrake** application. It almost universally recognizes all video and most audio formats (`https://handbrake.fr/`).

Just drag the file to be converted into the **HandBrake** window. It uses the term **Preset** for the conversion method. If you don't know what format to convert to, use the default **Fast 1080p30** option for NTSC countries, or you can create your own presets for PAL countries.

At the bottom of the window, next to the **Save As** heading, is the path that the converted file will be saved to. Use the **Browse…** button to select a location to save to.

When you have set these, use the **Start** button to start the conversion or add to a queue, and then click **Start** if you have a batch of files to convert.

Figure 1.14 – The HandBrake window

Which video format is best for which purpose?

Some video formats are more suitable for different purposes than others. Some are better as camera clips, and others are better for editing or delivery (export). This section will delve into various file formats and their respective strengths for different applications. Let's get started:

- The following are the formats best suitable as camera files. The most common file formats for entry-level cameras are AVCHD and MP4. However, different brands and more advanced cameras will have proprietary formats:

  - Sony camera formats are AVCHD, MP4, DV, XAVC S, XAVC S HD, HDV, MPEG2, MPEG4, and ProRes RAW

  - RED cameras use R3D and REDCODE RAW

  - ARRI cameras use formats with the `.ari`, `.mxf`, and `.arriraw` extensions

  - Canon cameras use MP4 (H.264), MP4 (HEVC), HEVC, XF-AVC (`.mxf`), RAW – Cinema RAW (`.crm`), and `.mov`

  - Panasonic cameras use the following:

    - **HC**: AVCHD, MP4, MP4, iFrame, and `.mov`

    - **HDC**: AVCHD and 50p H.264

    - **HM**: MPEG4 and Apple iFrame

    - **SDR**: SD video or MPEG4

    - ProRes RAW

- The formats most suitable for editing are ProRes 4444XQ, ProRes 4444, ProRes 422 (HQ), ProRes 422, ProRes 422 (LT), and ProRes 422 (Proxy)

- The formats least suitable for editing are H.264, AVCHD, and any camera proprietary formats

- The best formats for delivery (export) are as follows:

  - H.264, H.265 HEVC, and `.MOV` (uncompressed)

  - ProRes 4444XQ, ProRes 4444, ProRes 422 (HQ), and ProRes 422

If in doubt as to which format your client expects or needs, just ask.

We have covered a lot of ground looking at video codecs and formats. Now is the time to look at audio files, as they are similar but somewhat different from video and are handled differently by Final Cut Pro.

Audio formats

Audio file formats or file extensions are containers or wrappers for audio codecs. As with lossy video file formats, most audio formats lose data in compression. Which format you choose depends on the balance you want to strike between quality and ease of use.

Common lossy audio formats are as follows:

- **Advanced Audio Coding (AAC)**
- **Apple Lossless Audio Codec (ALAC)**
- **Free Lossless Audio Codec (FLAC)**
- **MPEG-1 Audio Layer 3 (MP3)**
- Ogg (Vorbis)
- **Windows Media Audio (WMA)**
- Common lossless
- **Audio Interchange File Format (AIFF)**
- **Pulse-Code Modulation (PCM)**
- **Waveform Audio File Format (WAV)**

The following section looks at how you will view video files with a second monitor.

Second monitors

Organization of media is one thing, but more importantly, you need to be able to view the footage, which is why a computer's monitor is crucial. Obviously, size matters, and while you can easily edit on a laptop while out in the field, I would not recommend that as a permanent single-monitor solution. This brings to light the amazing advantage of utilizing a second monitor. Not only does a bigger monitor mean you can see more of Final Cut Pro but a second monitor also means you can see more of the specific parts of the Final Cut Pro interface. Personally, and more importantly, I think it's about the associated files that you need to refer to while using Final Cut Pro. You don't need to switch between layered windows, and instead, you can view them side by side with the extra screen real estate.

The following are the things to keep in mind when selecting a monitor for Final Cut Pro:

- **Color accuracy**: DCI-P3, sRGB, Rec709, or Adobe RGB (factory-calibrated)
- **Mac-optimized**: 109 PPI or 218 PPI
- Screen real estate suitable for Final Cut Pro
- Do you need one or more separate monitors?

- Is one widescreen monitor better than two monitors?

- A webcam

- **Calibration**: Whether factory-calibrated or manually done after purchase

I'll just touch on the first three bullets, as the others are self-explanatory.

Color accuracy is important for video work and must be your top priority, as it's not about what you see on the screen but, rather, how color is translated to the exported file. If your screen is inaccurate, say with a permanent blue tint, you would likely increase the red to compensate for what you can see on the screen. It may look fine on your screen, but when you export that file, it will show an increased red. If your screen was accurate in the first place and there was too much actual blue in the image, when you add the red, that would also export as the correct color.

There are color accuracy standards, such as DCI-P3, sRGB, Rec709, and Adobe RGB, and monitor manufacturers rate their monitors against those standards (100% sRGB, for instance). Monitors that do not show a rating are not color-accurate. It is an added advantage to have a monitor that is factory-calibrated with a certificate. To be fully accurate, you will need to calibrate manually from time to time. You need to balance your requirements versus cost.

A Mac-optimized PPI is a tricky one because virtually all non-Apple branded monitors, except one or two, will not be perfectly optimized for macOS. It's all to do with the **pixels per inch** (**PPI**). Monitors that do not match the macOS optimum of 109 PPI and 218 PPI will still display with full-color accuracy and resolution for the monitor; macOS will scale to suit. This, in turn, uses some processor power, but it is nothing you will particularly notice under most circumstances on a modern computer.

I would recommend that you consider the Apple Studio display as your main editing monitor for good color accuracy. It's expensive compared to other brands but does have a 5k resolution at the correct 218 PPI, with the advantage of a webcam built in. Depending on your budget, use the same for a second monitor, or opt for a 4K monitor and have macOS scale the PPI by navigating to **Apple** menu | **Settings (Preferences)** | **Displays** | **Default**. The lower-cost option is to consider an HD monitor at 2,560 x 1,440 pixels that will match the macOS needs. It will only be in an HD resolution, but it is fine to display supporting documents for Final Cut Pro editing and will be at a significantly lower cost.

To achieve the best use of screen real estate suitable for Final Cut Pro, two 27" monitors are recommended. A 32" monitor would just about give enough space, but two of them might start to stretch your budget. If cost is not an issue, then two Apple 32" XDR monitors would be the ultimate choice.

The following subsection shows you how to use a second monitor so that different Final Cut Pro windows show on different screens.

Having different windows on each display

When in Final Cut Pro and you have two displays connected, an icon of two overlapping monitors will show above the **Inspector** window:

Figure 1.15 – The overlapping monitors icon

You can also go to the **Window** menu | **Show in Secondary Display**, where you will find the following three options – **Browser**, **Viewer**, and **Timeline**. These can be ticked to activate them, but only one can be selected at a time. I prefer **Timeline** on my second monitor when I have many layers of connected clips and multiple audio tracks. The thin timeline under the browser and viewer, when only one monitor is used, requires continual adjustments to the height of the timeline. The following screenshots show the browser and viewer on the main monitor and the timeline on the second monitor:

Figure 1.16 – The main monitor

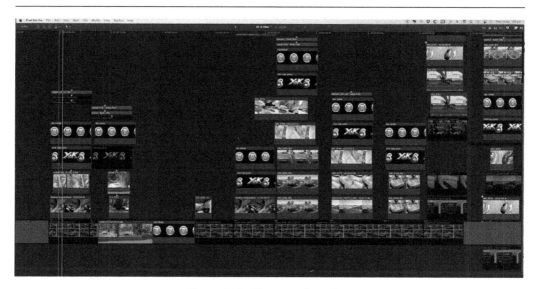

Figure 1.17 – The second monitor

As a further option, if your Mac has an HDMI port, you will be able to use the second monitor as a standalone viewer window while still having a viewer on your main monitor. If you're on a budget and just want a second monitor so that you can refer to text files while you are editing in Final Cut Pro, give some thought to using Sidecar on an iPad. It will be at a high resolution for text, and your mouse and keyboard will work on the iPad, but Final Cut Pro won't recognize it as a second monitor. You will need a 5th-generation iPad, an iPadOS of 16.2 or higher, or macOS 13.1 or higher.

While a second monitor can help the efficiency of your work patterns, it's equally, if not more, important to employ the best types of devices to store files on for the fastest access to Final Cut Pro. The different options for suitable storage disks are outlined next.

Types of disks

As you saw earlier in this chapter, SSDs are the best type of external disk for editing, but they are still somewhat expensive. So, there is still a place for spinning disks for archiving or backup purposes. At a pinch, a library on a spinning disk connected by USB-C or even USB 3 will serve the purpose for short projects, or quick corrections of previously completed projects in 4K or less.

RAID is a different story. Simply put, RAID combines several disks together to share the load, as it were. The biggest benefit is for spinning disks, as the mechanical process is duplicated so that more platters can be accessed at the same time. This results in the read and write speeds being faster. However, RAID still relies on the speed of the connection to the computer. If you are buying a new RAID setup, consider Thunderbolt technology version 3-4.

The added advantage of RAID, other than RAID 0, is that it allows data on a disk to be duplicated. If a disk in RAID fails, it can be replaced without losing data, which is called **redundancy**. In larger systems, an individual failed disk can be removed, without shutting a system down.

Whatever RAID of spinning disks you use, it will have nowhere near the transfer rates of an SSD. Currently, costs are high for SSD RAID, and they will become a force in the future but more so for their redundancy advantages.

RAID 0 is by far the fastest, but without any redundancy, it's purely a method of increasing transfer speeds. If you want both, I suggest RAID 10 when looking for speed but still needing redundancy. Four drives set at RAID 10 will have two drives mirrored, holding half the data, and the other two drives holding the other half.

From a technical point of view, RAID 0 uses striping, which distributes data blocks across several different disks. This manipulates the speed of multiple disks. The more disks you add to the group, the faster it'll be. The downside is that you will still need to back up the RAID. If any drive fails, all data will be lost.

RAID 1 mirrors data between two disks. It's mostly used with two disks; the read speeds are good since there are two drives available to access your data. RAID 1 is best combined with a hardware controller rather than a slower software-based RAID.

RAID 5 requires three drives, where a portion of the data is distributed over the three disks so that when one disk fails, the remaining drives can recover data that was on the failed drive.

When it comes to **Network-Attached Storage** (**NAS**) systems, things are quite different. At present, it's unlikely that you will use SSDs. NvMe Flash NAS systems are available at a considerable cost, offering a capacity of up to 288 drives, with 15-TB capacity per drive.

The advantage of conventional NAS systems is you will get a massive storage capacity and optionally built-in RAID. Even though conventional NAS systems use spinning media, some systems reach read/write speeds of 8,000 MB/s.

You need to ensure that macOS systems on all computers at least meet Final Cut Pro 10.4.x system requirements. Conventional NAS systems are best suited for 1080p projects. Mostly, they will be slower than physically attached disks while being expensive to set up and maintain.

The storage of the future is internet-based. I will discuss collaboration using Dropbox in *Chapter 19*. Final Cut Pro's library is stored on the cloud, and projects are edited directly from the cloud. The media is not on your computer or attached to external disks. The advantage is that all members of the Dropbox account can access the live project. Bandwidth is not a great issue once media is uploaded to Dropbox, as the editing instructions are small and sync to Dropbox almost immediately.

How much storage is enough?

As I discussed earlier, the preferred method of working with Final Cut Pro is to keep the application on the internal SSD (by default, in the `Applications` folder), and create a new Final Cut Pro Library on external SSDs. Then, before you venture to create each new library, it is a good idea to check how much storage will be required for the projects in that library. There are many variables, but to keep it simple, if you ask Final Cut Pro to optimize media (refer to the *Exploring settings* section in *Chapter 2*) as it is imported, expect that a 1080p project of 1 hour at 30 FPS will take up 60+ GB of space on your disk. If the project is 4K, 1 hour at 30 FPS will take up around 300 GB.

This is a perfect time to introduce the concept of proxy media, as it takes up less storage than optimized media and is just as smooth to edit. The compromise is that there is a drop in the quality of what you see while editing, compared to when you edit with optimized or original media.

Proxy media is the term for media used when you are actually editing with a smaller file format, taking up less space and causing less stress on the computer's processor. Proxy is the format that you can ask Final Cut Pro to convert original media to during the import process (again, refer to the *Exploring settings* section in *Chapter 2*).

When the edit is completed, before you export it, Final Cut Pro will prompt you to switch back to the original or optimized media. Everything you have edited in the proxy form is then matched, behind the scenes, with the original or optimized media for the export to be done at full quality. Optimized media is usually skipped when you use proxy media. However, you can have original, optimized, and proxy media. You must have at least one of either optimized or original media.

Proxy media is especially useful for multicam edits at 4K or higher. If you use original media, depending on the number of cameras in the multicam and the power of your computer, you may experience dropped frames during the edit in the timeline.

This whole process and how to set up optimized or proxy media editing formats is discussed in *Chapter 2*.

Summary

This was a particularly technical chapter that you should remember to refer back to. You should by no means try to remember all these details, as an abundance of the information is background material or historical data. The information that is important to retain includes the `Users` folder, where Final Cut Pro locates its files. You should know how to access the `Users` folder for emergency recovery of media, as well as be able to install and view the plug-ins used by Final Cut Pro. Equally important are the locations that you can choose to store Final Cut Pro's library and, most importantly, understanding the library concept as a whole.

You need to have a broad understanding of the different file formats and how they are either best suited as camera files, editing formats, or for export. The differences between the ways that files are compressed will give you an understanding of when to use those files, and when indeed you will need to convert them for best use within Final Cut Pro.

Finally, you should leave this chapter understanding the types of storage devices that will make your editing process go smoother.

If you go away with nothing else, you need to understand the Final Cut Pro library design concept and how and where it stores media. You will need to build on the concept when its organizational structure is discussed in *Chapter 2*, which also discusses how media is sorted and how Final Cut Pro transcodes media into formats that simplify the editing process.

2
Organizing Media

This chapter concentrates on the unique ways in which media is organized within the Final Cut Pro database. Organization within the filming industry's terminology is known as **logging**. In this chapter, you will learn about the distinctive sub-classifications in which different categories of media are separated to give you quick access during the editing process. The importance of this separation becomes even more apparent as the number of editors that require access to a project increases to share the workload. This chapter is principally about organization, but it is also about how media is sorted and where to find the metadata that refers to the creation of the camera clips. You will be introduced to how Final Cut Pro transcodes media into **optimized** and **proxy media** formats that simplify the editing process. You will become familiar with the **Settings** | **Preferences** setup and its implications, and you will understand the positioning of the project in the timeline and how the timeline index gives you quick access to the clips and effects in the project. You will learn about the two types of playheads and how they interact with each other.

You will also be shown how to sort the view of the browser so that the most useful clips are at your fingertips.

In this chapter, we will cover the following topics:

- Libraries and events
- When and why to log footage
- Favorites
- Keyword Collections
- Smart Collections
- Folders
- Templates
- Search
- Colored lines on browser clips

- Removing media from categories

- Browser filters

- Sorting the browser

- The Open Clip view

- Shortcuts for media actions

- Clip and library information

- Settings/preferences

By the end of this chapter, you will understand the relationship between a library and the events that are contained in every library. You will be clear on how Final Cut Pro uniquely indexes media into separate categories, allowing you to promptly select the most useful clips as you start editing in the timeline. You will learn how to create templates of libraries to save redoing the same setups time and again on future projects.

Understanding libraries and events

Organization is the key to exceptional video post-production, and Final Cut Pro contains a unique set of tools to ensure that media remains well organized. Traditionally, this organization is known as **logging**. As you saw in *Chapter 1*, all media is stored within a Final Cut Pro **library**. A town's public library contains many books, magazines, DVDs, and other items. The town library categorizes everything into different sections inside the building – for instance, fiction, non-fiction, sports, and so on. Final Cut Pro uses a similar method of categorization to store all of its contents. It uses **events**, **Favorites**, **Keyword Collections**, and **Smart Collections**, to which you give appropriate names to gain quick access to the contents when you are editing. The Final Cut Pro library also contains thumbnails representing Final Cut Pro's projects.

As you saw in *Chapter 1*, you have the choice of where you create a library. The industry standard recommends having a Final Cut Pro library on external SSDs rather than on the computer's internal disk.

Initially, we are going to concentrate on the relationship between a library and an event, and then we will cover events, favorites, Keyword Collections, Smart Collections, and projects.

The first and most important thing to remember is that a library contains everything. It is at the top of the hierarchy; the other classifications are just parts of what is in the library. When you select a library in the browser sidebar, you will see everything inside that library, including thumbnails that represent a project that has been opened in that library. The project thumbnails have a chevron effect at the top:

Figure 2.1 – The chevron effect

As you are already familiar with the basics of editing in Final Cut Pro, you will know that the browser includes the media that is to be used in the project. This knowledge has allowed you to edit and complete projects. In my years of teaching Final Cut Pro, I've found users are unsure about the relationship between the different categories in which to store media. When you select the **Library** button in the browser sidebar, you will see all of the media and project thumbnails in the right-hand side window in the browser.

> **Important note**
>
> To concentrate your view on the browser, it's a good idea to deactivate the Timeline and Inspector from the view to have more space on the display to see the browser. To do this, select **Window | Show in workspace**. Untick the Timeline and Inspector, or press the shortcut button at the top of the Inspector (as shown in the red outline in *Figure 2.2*):
>
>
>
> Figure 2.2 – The browser and Viewer activated, and the Timeline and Inspector deactivated

I want to clear up any confusion about what an event is. You will have noticed that whenever a new library is created, an event is automatically added to the sidebar below a folder named Smart Collections (there'll be more on Smart Collections later). The event is labeled with the day's date. *Figure 2.3* is an example of the library structure, which you will see more of in *Chapter 4, Pre-Editing a Rough Cut*:

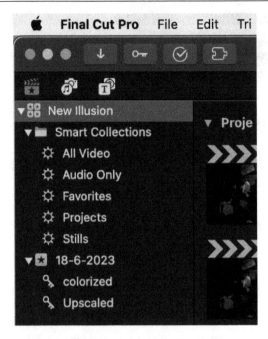

Figure 2.3 – An example of the library structure

I previously discussed the similarity of the Final Cut Pro library to a brick-and-mortar library. If you think about it, the town library is not just an empty space; it is made up of rooms. Even if it were just one open space, that space would be a room. Those rooms, in turn, contain the library's different categories. Similarly, a Final Cut Pro library is made up of rooms, which it calls events, and it must have at least one event (room).

When the architect designed the town library, they would have allocated different uses to different rooms. You do the same with Final Cut Pro events. You have the option to make use of them in any way that you wish. This flexibility, in turn, leads to confusion as to what they can be used for. I suggest that you open your mind to the possibilities, as perhaps the hardest part about understanding the relationship between a library and an event is how to make use of them.

In the real-world analogy, you would expect a library to have lots of rooms, purely from a practical prespective in having to contain lots of books. It would be unlikely that there would be a library with one room containing only a single category of books. However, in the Final Cut Pro analogy, there is no reason why you could not have a library with just one event, containing just one video project. The decision is up to the individual editor. In contrast, it is just as viable to have one library with multiple events with just one video project in each, or even one library with multiple events with multiple video projects in each. All are equally practical; you decide in your workflow.

There appears to be no limit to the number of events that can be in a Final Cut Pro library, but purely for practical reasons and to avoid any operational slowdown in Final Cut Pro, I would not have too many within any one library. I have had a library with over 40 events running concurrently, with no slowdown. You don't need to be nervous about it.

So, in summary, an event is a room or subcategory in a library. Referring back to the description of a physical town library, within each room, you can have different sections with categories of different styles of books (media). Within a Final Cut Pro event, you can also have different sections that are similar to the physical library's index. Final Cut Pro has ratings and sections that are categorized as Keyword Collections. Finally, there is another section that only exists in the digital world, called Smart Collections. All these sections can be contained within separate folders, as shown in the following example:

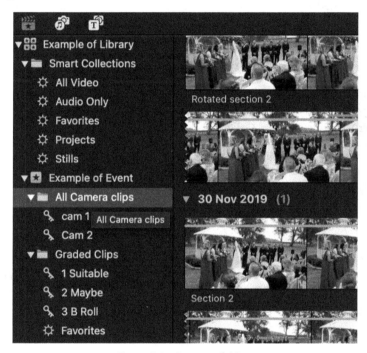

Figure 2.4 – Separate folders

Let's look at these in order. Now that you have your media in an event, how do you categorize the different types of media? How do you have footage of lions in one section and tigers in another so that when you are editing, you can find the animal that you need in the edit, quickly and easily, at the initial assembly or rough cut stage?

The next section discusses why you need to log clips. Logging is the film industry's term for organizing footage so that it can be more easily located during the editing process.

When and why to log clips

The decision on whether to log clips or not is best taken before ingestion of the footage. It is a simple choice, mostly based on the size and length of the proposed video. The decision will affect how you ingest the footage as well as the amount of time you intend to spend logging and organizing the imported media. Ingestion for a simple video is best done by dragging clips directly into the clip browser. For very basic edits with just one or two clips, the footage can even be dragged directly into a project in the timeline.

The rule of thumb should be, "The smaller and shorter the proposed video, the less need for logging." After all, logging is carried out so that footage is in an orderly classification, allowing you to access it quickly during the creative part of the editing process.

The more complex the edit, the more you will need to have *footage* and *B roll* in categories so that you are not searching through the browser for clips to add to the timeline.

Final Cut Pro offers various methods of logging imported clips with a simple selection, using the *F* key to add clips and portions of clips to a *favorites* category. There are also more specific categorizations using Final Cut Pro's unique Keyword Collections.

The next section covers simple categorization using the *F* key to save favorite clips, as well as portions of clips, which can be accessed from the **Favorites** category of the browser sidebar.

Favorites

The first and simplest way to categorize media is to use the Final Cut Pro **Favorites** feature, using its *F* keyboard shortcut. **Favorites** will contain the best clips that you will use in the assembly stage. When you choose a clip with a library selected in the browser sidebar and press the *F* key, the clip is categorized in a separate section called **Favorites**. It still remains accessible in the main library but is more easily selected from **Favorites**. You should think of the **Favorites** section as an index to quickly locate a clip that is also in the main library.

The rating as a favorite method

First, you need to put some media into an event; either create a new event (*Option + N*) or use the event that was created with the library.

Select a portion of a clip or group of clips, and press the *F* key. The clips will have a green line across the top of just the portion of the clip that has been selected:

Figure 2.5 – The green line

Behind the scenes, the clips have been categorized into an index called **Favorites**, and you can view them in two ways. The first way is to expand the **Smart Collections** button below the **Library** button in the browser sidebar:

Figure 2.6 – Smart Collections expanded

What's important to note is that not just a whole clip can be categorized as a favorite; portions of clips can also be stored in the **Favorites** category. The ramifications of this is that several portions of the same clip can be stored in **Favorites** and shown as separate clips. For instance, if you have a long interview, you can store just the parts of the interview that are suitable for the edit. This means that you can just pick from the good parts of the interview rather than the whole time that the camera was running.

The adding to favorites method

You can select a portion of a clip by either using the skimming option, which involves clicking and dragging a yellow outline over the clip, or by pressing the *I* key for the start of the portion and the *O* key to set the end of the portion. The same yellow outline will show on the original clip in the browser, just like when using the dragging method.

How to use Favorites

Select the **Favorites** button in the sidebar under **Smart Collections**, and you will see the favorited selections in the browser's right-hand side panel. It's as simple as that.

The second method of viewing favorites will introduce you to a way of sorting the contents of the browser's right-hand panel.

At the top-right of the browser window, you can see a group of icons with the words **All Clips**. Click the double chevrons to the right of **All Clips**:

Figure 2.7 – The double chevrons

Select the **Favorites** button:

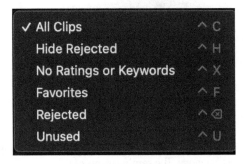

Figure 2.8 – Selecting Favorites

You will now see the clips that you previously favorited. This is your introduction to Smart Collections, which will be covered later in this chapter.

As you can see, the **Favorites** feature is easy to select with just a keystroke, but beware, as the selection includes all the clips in a single category. Everything you favorite goes under one index heading. This will be counterproductive if you are trying to keep the previously mentioned lions and tigers as separate categories. To solve that dilemma, there is a further method of isolating different types of media, called **keywording**.

Understanding Keyword Collections

Welcome to the concept of keywords. As the term suggests, different words are used to categorize different selections or different indexes. This concept makes it easy because you use the actual word of the item you are separating. The process of establishing a Keyword Collection is not as easy as it is for favorites, which have already been set up for you, but once it is set up, it is easy to add new media to the Keyword Collection.

Keyword Collections are specific to each event and can be created before you need to use them, or on the fly as the need occurs. In most cases, you are much more likely to set them up at the time you need them.

Keyword Collections are at their most useful at the pre-edit stage for storing clips and the B roll. The sorting process ranks the most useful clips for the edit. You will see more about that and the ways to see different views of the media later in this chapter in the *Browser filters* section, and in much more detail in *Chapter 4, Pre-Editing a Rough Cut*. Here, you will see how to sort clips that are categorized with my preferred labels – **Best**, **Suitable**, **Maybe**, and **B Roll**. I use the **Favorites** feature for my **Best** category. **Favorites** has the convenience of the keyboard shortcut (the *F* key). Then, **Suitable** clips can be added to a suitable Keyword Collection. Finally, **Maybe** clips also require another Keyword Collection, as does **B Roll**. The following section gives more detail.

Creating Keyword Collections

To set up a new empty Keyword Collection, select the event that will contain the Keyword Collection. Under the **File** menu, select **New | Keyword Collection** (*Shift + Command + K*).

Figure 2.9 – A Keyword Collection

The Keyword Collection will be added inside the event. Give it a name to suit the media that you will later add to it.

You will most likely use the following method of setting up a Keyword Collection. Select an event, click a portion of a clip or a complete clip(s), and press *Command + K*, and then a **Keyword Editor** window will appear. You can also right-click on an event to set up a Keyword Collection.

Type the word you want to use as the keyword, and then click the red button at the top-left:

Figure 2.10 – Typing the word to represent the Keyword Collection

The Keyword Collection is added inside the event. Note that a key symbol is placed beside each Keyword Collection.

Figure 2.11 – Keyword Collections shown in the sidebar

Now, you can drag clips of different subjects into each Keyword Collection to have them available separately.

The same principle of portions or whole clips applies to Keyword Collections just as it does to Favorites. However, rather than just having one category to select from when using Favorites, a different Keyword Collection will allow you to store the **Suitable**, **Maybe**, and **B Roll** categories, which I will discuss in much more detail later in this chapter. I suggest that you use **Favorites** as your choice for the best clips because it shows a green line to differentiate them:

Figure 2.12 – The green-colored line

Final Cut Pro considers Keyword Collections so important that it positions the button to open a **Keyword Collection** window in one of the most prominent places in the interface – right at the top, next to the **Import** arrow. Click the button to see the content of a Keyword Collection:

Figure 2.13 – Opening the Keyword Collection in blue

An alternative method of opening the **Keyword Collection** window is to click the keyword button in the browser sidebar; to select the clip in the browser, press *Command + K*. Clips or portions can also be in any number of other different Keyword Collections. All the keywords with which a clip is associated are shown in blue. To remove the clip from the Keyword Collection, click on it in the top panel of the **Keyword Collection** window and press the *Delete* key. It's also very useful to set up keyboard shortcuts to use when adding clips into a collection, similar to how we use the *F* key to add to Favorites.

Adding shortcuts to Keyword Collections

In the **Keyword Editor** window, if all number fields are empty, then you can add up to nine keyword shortcuts by typing keywords with a comma separator. For example, typing `lion, tiger` will add **lion** to the first shortcut and **tiger** to the second:

Figure 2.14 – Keyword shortcuts

In my opinion, the unique Keyword Collection is the jewel in the Final Cut Pro crown, making the editing process smoother, quicker, and easier than any other **Non-Linear Editor** (**NLE**).

Keyword Collections can also represent folders that contain multiple files. You can set a folder when you are ingesting clips by ticking the **From folders** option, next to **Keywords** in the **Import** settings window:

Figure 2.15 – The From folders option selected in the Import settings

Keyword Collections are a real benefit in differentiating media, but they do require you to drag media into different collections. There is a smarter way to make Final Cut Pro separate and categorize media without any input from you. It does require you to set it up, but once established, the process happens automatically. It's called Smart Collections.

Smart Collections

In the context of the real-world town library analogy, **Smart Collection** categories don't exist, as they are a digital process. Because Final Cut Pro is a digital application, it can sort items in a selection based on user-defined search attributes.

At the beginning of this chapter, you saw how to add to **Favorites**. You will have noticed that **Favorites** is within a folder called Smart Collections in the browser sidebar. There are five Smart Collections within that Smart Collections folder – **All Video**, **Audio Only**, **Favorites**, **Projects**, and **Stills**. These are set up by default and have the following functions:

- **All Video** shows no audio and no stills (photos), only video clips (including project thumbnails)
- **Audio Only** shows only audio
- **Favorites** shows the clips you have favorited
- **Projects** shows the project thumbnails only
- **Stills** shows still images (photos) only

Figure 2.16 – The default contents of Smart Collections

When audio, video, and stills are imported into Final Cut Pro, the default Smart Collection is automatically filled with the appropriate content, without any input from you. More importantly, you can set up your own Smart Collections for your personal categorization of media. Let's assume you would like to have a separate folder with different camera clips. For this exercise, I'll refer to two cameras. One camera uses the clip name clip_#1 and so on, and the other uses Clip0001 and so on.

What is a Smart Collection?

The concept of Smart Collections is used in many different Apple applications, such as the Photos app, the Music app, and the Apple Mail app. In fact, it's not just Apple that uses the concept of Smart Collections or, as Adobe calls them, **Collections**. You will find Collections in Adobe Lightroom. Other applications might call the concept **Smart Objects**.

The term *Smart Collection* is used when a set of data is matched with defined criteria. In a Final Cut Pro example, when metadata meets the set criteria, it is automatically added to a folder known as a Smart Collection. This means that when the media meets the criteria, it will always be in the Smart Collection. The Smart Collection contains the media without any input from you. It can't be added manually, and it can't be removed without the set criteria being changed.

The criteria that you use to set up a Smart Collection are extensive and varied, as you will see in the next section on adding a Smart Collection.

Adding a Smart Collection

Select the **Event** tab you want to add to, and then, from the **File** menu, select **New | Smart Collection**. You can also use the right-click shortcut on **Event**. A **Smart Collection** item is added to the event. Note the gear symbol, indicating it is a Smart Collection. Only media from within the event can be added to the Smart Collection.

Figure 2.17 – A new Smart Collection

After giving the Smart Collection a name (I'll call it Cam 1), you can double-click it and select the **Text** option from the window that opens:

Figure 2.18 – Smart Collection: Cam 1

Select the **Includes** option, and don't forget to add the clip numbers. Type clip # (be sure to leave a space before the # character):

Figure 2.19 – The Includes option

Create another Smart Collection, and call it Cam 2. Type Clip0 in the **All Text** field.

Camera clips that have three digits matching clip # or Clip0 will be added to the different Smart Collections, and whenever new camera clips with those attributes are imported, they will automatically be added to those Smart Collections.

You can see a button at the bottom of the window called **New Smart Collection**. I'll discuss that in more detail later in this chapter when we look at searching.

At this stage, I'm sure you will be already thinking about how unwieldy all these Keyword and Smart Collections could be in the sidebar. This is where folders come in.

What are folders?

The Keyword Collections and Smart Collections categories can be further contained in folders, which will avoid confusion in the sidebar, and those folders can, in turn, accommodate other folders.

The added advantage of using folders to organize the other categories is that when you select a folder in the sidebar, all the contents of the Keyword and Smart Collections inside the folder show on the right-hand side of the browser window. Of course, this applies when you select a library and an event as well. All the content inside the hierarchy of groups is displayed, as seen in the following screenshot of a folder with three cameras included:

Figure 2.20 – A folder containing three different cameras

Folders, just like Keyword and Smart Collections, are specific to each event. This means that by selecting an event at the top level of your hierarchy, you will see all the contents of the folders and the Keyword Collections within. The planning of the levels and hierarchy structure is discussed in more detail in *Chapter 4*.

Now that you have learned how to use the organizational structure of a library and all the containers within, the following section will show you how to set them up just once by creating a template, instead of redoing it each time you create a new library.

Templates

It's easy and convenient to create templates of a library structure so that they are available for you to use for any future library.

Creating templates

You can create templates for future use by setting up a new library and setting up the structure of events, folders, and Keyword and Smart Collections to suit your workflow. Then, you save the empty library to a location that you will remember. Next time you want to use that empty library structure as a template, right-click on the empty library in the Finder and select **Duplicate**:

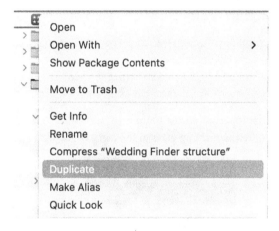

Figure 2.21 – Duplicate in the Finder

If there is no media in the template yet, it duplicates immediately. If you were to duplicate a working library containing media, you would need to wait for some time. Select the newly duplicated library, give it a name, and double-click it to launch the template in Final Cut Pro.

This is a brilliant way of separating camera footage shot on your favorite cameras into Smart Collections in Final Cut Pro. Just by importing the camera footage, it will automatically be added to the appropriate Smart Collection.

The notion of templates is based on the way that you adapt the Final Cut Pro organizational structure to suit your editing style or styles, should you be involved with different types of editing needs. If you are a contractor to different clients, you will likely set up templates for each of the clients' edit types. Templates really come into their own for wedding video edits, as you will see in *Chapter 9, Project Workflows – Pace and Structure*, when I discuss different workflows.

It's great to have all your media separated into different collections, but how do you find a particular clip quickly if you forget which category it is stored in? This is even more important for Smart Collections, where the media is stored without your input. In the next section, you will see how to search for media without knowing which category it is stored in.

Using the Search functionality

The **Search** feature allows you to quickly access the hierarchy structure discussed previously. You will not likely remember where you have categorized all of your media, especially if you are coming back to an edit after some time. A quick suggestion is to look at the structure of the browser sidebar; noting the different events, folders, and Keyword and Smart Collections will give you a clue as to where you may have stored different categories of clips.

If you are unsure, rather than fumbling through the categories, it is best to use the **Search** feature. When you search in a library or an event, all the folders within, including Keyword and Smart Collections, are searched as well. You don't need a hierarchal structure for **Search** to be effective; it can be used on single events as well.

The **Search** input field is at the top-right of the main browser window, signified with a magnifying glass. If you don't see it, click the magnifying glass to the right of the film strip icon:

Figure 2.22 – Clicking the magnifying glass icon

When you type a value in the **Search** field, it will search within whatever option is selected in the browser sidebar – even inside the categories contained within the selected option, as previously mentioned.

By default, **Search** displays *all* the clips that match, not just the name of the clip. As an example, if you type clip, all the media that includes the word clip in the name will be filtered and displayed in the browser window. All other files will be hidden. The following figure shows clip in the **Search** field:

Figure 2.23 – An example of a filtered search

The key to **Search** is the word *filter*. The first thing that may initially confuse you is that if you search on a selection in the sidebar that does not contain any word or part of a word that you type, the browser window will be empty. This is a real trap if you are not familiar with the filter searching method.

It should be noted here that the **Search** field above the browser only searches in the **Media** browser. There are separate search fields for the contents of **Timeline**, known as **Timeline Index**, which will be discussed later in this chapter. There are also separate **Search** fields for the **Effects** browser and the **Transitions** browser, which will be discussed in *Chapter 7, Titles, Effects, and Generators*. All the **Search** fields use the same methodology of filtering the results as the **Media** browser does.

Now that you understand the logic of the **Search** feature, let's look at the other filtering methods that you can choose to find material deep within the **Media** browser. You had a brief preview of the Boolean options when we looked at Smart Collections. It is, in fact, the same mechanism that the **Search** feature uses.

Filtering method 1

To show the Boolean options, click the folder icon to the right of the **Search** field:

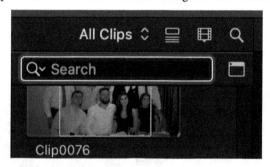

Figure 2.24 – The folder icon

A window will appear, titled **Filter**. Since you most recently actioned the default **Text** search with the **Includes** option, that will still be selected:

Figure 2.25 – The Text field with the Includes option

You can choose different types of filters by clicking the + sign on the right. As **All Text** is selected at the moment, let's look at the options there. By clicking the double chevron, you will be able to choose other subheadings rather than **All Text** – **Notes**, **Names**, and **Markers**:

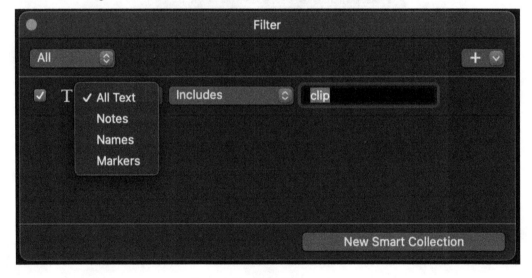

Figure 2.26 – The All Text options

If you select the double chevron next to **Includes**, you will see the **Does Not Include**, **Is**, and **Is Not** options.

If you need to only filter some names and not others, select the **Does Not Include** option.

For example, I want to filter all files that have **IMG** but don't want to include the image named IMG_123. Click + and select **Text**. A new line will appear; here, select **Names** and **Does Not Include**, and type 123. The **All** button needs to be selected at the top-left. That means all occurrences of the search filters need to match with both criteria. If you had **Any** selected, then either criterion would match the instruction. You will have noticed that I searched for img and found IMG, as **Search** is *not* case-sensitive.

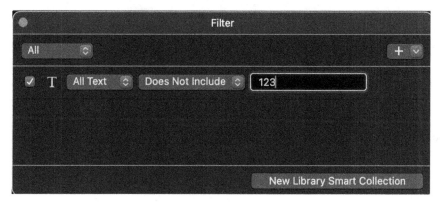

Figure 2.27 – Does Not Include

The **Search** function is not all about **Text** searches. I mentioned in the previous *Smart Collections* section that you can use it to create your own Smart Collections. Now, I'll create a Smart Collection to hold rejected clips. (An explanation of rejected clips is provided in the next section.)

Click the folder icon to the right of the **Search** field.

Figure 2.28 – The folder icon

You will find that the **Text** option is preselected. I don't want to use this though, so untick the checkbox on the left that selects that criteria. There is also the – (minus) button to remove criteria. Using the drop-down chevron, select **Ratings**.

Figure 2.29 – The Ratings dropdown

Select **Rejected**, and click the **New Smart Collection** button. An untitled Smart Collection displaying any rejected clips appears as an **Untitled** Smart Collection in the browser sidebar.

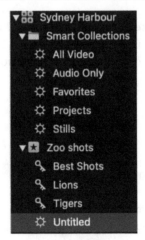

Figure 2.30 – The Untitled Smart Collection

You can rename the **Untitled** Smart Collection `Rejected` and even move it up into the `Smart Collections` folder:

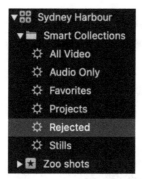

Figure 2.31 – Rejected moved to the Smart Collections folder

If you want a **Rejected** Smart Collection to appear in another library in the future, don't forget to create a template, as in the earlier section in this chapter.

As you can imagine, the criteria for **Search** can become very detailed. It is unlikely you will use all the options, but the options are there if you need them.

As well as being able to search for media, there are different visual clues to tell you where media is stored in the different categories. The colored lines that show on clips are one of those clues.

Colored lines on browser clips

This is a short list of what the colored lines represent in the browser clips. The reason for keeping this as a separate section is to give it a heading that you can refer back to when a question is raised about what a certain color represents. Let's look at the color meanings:

- **Green**: The clip has been added to **Favorites**
- **Blue**: The clip has been added to a Keyword Collection
- **Red**: The clip has been added to the **Rejected** category
- **Purple**: The clip has been analyzed to find people

- **Orange**: The clip has been added to the visible timeline

Figure 2.32 – The colored lines on media clips

As you saw in the list of colored lines, there is an orange line that tells you whether a browser clip (or a portion of a clip) has been added to the current project being viewed in the timeline. This means that you can quickly see what clips have already been added to your project so that you don't double up with the same clip by mistake. This is known as **Used Media Ranges**. I feel that this is absolutely indispensable to see in the browser. Unfortunately, it is not turned on by default. **Used Media Ranges** can be turned on from the **View** menu (**View** | **Browser** | **Used Media Ranges**) – make sure it's ticked.

Analyzing for people

When importing clips, you can instruct Final Cut Pro to categorize them as one-person shots, two-person shots, and groups by ticking the **Find people** option. The analysis of one-person, two-person, and group shots is where AI looks for the number of faces in a clip to place them in different categories. The following figure shows the settings for importing:

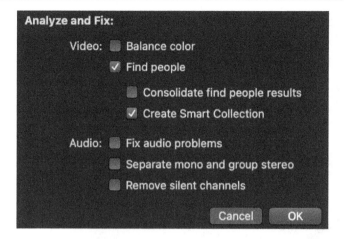

Figure 2.33 – Find people under Analyze and Fix

The following figure shows the settings for the **One Person**, **Two Persons**, and **Group** categories that are included in the **People** search filter:

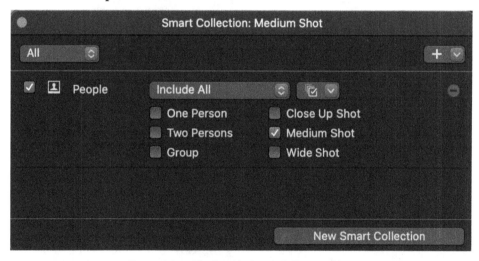

Figure 2.34 – The People Smart Collection filter

Markers

The use of markers in the browser gives a visual indication similar to the colored lines. Markers are particularly useful in a **List** view, as the name of the marker is shown in the list:

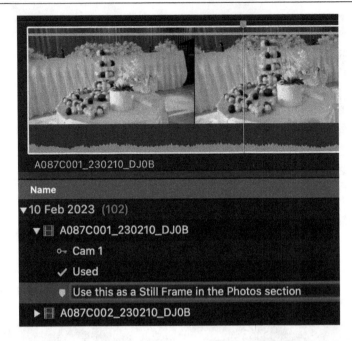

Figure 2.35 – A marker showing a reminder note in a List view

In the **Thumbnail** view, you will see a reminder in the thumbnail, as shown in the following figure:

Figure 2.36 – A marker showing a reminder note in the Thumbnail view

Up until now, I've shown you how to add media or portions to the different categories, but there seems to be no obvious way of removing the clip selections for each category. You will see how in the next section.

Removing media from categories

In this section, we will look at some simple steps to remove media from the various categories.

Let's consider them in order:

- **Favorites**: To remove a favorited clip, press the *U* key – it unrates both **Favorites** and **Rejected** categorizations. **Unrating** means the media is no longer rated as **Favorite** or **Rejected**.

- **Keyword Collections**: Select the Keyword Collection to remove it in the browser sidebar, and press *Command + K*. When the **Keyword** window opens, select the keyword in the top field of the window, shown in blue, and press *Delete*.

- **Rejected**: Press the *U* key; this is the same method of unrating used for **Favorites**.

- **Smart Collections**: Smart Collections are a little harder to remove because the clips are added automatically, as per their attributes. You would need to change those attributes, such as the name of a clip. If you had a Smart Collection that collected all clips named IMG, you could rename them to remove them from that collection. However, from a more practical point of view, if the clip wasn't wanted at all, then you could trash it. Right-click on the clip and select **Move to Trash**, or press the *Command + Delete* keys.

There is a further way of filtering how clips are displayed in the browser. You had a taste of these filter groups in the *Favorites* section earlier in the chapter. The following section will show you how to filter clips that are on view in the browser.

People shots can be removed by double-clicking the shot listing in the sidebar and unticking the unwanted shot.

Media contained in categories is one method of sorting clips. These categories are then able to sort themselves as per your will, which we will see in the following section.

Browser filters

Up until now, we have been looking at the media in the browser under the listing of **All Clips**. You saw that you could change that filter to **Favorites**. The other filter options are **Hide Rejected**, **No Ratings or Keywords**, **Rejected**, and **Unused**:

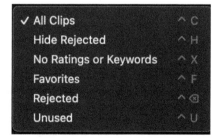

Figure 2.37 – The filter options

The filter headings don't explain a lot about what they do at first glance. Let's decipher what they do by looking at them in order. **Hide Rejected** refers to clips that have been hidden by using the *Delete* key – yes, the *Delete* key! Let me explain.

You would think that if you deleted a clip in the browser, it would go in the trash. To be clear, deleting from the browser *does not* trash media. It stores the clip in a hidden category called **Rejected**. It's so well hidden that you can't even access it. Well, that's not quite true – I'll show you how to use a filter to view hidden files, as there is no Smart Collection, such as **Favorites**, that shows you the hidden **Rejected** clips. Any clips that have been rejected show a red line across the top of the browser thumbnail.

You will recall that I showed you, in the previous section, how you can create your own Smart Collection to hold **Rejected** clips. The browser filters will also quickly display all clips other than **Rejected** clips – **Hide Rejected** in that filter.

No Ratings or Keywords is a way of only viewing media that is *not* in a Keyword Collection, a favorite, or in the **Rejected** category. You would use this filter to check that you have not missed any clips when you have finished rating clips as **Best**, **Suitable**, **Maybe**, and **B Roll**. You will learn more about ratings in *Chapter 4*.

The filters

The filter for **Favorites** speaks for itself – it just shows media that you have categorized by pressing the *F* key. As you saw in the *Keyword Collections* section earlier, I used **Favorites** as an option to set up my **Best**-labeled Keyword Collection.

Rejected clips can also be filtered by this option, adding a different way of viewing unwanted clips other than by the **Rejected** Smart Collection that I created earlier in the *Using the Search functionality* section.

Unused is the last in the list of ways to filter how media is viewed. **Unused** specifically refers to clips that are not included in the currently active project in the timeline. So, to be clear, this is completely different from **Rejected** clips in the browser. **Unused** gives you a heads-up so that don't miss any important clips by mistake. Don't get confused between the two.

An opposing way of filtering the browser is to change the order in which media is displayed and, in turn, show the clips to see them in a specified order. The next section looks at the ways to sort as well as the differences between the **List** and **Thumbnail** browser views.

Sorting the browser

To understand the principle of sorting, it is first best to consider two methods of viewing media in the browser – the **List** view or the **Thumbnail** view. Up until now, I have only discussed the ramifications of using the **Thumbnail** view. It is highly visual compared to the **List** view and, as such, is the view that most video editors would prefer to use.

After all, we are visual people. Aren't lists for people working in databases? Well, let's get real here – Final Cut Pro is a giant database, so the **List** view takes advantage of all those database facilities. To select the **List** view, click to the right of the browser filter selections.

Figure 2.38 – The List view icon

When you look at a **List** view, the visual part of the clip, which is selected in the list, indicated by a blue horizontal bar, is displayed at the top of the viewer:

Name	Start	End	Media Duration	Content Created	Camera Angle	Notes	Video Ro
▼Projects (1)							
🎬 Apple Motion's most important Feature	00:00:00:00	00:11:09:07	00:11:09:07	27 Jun 2022 at 6:30:29 pm			
▼No Data (6)							
▶ 🎬 First Clip	00:00:00:00	00:01:38:15	00:01:38:15	28 Jun 2022 at 9:40:19 am			Video
IMG_9482	00:00:00:00	00:01:34:00	00:01:34:00	28 Jun 2022 at 9:28:30 am			Video
IMG_9482 copy	00:00:00:00	00:01:34:00	00:01:34:00	28 Jun 2022 at 9:28:30 am			Video
IMG_9483	00:00:00:00	00:27:35:01	00:27:35:01	28 Jun 2022 at 9:27:39 am			Video
IMG_9483 copy	00:00:00:00	00:27:35:01	00:27:35:01	28 Jun 2022 at 9:27:39 am			Video
🎬 Second Clip	00:00:00:00	00:27:49:06	00:27:49:06	28 Jun 2022 at 10:10:54 am			Video
▼MPEG-4 movie (1)							
🎬 Filmage 2022-06-28 130739	00:00:00:00	00:00:22:24	00:00:22:24	28 Jun 2022 at 1:07:11 pm			Video
▼Media File (1)							

Figure 2.39 – The List view

What is different from the **Thumbnail** view is the amount of information that can be displayed in the list. Directly under the visual image are headings, in a slightly lighter gray, for each column in the list. There are a number of default headings. The options that hide behind the scenes are almost mind-boggling. Right-click on any column in the heading bar to reveal the options:

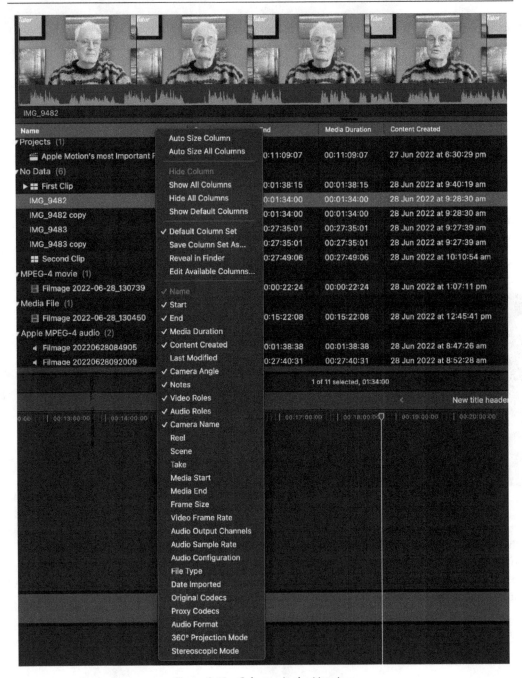

Figure 2.40 – Columns in the List view

The headings that are currently selected are ticked. You can add or remove any that you would like as a column in the list. They can be selected in ascending or descending order by clicking on the light gray heading bar at the top above the column that you wish to adjust. In turn, the columns can be reordered horizontally by dragging the light gray heading left or right until it is positioned in the optimum position to suit your editing style. Select **Edit Available Columns…** | **Column Set Editor** for a vast selection of further metadata:

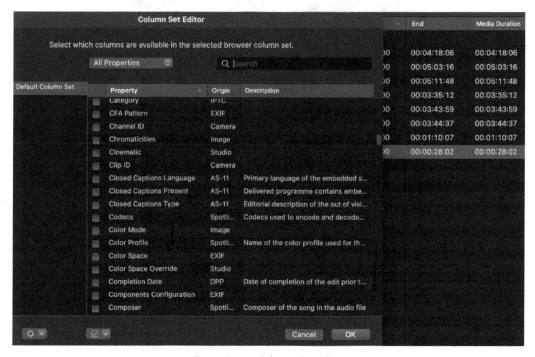

Figure 2.41 – Column Set Editor

To return to the **Thumbnail** view, click the same icon that you used to enter the **List** view.

To adjust the sorting order of clips when viewed in either the **List** or **Thumbnail** view, click the film strip icon to the right of the **List** view:

Figure 2.42 – The film strip icon

The sorting order gives you the option of how you would like media to show in the browser; firstly, it can be modified by how the media is grouped, and then, secondly, on how those groups are sorted:

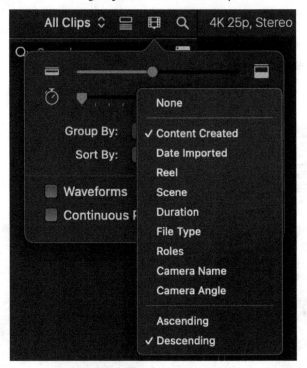

Figure 2.43 – Group By and Sort By

The window offers some other viewing options as well. The top slider adjusts how big (in height) the clips will show in the browser, and the second slider, with the stopwatch logo, shows how many video frames are shown in the browser. When the slider is on the far left, a single thumbnail contains all frames, and on the far right, the slider will allow every frame in the clip to be shown. This gives you the option to see more of the browser clips when you are pre-editing the initial assembly and the rough cut.

As you have seen, the browser is the preferred place to distill media into categories that will eventually appear in the rough cut, so you need to have a good view to see the details within the media.

By increasing the height and number of frames on view, you have a better chance to accurately find the beginning and end of the portion of a clip that you are going to categorize as a favorite, or in different Keyword Collections.

Within this same window are options to group media in the browser. As an example, if you select **Content Created**, the clips will be viewed by the dates that they were filmed. Then, in turn, you can sort those dated groups by the clip name or duration:

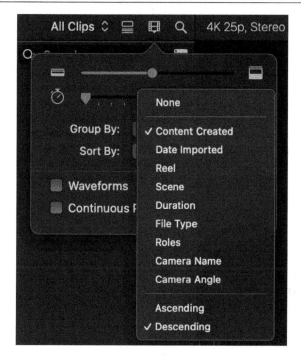

Figure 2.44 – Waveforms and Duration

The **Waveforms** checkbox will allow audio to show waveforms on video clips that have audio attached. Audio-only clips always show the audio waveforms. My suggestion is to keep this off, as the waveforms are not normally that important to see in the browser clip – there's no point stressing out the computer more than necessary.

There is an alternative method of viewing (and, in fact, adjusting) browser clips before they are edited in a project in the timeline. This is the **Open Clip** command, which you will be shown in the next section.

The Open Clip view

The **Open Clip** view is something that I suggest you use with real care, as it changes a browser clip before it is used in the project.

> **Note**
>
> The **Open Clip** view cannot be used to categorize clips in any of the indexes that have just been discussed. It can only be applied to individual whole clips, as it does not recognize portions of clips.

The **Open Clip** view will let you add and adjust color and audio effects in the browser clip itself. Think of this as a means of changing the color and audio attributes as if this task was done before importing a clip into Final Cut Pro. You can even add more than one video clip to blend multiple clips together.

I frequently use **Open Clip** to sync video clips with external audio recorders so that the clip is synchronized in the browser before it is added to a project in the timeline.

As I warned previously, be sure you know what you are doing, as once a clip that has been modified with the **Open Clip** command is added to a project, it is fixed in that state, even if the clip is later modified in the browser. Once a clip is added to a project, it is in a **Printed** state. It's fixed in the condition it was in in the browser before it was added to the project.

A potential use of **Open Clip** is to change the color of browser clips before they are used in an edit. An example of a use for **Open Clip** is where camera clips appear overexposed when there is not a suitable readily available **lookup table** (**LUT**) that would instantly adjust the color grade in the browser.

By adjusting the exposure of a clip with the use of **Open Clip**, all uses of that clip in projects within the current library will have the exposure correction burnt in.

Using the Open Clip function

To use **Open Clip**, select a clip in the browser, and from the **Clip** menu, select **Open Clip**. A copy of the clip will temporarily open in the timeline, with the video portion and audio as separate tracks. Effects can be added from both the video and audio **Effects** browsers. You can use the Inspector to modify those effects. You can even drag other video and audio clips into the temporary **Timeline** view.

Figure 2.45 – Use with care

You will be warned, as shown in *Figure 2.45*, that you are changing the browser clip.

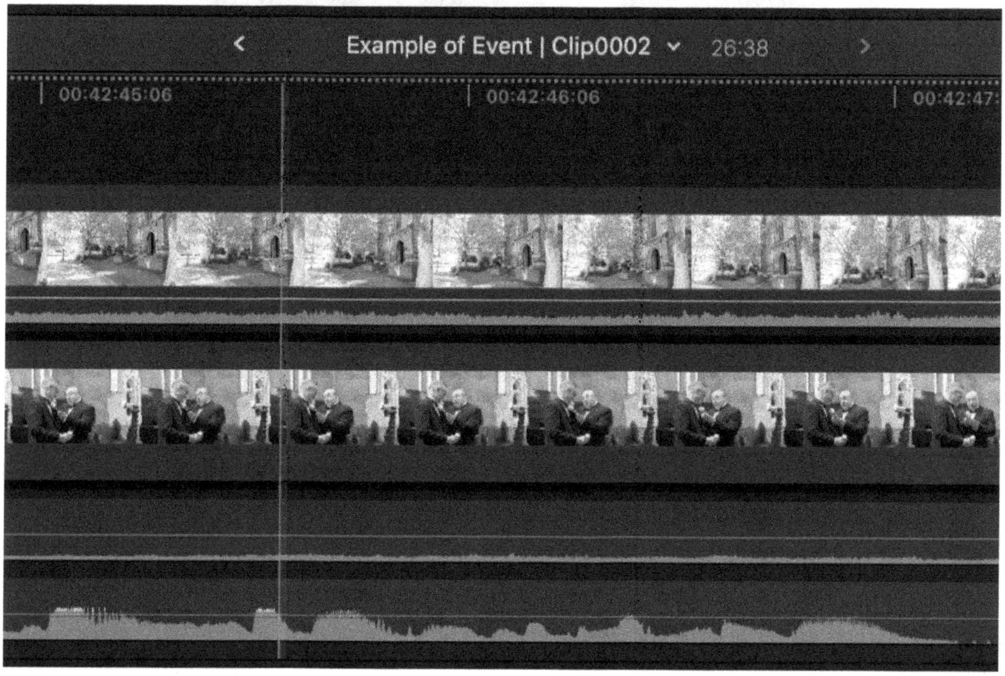

Figure 2.46 – How Open Clip shows in the timeline

Now that you have seen how to view media in the browser, you will need to action those clips, and this next section looks at a shortcut to the actions that you can perform on browser clips.

Shortcuts for media actions

Right-clicking on browser clips will offer the following shortcuts. The choices depend on whether one or more clips are selected. *Figure 2.47* shows when two clips are selected:

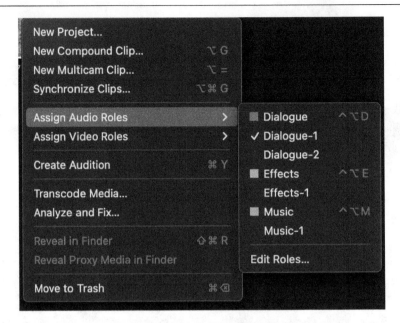

Figure 2.47 – Roles selected when right-clicking media in the browser

The first four choices are fairly self-explanatory, and they will be explained in detail in *Chapter 4* and *Chapter 7*.

Roles are unique to Final Cut Pro and are a much-underrated feature that deserves a brief explanation. You have just looked at categorizing media in the browser, and roles are a way of categorizing timeline audio clips in a similar manner to labeling browser clips. As you know, Final Cut Pro does not have independent tracks like other NLEs; it has a main magnetic timeline with clips connected to it.

The **Roles** feature allows you to apply different categories to audio clips connected to the main magnetic storyline. As of version 10.7 of Final Cut Pro, video clips in the main storyline with audio attached can have the roles categories attached to the audio portion of the clip. Think of roles as a type of label or category for audio clips in the timeline – it's not too dissimilar to the concept of categorizing clips in the browser. The real advantage of roles is when it comes to exporting audio, as you can differentiate audio tracks, based on the role label that has been applied to them. Roles are ideal for exporting videos with different language translations. You can also display a role by name, in the timeline, by using the timeline index. You will learn much more details about roles in *Chapter 4*.

Transcoding media

An integral part of how media is processed by Final Cut Pro, as discussed in *Chapter 1*, involves editing **original** media, **optimized** media, and, for the purposes of reducing the load on a computer's processor, **proxy** media.

As a regular user of Final Cut Pro, you will be aware of how to import footage and make Final Cut Pro transcode it to optimized or proxy media for ease of editing. As a reminder, this is done by selecting the options in the **Import** window, or **Import** in the **Preference** setting.

As noted in *Chapter 1*, proxy media takes up less storage than original or optimized media and is just as smooth to edit. The compromise is that there is a drop in the quality of what you see while editing, compared to when you are editing with optimized or original media. The different choices of proxy affect that quality quite significantly.

Proxy media is the term used for media when you are actually editing with that smaller file format, taking up less space and causing less stress on a computer's processor. **ProRes Proxy** is one of the format choices that you can ask Final Cut Pro to convert original media to during the **Import** process, or when you right-click and ask it to transcode. You can also transcode to optimized media, although in most cases, it is more practical to choose just one option, either optimized or proxy media.

There are different quality options for proxy media, and there are specific uses for those. Mainly, you would only use the low-quality proxy media options if file size for transfer over the internet is an issue.

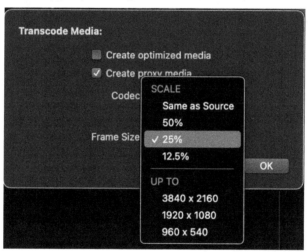

Figure 2.48 – Transcode options

The following example will explain it clearly for you. Recently, I was asked to edit an event sent from Iowa, USA, while I was based in Sydney, Australia. The main motivation was to do with the time difference. I was editing in Australia during nighttime in Iowa. I could receive the media at the end of the day in Iowa time, which was early morning in Sydney time. I could complete the edit while they slept in Iowa and have it back to them before they woke in the morning. The big issue was the time it took to get large files transferred over the internet.

This is where proxy media provides a solution. The shooter transcodes the clips to the smallest practical proxy size. The options are **ProRes Proxy** (just known as **Proxy**), which can be as small as **12.5%**. Also available to choose from is **H.264**, which has a higher compression format, resulting in even smaller file sizes. As an example, **ProRes Proxy** at a **50%** resolution is 70% smaller than optimized media. **H.264** at a **50%** resolution is 90% smaller than Final Cut Pro's optimized media. The **12.5%**-sized proxy is just too hard to see any meaningful detail for editing, never mind color correction. For my example, I opted for **ProRes Proxy** at **25%** of the size of the original footage. That is good enough to clearly see where to cut and make educated judgments for color correction.

The output was for the event attendees to see the previous day's activities, so the content was the main issue. The transfer time to receive the footage over the internet was less than an hour for all the day's footage. After the edit, the project was not exported in the normal method but exported as an XML file (**File | Export XML**). The real advantage of XML is that it's so small, it takes only seconds to transfer as an attachment in an email. The shooter matched the XML to the original footage in his Final Cut Pro library. He then exported the project as **H.264** and published it before the attendees from the Iowa event woke up for the day. That's the power of proxy media.

If you use proxy media, you need to change back to optimized or original when the edit is completed, and before you export. Final Cut Pro will prompt you to switch back. Everything you have edited in the proxy form is then matched, under the hood, with the original or optimized media for the export to be done at full quality. If you are using proxy media, it is unlikely that you will also need optimized media unless the original media has been deleted. However, it is possible to have original, optimized, and proxy media. You must have at least one of either optimized or original media.

As you have seen so far in the chapter, the browser is where you can view media. You've learned how to sort and filter the views of the media; now, it's time to see how to view the metadata information about libraries and clips in the Inspector.

Exploring clip and library information

As previously stated, Final Cut Pro is, at its heart, a database, so there is a vast amount of metadata that you can access from the Inspector. This type of information is different for clips and libraries. Clips show information about how they were created on the camera as well as offering fields where you can add information. Library information has more to do with where and how a library is located on a computer.

Figure 2.49 – Clip information in the Inspector

A method of exploring clip information

Select a clip in the browser sidebar, and make sure that the **i** letter in the circle is active in the Inspector (if the circle is blue, it's active). At the bottom-left of the **Inspector** window is a drop-down button. The default selection is **Basic**; change this to **Extended**.

The following is the information you will be most interested in. Let's start at the top of the window. In the gray bar is the clip aspect ratio in pixels, with the frame rate at which it was recorded. When a clip is selected, the aspect and frame rate always show at the top-left of the viewer window, next to the **Search** magnifying glass.

Figure 2.50 – The clip aspect ratio

Further down the list in the Inspector, you will see that there is fixed information that you can't change and options that you can add or change. The latter appear as either a blank field or as a drop-down menu that you can choose from.

Working your way down the list in the Inspector, the first open field is the **Notes** field. You will recall, from the *Sorting the browser* section earlier in this chapter, that you have the option to view clips in a **List** view. One of those list headings is **Notes**. In my opinion, the ability to attach notes to a clip is a much-underrated feature, although it is one thing to add notes but another to remember that they are there.

There are options to change the roles. These will be discussed in detail in *Chapter 4*. The next important field is **Camera Name** (which you will use in *Chapter 8*). Then, there is the **Camera LUT** field, which you will learn more about in *Chapter 13*.

At the bottom of the window, you can see the event and location that the clip is contained in, but more importantly, you can see the status of the **Original**, **Optimized**, and **Proxy** media. There is a **Transcode Media…** button as an alternative way to transcode the media, rather than the right-click method within the browser window, as detailed earlier in this chapter.

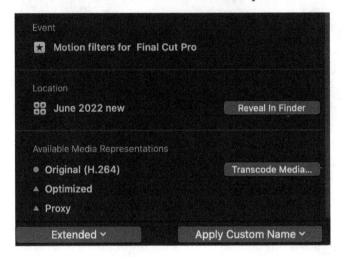

Figure 2.51 – The bottom view of the information in the Inspector

Information that is equally as important to be aware of before diving into the editing process is how to set up **Preferences**, recently known as **Settings**. This will be the last section of this chapter.

Exploring Settings/Preferences

Prior to macOS version 13 and Final Cut Pro 10.6.5, *Settings* were known as *Preferences*. They allow you to personalize the way that Final Cut Pro is set up. Settings can be accessed under the **Final Cut**

Pro menu; it's the second item, called either **Settings** or **Preferences**, depending on your version of Final Cut Pro and macOS.

There are five tabs. The first is **General**, where you can change the time display in the timeline. This is usually set at HH:MM:SS:FF – hours, minutes, seconds, and frames. This is the normal setting; the latter *frames* are dependent on the frame rate of the project in the timeline. The others are standard, as their words imply. You may need the second choice under the time display option will add subframes when working with audio, where there are many extra frames, known as **subframes**, of audio within a single frame of video.

The second tab is the **Editing** tab. You may wish to adjust the default duration of still images that are added to the timeline and the duration of transitions in the timeline:

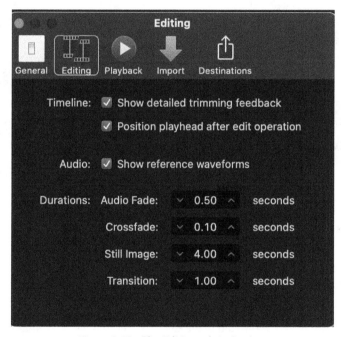

Figure 2.52 – The Editing tab in Settings

The third tab is the **Playback** tab, which is where you will most likely make the most changes.

Background render and **Player Background** are usually the settings that you will change to suit your needs.

Background render allows you to choose whether the rendering of the timeline takes place when the computer is at rest and you are not editing. The **Start after** option starts the render after a set time from when you last made changes in Final Cut Pro. If you do decide to turn on **Background render**, don't make the start time too short; otherwise, the rendering will turn on and off almost continuously. If you do use **Background render**, set the start time to a least one minute.

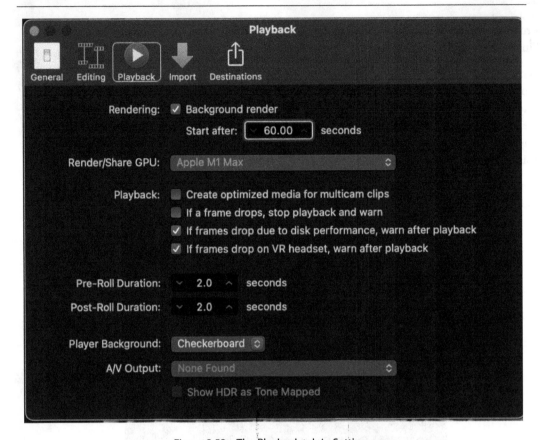

Figure 2.53 – The Playback tab in Settings

My preference is to avoid using **Background render**, as it substantially increases the size of the Final Cut Pro library. The setting is principally to aid slower computers by speeding up exports, because the timeline will be at least partly rendered during the downtime or during the editing process.

Player Background changes the background in the empty viewer from black to white or checkerboard. The latter is handy for seeing the edges of clips that may not fill the whole viewer window when a clip is resized or rotated.

Figure 2.54 – The viewer showing a checkerboard background

The fourth tab, **Import**, has the same settings as in *Chapter 4* (ingesting the media).

You should note that some changes within the interface will stick at the last setting for a new library or project, even if Final Cut Pro is quit and reopened. Frustratingly, there are some settings that don't stick. The main one for me is the height setting for the timeline. Any new project will return to the default.

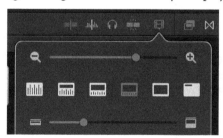

Figure 2.55 – The default timeline height and duration settings

The height and duration need to be reset for each new project.

Figure 2.56 – Settings need to be reset after quitting

The other frustrating default reset is in the browser. Whenever Final Cut Pro is quit and reopened, the height and duration of browser clips return to default.

Final Cut Pro is very sparse with the settings that you can adjust – maybe that is a good thing in that you don't have the temptation to change things that you don't know about. I would take that thought as a warning to not meddle in areas you are not familiar with. The **Help** tab in the main menu bar, provided by Apple, is well worth visiting regularly.

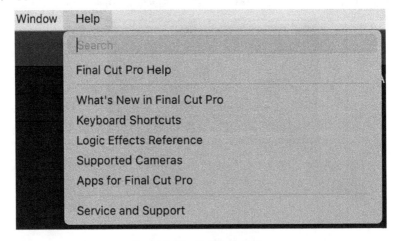

Figure 2.57 – The Help menu

The fifth and final tab is **Destinations**, which focuses on the methods of exporting a completed project from Final Cut Pro. Check out *Chapter 1*, to know which video format is best for which purpose for a refresher on what types of video formats you can use to export a project under this tab.

Summary

As with *Chapter 1*, this chapter is rich in reference content that you will need to engage with from time to time. You saw that Final Cut Pro's unique set of tools ensures that media remains well organized, with all of it being stored within a library and then in events, favorites, Keyword Collections, and Smart Collections. You saw how to create templates to ease the setup of future edits, along with searching routines and ways to sort media in a browser. There was information about how and why to transcode media for ease of editing. We discussed options on how the view of the browser can be adjusted to suit your needs. You saw how Final Cut Pro allows you to become very detailed in how you categorize clips and the rating of those selections. You will have realized that it is useful to spend time sorting when working on longer and more complex projects, but for shorter videos, you should let your instincts prevail and start editing as quickly as possible.

We explained the different colored lines that appear on clips, as well as how to remove clips from indexed categories.

You saw how to access metadata about clips and libraries in the Inspector, and we also gave a brief explanation of the **Preferences/Settings** window.

The main message to take away from this chapter is how uniquely flexible Final Cut Pro is at organizing media, and how you can adapt that flexibility to suit your editing style and workflow.

The next chapter will introduce you to methods that you will use to plan your edit, as well as the information you should be asking shooters to provide you with.

3

Planning the Video Story

Video is the new preferred medium of storytelling. In this chapter, you will see how a video story comes to life and how Final Cut Pro assists in the planning process. When planning videos, we need to understand traditional human story types as well as other story types, such as slice-of-life, commercial, instructional, and social media. When you are planning your video, it helps to see where it fits in terms of the types of stories that are universally recognized. In this chapter, you will learn about the different types of stories and how videos can uniquely tell these stories. You will see how the most important consideration is to uncover who the intended audience is. You need to plan your story with that target audience specifically in mind by creating a persona in your mind (a persona is an archetypal person that represents a group of individuals). Throughout this chapter, you will be shown different types of video styles and how to plan for those different styles. You will be presented with story types and structures for commercial-style videos, along with human story styles with varying plot types. Finally, when the tried-and-true, nuts-and-bolts planning is complete, the conceptual ideas can be moved into the storyboard, where you can flesh them out with tactile shapes and sequences.

Of course, much of this will be out of your control if you are not involved with the shoot and your first involvement is when the footage is sent to you. Whatever the case, you will learn that you still need to plan how to build the footage into a video story unless the storyboard and the video plan are provided as part of your brief.

In this chapter, we're going to cover the following main topics:

- A story is a journey
- What you should remember when planning a story
- Planning for different types of videos

By the end of this chapter, you will be able to recognize the various types of video stories. Understanding their characteristics will help you come up with an idea of how your story can be systematically arranged into an order that will give it the substance needed for a compelling video. You will understand how dramatic and commercial videos require different approaches to the planning process. You will also be aware that the audience for your video needs to be recognized before you start the planning process. Finally, you will know how to keep that audience persona in your mind throughout the planning as well as the editing process.

A story is a journey

Past generations learned how to write a letter or a narrative in school, but the current generation of students is learning how to create movies. Not to say that writing is not important, but the visual aspect is becoming more of a significant factor.

A story can be thought of as a journey, and no journey can start without a plan. You can't journey anywhere without knowing where you are going. Even an off-the-cuff *let's go out today* is the start of a plan. If you are the original planner of the video, your first decision is what type of story the video is going to tell. Just as in a literary composition, a video that tells a human story will be of a fixed set of story types.

Once you've started putting together a draft of what the video is about, it's time to explore the different plot ideas.

What are the types of stories?

There are differing opinions on how many story types exist. Some say there are only two types of stories:

- The **popular type**, which is made up of fairy tales, animal tales, fables, myths, and legends
- The **literal type**, which includes realistic stories such as the mystery, historical, romantic, police, and fantasy genres

Most commentators agree on the following classifications. These can overlap, so your video story could fit in more than one classification:

- **Fairy tales**: These portray events that are not real; they usually have a happy ending.
- **Animal tales**: These are stories with animals that have human personalities.
- **Traditions**: These are usually critical of the current or a past society, often told with satire or humor.
- **Fantasy**: These stories are based on magic, where the characters or their environment have magical abilities.
- **Realism**: These concentrate on day-to-day, unembellished contemporary life.

- **Mystery**: These stories coerce the viewer into the feeling of intrigue, which can include the feeling of living the character's experiences as if they, the viewers, are part of the story.

- **Horror**: Fear is the key to this story type and intends to induce terror. Again, this can be done by hooking the viewer into experiencing the events as if they were the character.

- **Comedy**: These stories are intended to make the viewer laugh.

- **History**: These stories are not just about historical facts – they can also be about fictional events that a historical person may have experienced.

- **Romantic**: These stories mainly revolve around the love between two characters and how other events affect them.

- **Police**: These stories involve a crime or solving a predicament. They do not necessarily portray the police.

- **Science fiction**: These stories are commonly set in the future, but also in the present with fictional technologies.

Why classify stories?

The principal reason to classify your video story is to give you somewhere to start in your planning process. As you proceed through the planning process and develop a plot, you will likely find that you have overlapped with more than one of the other classifications.

It is well known that dreaming up the original concept of anything is easy, but it's the implementation that is much harder. Once you have the idea in your head, how do you start documenting? How do you proceed? It's at this point that you need a plan. The difficult part is deciding what to start with. Your mind will be either so full of ideas that you can't decide or, more likely, completely devoid of anything concrete to use as the actual starting point. The preceding classifications can give you some clues about what you could include. The initial thought hurdle will be overcome, and your creative juices will flow.

The various types of stories are not isolated; they will exist alongside and overlap with other story types, as you will discover in the following section.

Drama stories

All drama stories have several shared elements that can involve a person or persons working toward a greater desire or goal or a provoking event that takes the person out of their comfort zone. There is rising action, where the person is tested in some way. There is also, most likely, the fear of failure, but it always has some resolution, good or bad.

The person can either achieve their goal or not, but to fit the mold of a drama story, you need some conflict. Otherwise, there is no story, just a series of events, and this won't hold your audience's attention.

Human stories

A story may or may not refer to real events; fiction can be added to the mix. The narrative of a human story in video form is different from a book in that it is mainly told through images and sounds that are linked together to give a flow and meaning to the video. The story structure is made up of three parts, commonly referred to as the beginning, middle, and end.

The beginning introduces the characters and portrays their desires or goals.

The middle shows the the characters in a state of confusion when they are out of their comfort zone.

The end is when a solution is found (or it is determined that one cannot be found).

Human story versus commercial videos

As well as traditional human stories, we also have slices of life, such as interviews and wedding videos. Non-human stories – let's call them commercial videos – have a different planning routine that is quite unlike that of traditional human stories.

First, I'll consider commercial videos, describe how you should approach the planning process, and point out the areas where commercial videos overlap with human story videos.

A consideration that affects the planning of any video is who will watch it. The people who watch your video are known as the target audience. You can get a better idea of who that intended audience is by being aware of the different plot types, as covered in the next section.

What are the types of plots?

Just like story types, there are multiple genres that plot types are employed in, as shown here:

- **Life or death**: Adventure and thriller/action video stories.

- **Life or a fate worse than death**: Horror or mystery video stories.

- **Love or hate**: Romance/love video stories.

- **Achievement or failure**: Performance/sports video stories.

- **Maturity or immaturity**: Coming-of-age video stories.

- **Good or evil**: Relating to the polar opposites of good and bad.

- **Temptation/morality video stories**: The scenes will include propriety conventions, along with either ethical or non-ethical characters. Use conventional moral views to flavor your video's concepts.

- **Action/thriller videos**: The plot of an action video involves an event or action that has caused some wrong to be done to or by the main character. The resolution is how the character rights the wrong or gets revenge. A subtype of an action plot is the adventure video, which revolves around an object, place, or person important to the characters and determines how the plot develops and its ultimate resolution. Thriller and adventure videos need to have moments of *life or death*, or *a fate worse than death*.

- **Horror story**: This plot type has fictional characters who are trapped with someone or something deviating from the norm by way of shape or behavior, often a monster. The plot needs to have moments of *life versus a fate worse than death*.

- **Mystery story**: All mystery plot video types feature an event where a crime is discovered. The plot needs to have *life-threatening or a fate worse than death* moments.

- **Romance/love story**: These stories usually involve a conflict where couples are meeting or breaking up. A love story needs to have equal moments of love and hate, anger, disillusion, or dislike.

- **Achievement or failure**: Videos of this type are about a person's ego and their success in achieving something outstanding. There will be a challenger of dubious intent. There need to be as many moments of near failure, or actual failure, as there are of achievements.

- **Coming-of-age story**: These videos are about teens or young adults in the process of reaching adulthood by reflecting on their lives. The plot needs to have moments where their developing maturity conflicts with immaturity. These stories usually have a happy ending.

- **Temptation/morality story**: This type of video plays on selfishness and the resolution to give in to temptation or resist and feel morally rewarded. The character does things they know are wrong, for benefit or not.

Parallel editing style

While not a story type, you should be aware of the parallel editing style, which jumps between two or more different scenes happening at the same time. It can increase the feeling of suspense and the pacing of a scene. This style is best used in the drama, mystery, and suspense types of plots.

To summarize the types and how to use them, use a mix of the different types of stories in longer videos, where you can include sub-stories or parallel stories, to allow a change of pace. Try not to mix the types for short-format videos as you are likely to confuse your audience.

What you should remember when planning a story

You need to be aware of several factors that will affect how you plan your video. Once you understand the following information, you will find planning much easier.

Knowing your target audience

All video stories, both human and commercial ones, need to be tested for their appeal to the target audience. *There is no point in trying to sell fridges to Eskimos*, would be one way to put it. It's not just who the audience is but, more importantly, the attention of the audience or how long they will watch your video. A video about politics is unlikely to hold the attention of a very young audience. A documentary on cars is unlikely to attract people who have no interest in driving.

Don't fall into the trap of thinking that the target audience is only a pre-production concern. As the video editor, it is just as relevant for you to keep the persona of the target audience in mind as you progress through the edit. You may not have to go through the following research process if you are not involved with pre-production. Hopefully, it will have been done for you by the pre-production department. Make sure they communicate to you who they have established as the target audience. Don't settle for something too wide. Terms such as *all males* or *only children* are not a workable target. Of course, if you are a one-man band and responsible for everything, then read on.

You need to research who your intended audience is and how they will have access to the completed video. From this point in this chapter, the discussion will mostly focus on the commercial type of video. Even if you are planning a traditional human story video, you will understand the absolute importance of identifying the target audience for your video and understanding their needs and aspirations. When you visualize the persona of the intended viewer, it becomes easier to plan what they will want to see in the video.

Now, from a commercial aspect, it is important to quickly grab the viewer's attention; this is called the hook. This will encourage them to continue viewing the video. Even human video stories should make use of the hook. It is within the first few scenes of the video. Just think of a James Bond movie.

Sourcing the target audience for commercial videos is not an easy task but you must figure this out. It will require research, experimentation, and planning. Even if you have a target audience in mind, you need to research whether they are the most appropriate to appreciate and benefit from your video.

Because it's such an important step in planning your video, the following are some ideas to consider. You need to consider a combination of these, not just one:

- You should contemplate the demographics and goals of your target audience, taking into account how your product will assist them.
- You should conduct some focus group research to see who is interested in the video's topic. Use Google and social media platforms.
- If you are creating videos for your business or client's businesses, talk to their salespeople to see what their customers are asking about.

Once you have information about the potential audience, create a persona (a persona is an archetypal person who represents a group of individuals). You should define most of the following traits for a persona, not just one or two:

- **Demographic information**: Age, gender, location, and income
- **Personality details**: Qualities and traits that make them an individual

- **Challenges**: What affects their day-to-day routines?
- **Resolution**: How will your video solve their problems?

As an editor, now that you have the persona, whether it was handed to you by the client or you built it yourself, you need to put it to use while you're planning how the edit will proceed.

Planning the edit with the target audience in mind

The following list will be useful for you when you're planning a video so that you can keep the target audience in mind:

- **Grab their attention up front**: In today's instant gratification world, you only have seconds to capture your audience's attention. Use a hook to make sure that the first five seconds of the video grab their attention. Avoid drawn-out intros or animated logos. They are just fluff and mainly just appeal to your sense of personal satisfaction with the video. They do the opposite of gaining attention. Place the best clips first.

- **Respond to customer feedback in videos**: Plan a video that reveals a behind-the-scenes viewpoint of the product or service that will appeal to your audience. Think of it as a back story, an explanation of why the product exists, or its history – perhaps its environmental benefits or social virtues.

- **Use videos from satisfied customers**: The most unique and relatable way to appeal to an audience is to use their videos. Try to get customers talking about and using the product, preferably with videos they have shot themselves. These are much more authentic than commercially shot high-quality shots.

- **Plan videos as content for marketing emails**: This allows your organization or your client's company to use videos in combination with email marketing. Split up the content into several short videos. Content that runs for 10 minutes will receive many more views when it's edited into five 2-minute videos than one long 10-minute video. Short videos with common title effects and logos are quick to duplicate, so your editing time will be reduced. The added benefit is that you have provided your client with five videos and not just one. They will think they are getting more for their money.

- **Create a video series**: Similar to videos as content for marketing emails, a video series around a theme can be highly effective. As stated earlier, instant gratification is in vogue, but even so, staggering the release of videos not only keeps the viewer hooked but also builds anticipation for the next video.

Once you have established who encompasses your target audience, you will be able to craft your videos to suit them. Then, eventually, you will need to know how to reach the target audience, but that comes much later and will be covered in *Chapter 9*. In the meantime, there is an assembly edit to do in Final Cut Pro.

Creating storyboards

As with scripts, storyboards are produced before filming commences. So, if you aren't the shooter, this will have been done before the editing stage. I will introduce storyboards here for those who are both the shooter and the editor.

While planning a video, there will be ideas flashing through your head from all directions. So, when it comes to the actual shoot, you need to be focused on what you are about to shoot. In the case of a traditional story, shots are frequently filmed out of sequence. Commercial videos are more likely to be shot in sequential order.

To create a video storyboard, you take the thoughts that are in your mind and add characters and activities, in chronological order. The storyboard represents the shot order but not necessarily how the finished video will unfold. The added advantage of a storyboard is other people can understand your pattern of thoughts as they become tactile images. Storyboards can be drawn on paper or with software, both online (https://www.storyboardthat.com/) and locally on your computer (https://wonderunit.com/storyboarder/download/).

Once you have drawn the images of each action sequence, you can add scene-related details, such as extra notes or comments to make it clear to the team. Use rectangles that are of the same aspect ratio as your video – that is, 16:9:

Figure 3.1– Storyboard – photo by Nasim Keshmiri on Unsplash

Final Cut Pro has a storyboard feature called placeholders, built into the **Elements** category of **Generators**. During rough-cut editing, media may not be available yet. Placeholder clips can be used as a substitute shot until the missing footage becomes available. A placeholder can be customized to different shot sizes and backgrounds. You can use placeholders to indicate shots that need to be added to the timeline, such as a wide shot or a mid shot of two people. See *Chapter 4* for details:

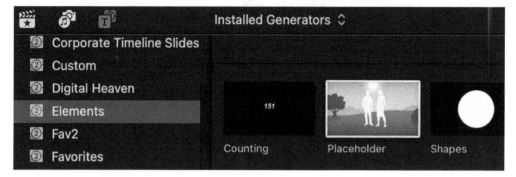

Figure 3.2 – Placeholders

In addition to commercial-style videos, you will also need to consider planning for other types, such as documentaries and interviews, as outlined in the following section.

Planning for different types of videos

Different types of videos will have different planning processes. The following subsections look at different types of video styles, laying out some ideas for the specific planning required.

Documentary videos

If you were involved in shooting the documentary, you would have gone through the process of defining a target audience, so you would be more aware of how the clips will be organized.

Try to arrange the media chronologically, usually according to the storyboard, which will give you a pattern to follow. You will be able to set up the footage as described in *Chapter 2*. In most cases, all the planning has been taken out of your hands, so after organizing the footage into categories, you will need to follow the procedures described in *Chapter 4*.

Interviews

When it comes to planning, and you are editing another shooter's footage, interview videos follow similar lines to the documentary type. However, in many cases, you will also be the shooter, so you will need to plan the shoot. If you are not the shooter, it may be good to ask the shooter to follow the steps discussed in this section. But before you jump in, check how experienced the shooters are. It's not going to end well if you start trying to tell an experienced camera operator how to do their job. Otherwise, if you feel they will accept your input, you will benefit from receiving footage taken as follows.

Conducting interviews with one camera

The following list outlines some tips that you can utilize:

- Set the interviewee to the side in the mid shot. If there is a separate interviewer, position them to the right of the camera when the interviewee is looking away from the camera. Otherwise, if the interviewee is looking directly into the camera, set the interviewer behind the camera just to the side.

- If you shoot in 4K and edit in HD, you can resize the image in the **Viewer** area without quality loss. The different sizes let you edit the video without visible jump cuts. You can change the size of alternative shots by using **Transform** to give the impression that you are changing angles (see *Chapter 9*).

- It is best to use lapel microphones that are connected to either external recorders or a camera (if to a camera, preferably to one track in the main camera). A lavalier microphone or lapel microphone is a small microphone that can be clipped to a collar to allow hands-free operation. You don't need stereo as mono is just as effective for a single-person interview. If you have two people, then each can have their own channel in the camera or recorder.

- If you are the interviewer, stay off camera and preferably don't use the recording of your questions in the edit. Ask the interviewee to wait 2-3 seconds after you ask the question and then ask the editor to display the question as a title at the start of the interviewee's answer. For example, you might ask, *"Do you often meet other staff socially?"* The answer might be, *"Yes, I've met the other staff at office Christmas parties."*

Conducting interviews with two cameras

The main camera is set as described in the *Conducting interviews with one camera* subsection. The second camera should be set to a profile shot but not at too much of an angle (90° is too much). Its angle should be just enough to look different from the main camera. Full profiles look unnatural. Set the second camera wider than the (mid-shot) main camera. The two cameras will be synced together in Final Cut Pro (see *Chapter 8*).

As with the one-camera suggestions, the following tips will assist you when using two cameras:

- **Study the questions**: You will most likely have been provided with the questions to ask the interviewee by your client. You need to study those questions so that you are familiar with them, not necessarily memorizing them word for word but at least understanding the context.

- **Choose the look**: Establish whether the interviewee looks into or away from the camera. Make it consistent; a mix will usually not work well. If the interviewee decides to look down the lens, stick with that. If they look away, you will need to reshoot that section or cover it with B roll in the edit.

- **Ensure that the interviewer and interviewee are at ease**: Ask everyone to close their eyes and take three deep breaths before starting. This helps both the interviewer and interviewee focus. It also helps block out the cameras and equipment from the interviewee's mind. Tell the interviewee to relax their shoulders and count down before they first speak.

- **Shoot B roll**: B roll is a term used for secondary footage that has some relationship to the main subject matter. As an example, the B roll that's used for an interview could be images of items discussed in the interview. B roll is used to hide the jump cut away from a long, uninterrupted shot of someone talking to a camera. An example of B roll is the use of the interviewer nodding to hide the jump cut of the interviewee's head and body changing positon from one scene to the next. Shoot as much B roll as time allows. If none is available at the shoot, you need to source footage from the client. If you have to edit with limited or no B roll, and the footage is 4K, you can set the Final Cut Pro project to 1,920 x 1,080, which will allow you to cut and increase a timeline clip by up to 150% without losing resolution. Then, at the next cut, take it back to normal. B roll also helps give some variation from one long scene of just a talking head.

Wedding videos

Wedding videos are usually structured in a very similar way. They are the most recognizable pattern of any video I have edited, and it is ideal to use the template suggestions I included in *Chapter 2*. For the following example, I will assume you are not the shooter.

The organizational planning for a wedding video is minimal and takes care of itself when you use a template. It is a structured library that can be duplicated in **Finder** and double-clicked to launch in Final Cut Pro. The template library has **Keyword Collections** and **Smart Collections** for you to import for the different parts of the wedding day, preparations, church, photos, and reception. From there, you can proceed as described in *Chapter 4*. The different parts of a wedding day should be edited in separate projects and then combined before being exported.

If you don't use a template, I suggest that you copy all the files from the camera into separate folders in the Mac's **Finder**. Then, provided you have **From folders** ticked in the **Import** window, as shown in *Figure 3.3*, when you import the media into a new library in Final Cut Pro, it will be organized for you in **Keyword Collections**, which can be directly accessed in the pre-edit:

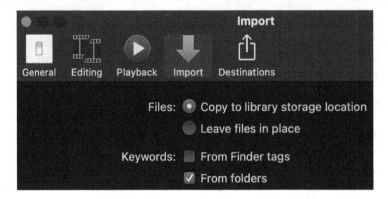

Figure 3.3 – From folders selected

This will be covered in full detail in the wedding video workflow in *Chapter 9*.

Social media videos

Social media videos continue to grow in popularity. Special planning is required when you are considering an edit where social media is the intended viewing destination. The editing style needs to create trust and connections between brands and customers, develop brand loyalty, improve lead generation, and stimulate comments on social media platforms.

As with all forms of video planning, it is a good idea to keep these tips in mind so that you cover all the material needed in the planning process:

- Know your objectives and audience. As with any plan, as you have seen, you need to know your audience as well as be clear on the objectives you specifically want to achieve: brand awareness, initiate conversations, entice new followers, and achieve more sign-ups and website visits.

- Try to make a good first impression. You need to describe the main subject and present the hook within the first few seconds, no more than five seconds. Make sure that the images, either the video or stills, are compelling and match the voiceover.

- Show the logo and tag lines as overlays of the first video frames. Don't have title-only clips. Incorporate the heading or title as part of the first few video images.

- Vertical videos can be broken into three panels: top, middle, and bottom. The top panel can have the logo or brand image on a plain background, the middle panel is for the video, and the bottom panel can have the title or other explanatory text again on a plain background.

The following figures show some examples of a vertical video:

Figure 3.4 – Text in panels on a vertical video

Figure 3.5 – Text without panels on a vertical video

- Keep the video short and focused. Keep social media videos to 1-3 minutes. 1-minute vertical and square videos are good for TikTok, Instagram, and YouTube Shorts. If the subject is complex, maybe consider 6 minutes at the most. Otherwise, break it up into parts and post them separately or as a series.

- Videos should grab the audience's attention as well as present the message to influence viewers to act promptly, the all-important factor. It must have value; otherwise, viewers will not come back to view further videos. Remember the phrase content is king.

- Plan for different formats. Social media is all about vertical and square video formats. That doesn't mean you can't use 16 x 9. The answer is to plan for the three different formats. Start with a 16 x 9 project, and don't stress too much if you go over the 1-minute barrier. Then, you can convert to vertical or square with the automated **Smart Conform** feature with the **Duplicate as…** command in Final Cut Pro.

Let's see how this is done:

I.   Right-click on the 16 x 9 project and select **Duplicate as…**. The window shown in *Figure 3.6* will appear.

II.   Change **Video** to **Vertical** (or **Square**).

III.   Change the resolution to **1080x1920** for vertical (**1080x1080** for square). The most important thing to remember is to tick **Smart Conform** (*see Figure 3.6*). It's not selected by default. Final Cut Pro uses AI to center what it thinks is the main image:

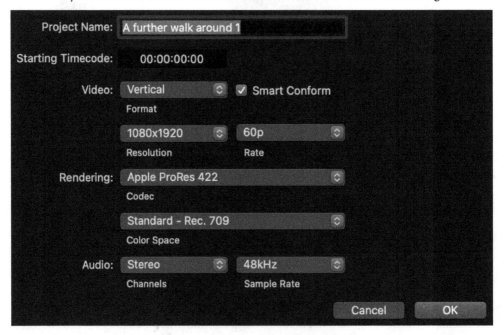

Figure 3.6 – Smart Conform and settings for vertical video

You can manually move clips that are not positioned automatically by using the **Overlay** button (*see Figure 3.7*):

Figure 3.7 – The Overlay button

The **Overlay** button shows the hidden edges, allowing you, if needed, to manually center the prominent image in the vertical part of the video (*see Figure 3.8*):

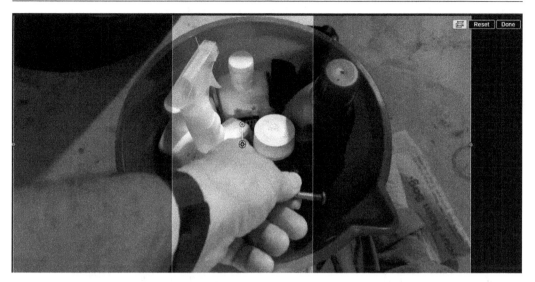

Figure 3.8 – The Overlay button showing the parts of the clip not in view

- Use subtitles. Adding subtitles has advantages at several levels. If you have a global audience, translations are important. The **Roles** feature in Final Cut Pro will allow separate audio tracks in different languages (see *Chapter 4*). Social media platforms are mainly viewed on mobile devices, with the sound turned off, so your message could be lost without subtitles. *Figure 3.4* shows the top and bottom panels. Use the bottom field in a vertical video for the subtitles that you add. *Chapter 16* will discuss an application called Captionator that allows you to add captions easily (see *Figure 3.9*):

Figure 3.9 – Vertical video using Captionator

YouTube videos offer a built-in option for automatic subtitles. If you use it, be sure to manually edit the subtitles. This is because even though the speech-to-text option is accurate, it does not punctuate subtitles, so sentences run into each other, and the meaning quickly gets lost.

You need to consider the consequences of adding your own subtitles in the bottom panel of the video as automated subtitles from YouTube and other social media will likely overlap and make your subtitles unreadable:

Figure 3.10 – YouTube subtitles hiding the text on the video

- Call to action. You might have heard the advice end with a call to action. It's more important with social media videos to have the call to action placed just after the hook and before the real content of the video starts. A social media audience is savvy enough to switch off before the end of the video just as they feel it is winding down, or sometimes they just get distracted with something else and switch. If you haven't placed your call to action by then, the whole purpose of the video is lost.

Now that you have seen a list of the steps to follow when planning for social media videos, the next section describes planning ideas for instructional videos.

Instructional videos

An instructional video is any video that illustrates a procedure, teaches concepts, imparts knowledge, or educates. There are subtypes of instructional videos. They have different names, but the intended outcome is the same:

- **One-topic videos** focus on a single subject. They are best used in a series of short videos.

- **Tutorial videos** give explanatory instructions with illustrations.

- **Training videos** are designed to improve skills. They are the most effective when they use real people or animations of people.

- **Explainer videos**, as the name suggests, explain something visually. Complicated items are broken into simple forms.

- **Lectures** are likely longer than tutorial videos and may hold the audience's attention for longer.

The key to instructional videos is to have a script to follow. This is imperative if you are shooting the video, but just as important for the editor to be able to follow how the video was intended to be.

Now, let's look at some tips to help an instructional video hit its mark:

- Add arrows, shapes, lower thirds, lists, and titles, generally known as **callouts**, to highlight key moments in the video (see *Figure 3.11*):

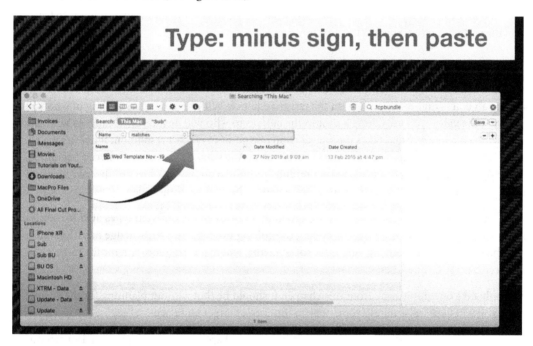

Figure 3.11 – Callouts

- To explain a concept while pausing the video clip, split the clip. In Final Cut Pro, use *Option + F* to apply a freeze frame. You can extend the freeze frame by dragging the duration.

- You can speed up and slow down parts of the recording (see *Figure 3.12*) by using the *Shift + B* keys. When using *Shift + B*, Final Cut Pro will action the blade speed command; drag to change the speed. Refer to *Chapter 5* for details:

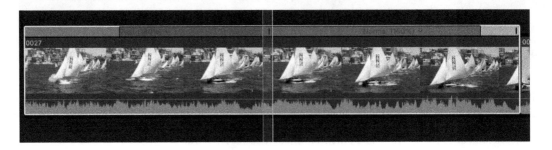

Figure 3.12 – Blade speed – different speeds in the same clip

- Add an explanatory title clearly outlining what the video is about and what it intends to teach the audience (see *Chapter 7*).

Summary

Planning an edit is highly dependent on the target audience. Without an understanding of who will be viewing the video, you are taking a shot in the dark as to who will be interested in it. As with any story, a video is a journey that takes the viewer from one point to reach a resolution. It doesn't matter whether the video is a drama story or a commercial video. Any story should typically have a beginning, to introduce the viewer to the story, then a middle, to inform about the object of the story, and an end, to give a resolution to the information presented in the middle of the video.

To understand the planning process, it is important to be aware of the different types of video stories and how these types should be treated during the editing process. This knowledge has its greatest need when it comes to producing videos for social media, where it is so important for the format and the aspect ratio to be fixed.

If you only take one thing away from this chapter, it should be that without planning for the correct viewer, you will likely miss telling your story to the correct target audience.

The next chapter follows from the planning exercises in this chapter to the more practical instructions on how to pre-edit the rough cut while focusing more on the Final Cut Pro methods of doing things.

4

Pre-Editing a Rough Cut

In the first three chapters, we concentrated on discussing processes from a broad perspective rather than just the Final Cut Pro way of editing. This chapter focuses on Final Cut Pro and the actual steps you will use to pre-edit and create an **initial assembly** and then a **rough cut**. The initial assembly is added to a project in the timeline. Before you start the procedure of adding clips, it is important to know how to navigate the timeline and understand the terminology of a Final Cut Pro project.

This chapter and *Chapter 5* will explain how to approach the assembly of the media that you have spent time categorizing and rating. Your personality is now coming to the fore, and even though there is a process defined for you, it's more important that you do it your way.

You will see how the pre-edit is the process of preparing the best of the media to be added later to the initial assembly. The explanation of this early stage of the editing process is divided into three distinct routines in this chapter, rating the media and then separately using that rated media to produce an initial assembly, which, in turn, becomes the rough cut.

You will learn the difference in how audio or dialogue-focused videos (interviews) are assembled compared to videos that are picture (action)-focused. When an initial assembly project is complete, you will transition it to a rough cut either as a separate project or continue working on the initial assembly project.

The term *rough cut* almost needs no definition as it includes all the significant components of the footage, positioned in sequential order, that will make up the basis of the story. The media from the initial assembly, which was assembled without taking care that it was cut at the best frame, is now tuned in the rough cut, concentrating more on how a cut relates to the clips before and after. This will likely take some reordering of clips as well as adjusting the editing points. Removing unwanted media from the initial assembly is the key to generating a clean rough cut project in the project. Special and sound effects, graphics, music, color correction, and audio sweetening are all done after the rough cut is fixed at **Picture Lock**.

In this chapter, we're going to cover the following main topics:

- The steps from importing to rough cut
- Ingesting the media
- Logging
- What are projects?
- Adding clips to the project
- The initial assembly
- The rough cut

By the end of this chapter, you will be able to recognize the various types of video stories and understand how their characteristics will help with suggestions of how your story can be systematically arranged into an order that will give it the substance needed for a compelling video. You will understand how dramatic and commercial videos require different approaches in the planning process. You will become aware that the audience for your video needs to be clearly recognized before you start the planning process. You will learn how to retain that audience's persona in your mind throughout the planning and editing processes.

To understand the rough cut as part of the post-production process, it's important to note the steps building up to the rough cut.

The steps from importing to rough cut

The following is the order of how the full editing process takes place to produce a worthwhile video production.

Steps in video post-production

The post-production process involved the following steps:

1. **Ingesting or importing the media:**

   While this is not strictly part of the pre-editing process, ingestion needs to be done before everything else. If you feel unsure of the organizational structure, refer to *Chapter 1*.

2. **Organization or logging:**

   The imported media is shot in the order of the storyboard, which will be different from the sequence order of the final video. Logging categorizes the media with labels rather than the order in which it was shot.

3.   **Initial assembly**:

The logged footage is moved into the approximate order that will resemble the order in the final video.

4.   **Rough cut**:

The rough cut has the same key scenes as the initial assembly but gives more attention to pacing. The rough cut shows any holes where more footage may be needed. These holes will be filled with still images or **placeholders** to represent what new shots are required.

5.   **The final cut**:

In the final cut, all effects are added along with color, audio corrections have been made with graphics, and titles are ready for export.

Who does what?

Depending on the scale and complexity of the production, there can be just a sole editor who needs to have all the skills, or multiple assistants and specialists for color, audio, and graphics.

In a large production, *steps 1–3* could be handled by assistants under the guidance of the executive editor. The main editor will be directly involved with *step 4*, the rough cut, and fully involved with *step 5*, the final cut. Specialists will be involved for color, audio, and graphics. The middle ground is where the production is processed on a collaborative basis between two or more fully versed editors (see *Chapter 15*).

The browser or the timeline

Depending on your preference and, perhaps more importantly, the scale of the production, the pre-edit for long-form videos would normally be done in the browser. But for short videos with limited footage, it could be easier to accomplish it in a project in the **timeline**. As you will see as you read through this chapter, you will make your own decisions as to how you approach the process.

In some cases, the time invested in creating categories, such as **Keyword** and **Smart Collections**, would be better spent jumping straight into creating a project in the timeline, adding the full clip, and cutting out the unwanted material from the project in the timeline.

Initial assembly or rough cut

If there is one truth about editing in Final Cut Pro, it's that there is no single way to treat every edit: *there's no one method to suit all*. It's mainly about the length of the video, but how you work best comes down to your personal preferences. What's important is to keep your mind open to the different ways that editors work because you may have been missing something up to now. But don't change just because someone else is doing it in a particular way.

So, you can appreciate that there are different methods of editing; this chapter, though, is about showing all the formal ways of doing things. Creating an initial assembly clip or moving straight to the rough cut is a case in point. You do what works for you. Longer and more formal edits will have both an initial assembly and a rough cut. This is a good opportunity for the assistant editor to start the initial assembly and then the executive editor can tune that into the rough cut.

If you are a sole operator, you will most likely jump straight into a rough cut. In some cases, it will be quicker and easier for you to dump the footage from the camera directly into the timeline and just cut out the unwanted material. If you are keen to get on with the edit without too much, or any, pre-editing, I suggest that you take the time to read through the following pre-edit methods as it does no harm to know how others approach the edit in Final Cut Pro. The next section starts from the beginning, ingesting the media.

Ingesting the media

For longer-form videos that require categorization and grading of clip quality, there are two distinct methods of ingesting media into Final Cut Pro. One is to pre-assemble the folder structure in Mac's Finder and then, when they are imported, Keyword Collections will be set up automatically for you to use in the initial assembly. These Keyword Collections will take on the name of the folder that you set up in the Finder. The second method is to drag the footage into the Keyword Collections that are discussed in *Chapter 2*.

There is a simple variation for really short videos. Video clips that are in any Finder folder can be dragged directly into a project in the timeline. A direct drag is also a good option for importing single clips, stills, or music clips when a video is nearly complete and just needs something done to fill a gap.

Ingestion using the **Import** window will achieve the same result as the first method, but dragging is best if you are creating Keyword Collections in the Final Cut Pro browser.

Setting up media folders in the Finder

The technique of setting up media folders in the Finder is implemented before the media has been transferred from the camera. You will add the media to a Finder folder, then add separate folders for different cameras, as well as folders for all the different classifications you would like to be in the Final Cut Pro browser.

> **Note**
> Folders need to have footage in them to be recognized in the Final Cut Pro browser's sidebar.

For shoots over several days, you can create folders for each camera on each day. It is a good idea to make a template by duplicating the folder structure for future use. This method is a suitable alternative for long-form videos.

Let's take a look at the steps to create a new folder in the Finder:

1. After you have created a new Final Cut Pro library, open the folder that you want to store the media in, right-click in an open area, and select **New Folder**:

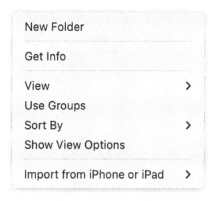

Figure 4.1– New Folder

2. Name the folder `all cameras`.

3. Double-click the `all cameras` folder to open it, right-click again to create a new folder, and name it `cam 1`.

4. Right-click again in the open area of the `all cameras` folder and create a new folder called `cam 2`.

5. Continue until all your cameras have a separate folder. If you have footage from several days and want to separate it, create folders for each camera on each day.

    You can either create all the other folders for different classifications here, in the Finder, or do that when you start the pre-edit in Final Cut Pro. I strongly suggest you duplicate the folder structure for future use. This can be achieved really easily. As you have done all the hard work by creating the structure, why repeat it all again next time? To create a template, right-click on the `all cameras` folder and select **Duplicate**.

> **Important note**
>
> Make sure to duplicate the folder structure before you add any media into the folders. Otherwise, the media will be duplicated as well.

There is another useful advantage of setting up a highly detailed template: empty folders are not transferred to the browser when you import. This means that you can decide what folders are used for different jobs because only the ones with content will appear on the Final Cut Pro browser's sidebar.

Finder's tags and color options are also recognized and transferred to the browser's sidebar. They are useful for tagging individual files and not just folders. They also show up as a Keyword Collection on the browser's sidebar.

6.   Finally, while still in the Finder, transfer all the camera footage saved from the camera cards into the appropriate folders. My suggestion is that you have this Finder folder structure set up well before the footage becomes available from the camera.

In *Figure 4.2*, you can see what a detailed folder structure for a wedding edit would look like:

Figure 4.2 – Finder folder structure for a wedding video

7.   The next step is to ingest the structure by dragging it into **Event** in the Final Cut Pro browser's sidebar, or using the **Import** window and selecting **Event** to add to.

In *Figure 4.3*, you can see how that same Finder structure will appear in the Final Cut Pro browser window:

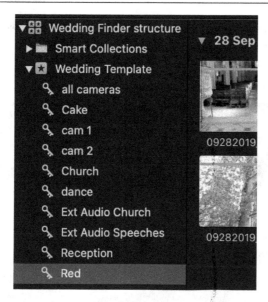

Figure 4.3 – Structure after import in the browser sidebar

Note that the Maybe needed and Suitable for folders are not displayed because no content was added to them in the Finder. Also, notice the Red tag, which contains individual clips within the cam 1 selection, meaning those clips are in the cam 1 and Red tag Keyword Collections.

Importing media directly

Alternatively, you can create the structure in the Final Cut Pro browser, as you saw in *Chapter 2*. This technique allows you to import media directly into the Final Cut browser and categorize it within Final Cut Pro. This is certainly the preferred method for shorter, less formal edits. The categorization structure discussed in *Chapter 2* is more useful for longer videos.

For short videos, the time spent creating categories such as Keyword Collections and Smart Collections would be better spent jumping straight into the pre-edit.

Let's take a look at how to directly import media:

1. As you will recall from *Chapter 1*, the Final Cut Pro library is at the top of the hierarchy structure, and **Event** is a subsection. The footage is imported into an event, which is given a suitable name. In this case, we'll call it Main Edit. Select Main Edit from the browser's sidebar.

2. Right-click or select **New Keyword Collection** from the **File** menu. Name it cam 1.

3. Follow the same procedure to create a cam 2 Keyword Collection. Repeat the steps for all cameras or audio recorders.

4. Drag the first camera's folder or individual clips into the cam 1 Keyword Collection and the second camera's folder or individual clips into the cam 2 Keyword Collection. Do the same for all cameras and audio recorders.

In *Figure 4.4*, you can see what the folders look like in the browser's sidebar:

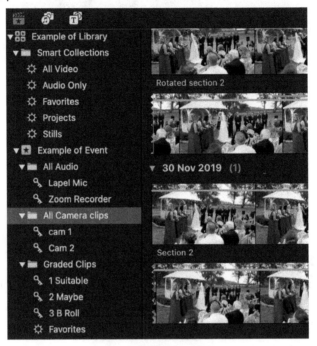

Figure 4.4 – Folders in the browser's sidebar

5. You can now rank these clips into grades. Name them as follows: Suitable, Maybe, and B Roll Keyword Collections. To create new Keyword Collections for each of the four grades, select **Main Edit** and right-click or select **New Keyword Collection** from the **File** menu.

In *Figure 4.4*, you can see a suggested hierarchy for a wedding classification. The event has three folders: All Audio, All Camera clips (this will be useful when it comes to multi-cam editing of the individual camera's footage; see *Chapter 8*), and Graded Clips (you will see in the next section how to add **Favorites** to the Graded Clips folder).

Logging

When working in Final Cut Pro's browser, you will sort clips that are categorized as **Best**, **Suitable**, **Maybe**, and **B Roll**. Depending on your workflow, you may want to have other categories; it's your choice. I use the **Favorites** feature for my Best category.

As you saw in the *Ingesting the media* section, there is considerable flexibility in how you make use of the different categories, something similar to the library and event flexibility. But with flexibility comes indecision, so to give you some help, I'll give some actual examples with appropriate names that you can use.

Categorizing the clips

My suggestion is to have at least four categories where you can store the different clips depending on their suitability for the edit.

Different types of edits will have different levels of need and practicality. The different roles run from a sole proprietor editor right through to the Hollywood blockbuster team of editors. Most people will be in the former position, there are quite a few in the middle, and not many in the latter. Production houses will have their own workflows. But if you are responsible for setting up a workflow, here are a few tips.

The sole trader is a *one-man band*, but as productions grow in size and the number of staff members increases, they will need assistant editors and even junior assistants to the assistant editor. Whatever the case, the four main category principle applies. What you call them is your choice. What these categories represent is what's important.

For the quality of the footage and suitability for the edit, I call my categories **Favorites**, **Suitable**, and **Maybe**, and I set another category for **B Roll**. `Favorites` is for outstanding clips that will surely be used. `Suitable` is for most of the other clips, and `Maybe` is for clips that could be used if there is a need for extra media.

Many editors use the **Good**, **Better**, and **Best** labels. These are fine to use if you want. I know it's splitting hairs, but to me, *Good* represents my idea of clips that will only possibly be needed. I feel that *Better* is more closely represented by the word `Suitable`, and `Favorites` says it all. But as I said, it's your choice.

`Favorites` has the convenience of a keyboard shortcut (the *F* key). When a clip is added to `Favorites`, a green line appears at the top of the thumbnail in the browser. Then the `Suitable` clips would be added to a `Suitable` Keyword Collection. Finally, the `Maybe` clips would also require another Keyword Collection, as would `B Roll`.

The added advantage of this categorization is that you will be able to see, in one place, all the actual Keyword Collections on the sidebar when you start the rough cut.

Grading the clips

Once the appropriate clips are in the various Keyword Collections, a blue line appears at the top of every keyworded clip. To complete the pre-edit process, you need to check that you have favorited or keyworded all the clips ready for the initial assembly or rough cut. To display all the clips that are not in `Keyword Collections` or `Favorites`, select the **Event** button on the browser's sidebar and change the browser filter to **No ratings or Keywords**. All the clips in Favorites and Keyword Collections will be hidden. The clips that have been missed and not rated are displayed and can then be added to the appropriate keyword collections if needed (clips only in a Smart Collection and with no other rating will still be displayed when the browser filter is set to **No ratings or Keywords**).

Next is the rating process, where we evaluate the sections of the clips and add them to the appropriate Keyword Collection.

Let's see how the grading process is done:

1. For the best results, make the browser as large as possible and increase the size and duration of the thumbnails. Select the **Filmstrip** icon at the top right of the browser and set the size slider to 50% and the duration to **30s**.

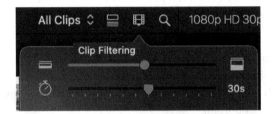

Figure 4.5 – Clip height and duration in the timeline

2. In the top menu, click on **Window** | **Show in workspace** and untick all items except the browser and sidebar. If you have two monitors, you could put the browser on the secondary display. I find that with a 27" monitor, I prefer to have both the browser and the viewer together by unticking all the others in **Show in workspace**.

3. You may not like the skimmer, but for this operation, it is brilliant. I suggest that you at least give it a go and try it out. Skim through the footage by hovering the mouse over the clip. The skimmer is a red line on the clip in the browser. Starting from the beginning of the clip, hover until you have a portion that you want to rate for the Favorites, Suitable, Maybe, or B Roll categories. Click at the beginning of the selection, hold and drag until the end of the selection, and then release the mouse/trackpad. A yellow outline will show your selection.

Figure 4.6 – Yellow outline

4. If it is your `Favorites` selection, press the *F* key. A green line appears across the top.

Figure 4.7 – Favorites green line

5. Don't be too concerned about how accurate the cuts are, within reason. It is best to be close, but don't waste time being really accurate. The key point is to portray the salient reason for your choice. There will be several takes, particularly of the same close-up shot, or establishing shots. Include all your favorite selections from all cameras. The best of these should be added to `Favorites`. Others can be added to `Suitable`, `Maybe`, or `B Roll` by clicking inside

the yellow outline and dragging to the appropriate keyword. A faded yellow outline is retained on the clip after you have marked the in and out range.

Figure 4.8 – Faded outline retained

6. You will note that the Favorites folder does not appear in the same place on the sidebar as the Suitable, Maybe, and B Roll folders. This can be rectified by dragging the Favorites folder from Smart Collections into the Graded Clips folder. A copy of Favorites will now reside in both but be more easily seen alongside Suitable, Maybe, and B Roll in the Graded Clips folder.

> **Note**
> When you drag any Smart Collection, such as Favorites, to an event, clips marked as a favorite from that event will be displayed, whereas when you select Favorites from the Smart Collections folder, it will display all the favorited clips from the entire library.

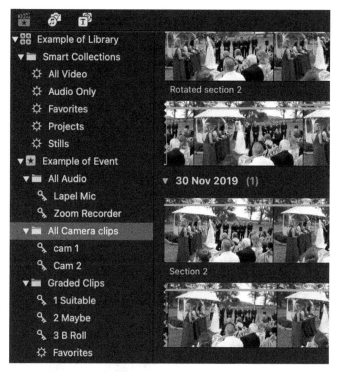

Figure 4.9 – All Camera clips selected

7.   To drag and add clips to the Keyword Collection, you can set up keyboard shortcuts, which will not only save time but also minimize possible mistakes when dragging to the incorrect Keyword Collection.

Let's see how keyboard shortcuts can be used to add clips. Select any one of the keywords in the sidebar and press *Command + K.* The keyword selection window will open.

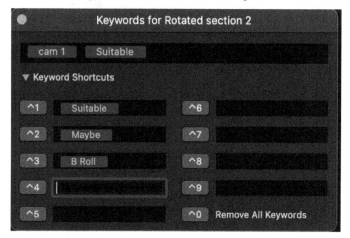

Figure 4.10 – Keyword shortcuts

Now type Suitable, Maybe, and B Roll. This will allow you to press *Control + 1* for Suitable, *Control + 2* for Maybe, and *Control + 3* for B Roll.

Shortcuts can be used to add keywords, but when you reach a completely unusable section, press the *Delete* key. The deleted section is not actually trashed; it's moved to the Rejected category.

This is where the sorting options are useful. From the top of the browser, select the drop-down menu that normally says **All Clips** and select **Hide Rejected**. To view those rejected clips, change the selection in the drop-down menu.

Upon selecting **All Clips**, the red line will show the rejected clips, and the green line will show the favorites. You can see all favorites in the dropdown. These are the ones you will use the most in the initial assembly. You can also see the last section that has been selected when returning to the clip in the browser, even if it wasn't the last clip actioned. The selection is retained until another is selected in the same clip.

Figure 4.11 – The selection is retained

In a perfect world, all the original clips will either be separated into one of the four categories or rejected. It's important to work through the whole clip, and it's best not to miss any part.

If you are not a fan of the skimmer, then instead, you can use the *I* and *O* keys to select in and out points in the same way as the skimmer was used earlier. Everything works the same.

Now that the clips are graded, you mostly consider the Favorites clips for the initial assembly and, for now, most likely ignore Maybe and B Roll until the rough edit.

So far, we have concentrated on the media in the browser. From this point, the media will be assembled in sequential order in a Final Cut Pro project. Before jumping into the procedure for the initial assembly,

I would like to take a timeout to discuss a Final Cut Pro project, compared to the terminology used by **Non-Linear Editors** (**NLEs**). If you are happy with what you know about projects and how they differ from sequences (the term that some NLEs use) then jump forward to the *The initial assembly* section.

What are projects?

The meaning of the word *project* in the context of Final Cut Pro (X) compared to the legacy Final Cut Pro 7 can be confusing, as the legacy meaning of the word is different from the Final Cut Pro (X) interpretation. There is a similar difference in the definition of the word *project* between other NLEs and Final Cut Pro, too. In Final Cut Pro, a project is contained within an event, which is contained within the library. The other NLEs have **bins** and **sequences**. Think of bins as events and sequences as projects in Final Cut Pro. The word *bin* is a carryover from the days of film, before digital, where the reels of film were stored in a bin.

The structure of the legacy version of Final Cut Pro also had *project*, rather than *library*, at the top of the hierarchy, with a sequence being more of a project in the current version of Final Cut Pro.

One of the other differences in Final Cut Pro is that the thumbnail representing the project can be seen in the event along with the media. This means that projects in Final Cut Pro belong in **Events**. When a new project is opened, you are required to nominate which event it is to be stored in. You can recognize a project's thumbnail by the chevron/herringbone across the top. Double-clicking the thumbnail opens the project in the timeline.

Figure 4.12 – Herringbone across the top of a project thumbnail

If you have or are a current user of legacy Final Cut Pro or another NLE, then you need to be aware of the differences in the meaning of the words *bins*, *projects*, and *sequences*.

Projects in Final Cut Pro are opened in the timeline. The next section explains how the Final Cut Pro timeline operates.

Adding clips to the project

As this book is aimed at the current users of Final Cut Pro, it is unnecessary to explain all the normal methods of adding clips to a project in the magnetic timeline, but I feel it is important to review the concept of the connected clips and the associated three-point edits.

Connected clips

Connected clips are exactly what they say they are: connected to the main (primary) story. The connection point (shown by the red arrow in *Figure 4.13*) is very small and hard to see. Being able to see the connection point is made even harder by the fact that it is blue on a black background. The default position of the connection point is at the beginning of the connected clip. The connection point can be repositioned to attach to a different point or another primary clip by holding *Command + Option* and clicking on the connected clip at the new location.

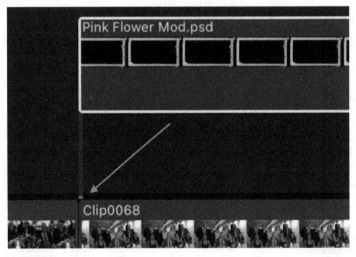

Figure 4.13 – The blue connection point at the default position at the beginning of the connected clip

It is important to note there is only one connection per connected clip, no matter how long the connected clip is. There is an issue to be aware of because each connected clip is attached to one clip in the primary storyline, so when the storyline clip is moved, the attached connected clip moves with it.

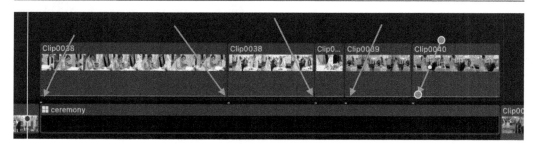

Figure 4.14 – Individual connected clips, each with their own connection points

You can group connected clips together to help prevent this. The shortcut is *Command + G*. When the connected clips are grouped, they can only be moved using the gray line at the top (see *Figure 4.15*). The group can be thought of as a secondary storyline with magnetic properties that are the same as those of the primary storyline.

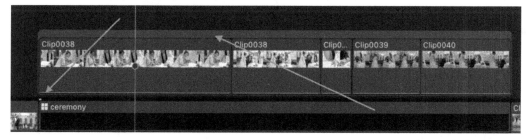

Figure 4.15 – The same clips grouped with one connection point and the gray line above it

If you need to remove a clip from the primary storyline without removing the attached connected clips, hold the *grave* (~) key (located under the *Esc* key.) You will see a new cursor icon symbol in the timeline.

Figure 4.16 – Cursor icon when holding the grave key

As of version 10.7 of Final Cut Pro, connected clips can be grouped together with the **Collapse to a Connected Storyline** command, as we will discuss in *Chapter 9*.

Connected clips are a key feature of the Final Cut Pro magnetic timeline, and you should embrace the concept because this is what makes Final Cut Pro such a fast video editing platform. The next section explains how connected clips feature when the three-point editing method is employed.

Three-point edits

Understanding connected clips will allow you to use a universal editing method called **three-point editing**. This gives you complete accuracy regarding where the connected clip will be placed in the timeline, including the duration of the connected clip.

The operation is simple. You need to nominate the **in** and **out** points of a clip in the browser (the clip needs to have a longer duration than what will appear in the timeline). At the same time, you need to nominate the position and duration you want the connected clip to fill in the timeline with *in* and *out* points. Simply press the Q key, and the points in the timeline are filled from the *in* point in the browser. *In* and *out* points are actioned with the *I* and *O* keys or using the **Range** tool. You can use *Shift* + *Q* to back-time from the *out* point.

You can use the same three-point edit principle to add a clip to the primary storyline at a set position and duration. You need to use the same principle to set the *in* and *out* points in the browser and the primary storyline. Press the *D* key to add the clip to the timeline using the *in* point reference from the browser; to move back from the *out* point to the *in* point in the browser, use *Shift* + *D*.

With your new knowledge of adding clips to a project, it's now time to learn how projects are handed in the timeline.

The timeline

It is important to be clear about the difference between the timeline and a project that exists within the timeline. Think of the timeline as a container for projects.

When you create a new project, an empty view appears in the timeline. Multiple projects can be active in the timeline, but only one is visible at a time. You can switch project views by selecting the left and right arrows at the top of the timeline in the middle of the screen. This is similar to the familiar *back* and *forward* buttons in an internet browser. The name of the current project on view is between the two arrows.

Figure 4.17 – The project on view is between the two arrows

The timeline view can be adjusted to suit your view with the **Filmstrip** tab above the effects browser and to the right of the timeline. The top slider adjusts the duration view of the timeline – in effect, allowing you to zoom in to see more detail or zoom out for a wider view.

Figure 4.18 – Adjusting the timeline view

Angles and clip names are for multi-cam editing (see *Chapter 8*). The **Lane Headers** checkbox ensures that audio lane headers are not obscured by other clips (see *Chapter 6*). A recent addition to this window is the **Duplicate Ranges** checkbox, which shows clips that have been added twice in the timeline. It shows a striped pattern at the top of clips that have been duplicated in the timeline.

Figure 4.19 – Striped pattern showing the duplicated clip

The other buttons next to the **Filmstrip** tab also control the timeline. To the left of the **Filmstrip** tab is the **Snapping** button, which determines whether the playhead snaps to an edit point or smoothly moves past. To the left of **Snapping** is the **Solo** button, which you can use to select just one clip while disabling the others. To the left of the **Solo** button is the **Audio scrubbing** button, which emits a sound when the skimmer is moved along the timeline. Finally, there is the **Skimming** on/off button.

Figure 4.20 – When activated, the skimmer is the blue button on the left-hand side

The skimmer and playhead are explained in the following sections.

The skimmer and playhead

There are two playheads in Final Cut Pro. When the **skimmer** is active, the **fixed playhead** sits at a certain location (indicated in white) in the timeline and stays until you move it (the skimmer is active by default). The skimmer playhead (indicated in red) moves as you hover the mouse left and right. There is a third color (yellow), which indicates that both the fixed playheads are in the same position.

Figure 4.21 – Fixed playhead icon

The fixed playhead can be scrubbed to any location in the timeline by dragging the top of the playhead symbol in the timeline. It will stay in place until you either drag it again or click on a different location. The clip is played from the playhead position.

When you play a clip in the timeline, it's the white playhead that moves along the timeline. When the playhead reaches the center position in the timeline, it's the timeline that now scrolls to keep the playhead visible in the center position. If you manually zoom into the timeline or move the playhead while it is playing, the playhead will slowly make its way back to the center position in the timeline. You can turn the scrolling timeline on or off in **Settings | Playback**.

The skimmer, when turned on, springs into action as soon as you activate the timeline and hover the mouse left or right to freely move over clips to play them at the speed of the mouse. You can preview clips in the timeline without changing the fixed playhead position. The skimmer takes priority over the fixed playhead when you are making edits in the timeline with shortcut keys. For example, if you have the fixed playhead at position one and move the skimmer to position two, then press *Command + B*, the cut will be at position two.

One of the most important things to learn when clicking on the timeline is where the fixed white playhead is located. As I've already described, when the skimmer is used, it becomes the active playhead for any cuts or what is displayed in the viewer. When you click on a clip in the timeline, the clip is selected with a yellow outline. The skimmer (the red line) is shown at the point you click.

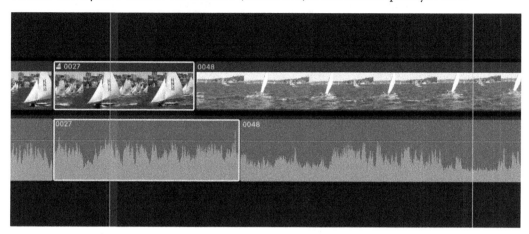

Figure 4.22 – The red line is the skimmer, and the white line is the fixed playhead

However, if you need to have the white fixed playhead at the point where you click, then use *Option + click*. The fixed playhead moves to the point where you clicked. This saves you the effort of dragging the fixed playhead to a position. Two actions with one click!

> **Note**
> If a clip is not selected, then clicking an empty space above the clip will place the fixed playhead at the skimmer position.

There is, however, a good reason to make the fixed playhead stay in position when you click without holding *Option*. The skimmer moves but the fixed playhead stays in place like a temporary marker for you to see where the last action happened.

You need to practice these different ways of selecting a clip in the timeline. It's important to know the difference because you can save yourself a significant amount of time by using *Option + click* instead of just clicking to select the clip.

Option + click in the browser makes no difference because any click always enters the fixed playhead at the clicked point. It's only the timeline click that results in a different action.

The skimmer playhead's functionality is similar. When the browser is active, if the mouse is hovered over any media other than a project thumbnail, it shows a red line. The fixed playhead will be white and can only be activated by clicking on the clip or by using the *I* and *O* keys for *in* and *out* selections, respectively.

If you find it difficult to get used to the skimmer, you can turn it off. The color of the playhead will be different. You can click on the timeline and the playhead will move to that position with the red line displayed. You can scrub as before by dragging the playhead icon. If **Snapping** is turned on, the line will become yellow at every edit point.

The timeline uses a timecode to be able to keep track of where the clips are within a project. The next section explains how to access and use the timecode to navigate within the timeline.

Timecode

The timecode is essential for regulating a clip's duration and where it is located in the project. As you saw in the *Settings/Preferences* section in *Chapter 2*, the timecode is normally set to **Hours**, **Minutes**, **Seconds**, and **Frames**. Immediately centered under the viewer is the key for accessing the timecode. Most of the time, it will simply show the timecode location of the playhead within the timeline, reading frames from the right-hand side. For example, **2:10** represents 2 seconds and 10 frames. The real power of the timecode is the ability to locate any frame in the timeline.

Let's see how to access the timecode:

1. Click on the timecode field. It appears empty with a blue icon in the form of the playhead.

2. Type in the timecode using the **HH:MM:SS:FF** format. Type 1:23:20 and press *Enter*. The playhead will jump to that position in the timeline. That's simple enough.

3. To make it simpler, type 1.23, with the period (.). When you enter the period (.), **00** is completed for you. In the same way, if you type 1.., two periods are equal to four zeros, which would give you **1.00.00** (one minute, zero seconds, and zero frames).

Figure 4.23 – Timecode showing 1 minute, 23 seconds, and 20 frames

One of Final Cut Pro's unique features allows you to quickly see where clips are in the timeline. The timeline has its own index. I find that my new students are vague about and completely ignore this most important function of Final Cut Pro. The next section covers the concept of the timeline index. You will find that throughout this book, I will continually refer to the timeline index as it has many **roles**, to play on words. (Roles are one of the most important uses for the timeline index.)

The timeline index

The timeline index is extremely underrated. It is one of the most powerful and unique tools in Final Cut Pro. If you need to find anything in the timeline, this is where you should go. You may initially think that it can only search for clips in the timeline, but it can search by all clips, just audio, just video, and, separately, only titles.

Let's see how we can use the timeline index.

Let's assume you have added a title to the project in the timeline and you don't recall where a clip is located with a brand name in it. Open the timeline index by clicking on the word **Index** at the top left of the timeline. Select the **Clips** tab, type the brand name, and the title will appear in the list. Click on the list and the timeline will jump to the position with the title you are looking for, and it will have a yellow outline.

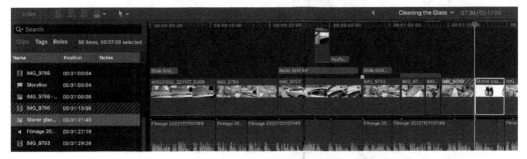

Figure 4.24 – Timeline index showing the highlighted clip

The timeline index also searches for markers that you have added to the timeline, such as markers waiting for a *to-do* action (indicated in red) and markers on which *to-do* has been actioned (indicated in green). Also searchable are chapter markers, which are not just for DVDs, as you will see in *Chapter 9*.

Perhaps the most useful thing for professional editing is the **Roles** feature, which you saw a little about in *Chapter 2* when discussing the browser. There will be more discussion on roles in *Chapter 5*.

Now, after discussing the timeline index and its positioning in the timeline, let's continue. In the next section, we'll cover the use of roles.

Roles

Who said that Final Cut Pro is not track-based? While the **magnetic timeline** replaces track-based video, the **Roles** feature uniquely allows audio to be separated into as many tracks as your heart may desire. Think of roles as labels that group similar clips so you can access them by the label. Roles can be used in both the browser and the timeline. There are separate **Roles** options for video and audio. Separate colors can be applied to each role, but audio colors have priority over video colors.

The workflow for roles is that they are created first with **Edit Roles,** by right-clicking on a clip in the browser or the timeline and selecting **Assign Audio Roles** or **Assign Video Roles.**

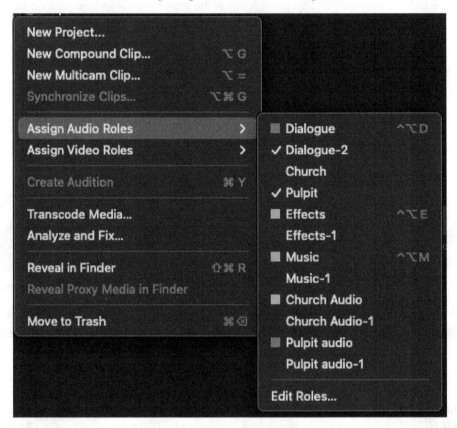

Figure 4.25 – Edit roles by right-clicking in the timeline

The **Roles** window will allow new roles to be created and sub-roles to be added.

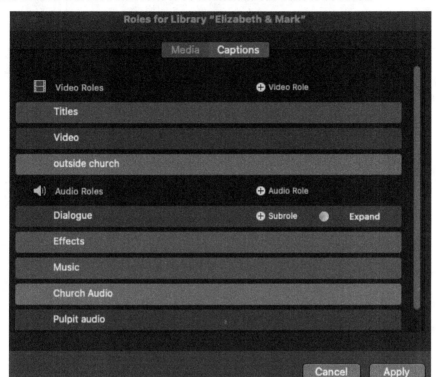

Figure 4.26 – Edit Roles window showing how to add roles

> **Note**
>
> If you are applying roles to multi-cam clips, this needs to be done at the base level, not the edited version of multi-cam.

Now, let's look at some of the advantages of roles:

- Roles are color-coded so you can quickly see the different audio tracks.
- Individual roles can be highlighted (called **focus**) so that all other tracks are squashed from view and the role in focus is featured, while the other tracks are still shown but on a smaller scale.
- Sub-roles are available. For example, audio from a series of interviews can have a role for all the interview audio, and the sub-roles would have the names of the different interviewees in different colors so they are visually different and can be highlighted using focus.

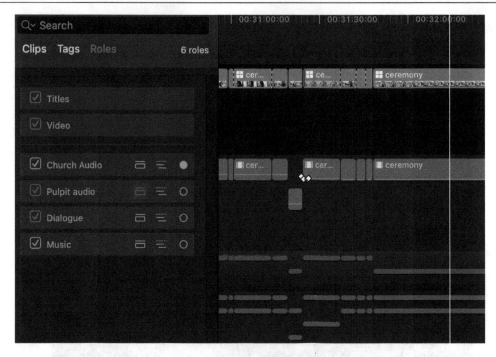

Figure 4.27 – Roles showing colors and sub-roles with the Church Audio focus selected

- Roles can be deselected on **Export/Share**. For example, different language versions can be exported separately.

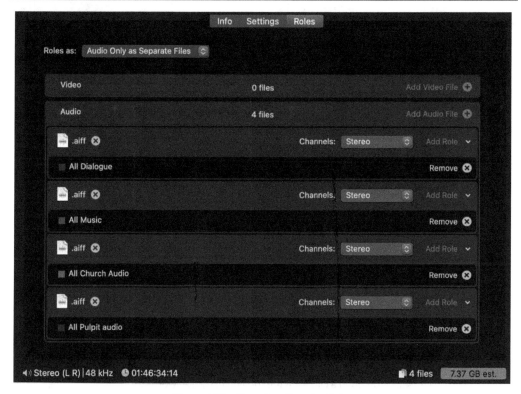

Figure 4.28 – Export options for Roles

See *Chapter 6* for a detailed workflow using roles.

Now that you have a full understanding of the Final Cut Pro functions that you can use when creating a project, it's time to use all that knowledge to start the initial assembly of the media.

The initial assembly

Initial assembly is the procedure in which you assemble the clips from the `Favorites` selection into an order that represents the chronological sequence of the video's original script. When the organization and grading have been done by an assistant editor, the initial assembly is possibly the first time that the executive editor is involved. For larger productions, the initial assembly gives the director the first chance to see the chronological sequence of the clips so they can ascertain whether the video is viable and whether more media needs to be shot.

If this is the first time the executive editor is involved, it's important that they view all the footage in both the `Favorites` and `Suitable` categories in the browser before committing them to the initial assembly project.

To review the footage from the Keyword Collections, select any keyword and press *Command + K*. This will open the **Keywords** window, and you can then see what Keyword Collection any selected clip belongs to. Once opened, the **Keywords** window stays open so you can check other clips or keywords. It stays open until purposely closed by pressing the red button in the top-left corner. Clips can be added to Keyword Collections by dragging or pressing *Control + #* for the appropriate keyword. The clips can be removed by deleting from the top line in the **Keywords** window.

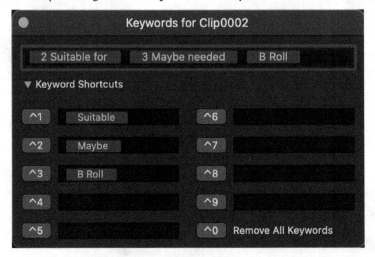

Figure 4.29 – Deleting a clip from the top line in the Keywords window

Initial assembly is where all that time we spent rating clips as Favorites or sorting them into Keyword Collections comes to fruition. As per the workflow discussed in *Chapter 2*, the best clips are labeled as Favorites and the others as Suitable or Maybe. The object is to get all the best clips into a new Final Cut Pro project.

> **Note**
>
> If you missed the workflow in *Chapter 2*, Favorites can be labeled by pressing the *F* key and removed from Favorites by pressing the *U* key.

If all the Favorites clips are dumped into a project, they will be added in the order in which they were shot.

Event-type videos work well with this approach because the filming is done throughout the day or days, and these videos are mostly going to be in the same order in the finished video.

However, this is not a suitable approach if you know the shooting order has no relationship to the chronological storyline. But then again, it may still be quicker and easier to work out than adding clips one at a time. This is because once the clips are in the initial assembly project's timeline, they can be quickly reordered.

You need to think this through before dumping all your media. However, not much time will be lost if you try it out and it doesn't work or is too confusing. You can always create another project and add the clips in a more conventional way. Just don't spend too much time deciding.

After the first reorder, make a duplicate of the project and try to reorder the clips differently. The object is to get a chronological storyline rather than a finished movie.

Assembling audio- or image-focused videos

If the video is audio-focused, with either dialogue or music, the audio is given priority in the assembly. You should make sure that the words match up and make sense, or that the music track is in the correct order. You could find that the visuals are out of sync; ignore that for now. You can add different visuals after the audio makes sense.

Interviews are a classic example of audio-focused content because the words can be taken well out of the order in which the interview was filmed. Obviously, you need to be sure the original meaning is retained.

A visual-focused video is what you would normally expect, and then the sequence of pictures is the objective of the assembly.

You could also be presented with an assembly that is a mix of visual and audio focus. My suggestion is to treat these as separate segments and assemble them separately. If the segments are large, you could consider separate projects for each segment.

Don't over-edit!

The biggest urge you will have is to over-edit. The initial assembly will be messy, just so you can quickly visualize the video. For sure, it's going to be too long as well as look clunky and crude. The initial assembly can run many hours longer than the final edit, particularly if it's a full-length movie.

You could also experiment with different takes and try some initial B Roll clips to help give the story some emphasis. If you are adding different takes, rather than replacing clips in the timeline, you can use Final Cut Pro's **Audition** feature so that you have the option to revert to the original take. I suggest you don't get too carried away with that feature because there is a fine line between an initial assembly and a rough cut.

The job at this stage is to get the chronological order in place, and then you can simply continue with the same project as a rough cut. I suggest that you at least duplicate the initial assembly with a new project that you call Rough Cut.

It's important to note, again, that if the video is not a long-form or complex video, all this may be overkill. You need to think about this before venturing into the initial assembly phase or even categorizing in the first place. You may call the initial assembly stage your rough cut and take it from there.

The rough cut

Now, let's look at the process of refining the initial assembly into the rough cut. But why have a rough cut when the clips have already been assembled in the correct sequence to tell the story? The main reason for both an initial assembly and a rough cut, for larger, potentially venture-capital-funded videos, is that the rough cut is used to get feedback and to allow investors to get a preliminary view of the video. The director will also get an early impression of the video to show them a sense of how the story flows and how long it takes to tell.

Smaller, sole-editor videos don't really need both an initial assembly and a rough cut, but it's your personal choice. Nonetheless, you should be getting some feedback from other people. Let your colleagues view the rough cut. It's best that they don't see the messy initial assembly. Ask them for constructive feedback; you don't want it sugar-coated.

The formal rough cut involves trimming excess footage and taking out unnecessary major scenes. It'll still be considerably longer than the final video. Don't take too much out; there's a fine balance. You may need it later in the final edit. Err on the side of caution because you can still remove clips when you refine the rough cut into the final edit. Your experience and intuition will show here.

Don't feel upset or embarrassed about the rough cut. It'll still be crude and not something that you will want in your resume. It'll have abrupt jump cuts, the audio volume will vary in places, and the color won't match. But remember, it is just another step in the process.

Much more than the initial assembly, the rough cut is more about how different scenes react with each other rather than just being placed next to one another. More emphasis is now placed on how scenes transition from one to the other. This will be even more refined in the final edit. For example, not just several shots of a bus driving along the road with a flat tire but also a close-up of the wheel, as B Roll, and a pan to the nail in the side wall of the tire.

Remember that the initial assembly, which was put together without taking much care about whether it was cut at the best frame, is now tuned in the rough cut, concentrating more on how a cut relates to the clips before and after. Removing unwanted media from the initial assembly is part of the process of generating a clean rough cut project in the timeline. Something to be aware of at this stage is that every editor will treat the process differently. This is where your unique style will come to the fore. Don't be afraid to do it your way. The steps suggested in this chapter are just a guide to show you how it could work for you.

Adding scratch music

Some editors like to add simple music tracks as placeholders to represent where the final music track will be in the final edit. I warn against this as it can give a different flavor to a rough cut when it is primarily being used for feedback.

Along with music, scratch narration can be included. Make sure it has the pacing that will be used by the professional voiceover actor.

While on the subject of placeholders, you will have times when the right shot is just not available for the rough cut. Rather than waiting for the missing media to arrive, you can insert placeholders where the shots are missing.

Placeholders

The Final Cut Pro **generators** have a selection of **elements** that can be inserted into a gap, giving meaning to the space that the placeholder will fill.

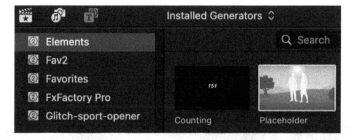

Figure 4.30 – Elements category in Generators

The placeholder is an appropriate storyboard, which shows representative images of people in close-up, mid-frame, and wide positions. Placeholders can give meaning to the rough cut instead of leaving a blank space in the timeline. You can add notes to placeholders explaining what characteristics the missing clip should have.

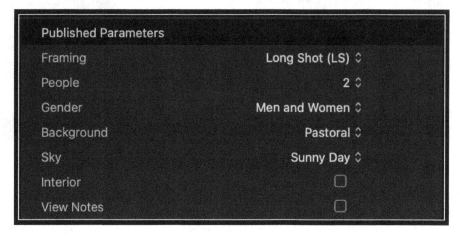

Figure 4.31 – Placeholder options

Alternatives to placeholders

There are simple alternatives to adding a placeholder:

- If you have a clip already in the timeline that you are not sure you will use, simply press the *V* key. The clip will darken in the timeline and the viewer will be black. Both audio and video are hidden. Press the *V* key to return the clip to un-hide the clip.

- To add a blank clip, press *Option + W*. A slug is added to the timeline, which can be adjusted in length.

- If you have a clip that you think you may want to use but don't want it to show in the timeline or you don't want to discard it in case you forget where to find it in the browser, you can simply drag the clip below the primary storyline. It will not show in the viewer and will still be there when you come back to revisit that part of the edit. Be careful about the audio as it will still be heard. It's best to fully reduce the volume.

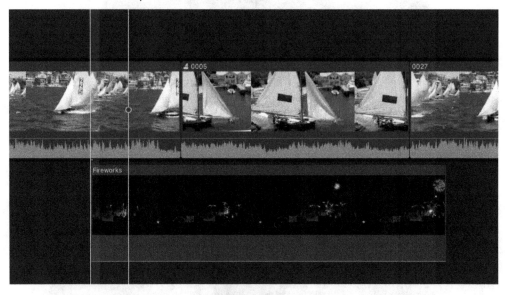

Figure 4.32 – The clip below the storyline is not displayed in the viewer

As you have been making many discretionary changes to the project, it is worthwhile to take a break and save a copy in case future changes destroy all the good work you have done so far. *Command + Z* is only useful for going a few changes back and is only effective for the current session. If you have quit and relaunched Final Cut Pro, *Command + Z* won't be of any use to you. You will see in the next section how to duplicate projects without sacrificing any disk space.

Duplicating projects

The rough cut is the time to consider more possibilities and become more adventurous and experimental. Don't be afraid to continue to duplicate projects as snapshots right throughout the editing process, as you will see in this section.

Figure 4.33 – Three ways to duplicate a project

There are three ways to duplicate a project:

- **Duplicate Project** creates a duplicate and keeps a memory of compound clips and multi-cam clips so that when a change is made in one of those formats, the change is effected in all of the duplicated projects. Care should be taken if you want to make changes to compound clips in duplicated projects, as all the changes will be reflected in all the earlier versions as well. For this very reason, I suggest that you work with snapshots.

- **Duplicate Project As...** is for changing the aspect ratio. It is particularly useful for social media projects.

- **Snapshot Project** creates a snapshot in time of the current project. I suggest that, for this situation, **Snapshot Project** is the safest option.

Let's see how to create a snapshot of a project. Select the project in the browser and right-click. A snapshot of a project is a new project with the same name as the original project and the date and time of the snapshot. Other than giving you a chance to refer to the state of earlier projects, the benefit is that each of these new projects takes up very little disk space, just a few MB, because it is only the database file that is duplicated. All the media remains the same unless you add more to the duplicated project. Remember that all the media is inside the same library.

Let's take a look at how **Snapshot Project** works.

Select the project that you want to snapshot in the browser. Right-click and select **Snapshot Project**.

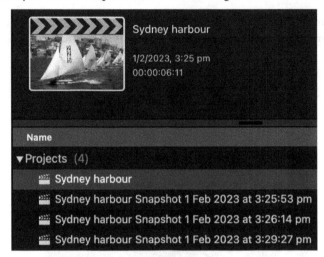

Figure 4.34 – Original project with two snapshots

You need to be clear about which project is in the timeline for you to continue editing. When you snapshot a project, there is no change to the project in the timeline. So, if the original project is in the timeline when you select **Snapshot Project**, it will be the original project that you will continue to edit. Take it from me, it is easy to mix the projects up.

My recommendation is that you treat the projects with *snapshot* in the title as backups and continue to edit in the original. If you need to go back to a snapshot to edit it, make sure you change the name of the project to show it is the main version.

In *Chapter 9*, I'll show you how to create a Smart Collection that only shows the original project and not the Snapshot projects.

Summary

We have covered a lot of ground in this chapter, from ingesting the media to having the foundations of the final edit at your fingertips. Along the way, we looked at the differences between an initial assembly and a rough cut, such as why you would have both and where time can be saved by combining them as one project.

We looked at some advanced ways to add clips to the project in the timeline, which is a container for projects, and saw how active projects can be brought into view in a similar way to an internet browser's style. Then, you were introduced to the timeline index.

You learned the difference between how Final Cut Pro and other NLEs use different words to represent projects and sequences, which is important for those who work with several different video editing applications.

The chapter looked at what should be included in the rough cut and how it shouldn't be too fine-tuned. Fine-tuning is for *Chapter 5*.

Once the rough cut has done its job, it will probably never be viewed again.

If you take nothing more from this chapter, make sure you recognize that your individuality and spirit are more important than the nuts and bolts of the steps listed in this chapter.

Part 2: Editing

Part 2 is about the refined cutting process to perfect assembling the rough cut. Effects and titles are added before the processes of color correction and audio sweetening. Finally, we will look at how a video is prepared for publishing.

This part contains the following chapters:

- *Chapter 5, Refining the Rough Cut*
- *Chapter 6, Fixing and Enhancing the Audio*
- *Chapter 7, Titles, Effects, and Generators*
- *Chapter 8, Setting Up and Editing Multicam*
- *Chapter 9, Project Workflows – Pace and Structure*

5

Refining the Rough Cut

In previous chapters, there was very little hands-on content, as the idea was to get you started with the software. This is about to change from this chapter onward, as from now on, the discussion will be on how to practically use Final Cut Pro. The previous chapter examined preparing the rough cut. The process involved adding the raw visual and audio-based media for the video and assembling it into a Final Cut Pro project. The refining of the rough cut to produce the final edit is the main focus of this chapter. In this chapter, we will look at and discuss techniques for cleaning up the rough cut using the tools in Final Cut Pro. You will learn that the final edit is a distillation of the story, removing material that is surplus to the edit while leaving just the right amount of content to strengthen the story. Then, once the duration of the fine edit is fixed (which is called *picture lock*), we can move on to adding effects, actioning the color correction, and audio sweetening.

You will learn about the most important requirements for the transition from the rough cut to the final edit, seeing how the flavor of the edit is affected by the pace and timing of the clips in the timeline and how those clips relate to each other. It's paramount that not only do the clips relate to each other in some way but the edit points between the clips smoothly transition from one scene to another, making sense without interrupting the flow of the story.

You will see that the process from rough cut to final cut does not start until the director and producer have signed off on the clip order in the rough cut. This applies equally to shorter and smaller productions as to large studio work. Even a solo editor working alone needs to make a conscious decision as to whether the sequence order of the rough cut is entirely as it should be.

Once you have a complete timeline with all the clips (or placeholders) in the correct order, you will be in a position to advance to the final edit – providing that you have the director's sign-off for the rough cut.

In this chapter, we're going to cover the following main topics:

- Understanding the remove, replace, and add actions
- Understanding the timeline view tools
- What is pacing?
- What is the **Total Running Time** (TRT)/picture lock?

By the end of this chapter, you will be fully aware of the need to remove, replace, and add clips to transform the rough cut into the fine edit that will become the core of your finished video. You will find that once the major changes have been made, you need to get down to specific details by using the Final Cut Pro fine-edit tools with techniques such as ripple, roll, slip, and slide edits.

The process of matching clips and pacing the video will be actioned in concert. All of the initial steps and the process of removing, replacing, and adding clips have an impact on each other in some way (albeit to a lesser degree for removing clips). You will find that clips are less likely to be removed and more likely to be replaced. However, there is no rule that prevents them from being removed at this late stage if the edit works better without them.

With the remove, replace, and add steps completed, you will then have what could be referred to as a fine edit. It's time for the effects to be added along with adding titles to clips. Once the fine edit is defined, it enters the stage referred to as **picture lock** or TRT, from there the edit will be sent off for special effects, coloring, and audio correction.

Understanding the remove, replace, and add actions

The three actions remove, replace, and add can be performed together as you work through the rough cut. In fact, you will also find that you might be tempted to smoothen the edit points as well, but stay away from changing the pacing until the other steps have been completed.

> **Note**
> For your peace of mind, note that when you remove or trim clips from the timeline, they are only removed from the project. The source clips in your library are not changed and you can always go back to them in the browser.

You may not have that many clips to remove, as candidates for removal should largely have been weeded out before getting to the rough cut. Also, keep in mind that it may not be the whole clip you need to remove, in which case you can just shorten the clip and leave just the important scenes in the timeline. As another alternative to removing, you can replace clips with others from the browser. The added advantage of replacing is that the duration of the timeline is left unchanged. I'll show you how to replace clips using the audition feature later in this section.

But first, let's look at the procedure for removing clips. If like me you have a lot of things to keep track of, your memory might not always manage to keep up. If you are removing clips from the rough cut, it is recommended to keep a note of what clips have been removed in case they need to be recovered later. You do this with markers, specifically the to-do marker in this case, as you will see in the next section.

Using the to-do marker

Before you remove a clip from the timeline with the *Delete* key, open the timeline index, make sure the **Clips** tab is activated, and select the clip in the timeline. It will be highlighted in the index. Select the clip name and copy it with *Command + C* so it can be pasted into the marker. Now, delete the clip from the timeline (you can do that from the **Index** tab, but it's better to do it directly on the clip in the timeline itself):

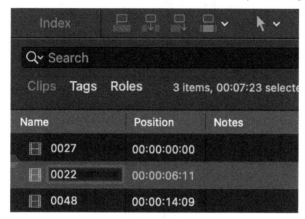

Figure 5.1 – Copy the clip name

At the edit point where the clip was removed, press *Option + M*. This will add a marker and open the modify window.

Paste the clip name that you have just copied. Select the middle tab at the top center of the modify window. The marker will turn red.

Figure 5.2 – Paste the clip name

This serves as a reminder to return to this to-do marker to complete an action. Upon ticking the **Completed** checkbox, the marker will turn green. Using these markers allows you to visually review the rough cut to quickly see where action is required.

When the playhead is at the edit point, adding a marker will place it on the first frame of the incoming clip. You might do this, for example, if you wish to be reminded that color correction is required. After completing the color correction tasks and ticking the **Completed** checkbox, the marker turns green.

It is important to note that in Final Cut Pro, markers are attached to clips. If you remove a clip, any markers on it will also be removed. If you desire a reminder that a clip has been removed, add a marker to the previous clip with a note that the following clip has been removed.

What's important here is that the to-do marker is used to remind you of two things: first, that a clip has been removed, and second, a reminder of the clip name so you can retrieve it later if needed. Just as a minor consideration, remember that you have the choice to leave the marker green or red. If you are certain that the removed clip will not be needed, set the marker to green, indicating no further action is required. You can still come back to it, but you are unlikely to need to. If you are unsure, then set the marker to red, so that you can quickly see where you might need to review the removal decision.

As well as removing clips, you will likely also need to consider replacing clips with others from the timeline. Final Cut Pro has a convenient method for this as well. It's called the audition feature; you will see how to use it in the next section.

Using the audition feature to replace clips

The best way to explain the audition feature is to say that it stores any number of different clips at one location in the timeline so that you can decide later which clip you would like to use at that point in the timeline.

To do that, follow these steps:

1. Locate the clip in the timeline that you would like to replace with another clip from the browser.

2. Select the whole browser clip or a portion of it, then, drag the browser selection inside the clip in the timeline. The cursor will change to a filmstrip icon with a green plus sign.

3. Select the **Replace and Add to Audition** option. The new clip from the browser will replace the view of the previous clip in the timeline.

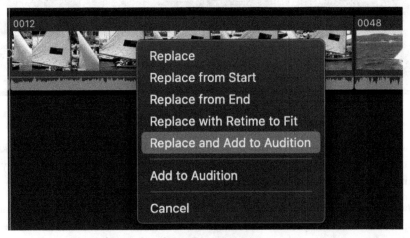

Figure 5.3 – Replace and Add to Audition

The duration will now be the length of the new clip, replacing the duration of the previous clip. Note the icon, shown in *Figure 5.4*, at the top left of the **0005** clip:

Figure 5.4 – Clip with audition icon in the top left

On clicking this audition icon, a new window appears with all of the clips included within the audition, through which you can scroll left and right. The dots in the middle of the window represent the number of clips in the audition, the blue dot indicating the current one on display.

Figure 5.5 – Audition window when the audition icon is pressed

You may have noticed that when you dragged the replacement clip inside the clip in the timeline, there was another audition option: **Add to Audition**. This is subtly different from the option you previously used in that it creates and adds to an audition but does not replace the current clip in the timeline. You would use this option to put a potential clip in the audition window "just in case" you might use it later.

> **Note**
>
> In *Figure 4.3*, you can see a number of different **Replace** options. When you use any of these **Replace** options, any effects added to the clip that was replaced are discarded. To avoid losing the effects and any inspector adjustments made to them, copy the clip in the timeline first using *Command + C*. After the clip has been replaced, select **Paste Attributes** (*Shift + Command + V*) and select the attributes that you want to paste into the new clip.

You can also create an audition in the browser to add to the timeline at a later date. This involves selecting the clips (or portions of clips) in the browser by holding the *Command* key, then selecting the **View** menu | **Audition** | **Create**.

Figure 5.6 – An audition created in the browser with the audition icon shown at the top right of the clip

Of course, you can add browser clips to the timeline with the same actions that you used to create the initial assembly and rough cut, by either dragging clips to the timeline or adding them more accurately with the *E*, *W*, and *Q* keys. Don't forget about the technique of the three-point edit of the primary storyline or the connected B-roll clips that we covered in *Chapter 4, Pre-Editing a Rough Cut*.

Once the biggest changes caused by remove, replace, and add actions have been completed and the chronological order is unlikely to change, you will mainly be fine-tuning the edit points between contiguous clips. This trimming process requires precision adjustments of as little as one frame at a time. We use the following methods in Final Cut Pro to trim edit points: ripple edits, roll edits, slip edits, and slide edits. These trimming methods require much more precise editing, so it's essential that you can view the timeline in much more detail. To do this, you will need to know how to control the timeline view with the following tools.

Understanding the timeline view tools

The height and duration of the timeline can be changed from the right-hand side of the center menu bar, by pressing the filmstrip icon. The top slider lets you zoom in and out of the timeline to see more or less detail. The six icons below this slider give you different configurations of video views compared to audio. The second, lower slider bar changes the height of the timeline.

Figure 5.7 – Timeline view tools

The *Command + +* and *Command + -* shortcuts are very useful to zoom in and out of the timeline in incremental steps. *Shift + Z* will show a fit-in-window view, so everything in the timeline fits in one window. The *Home* key and *End* key on extended keyboards jump to the beginning and end of the timeline.

Figure 5.8 – Home and End keys

The secret to a seamless edit is to have the action at the end of one clip flow into the following clip. A classic example of a transition between scenes is when a car drives out of the right side of the frame at the end of the first clip and then drives in from the left side in the second clip, giving the impression that it has seamlessly driven out of the first clip and directly into the second. Another is the classic door routine, where a person walks away from the camera into a doorway and the next clip shows them exiting the doorway and walking toward the camera. Whatever the specific detail, the cut needs to be smooth and not attract the viewers' attention. The principle is to hide cuts so the audience doesn't notice them happening. The perfect edit is one where no one notices it.

As a general rule, make your cuts on some action in the video or even on the peaks of the audio. Your objective is to distract the viewer with something that hides the cut from their mind. There are many things to choose from for this: someone sitting down, a head turning, a punch, a car driving by – just look out for some movement in the scene.

While hard cuts on some form of action are the traditional way that editors move from one clip to the next, it is beyond the scope of this book to dwell on the multitude of different cuts that are available to video editors (to list just a few: J-cuts, L-cuts, jump cuts, cross cuts, parallel edits, match cuts, and audio focus cuts).

What you do need to know are the methods of precise adjustment for modifying the edit points with the myriad of cutting methods at your disposal. The following sections outline the tools used for ripple, roll, slip, and slide edits in Final Cut Pro.

Ripple edits

You know now that clicking on an edit point highlights the left- or right-hand side of the edit point, allowing you to shorten or lengthen the clip enclosed by the yellow outline by dragging left and right.

Figure 5.9 – Edit points

When you drag this yellow highlight, you get a two-up display in the viewer window. The image on the left represents the last frame of the left-hand clip. The image on the right-hand side represents the first frame of the right-hand clip. For instance, if you have the previous clip highlighted in yellow, only the left of *Figure 4.10* will change, while the right-hand image will stay static.

Figure 5.10 – Two-up display in the viewer

That's fine for sweeping changes. You can, however, use finer control, although at a cost.

Single-frame changes can be actioned with the comma (,) and period (.) keys, which is the perfect solution for finite controls to shorten or lengthen a clip.

Figure 5.11 – Comma (,) and period (.) keys

There is a downside to using the comma (,) and period (.) keys rather than dragging, though: the single-frame method doesn't show the two-up window. It's a real pity. The other advantage of dragging is that you are shown the timecode duration of the clip and the amount of time you're adding to or removing from the edit point.

Figure 5.12 – Timecode duration of the clip and the amount of time
you're adding to or removing from the edit point

The ripple edit options are extensive, allowing you to do much more than just move the edit point with the **Select** tool. These options are available in the **Trim** menu:

Trim	Mark	Clip	Modify
Blade			⌘ B
Blade All			⇧ ⌘ B
Join Clips			
Trim Start			G
Trim End			H
Trim to Playhead			⌥ \
Extend Edit			⇧ X
Align Audio to Video			
Nudge Left			,
Nudge Right			.

Figure 5.13 – Ripple options in the Trim menu

You can review all the options on Apple's Support page: `https://support.apple.com/en-gb/guide/final-cut-pro/ver9847ec25/10.6.2/mac/11.5.1`.

So far, you have seen the changes you can make to either side of a clip independently of the connecting clip. The ramification of this is that the duration of the timeline changes every time you make a ripple edit. What is much more useful is the ability to modify both the **In** and **Out** points of the respective clips at the same time, giving you the ability to change how one scene closes and the next opens simultaneously. This is called a roll edit. This is very powerful as it doesn't change the duration of the timeline.

Roll edits

To use the roll editing technique, you need to activate the **Trim** tool by either selecting it from the toolset or pressing the *T* key.

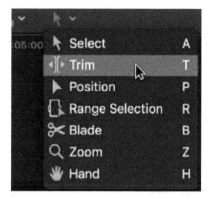

Figure 5.14 – Trim tool showing in the tool selection window

> **Note**
> Particularly useful is the ability to temporarily activate the **Trim** tool by holding *T* while you make the edit, and then releasing the *T* key. This has the major benefit of returning you to the previous tool selection rather than sticking to the **Trim** tool selection.

The following screenshot shows the double-sided **Trim** tool placed over an edit point.

Figure 5.15 – Trim tool location indication, plus the amount of change in the duration

Similar to the ripple technique, the timecode shows the change in the duration of your edit.

More information about roll edits is available from Apple's support page: https://support. apple.com/en-gb/guide/final-cut-pro/ver1632d9ae/10.6.2/mac/11.5.1.

The first two techniques that we've just examined showed changes to the edit point, whereas the next technique, slip edits, changes the content of the clip itself without changing the edit points or the total duration of the project. A slip edit changes what's inside the clip rather than the edit point.

Slip edits

A slip edit is perfectly explained in the context of a music video. Assume you have lined up the edits on the beat points, so you want the lengths of the clips to stay as they are, but you want to display a different scene from within a given clip. By moving both the start and end points of the clip simultaneously, you can select a different part of the clip to be shown without changing the length of the clip itself. Think of the determined length of the clip as a window; all you are doing is changing the scene shown in the window. As the name suggests, this technique slips the content with the clip itself. Of course, you could replace the clip with another from the browser, but if the scene you want is in the clip already in the timeline, a slip will do this more quickly. As shown in the following figure, the timecode highlights how much you have moved the content of the clip, + for movements to the right and – for movements to the left:

Figure 5.16 – The timecode shows the clip was slipped to the right

There is one final **Trim** edit technique, which affects three clips by moving the position of the central clip in relation to the other two. You could say that it *slides* the center clip over one of the other two without leaving a gap, and this is appropriately called a slide edit.

Slide edits

Imagine that you need to keep the duration of the total video unchanged, but one clip (clip 1) has some content that needs to be removed. You can slide a neighboring clip (clip 2) over the unwanted portion of clip 1. Clip 2 remains unchanged, but extra content from clip 3, to the other side of clip 2, replaces the duration that was removed in clip 1. Slide edits, though rarely used, are actioned with the **Trim** tool, but with the *Option* key held down.

Figure 5.17 – Slide edit showing the center clip moved over the
clip on the left and exposing frames in the left clip

This highlights the main point of this chapter: ultimately, there are no rules. If there were rules, then all videos would be the same, without any distinctive character. As we've seen, this part of the editing process is where you can apply your own style to bring out your creativity and put your own stamp on the production.

The different types of edits and styles of cuts that we've reviewed so far mostly affect the edit point. However, one of the important (if not the most important) ways a video comes to life and develops its own feel and character is with pacing. You are in control of this, and all the other members of the team are at your mercy. Let's look at some ways to help you with your pacing when editing.

What is pacing?

As the word suggests, pace concerns the video's momentum. It's not just the speed or velocity, but also the tempo – the cumulative effect of multiple edits. Speed, as opposed to pace, is more about quick and slow. Pace is more subtle and can be in the subconscious. as much as it can be physically seen.

I said there are no rules about how to implement pace in a video, but there are some conventions to give you some indications as to how the tempo of pacing can be implemented in your projects. But remember: it's a craft that you need to develop. It comes with experience and familiarity with the editing process. It can't be fully taught; it relies on harnessing your creativity.

The first thing you need to understand is that pacing does not refer to a change in speed. Moving from fast motion to slow motion is not the way to introduce pace into a video. Though high speed and slow motion could be added for extra effect, they have less to do with the overall feel of the video than pace does.

Consider these conventions

For quick-action sequences, rapid cuts are the order of the day. Slow scenes call for more moderate rates of cutting. Even so, you need to decide on the tone of a scene by using a certain pace that also enhances the expression of the meaning of the story, and not just a series of fast/slow cuts.

Action sequences may call for faster pacing, but slower rates of cuts can also create a powerful mood. Slow cuts will give a feeling of suspense, whereas normal-paced cuts reference normal life, the daily routine.

Once you introduce a faster pace, you need to be careful about how long it continues, as the viewer will need a break after a while – for this, a comedic moment can give a little relief from fast cuts to let the viewers catch their breath. Then, depending on what the story requires, move back to the fast-cut action, slow the pace down, or return it to normal. Your clips and audio will give you a clue on what is most appropriate.

So, to review, cut too fast and you'll lose people; cut too slow and you'll bore them. Use rapid pacing for intensity and excitement. Use slower pacing to relax the viewer and make them think about the story. If in doubt, err on the side of faster cuts, as it's more dynamic. For sure, boring your viewer is not something you want to do, but equally, confusing them with fast-paced cuts will wear them out and you'll lose their attention. It's best to vary the length of the clips in the timeline to garner emotional responses from the viewer as well as thrill them with action.

This next section looks at the tools that affect the pace, as well as changing the duration of clips.

Tools that aid pacing

The simplest method is the cut method itself. Final Cut Pro has both cutting tools and methods for shortening and lengthening clips in the timeline.

Cutting tools

The **Blade** tool was represented by a blade icon, but from Final Cut Pro version 10.5 onward, it is now a pair of scissors. It's located in the list of tools on the left side of the center bar.

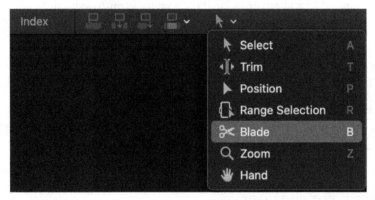

Figure 5.18 – Blade tool selected (shown as scissors here)

Blade is used, after selecting it in the toolset, by clicking on the required place in a clip in the timeline. It can also be used even when not selected in the toolset by positioning the playhead where you want to cut and pressing *Command + B*. **Blade** can be quickly activated by temporarily holding the *B* key, clicking to cut, and then releasing the *B* key so the selected tool returns to the previous one.

> **Tip**
> *Shift + Command + B* will cut through all clips at the playhead position, including connected clips. It's a great tool for the end of a sequence where there are a number of stacked connected clips, to ensure they all end at exactly the same frame.

When a cut is made, an edit point is created so you can then decide what to do with the new clips on either side of the cut, such as shortening, lengthening, or deleting them.

> **Note**
>
> Contrary to what you might expect, Final Cut Pro does not rest the playhead on the actual edit point. The playhead can only rest on a frame on either side of the edit point. By default, when you move the playhead or it snaps to an edit point, the playhead always rests on the first frame of the right-hand clip. If you want to move to the last frame of the previous clip, you need to use the left arrow key – just one press.

Dragging tools

You saw these tools in action in the sections examining ripple and roll edits earlier in this chapter. Just as a quick reminder, if an edit point already exists, clips on either side of the edit point can be individually dragged by clicking the left or right frame of the edit point to shorten or lengthen the duration of each clip independently. You need to use the **Select** tool (arrow) for that action.

When the **Trim** tool is selected and you click on the edit point, both sides are selected, so when you move left or right, you change the duration of both clips without affecting the total duration of the timeline. The comma and period keys will move the edit point one frame at a time.

Trimming (clipping) action

This is not a tool as such, but it is certainly one of the most convenient cutting actions: it trims, but not in the way the **Trim** tool does. This trimming (or clipping) action uses the playhead's position and cuts to an edit point on either side of the playhead, depending on which key combination you press. The convenience of this is demonstrated when you are playing through the clip, checking for places to shorten it – the playhead will already be in place when you choose to make your trimming cut. Should you decide to remove the portion of the clip up to that point, press the *Option + [* keys. The portion of the clip from the edit point to the left up to the playhead will be deleted. *Option +]* deletes the portion from the playhead up to the edit point to the right. This trimming action can be done on the fly as a video is playing, and even when skimming – this is very convenient for speedy edits. I will show you a method of setting a single key command for this most useful tool in *Chapter 18, Troubleshooting Final Cut Pro*.

Speed controls

Even though speed is not the biggest concern of pacing, it does have its place as an extra effect. Think of freezing an image to hold the viewer's attention, even for a few frames: this will increase moments of tension. Speeding up the clip gives the impression of the passing of time. Equally, you may want to introduce a slow-motion effect to bring home the action by showing all the motion that, in real life, would happen too quickly to be appreciated. These techniques are to be used with care and, in most cases, infrequently. However, it is quite common for a sped-up sequence of a fast-paced cityscape to be used as a transition between clips where there is a significant jump in time, say from the night to the following morning.

The speed controls are found in the center bar, under the viewer. They mainly speak for themselves.

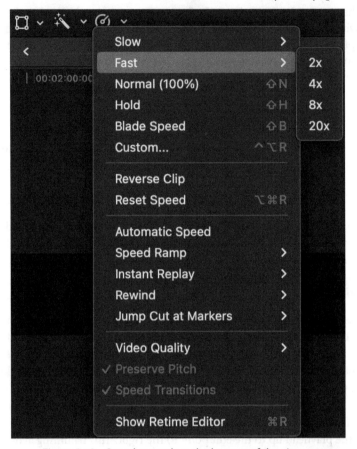

Figure 5.19 – Speed controls at the bottom of the viewer

Slow offers presets for **10%**, **25%**, and **50%**. **Fast** offers **2x**, **4x**, **8x**, and **20x**. **Hold** is a freeze frame that gives you the choice of speeding up or slowing down the part of the clip following the **Hold** frame. The duration of the held frame itself can be changed as well.

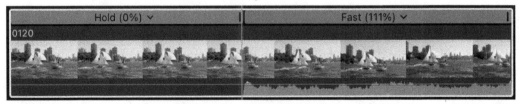

Figure 5.20 – Hold allows you to change the speed after the held frame

Blade Speed gives you the choice of speeding up or slowing down either side of the frame selected in the retime editor.

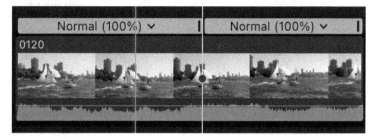

Figure 5.21 – Blade Speed is the most flexible of the speed controls

Speed Ramp offers a preset to slow down or speed up the clip from the playhead position to or from 0%.

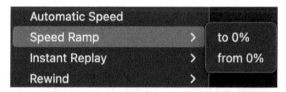

Figure 5.22 – Speed Ramp from normal speed to 0

There is a quick and convenient method to add a freeze frame with a default four-second duration to the timeline at the playhead position: simply press *Option + F*. You can change the default duration of the given still image in the Final Cut Pro settings. *Option + F* can also be used in the browser to add a freeze to the timeline as a connected clip.

Figure 5.23 – Option + F adds a freeze frame to the timeline

The fine cut stage has now become the final edit stage; it's just awaiting the effects plug-ins, titles, special effects, color correction, and audio sweetening. This stage is known as picture lock or TRT.

What is the Total Running Time (TRT)/picture lock?

TRT is the term for when the duration of a project has finally been determined and can be set in stone. From this point, external services such as color and audio correction can be actioned without the fear of the edit changing in duration. Picture lock is another term for TRT. I prefer to use the term picture lock as it better indicates a *final* state.

After the fine cut, the video is ready to be sent for finishing by color specialists, audio engineers, and special effects technicians. These specialists require the video to have a set duration, so no more changes to the timeline can be made. It's pretty much the point of no return for the editing team. Even as a solo operator, I suggest that you keep the same mindset: once the picture lock point is reached, don't make any duration changes to the edit. I know this is easier said than done, as one of the traits of an editor is always finding things to improve, but you have to sign off on an edit at some point. Make this the sign-off point to finalize the video's duration, so everything after this is solely about color, audio, and effects.

Summary

This chapter introduced you to the practical aspects of editing in Final Cut Pro. You learned about the tools to tidy up the rough cut and finesse your edit to the point where it now only needs the color correction and audio to be handled and the special effects added. Specifically, we saw how to remove, replace, and add clips to and from the rough cut. You were introduced to the audition feature, which lets you store selections of different clips in the timeline for a later decision. You saw how to use the to-do marker to remind yourself where these actions had taken place so you could restore what was removed if you needed to. You also learned about the edit controls associated with ripple, roll, slip, and slide edits.

One of the most important aspects of the fine edit is the decisions made about pacing throughout the whole video, as well as the relationships that clips have with each other, particularly how they transition to the following clip. Finally, you understood that your personality and experience can determine how you make the edit *yours*, and not just a copy of other people's works. You also learned about the conventions of pacing and how they assist you in controlling your version of the edit.

The main takeaway from this chapter is that attention to detail plus varying the pace and tempo of the edit are what make it a compelling video that holds your audience's attention.

Now that you have completed the fine cut and reached picture lock, the next chapter looks at the process of audio correction. In real-life projects, you may send the edit out to a specialist or fix the audio in-house. The next chapter shows how to correct audio with Final Cut Pro.

6

Fixing and Enhancing the Audio

In the previous chapter, we completed the rough cut, reaching a fixed duration and moving to *picture lock*, ready for the final stages of color correction and audio sweetening. This chapter takes a look at the more advanced methods of audio correction, assuming that the basic volume level adjustments are already known.

Good audio is more important in a video than the images themselves. Viewers will stop watching a video with questionable audio much faster than one with acceptable audio but marginal video quality. To help improve the audio of imported media, Final Cut Pro ships with a myriad of audio filters, mostly borrowed from Apple's own Logic Pro application. A deep understanding of all these filters and their options would take a lifetime of experience with audio, so this chapter will focus only on the most frequently needed filters with the thought in mind that the reader of this book will be unlikely to have the requisite knowledge of audio to understand all the filters. It is a fact of life that, generally speaking, video editors are not the best audio editors, so for any important audio editing, the project should be sent, with the use of roles, to audio experts just as it would also be sent out to the relevant experts for color correction and special effects.

This chapter will help you understand some of the more specific audio needs that you will read about in *Chapter 9, Project Workflows – Pace and Structure*. This chapter will concentrate on the needs of the solo editor trying to fill the role of "Jack of all trades."

In this chapter, we're going to cover the following main topics:

- Audio in the browser
- Audio in the timeline
- Fixing audio vocal problems
- Suggestions when correcting audio
- Using XML files
- Exporting with audio-only roles
- Audio tips and tricks

By the end of this chapter, you will have learned how to apply the common audio filters to sweeten any audio as well as special filters that may help recover badly recorded audio with distracting background noise. The most important piece of knowledge you will gain is the difference between the source **decibel (dB)** level reading and the adjusted output dB level. You will also understand when you are out of your depth with audio and how to prepare your edit to be sent as an XML file to audio experts for a more professional result. As a solo editor, you will learn the basics of sending the audio-only output to external audio correction applications such as Audacity – see *Chapter 17, Supporting Software Applications for Final Cut Pro*, for more on this. You will also learn about the differences in audio correction for vocal-based videos compared to the needs of a music-focused video.

Understanding audio in the browser

Audio levels can be adjusted in the browser, which is useful for dialogue and music videos when the levels are low. You should also be aware of the option to display waveforms as these give you a visual representation of the audio.

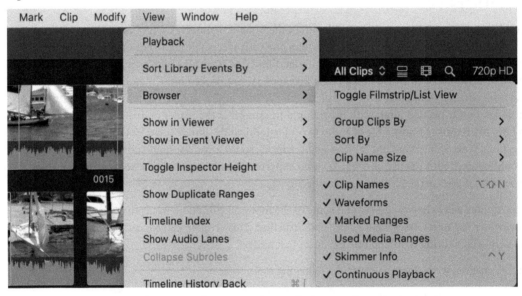

Figure 6.1 – Browser setting to display waveforms

The default audio level in a **Browser** clip, as it is imported, is at the level set on the camera. This will show as **0.0** in the inspector when the clip is selected in the browser.

Figure 6.2 – Browser volume level adjustment in the inspector

Even though the dB level shows in the inspector as **0.0**, the audio meters will show a different level. The default meters are small and shown below the viewer to the right of the timecode. It is advised to click the default meters to display them in a larger form beside the **Effects** or **Transition** browsers, as shown in *Figure 6.3*:

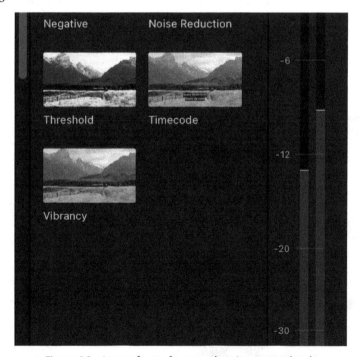

Figure 6.3 – Larger form of meters showing output levels

This is perhaps the most important lesson to learn in this chapter. It may be confusing to you that both are measured in dB readings. It's a fact of life that you have to live with. The important thing is to understand the difference and be really careful you don't mix them up.

The source level from the camera, as shown in *Figure 6.2*, defaults to **0.0**. That's the same whether it's a scream or a whisper. We will name it the Source Level. The **0.0** value can be adjusted up or down. Its maximum is +12, with its minimum going past -90 to read -∞ (no sound):

Figure 6.4 – Volume displaying as -∞ dB (no sound)

Don't worry about +12 being the highest volume, as there are many ways of increasing this, but at the cost of also increasing the ambient background noise present in the location being filmed, as well as the internal noise of the microphone (this is heard as a soft hissing sound). There are filters that I will show you that can help reduce those noise levels but not eliminate them. Though, in the scheme of things, they can appear to be quite magical at times. We will see more on this later in this chapter, in the *Audio filters* section.

Let's get back to the difference in the dB levels: now you understand the source level, let's look at the output level as shown by the audio meters. The output levels effectively range from -60 to 0 and up to +6. The measurements show the volume level that your video will be exported at, hence being known as the **output level**.

Figure 6.5 – Audio level showing as -∞ (no sound) in a timeline clip

There are differing opinions as to what is the optimal maximum output level. Whatever you decide, it must *not* be more than 0, as any audio above that level will be cut out completely, or even worse, there will be an audible static pop, then no sound. From a practical point of view, the peak reading should be between -12 and -6 dB at most on the Final Cut Pro meters, as shown in *Figure 6.3*.

Now you know about the levels, the next section will show you how to read the meters so you can set them at the optimum levels.

Reading the audio meters

The vertical green bars move up and down while the video is playing, reflecting the volume as it changes. At the very top of the green bars is a white horizontal line that floats just above the green bars to indicate the recent peak readings:

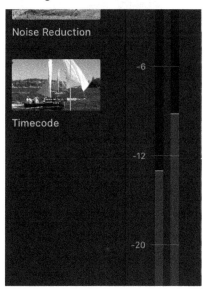

Figure 6.6 – White vertical peaks

If the volume levels are too high and reach above 0, the red indicator will show at the top of the meters. The red indicator stays alight until you play another clip, so you know that the 0 level has been passed.

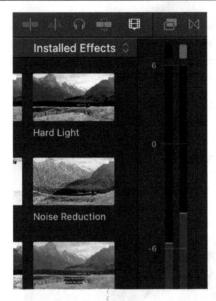

Figure 6.7 – Red warning light

When you adjust the level of the audio in a **Browser** clip in the inspector and add the clip with the adjusted volume to a project, it will show the adjusted volume, not the default 0.0 dB.

There is an alternative way to adjust the volume of a **Browser** clip as well as adding audio filters to that clip. In fact, you can also add video filters and make other modifications: it uses a feature called **Open Clip** from the **Clip** menu. **Open Clip** was discussed in *Chapter 2, Organizing the Media*.

Select the clip in the browser and go to **Clip | Open Clip**. The clip shows a temporary view in the timeline. Add any filter that you want at this point.

Now that you have seen the primary, albeit limited, ways of adjusting audio in the browser, the next section shows you the full extent of audio correction functionality in Final Cut Pro.

Audio in the timeline

As a current user of Final Cut Pro, you will be aware of how to drag the horizontal audio line to adjust the volume level within a clip, and how aggressively the volume changes when you drag. There is a simple way to control that by holding the *Command* key while you drag. The changes will be far more composed.

When you drag the line, volume levels are changed for the whole clip, from edit point to edit point; however, there are also ways to change the levels within the clip. The easiest method is to use the **Range** tool. Hold the *R* key down, hover over the point where you want to start the change in volume, then click and drag to the end of where you want to make the change. A yellow outline will enclose the area to be changed, as shown in the following screenshot:

Figure 6.8 – The Range tool for adjusting within a clip

Drag the horizontal line to the new volume level and you'll see that auto-fade transitions are entered for you. When you click away, you will be able to adjust the fades by dragging any of the four keyframe dots.

Under normal circumstances, audio volume levels are adjusted at the frame rate of the video, but when even greater accuracy is required, audio can be adjusted at the sub-frame level.

Sub-frame audio fine-tuning

Video frames are linked to the frame rate at which the video was shot – conventionally, 30 frames per second for NTSC or 25 frames per second for PAL. You will have heard that the smallest fraction you can go down to is one video frame. When you zoom into the timeline with the *Command + +* shortcut, you will eventually see a light-gray highlight indicating a single frame (*Figure 6.9*). At this zoom level, you can move one video frame at a time with the left and right arrows on the keyboard.

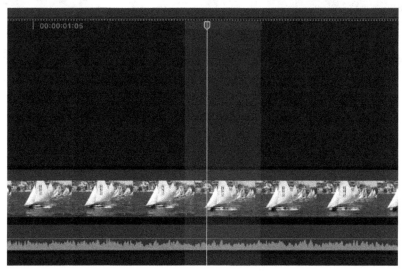

Figure 6.9 – Single video frame within the lighter gray highlight. Audio
is extended from the combined video/audio track

Although it's accurate to consider a single frame as the smallest unit in video, the same does not hold true for audio. In an NTSC video, audio adjustments can be made at a finer level, specifically $1/80^{th}$ of a video frame. To navigate at this sub-frame level, you can use the *Option + left or right arrow* keys. To navigate at the sub-frame level, make sure **Zoom to Samples** is checked and **Time display** is set to **Subframes** in the **Preference** panel.

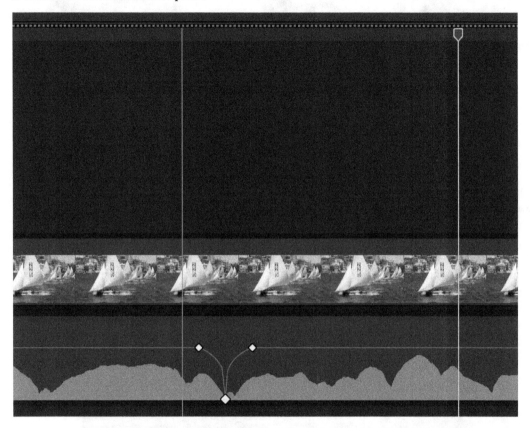

Figure 6.10 – Moving by one audio sub-frame with Option + left arrow key

The key to adjusting and correcting audio effectively is to use filters. The next section shows where to find audio filters in the inspector as well as the **Effects** browser.

Audio filters

Any audio filters can be dragged inside the clip in the timeline, and they can then be adjusted in the inspector, under the **Effects** subheading.

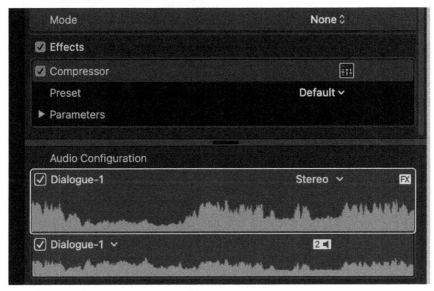

Figure 6.11 – An audio effect added under the Effects subheading in the inspector

When you have multiple audio tracks, as in a multicam edit, you must drag the filter directly onto the track in the inspector. If you drag it to the timeline, it will only affect the audio that is part of the video track.

The following figure shows effects added to the track in the inspector rather than the timeline:

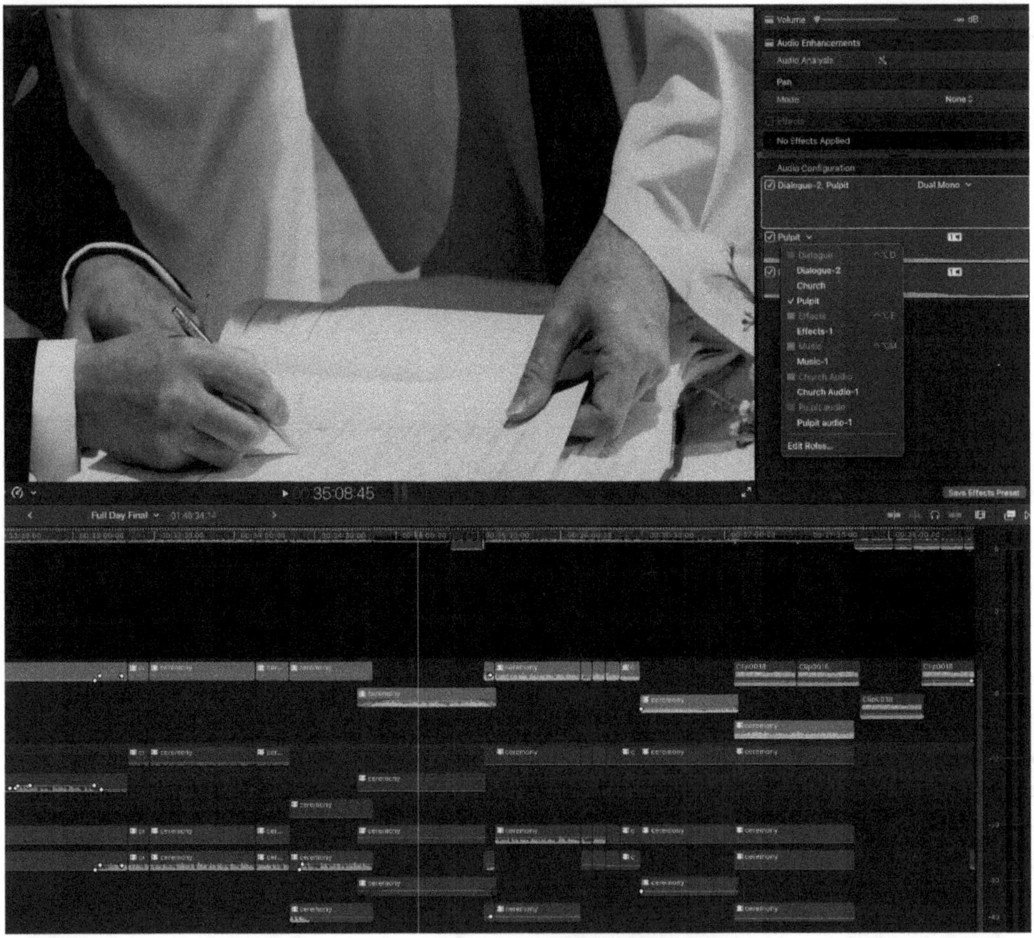

Figure 6.12 – Multiple audio tracks

When working with the audio that is part of a video clip, it can be helpful to show the audio expanded from the video. When expanded, the audio shows more details than it does when viewed with the video clip.

Expanded audio

A video track with audio or a multicam clip with many audio channels can have the audio track expanded in the timeline or just show the audio as part of the video track, as in *Figure 6.9*.

When you right-click in the timeline, a menu with options to expand and collapse audio appears. There are two expansion levels, depending on whether the timeline clip just has audio that is part of the video track or there are separate audio tracks:

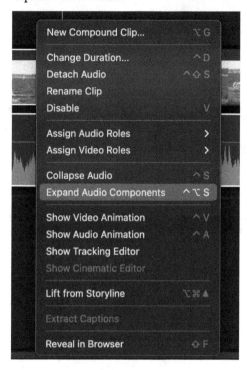

Figure 6.13 – Expand Audio Components is shown for multiple audio tracks

Any audio that is part of a video clip, as shown in *Figure 6.14*, can be expanded to show as a separate track while still being synced to the video. Think of it this way: if the audio was recorded by the camera, then it becomes part of the video clip. Audio recorded separately is independent.

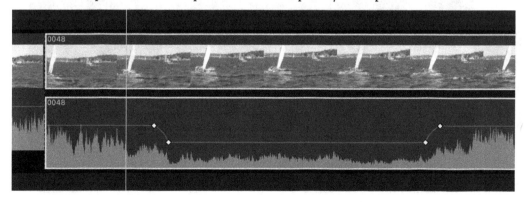

Figure 6.14 – Audio that is part of the video clip showing as expanded while still being synced

This allows you to edit **J-cuts** and **L-cuts**, where the audio is cut at a different point from the video. In the following figure, the **Trim** tool has been used to roll the video cut to the right of the audio cut:

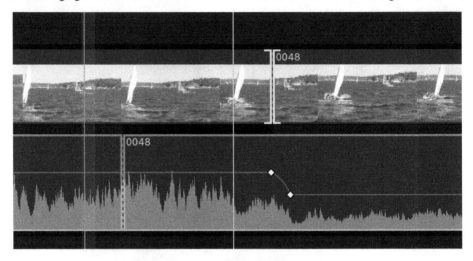

Figure 6.15 – J-cut

Audio that is expanded can be dragged under different video clips, which will either overlap the audio in the video or replace it. If you are overlapping audio, you should fade from one clip to the other. Final Cut Pro has fade handles built into each video clip. In the following figure, the expanded audio from clip **0005** has been dragged under clip **0048** for an L-cut:

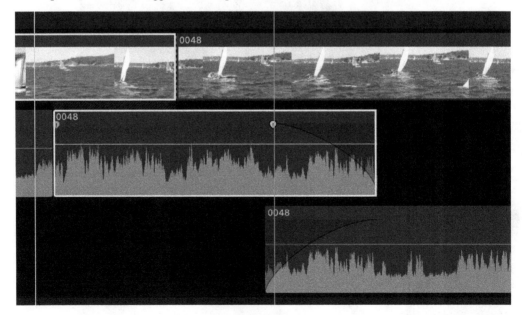

Figure 6.16 – L cut

In *Figure 6.17*, we can see the same view but with the expanded audio collapsed, showing the audio from clip **0005** hidden, but it will still be heard, even though there is an apparent gap where the audio does not show. This is always something to watch out for, and I suggest that if you have extended audio in your project, you don't collapse the clip. If you find yourself in this situation and can't recall which clips were collapsed previously, select the whole timeline with *Command + A* and press *Control + S* and all clips in the project will be expanded. You can collapse them all again with the same shortcut keys.

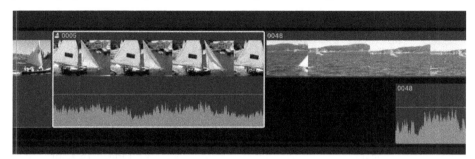

Figure 6.17 – Collapsed audio showing as a gap in the timeline

Expanded audio is still in sync with the video. You will need to right-click and select **Detach Audio** (see *Figure 6.13*) if you need to move the audio to a different position from the video. I would practice caution when detaching audio unless you have no other choice. **Detach Audio** makes the audio out of sync with the video, with no easy way to sync it back up (other than adding the video again, with audio still attached, from the browser). To find the clip in the browser, right-click and select **Reveal in Browser** (see *Figure 6.13*).

The following figure shows a multicam project with several tracks expanded. These can be shown or hidden again by checking them in the inspector, as in *Figure 6.12*.

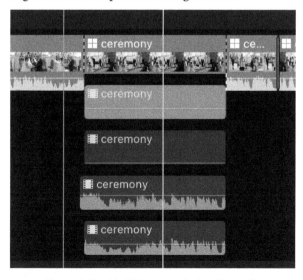

Figure 6.18 – Multiple expanded audio tracks

Now that you have a foundational understanding of how audio is adjusted in Final Cut Pro, it's time to look at how to correct problems with the audio. The commonly heard saying is, "*It can always be fixed in post-production.*" This is most often used as an excuse for not reshooting when audio problems are noticed on set. I can tell you that this saying is only partly true. Some things will be fixed in post-production, but it's always best to have good audio from the start rather than trying to fix things that may have been really easy to re-record on set.

Without a doubt, bad audio is the biggest problem you will be confronted with and have to deal with. You will be expected to fix what you receive, so most of the rest of this chapter will look at the common issues that will need repair.

The results will vary: some will be OK, some will be borderline, and some may be best to send off to audio experts. Some will just not be acceptable no matter what and will require new audio recordings or some filler to be made.

In major drama productions, there is a process called **Automated Dialog Replacement (ADR)**. Various software applications sync up two pieces of audio. The process is done offline, with actors watching the scene and then repeating the same lines in the same way as originally. The software adjusts the new recording to match the original version exactly in timing.

Final Cut Pro allows the export of audio only for the ADR process as **Audio only Roles**, which I will show you later in this chapter, in the section titled *Exporting audio-only roles*).

When you receive the new recording from the ADR process, add it to the project by placing it below the original clip in the timeline, and the clips will be in sync. You can even check the timing by playing both clips together. When you are happy, just reduce the audio of the original clip.

There are often hard decisions to make where you as the editor are in a no-win situation. If you can't fix the audio issues, you will be seen as inadequate; if you do fix them, nobody will notice. This is, after all, the fundamental result of video editing – nobody should notice your work.

Fixing audio vocal problems

In this section, we will learn how to fix audio problems, particularly the following ones:

- Ambient background noise
- Voices with variable volume levels
- Wind noise
- Echoes
- Distorted voices
- Ums and ahs, coughs, and sniffs

Ambient background noise

You will get the best results by using audio filters to fix ambient background noise problems. In most cases, other than the worst types of noise problems, you will produce something that will feel like magic, and everyone else will just say, "*Well done.*"

The first filter to try is the inspector's **Noise Removal** filter. It's built into the main body of the inspector so there's no need to add it from the **Effects** browser.

Figure 6.19 – Noise Removal in the inspector

When you activate the effect, it defaults to **50 %**. I suggest that you reduce the slider to around **45 %** as **50 %** tends to give a bit of a helium-inhaling effect. **Noise Removal** works best on consistent noises that don't change much in pitch. The biggest issue with this filter is that voices located far away from the recording device will sound somewhat distorted. You could try to reduce the slider further or try the next magic effect, called **Voice Isolation**.

Voice Isolation is a relatively new filter and is built into the inspector. You should give it a try even if you get reasonable results with **Noise Removal**:

Figure 6.20 – Voice Isolation in the inspector

> Warning
> **Noise Removal** and **Voice Isolation** do not work well together.

When you check **Voice Isolation**, as shown in the preceding screenshot, you will also get a **50 %** default setting on the slider. In my own experience with frequent use of **Voice Isolation**, the results are nothing short of outstanding. I have had occasions where I have been able to remove the sound of a plane flying overhead, with the slider up to **90 %**. I find that **Voice Isolation** works well with non-constant background noises – much better than **Noise Removal**. **Voice Isolation** will not remove all types of noise and is not good with wind noise. It has issues with vocal music tracks and also crowds of people in the background talking behind your subject's voice. If there is one voice with a prominent mechanical noise in the background, for example, you will do well with this filter, so give it a try.

Voices with variable volume levels

Variable volume levels are also a problem area that can be fixed reasonably easily. You will come across this issue frequently where a person's voice fluctuates. It usually happens when the actor is shy or uneasy with the situation. You will find this is a common issue in interviews where the person is not comfortable in front of a microphone. The issue will show when your meter peaks are mostly at a good level, but some words are just too soft and drop below -20. The filter to use here is **Compressor**.

Using the Compressor filter

From the **Effects** sidebar, select **Levels**, and drag the **Compressor** effect into the clip on the timeline or onto the audio track in the inspector:

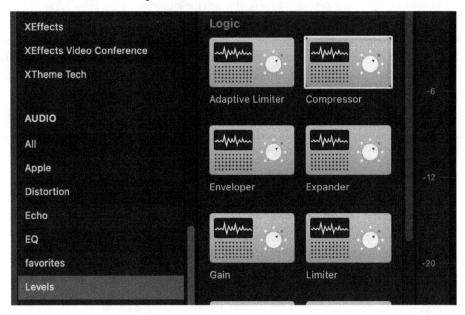

Figure 6.21 – Compressor in the sidebar's Levels panel

Most of the time, this filter will work well with the default settings, though you also have a number of presets that you can try:

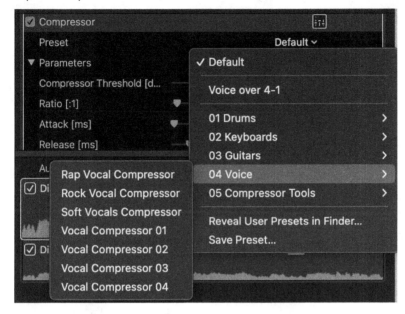

Figure 6.22 – Compressor in the inspector with Voice options

At the top of the **Compressor** options, you will notice a small icon that looks like a calculator:

Figure 6.23 – Adjustment icon

Clicking on the icon will let you customize the **Compressor** settings. See *Chapter 10, The Inspector Controls*, for an explanation of using **Effects** to personalize the different filters. Each effect will have unique panels, as shown in *Figure 6.24*:

Figure 6.24 – Panel for Compressor

There are two side effects that you may experience with **Compressor**. Background noise may increase, particularly if you have used the **Noise Removal** filter. The second issue is that the louder parts of the dialogue may now be too high on the dB meter.

Fixing the side effects of the Compressor filter

The first issue will be to balance out the **Noise Removal** filter with an adjustment to the **Compressor Threshold** value. Click the drop-down triangle next to **Parameters** in **Compressor** if you don't see **Threshold**. You will need to adjust both the **Noise Removal** slider and **Threshold** until you get a satisfactory result.

The second issue, concerning the meters peaking, can be resolved with the **Limiter** filter. It is also in the **Levels** panel of the audio effects. Drag it as you did with the **Compressor** filter. There are presets to choose from; I suggest you use **For Vocals**. The principle behind **Limiter** is to attempt to reduce any peak above the threshold to the threshold level. I suggest you test a section of the audio in the clip after adjusting the **Gain** control under **Parameters** inside **Limiter**.

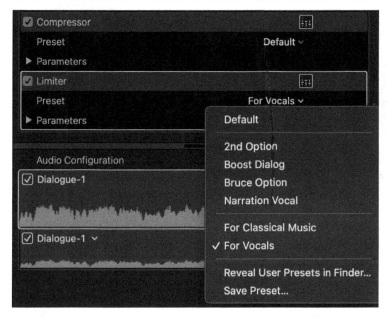

Figure 6.25 – Limiter in the inspector

Wind noise

You will find wind noise very hard to remove, even partially. It tends to overlap the same frequencies of the human voice, so filters will cut out both. There are a number of plug-ins available to purchase that will do an excellent job of removing wind noise. Toolfarm has a number that you can consider if required: https://protect-eu.mimecast.com/s/jWm8CV5k2CxQl0AIzS5Gu?domain=toolfarm.com.

If you only want to use the default filters in Final Cut Pro, you should use **Denoiser**. It has similar features as **Compressor** and **Limiter** and is found in the **Specialized** panel in the **Effects** sidebar. There are presets but I find that to reduce wind noise, it is best to try the **Noise Type** slider. Since there are so many different levels of wind noise, there is no magic setting. In reality, you will only be able to reduce low-volume wind noise; you will never be able to extract hurricane-level sounds.

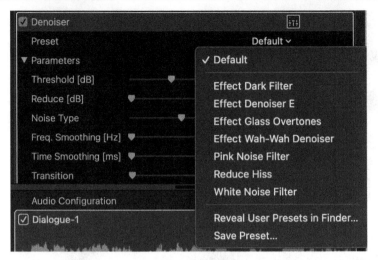

Figure 6.26 – The Denoiser panel in the inspector

Wind noise can sometimes occupy the low frequencies of the spectrum and, if so, those frequencies are not always present in human voices. If the wind noise appears to you to be at a low frequency, try this approach: drag the **Remove Low Frequencies** effect to the clip and drag the slider high, say to **90**, and set the **Voice Isolation** filter to **50 %**. If the wind noise is in the higher frequencies, try the same with the **Remove High Frequencies** effect.

Echoes

This problem is the hardest to remove. Final Cut Pro doesn't have any filter that can really help you but there are various plug-ins available for different suppliers. **EchoRemover** by CrumplePop (`https://www.toolfarm.com/store/cart/referral/referrer/VTUTOR/url/boris_fx_crumplepop/target/buy`) is a plug-in that uses AI to remove echo from your audio in Final Cut Pro. This plug-in is discussed in *Chapter 12, Using Third-Party Plug-Ins*.

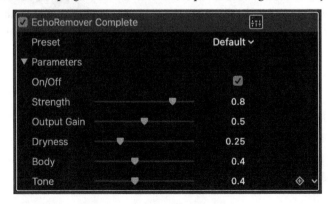

Figure 6.27 – EchoRemover in the inspector

Distorted voices

The filters for use with distorted voices include **Voice Isolation** and **Noise Removal** as well as **Compressor**. There are **Noise Gate** filters and **Pass** filters that may also help. I have a trick of using a filter that introduces distortion and then winding back all the settings. It works well with recordings featuring many voices, and where the recording is muffled. Use the settings shown in the following figure:

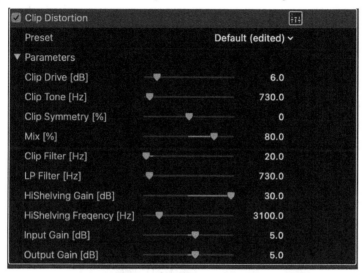

Figure 6.28 – The Clip Distortion panel in the inspector

You will need to adjust **Output Gain** for the volume level. In *Chapter 10, The Inspector Controls*, I'll show you how to create a preset from these settings and save it in the **Effects** browser so you can use it over and over.

Ums and ahs, coughs, and sniffs

These sounds are known as *fillers*. To remove fillers, which only take up a few frames, you will need to cut them out rather than apply a filter. Use the **Range** tool to select the duration of the filler's sound. Drag the volume line down inside the range, and if necessary, you could fill the gap with the **Speed** tool, but not with a setting greater than **2x**. The procedure is discussed in detail in the *Interview workflow* section of *Chapter 9, Project Workflows – Pace and Structure*.

There are many quick fixes for audio that will save you an incredible amount of time. The next section has some suggestions to quickly correct your audio.

Suggestions for correcting audio

There are a number of methods to correct audio, and in this section, we will look at some of them.

Settings for the audio meters

Always set the audio meters to their maximum display size to the right of the **Effects/Transitions** browsers (*Figure 6.30*). This is done by clicking on the default meters below the viewer, as in *Figure 6.29*:

Figure 6.29 – Default location of the small audio meters

Click on the small meters and they will move to the right of the **Effects/Transitions** browsers:

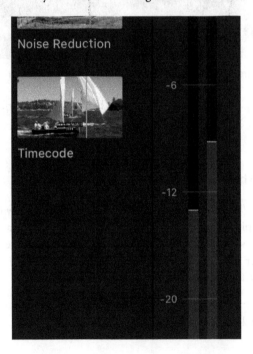

Figure 6.30 – Best location for the larger audio meters

The following are some other suggestions to consider:

- Keep the mix of dialogue audio between -8 and -15
- Keep the maximum peaks at -6
- Set the music to somewhere between -12 and -20
- Make sure any background music behind dialogue is set between -20 and -30
- Keep sound effects between -10 and -20; they can spike to -6

One of the most frequent audio issues that will need correcting is when the audio volume has been recorded too low. The next section discusses some fixes.

Simple methods to increase low volume

Earlier in the chapter, we showed that the maximum audio level in the timeline is +12. There are a number of simple ways to raise this higher than +12:

- In the inspector, check **Loudness**.
- Duplicate the **Timeline** clip by holding the *Option* key and dragging down below the clip to create a copy. You can do that any number of times.
- Use the **Gain** filter, which is found in the **Effects** browser under the **Levels** panel.

The obvious consideration is that when you increase the volume of what you want to hear, you also boost the volume of the microphone's internal noise along with any background noise.

Loop playback

Loop playback is really useful to play back a section of audio over and over while you change the setting of an effect in the inspector. It is much easier to appreciate a change in the audio when you are hearing the same sound over and over. Here's how to do it:

1. Go to **View** | **Playback** | **Loop Playback** or press *Command + L*.
2. With the **Range** tool, select a section of a clip to play back as a loop.
3. Position the playhead over the section to be looped, then press the slash (/) key, which is the shortcut key to **Play Selection**.

Now, as you make effect adjustments in the inspector, you will hear the changes live as the loop plays continuously.

Another common audio issue to correct is room noise, as discussed in the next section.

Removing room noise

Earlier in the chapter, we looked at the general **Noise Removal** filter. Room noise has a particular range of frequencies that often overlap with voice frequencies, so it is helpful to have a filter that takes into account when someone is speaking, rather than removing all the frequencies during dialogue as well.

The filter to use is called **Noise Gate**, found under the **Levels** category in the **Effects** sidebar. Drag it onto the clip and open the panel from the inspector, adjusting the settings to those shown in *Figure 6.31*:

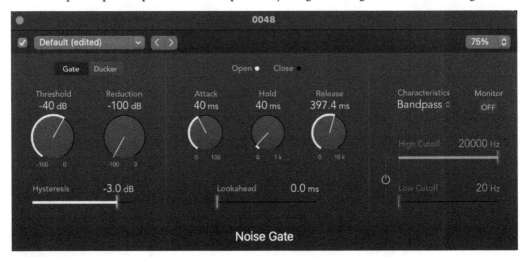

Figure 6.31 – The Noise Gate panel

Removing high and low frequencies

Since the human voice doesn't feature really high and low frequencies, these frequencies can be removed from the audio. This will cut out unwanted sounds that are not dialogue. You can use the following method when editing dialogue-based videos:

1. To remove high and low frequencies, add the **Channel EQ** filter to the clip, and in the inspector, click the calculator-like icon at the right of the screen.

Figure 6.32 – The icon opens the adjustment meters and panels

2. The **Channel EQ** window will open up, showing a horizontal line extending across a range of frequencies. Click on the left side of this line and drag the low frequencies to about **100**, as shown in *Figure 6.33*. Next, drag the high frequencies on the right to **5k**. You could also reduce the sharp peak that can occur at about **1k** by dragging down on the center line. This will remove possible essing sounds that can occur in vocal recordings. If you have a problem with ess (*S*) sounds, they can also be removed with the **DeEsser** filter.

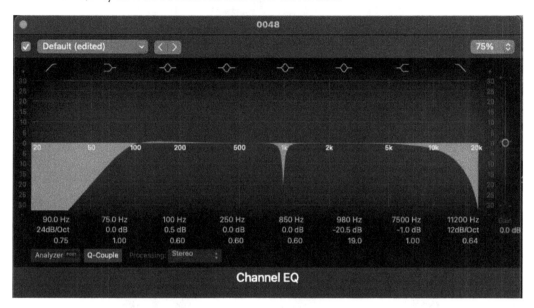

Figure 6.33 – Using Channel EQ to remove high and low frequencies

Sweetening male and female voices

The objective here is to enhance the male voice separately from the female voice.

I've used **Channel EQ** for this. Use the settings shown in *Figure 6.34* and *Figure 6.35*. Drag **Channel EQ** onto the clip in the timeline as usual and click the *meter* icon to open the **Channel EQ** meters.

Select the preset in **Channel EQ** in the inspector. Select **05 Voice** and you can choose between three versions for male and two versions for female, as shown in *Figure 6.34*:

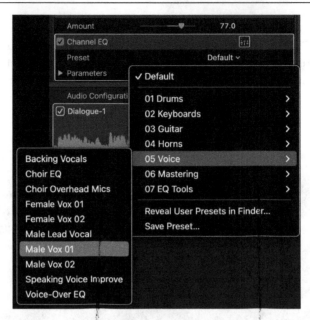

Figure 6.34 – Male Vox 01 selected in the inspector

You are able to make your own modifications to the preset in the panel that opens, as shown in *Figure 6.35*:

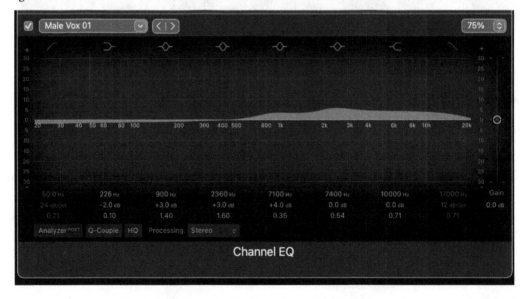

Figure 6.35 –The default settings for the Male Vox 01 preset

Reducing the music

Just as we were able to improve the human voice frequencies in the previous section, it is also possible to reduce levels in a music track to let the voice stand out, while the music will be strong at frequencies not used by the voice. The process with **Channel EQ** is the same as before. The new settings for use with the music track are shown in the following figure:

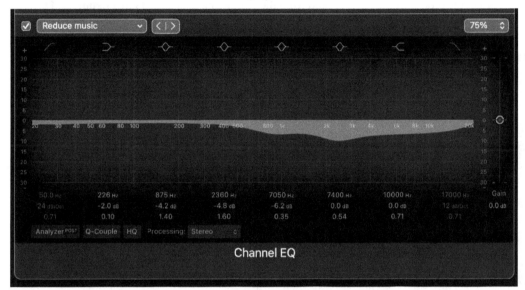

Figure 6.36 – Reduce music behind voices

This chapter has concentrated on how to work with and correct audio as a solo editor and become capable of taking on all the editing roles. However, there are going to be times when it will be more practical to refer to a more specialized professional. The following section shows ways to send the audio to experts.

Using XML files

XML files are industry-standard text files that contain all of the information about your edit and are exchanged between Final Cut Pro and third-party applications, such as Logic Pro. Follow these steps to export an XML file from your project:

1. Select the project in the browser, and from the **File** menu, navigate to **File | Export XML**.

2. Save the XML file to your preferred location on your computer.

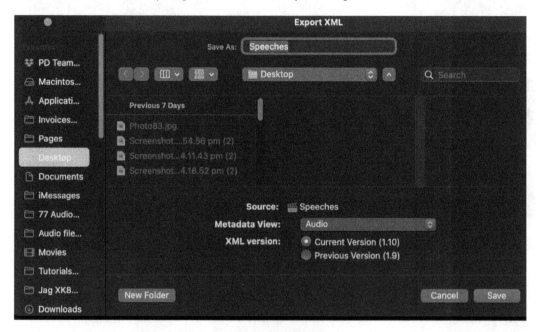

Figure 6.37 – Export XML

3. When the pop-up menu appears, select **Audio** in **Metadata View**, then select **Current Version**, unless advised differently. (Note that you may be asked to select another option by the audio professional you are sending the XML to.)

4. If you are sending the XML file to Logic Pro, choose **File | Import | Final Cut Pro XML**, then choose the file in the **Import** dialog. When you import Final Cut Pro sequences into Logic Pro, volume and stereo pan automation are retained.

When sending audio as an XML file, you can also export audio only by using the **Roles** feature.

Exporting with audio-only roles

Roles are located in the **Index** panel for the timeline and are a convenient method of sending a full Final Cut Pro file to be used in third-party applications that don't support XML. Make sure that you have assigned the audio to separate audio roles. Here's how to do it:

1. Select the **Share** menu, and then select **Export** or **Export Master File**.

    You will be presented with three tabs across the top: **Info**, **Settings**, and **Roles**.

2. Select the middle **Settings** tab and set **Format** to **Audio Only**.

3. Select the **Roles** tab on the right. It will default to **QuickTime Movie**. Set **Roles as** to **Audio Only as Separate Files**.

Figure 6.38 – Exporting audio-only roles

By following the preceding steps, individual `.wav` files can be produced and then imported into any audio editor. *Chapter 17, Supporting Software Applications for Final Cut Pro*, details how to do audio corrections in Audacity.

If you only have one track of audio to export, follow the preceding steps up to *step 3* and you can then select any of the audio formats and export directly:

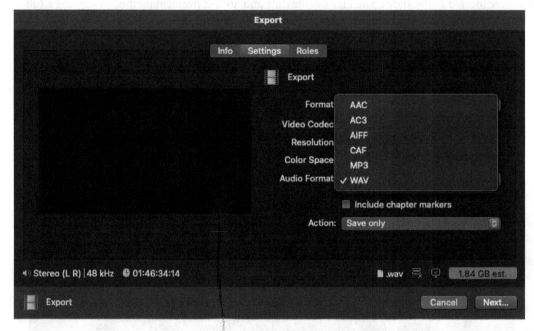

Figure 6.39 – Exporting single-track audio only

So far in this chapter, you have been shown audio fixes for specific problems. This last section has a list of general tips and tricks for quickly modifying and fixing audio issues.

Audio tips and tricks

The following are some tips and tricks to modify and fix audio issues:

- A shortcut for controlling volume levels in the timeline is *Control* + + and *Control* + - to raise and lower the volume level by 1 dB, respectively.
- Hold the *Command* key to manually raise and lower the volume levels one dB at a time when dragging the horizontal volume line in a timeline clip.

- To silence audio in a clip, go to **Modify | Adjust Volume | Silence (-∞)**:

Adjust Volume	>	Up (+1 dB)	^ =
Adjust Audio Fades	>	Down (-1 dB)	^ -
		Silence (-∞)	⌘ S
Add Keyframe to Selected Effect in Animation Editor	⌥ K	Reset (0dB)	⌥ 0
Change Duration...	^ D		

Figure 6.40 – Silencing a clip

- To reset the volume level to zero, go to **Modify | Adjust Volume | Reset (0dB)**:

Adjust Volume	>	Up (+1 dB)	^ =
Adjust Audio Fades	>	Down (-1 dB)	^ -
		Silence (-∞)	⌘ S
Add Keyframe to Selected Effect in Animation Editor	⌥ K	Reset (0dB)	⌥ 0
Change Duration...	^ D		

Figure 6.41 – Resetting volume to zero

- To adjust the auto-fades between multiple clips with audio, select the multiple clips and go to **Modify | Adjust Audio Fades | Crossfade** (shortcut *Option + T*):

Adjust Audio Fades	>	Crossfade	⌥ T
		Apply Fades	F1
Add Keyframe to Selected Effect in Animation Editor	⌥ K	Remove Fades	⇧ 5
Change Duration...	^ D		

Figure 6.42 – Crossfade multiple clips with audio

- The absolute volume level allows you to set the volume to a specified level using the *Control + Option + L* shortcut. This is useful if you want to remove any keyframes or fades previously set. The desired level is entered when the + sign is shown in blue under the viewer. The same applies to the relative volume level.

Figure 6.43 – The location of the + sign to enter the new audio level

- Relative volume level is the most useful of the volume adjustments as it allows you to change the level of all the selected clips relative to each other. You can increase and reduce the volume by 1 dB at a time. So, by increasing by 1 dB, a clip set at 0 dB will become +1, a clip at -4 will become -3, and so on.

Summary

In this chapter, you learned about many advanced features of audio editing in Final Cut Pro, and in future chapters, these skills will be expanded and used with workflows, particularly in *Chapter 9, Project Workflows – Pace and Structure*. The skills learned included how to modify audio in the browser, understanding the principles of the different levels in the audio meters, and how to evaluate the dB readings for various types of audio. You also learned how to correct various audio issues, including removing background noise, fixing distorted voices and voices with variable volume levels, reducing wind noise and echoes, and removing dialogue fillers. You were given a number of suggestions to make your audio editing easier, as well as being shown some simple filter settings to simplify common correction needs. Finally, you saw how to export specific audio-only files via XML and roles.

If you take just one lesson from this chapter, it is to be aware of the distinction between the source level volume and the output levels, which are different, even though they are both measured in dB.

The next chapter will take you on a journey through the extras that you can add to your edit with titles, effects, and generators.

7
Titles, Effects, and Generators

In previous chapters, you did everything yourself; the total of your efforts has been created by your hand. In this chapter, we will look at enhancements that are built into the software so that you can add your media to them, adding flair to your edit without any extra effort. **Titles** are templates of animated routines that you just add text to; some are simple containers for basic text, while others are for short animations that you can also add to your video. **Generators** are also animations but are usually far more complex than titles. Think of them as little videos that you add to your video. They tell a short story – for instance, as an opening for your video with animations, somewhat like a Hollywood movie intro. There is another element we will cover in this chapter, known as **effects**, which change the look of your video. You were briefly introduced to audio effects in the previous chapter. With effects, there are also **transitions**, which smoothen the jump at the edit point between one clip to the next. Titles and generators are treated as separate clips in the **timeline**, whereas effects are added to the whole clip to make adjustments – for example, color corrections. **Transitions** are added between clips in the timeline to smoothen the cut between the clips. The distinction is conveyed in the Final Cut Pro interface by keeping the two groups in separate locations. Titles and generators are above the media browser and effects and transitions are in their own browser to the right of the timeline.

All the elements that this chapter teaches are known as **Plug-ins**. All Plug-ins can be adjusted in the **Inspector** window and will be discussed in detail in *Chapter 10*.

In this chapter, you will learn about the plug-in environment in Final Cut Pro. You will learn that there are default Plug-ins, and about those that you can buy to add to the different Final Cut Pro environments. You will be shown how to add text to the built-in titles and how to use the **drop zone** feature, which allows you to add your media to a title. You will learn how to create compound clips from standard titles that have had multiple effects added. You will also understand how video effects added to timeline clips can drastically change the look of clips. You will learn the conventions for the two different uses of transitions and how to limit overusing them. Finally, you will learn that older Plug-ins can cause problems as newer versions of Final Cut Pro are released.

In this chapter, we're going to cover the following main topics:

- What are titles?
- Text
- Generators
- Effects
- Transitions
- Plug-ins

By the end of this chapter, you will have a good understanding of Plug-ins in Final Cut Pro.

What are titles?

When I talk to new students, they know very little about titles in Final Cut Pro. I think this is because self-taught users of Final Cut Pro have just taken titles for granted and have not considered the full implications of what they can do and how to get the best use of them in Final Cut Pro. On that basis, I believe it is beneficial to go back to basics and discuss the intricacies of titles, even though this book is aimed at current users of Final Cut Pro beyond the beginner stage.

You can find the **Titles and Generators** button above the media browser; this is because titles and generators are treated by Final Cut Pro as clips when they are added to a project in the timeline. The **Title** button is third from the left at the top of the browser:

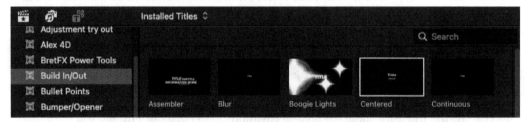

Figure 7.1– The Title button at the top left and the Centered title highlighted

Think of a Final Cut Pro title as a container into which you can add your text. A simple title, such as the **Centered** title, which can be found in the **Build In/Out** subheading in the title browser, simply adds a clip to the timeline for you to enter your text centrally. There is minimal animation, which can be disabled by unchecking **Build In** and **Build Out** in the inspector:

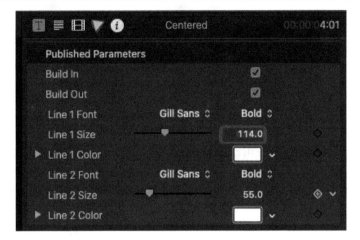

Figure 7.2 – The Centered title in the inspector

You can preview the animation by hovering your cursor over the **Title** thumbnail in the browser; as you drag the mouse, the animation will appear in the viewer. When you activate a title, it will include a default font, already selected. The *Animated titles* section will discuss the way that text is handled. The **Centered** title is about as basic as they come. All titles will have varying amounts of animation or options built in. You can use them or turn them off. Final Cut Pro titles are animated containers for text; they were created in Apple's Motion app. The next section discusses how to work with text in the title container.

Animated titles

Titles with large amounts of animation are generally known as openers and help you quickly create an introduction, giving your video a more professional feel than just a simple introduction title. These openers can range from very complex to just a second or so in length; usually, they will have drop zones for you to add your own media.

Drop zones

Drop zones can appear in titles, generators, and even effects. They appear intimidating but are just what they say they are – a place to drop your media. However, some versions of drop zones have different ways to add your media and move it within the zone. Some developers of drop zones are better at producing them than others.

There are rules about drop zones that will make them easier for you to use. The **Drop Zones** feature is shown in the inspector in the following figure:

Figure 7.3 – The Drop Zones feature has a downward-pointing arrow

You click in the drop zone to activate it; at this point, you need to be able to see the media that you want to put in the drop zone. If you open another part of Final Cut Pro to see the media, then the drop zone will deactivate. The simple thing to remember is that before you click in the drop zone in the inspector, make sure that the media is on show first. You can use clips from the media browser as well as the timeline.

The drop zone can accept still images as well as video. However, when using video, you need to be aware that its duration needs to be longer than that of the animation the drop zone represents. In other words, if the drop zone animation runs for 5 seconds, you need at least 5 seconds of video to play in the drop zone. If the video is not long enough, when the title animation is played, the video will freeze before the animation is finished.

Even if your video is longer than the duration of the animation, it's important to make sure you click on the video at a point that still allows enough time for it to play. The position that you click on is when the video starts playing in the drop zone. Some titles will have checkboxes for you to disable the drop zone:

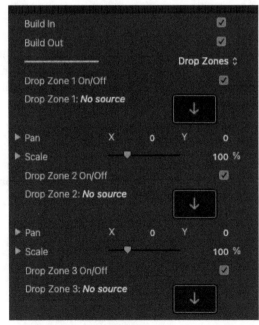

Figure 7.4 – A title in the inspector with checkboxes to disable drop zones

Some developers of animations with drop zones don't provide the ability to move an image within the window designated for the still or video. However, generally, there will be a way of moving the *X* (horizontal) and *Y* (vertical) angles in the inspector with sliders.

If you are not able to move an image added to the drop zone, you may be able to adjust its position by adjusting the *X* (horizontal) and *Y* (vertical) angles in the inspector (see *Chapter 10, The Inspector Controls*):

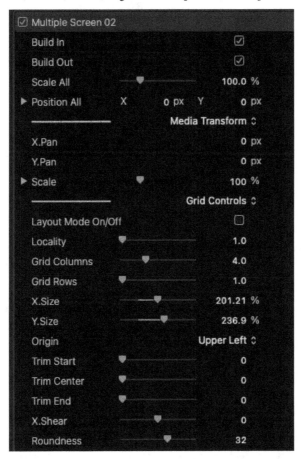

Figure 7.5 – An effect in the inspector with the X and Y sliders positioned

Some other titles offer the ability to both position by using the controls in the inspector and drag the image into the viewer. It is just a different way of doing the same thing. I suggest that the only way that you will become comfortable with drop zones in animations is to spend some time with each animated effect after you purchase it. I find that this defeats some of the purpose of an effect in the first place, which you purchased to quickly add something extra to the edit without having to spend the time building it yourself.

Of course, there is more to animated titles than just adding drop zones. They have animations that make it look as if you have spent a serious amount of time enhancing the video. Usually, there will be a fixed number of text fields in title animations. For fields that you don't need, just delete the text. If you want more text fields, don't be afraid to add some of the simple animated titles that ship with Final Cut Pro.

You can do this by adding a simple title as a connected clip above the animated title. This works because simple titles have a transparent background, which allows the main title in the track beneath to show through. If you want to use these combined titles as a theme for other videos, you can create a compound clip of the multiple effects. See *Chapter 8, Setting Up and Editing Multicam*, which discusses compound clips as a partial substitute for multicam clips.

Adding text to a title

The first consideration that you need to be clear on is that font and text are different terms; they are not interchangeable. Text includes all the characteristics, such as the size, the color, and the font. The font, which is just a typeface, is only one component of text.

There are clear conventions about the use of text in video, and this is because text in a video is different from printed text, even though we tend to treat them the same. Video is low-resolution compared to text printed on a page. This means that text in video, even 4K video, is pixelated. Also, text on a printed page is there for you to read for as long as you need to decipher it. You can decide how long you need to look at the printed page for your brain to understand the words.

Video is not only lower-resolution and slightly pixelated but also plays for a fixed time, which you have no control over unless you skip back to read it again or pause the screen. This means you have to decipher the text before it goes away, unlike printed text, which is there for as long as you need.

If your audience does not get to read the text, the message is lost, so presenting it correctly is key. The following list will assist you in how to present text in a title:

- Text in a video needs to stay on screen for as long as necessary, but not too long to be boring. It should be on screen long enough for you, the editor, to read it aloud twice.
- Make sure the text is legible, large enough, not italic, not script, horizontal not vertical, and not at an angle.
- Font sizes for HD video can be smaller than SD video, and 4K can be smaller again.
- Sans serif fonts are clearer to read than serif fonts.
- Make sure the text has a color that contrasts with the background.
- Light text should be on a dark background, and dark text should be on a light background.
- Avoid textured or patterned backgrounds.

- Avoid fancy fonts for important messages.

- Use an outline around text that is a warning message.

- Use the **Broadcast Safe** effect for broadcast and streaming.

- Use **Title Safe Zone** lines for broadcasts.

You enter the text in the inspector when the **T** tab at the top is blue (see *Figure 7.2*). Most titles will also allow you to adjust text with the **Text** tab highlighted – that is, when the text is outlined in white in the viewer.

Figure 7.6 – Text outlined in the viewer can be adjusted with the Text tab in the inspector

The **Text** tab is the icon with the horizontal lines on the left (shown in blue):

Figure 7.7 – The Text icon

When the **Text** tab is selected, it allows you the full gambit of text adjustments, including 3D text. These options will be discussed in *Chapter 10, The Inspector Controls*. In the next section, we will look at generators, which share many features that we discussed in the *What are titles?* section, including drop zones.

What are generators?

Generators are similar in some ways to titles in that they are computer-generated animations, created in Apple's Motion app. They are little videos within your video and are unique to Final Cut Pro. They provide animated sequences where you can modify and add your own media, in a similar way to titles. Think of generators as titles on steroids. You will also find drop zones available in the **Generator** inspector window.

The default generators include backgrounds, elements, solids, and textures.

Backgrounds

Backgrounds are full-screen, generated media that will fit any frame size, rate, or duration. They include the **Organic**, **Collage**, **Drifting**, **Clouds**, and **Underwater** types.

Drag the generator to the timeline and, in the inspector, select the **Generator** tab, where the **Title** tab was previously located:

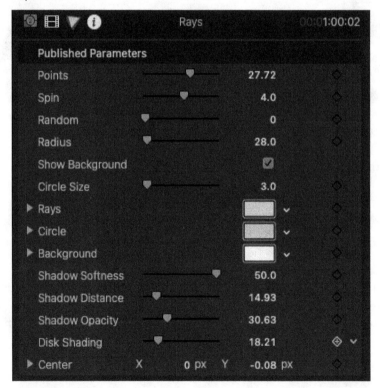

Figure 7.8 – The Rays background in the inspector with the Generator tab selected

The next category after backgrounds is elements.

Elements

Elements turn Final Cut Pro into a simple form of graphics editor.

Counting

One of the most useful generators is **Counting**, providing the **Number**, **Currency**, **Percent**, **Scientific**, **Spell Out**, **Binary**, and **Hexadecimal** options for counting up or down; these can be changed in the inspector. It's useful to show clients the length of a particular scene's duration:

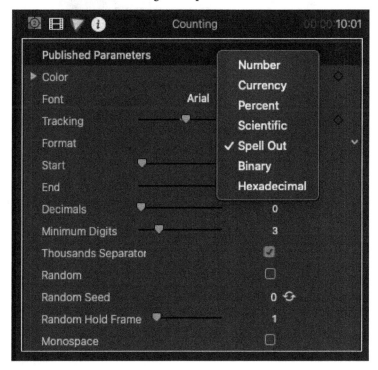

Figure 7.9 – The Counting background in the Inspector window with the Generator tab selected

Placeholders

Placeholders are perfect when you are preparing a rough edit, with a place in the timeline reserved for clips that you are still waiting to receive. Rough cuts were covered in *Chapter 4, Pre-Editing a Rough Cut*.

Shapes

The use of shapes gives you some basic graphic editing ability, where you can create 12 different forms. You can change the size, color, border, and drop shadow of a shape:

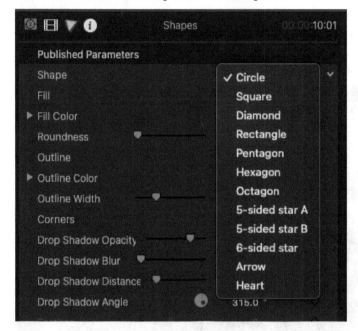

Figure 7.10 – Different forms of shapes

Timecode is the final section that I will discuss from the elements category.

Timecode

When you are sending a draft to a client, always make sure you add a timecode so that they can reference the exact point where they would like to make changes. This timecode shows from where the timecode generator is inserted in the timeline. You can change the title and position it anywhere on the screen:

Figure 7.11 – The timecode in the viewer

Solids and textures

Use solids to add a color below a clip that has an alpha channel (transparent background), most likely a title. The bright white background is used beneath still images or logos where there is no alpha background. They are smaller than a full screen, so the bright white fills in where black would normally be on both sides of the logo. Textures are similar to patterns, except they are a solid color. There are 12 texture themes with different options:

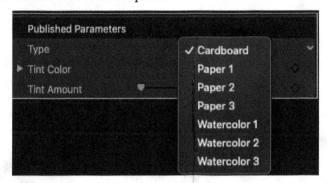

Figure 7.12 – Different choices in the Paper theme

While generators are little videos that play in your video, effects are add-ons that modify the way your video looks, while some effects have features that completely change the video, such as the **Keyer** effect, which allows you to work with a green screen. We'll discover them in the next section.

What are effects?

The **Effects and Transitions** browser is on the right of the timeline and can be activated with the two buttons on the far right of the center menu bar. The browser can show all the installed effects/ transitions or just those in selected projects:

Figure 7.13 – Effects for just one project or all installed effects

When effects are chosen in the browser, they contain both video and audio effects. The different titles for effects can be searched for at the bottom of the browser, by selecting **All** in the sidebar:

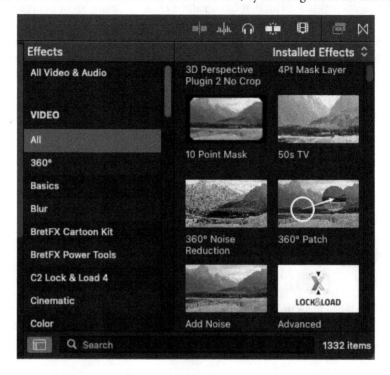

Figure 7.14 – The Search field at the bottom of the browser

As you hover your mouse across an effect in the browser, you will see a preview, within the effect thumbnail, of how it will look in the currently selected clip in the timeline. The effect is then dragged inside the clip in the timeline. Effects can also be added by selecting the timeline clip first and then double-clicking the effect in the browser.

Adjustments are made in the inspector, where you can reveal the effect settings for **Show/Hide**. You can turn the effect on/off with the checkbox. When you expose the chevron, you can modify a parameter and add keyframes. The effect can be deleted by ensuring that the yellow outline is shown and then pressing the *Delete* key:

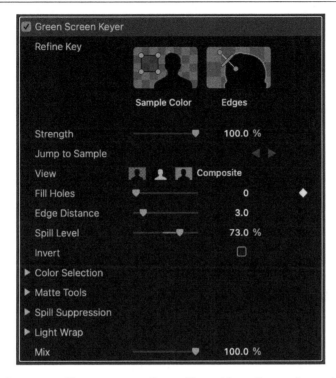

Figure 7.15 – The green screen Keyer effect, with a yellow outline and a
keyframe added at Fill Holes (the diamond-shaped button)

Effects are mostly concerned with ways to change color; however, some can make physical changes to clips in the timeline.

Effects categories

Effects can be categorized into two main groups, with the majority being linked to color and its various choices. The default subheadings include **Comic Looks**, **Color Presets**, and **Looks**.

Other effects are similar in concept to generators in that they include actions. These include **Keyer** to create a green screen, **Sharpen**, and **Masks**.

Effects are one of the components of a plug-in; they are employed within a clip in the timeline.

The next section looks at transitions, which are used at edit points only.

What are transitions?

By convention, the use of transitions should be kept to a minimum. The saying goes, "Just because you **can** doesn't mean you **should**." When you are new to video editing, it is very tempting to think that you are adding the wow factor by inserting transitions at every edit point. Not a good idea. The concept comes from the feeling that every edit point has a visual jump to the next clip. This comes from being too close to the edit.

If you are relatively new to editing, my suggestion is, after at least a few hours, to sit back and view the exported movie on another screen. Don't look out for the edits; try to view the movie as a complete story. If the straight cuts are jarring, then you need to do something to smoothen the edit points. That may or may not involve the use of transitions.

As you become more proficient at editing, you will realize that you don't need a transition effect to move from one scene to the next. There are a couple of things that professionals do.

First, at the filming stage, the camera operator will film scenes that flow to the next scene. Of course, that doesn't always happen, and as an editor, you will be given a clip with a scene that suddenly ends, with nothing useful to relate it to the next clip. Your choice is to find a point somewhere in the clip that will glide to the next scene, without losing the flow of the story.

If you can't find a flow from one scene to another, then consider a transition. It can be either a dissolve, a fade-to-black, or some effect to hide the jump cut. In a drama, it is very common to use some fast-moving cityscape as a cutaway transition. Another common practice involves integrating an entirely unrelated scene that becomes a thematic element for the video. That fast-moving effect signifies the passing of time. If you don't have the necessary footage, a longer duration of fade-to-black has a similar feel.

For interviews or dialogue scenes, where there is a change in subject, use a shorter fade-to-black (not too short, as that will be jarring in itself). Audiences can be so conditioned to seeing a fade-to-black that their eyes see the fade, but their brain doesn't register a cut.

Two categories of transition

There are two categories of transition – those that hide the cut, such as the ones discussed previously, or transitions that emphasize the cut as a change in the direction of the story in the video or a new beginning.

If this latter type of transition is required, then try out all those fancy swirls or wipes that are provided as part of the plug-in packs that you have purchased. If you only have Final Cut Pro's default transitions, explore the **Movements**, **Objects**, and **Wipes** sub-headings in the sidebar of the **Transitions** browser:

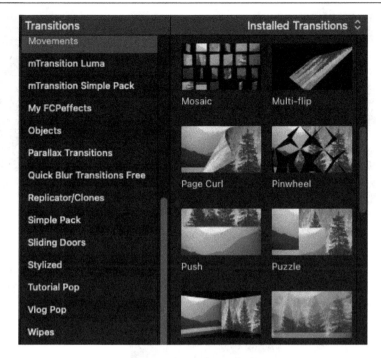

Figure 7.16 – The Transitions window showing the Movements category

All of the preceding categories of effects are known as Plug-ins, and all were written in Apple's Motion 5. The next section is about how you can acquire extra Plug-ins.

What are Plug-ins?

Plug-ins will be discussed in detail in *Chapter 11 and 12*. Many developers make Plug-ins for Final Cut Pro, along with other **Non-Linear Editors** (**NLEs**). Suppliers number in the hundreds; some are big organizations and others are sole operators. They all tend to offer some free Plug-ins, of limited value, to encourage purchasers to visit their websites.

All Final Cut Pro Plug-ins are developed using Apple's Motion 5 app. If you are a professional Final Cut Pro editor, I encourage you to purchase Motion 5. An introduction to Motion 5 will be provided in *Chapter 17, Supporting Software Applications for Final Cut Pro*.

Problems with Plug-ins

If there is one area that you should look at first for potential problems within Final Cut Pro, it is the status of Plug-ins. When Final Cut Pro is updated, it is common for Plug-ins to be rendered out of date. If you have recently installed an update and you have issues with Final Cut Pro, check the Plug-ins. Usually, after a major update, you will be given formal warnings when you open Final Cut Pro:

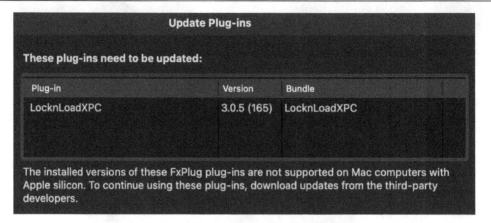

Figure 7.17 – A plug-in out-of-date warning

You can find the Plug-ins by right-clicking on the title, generator, effect, or transition and selecting **Reveal in Finder**. The default Plug-ins supplied with Final Cut Pro are not available for you to access as they are updated each time Final Cut Pro is updated:

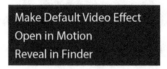

Figure 7.18: – Right-click a plug-in to select Reveal in Finder

The **Plug-ins** folder in the **Finder** area was discussed in *Chapter 1*, *It's All About the Media*.

Summary

In this chapter, you saw how the four different types of Plug-ins – titles, generators, effects, and transitions – can add extra information to your edit. You saw how these effects can save you a serious amount of time in having to build the animations or presets yourself. You saw how to make compound clips from standard titles that have had multiple effects added. Then, you learned that default Plug-ins are supplied as part of Final Cut Pro and that there are also Plug-ins available for purchase, or sometimes for free. You also saw how to add text to the built-in titles and how to use the drop zone feature, which allows you to add your media to the title. Additionally, you learned about the conventions for the two different uses of transitions and how to limit overusing them. Finally, you learned that older Plug-ins can cause problems as new versions of Final Cut Pro are released.

The next chapterwill show you how to combine a multicamera shoot, enabling you to switch between up to 16 camera angles from one timeline project. Multicam editing is also very useful with a single camera and an external audio recording.

8

Setting Up and Editing Multicam

This chapter will tell you everything that you need to know about multicam editing in Final Cut Pro.

You will learn about the specifics of editing multicam footage in a Final Cut Pro project, step by step, from importing the footage from your computer and categorizing the clips in your browser to combining the footage into a single timeline clip so that the different camera angles can be edited into a complete multicam project.

You will understand that there are two ways of viewing the multicam in separate timeline windows: the multicam angle timeline and the multicam project.

You will learn that a multicam edit has set procedures to ensure that synchronization is accurate. You will also learn when to make global modifications compared to modifying clips in the multicam project.

Next, you will learn about switching angles as well as adjusting those cuts for both video and audio.

Finally, you will learn how to simulate a multicam shoot with footage from just one camera.

The chapter will cover the following main topics:

- What is multicam?
- Suggestions for filming to suit multicam editing
- Settings before multicam editing
- Actions in the multicam angle timeline
- Editing the multicam project

By the end of this chapter, you will have learned how to edit footage from multiple cameras into a project in Final Cut Pro.

You will also know that multicam editing requires you to understand the settings and how to follow the correct procedures. The edit will fail if you do not understand the settings.

You will have also learned that multicam editing in itself is easy, but you need to understand the controls and that there are no shortcuts until you have the concepts clear in your mind. The process is not intuitive at first; you need to follow the instructions and fully absorb the reasons for the settings. If you are attentive in this chapter, you will become a multicam expert.

Finally, you will have learned how to simulate a multicam shoot from a single camera's footage.

What is multicam?

A multicam shoot uses multiple cameras to record the same subject or event from different angles and distances with the same audio source. A multicam project has those different camera angles as well as separate audio clips all combined and presented in the timeline as a single clip that can be cut from one camera angle to another on the fly or by selecting individual angles to switch the different cameras. Audio can either be fixed from one source or different sources and can be selected in the same manner as the video.

Final Cut Pro can edit up to 128 camera angles together in one multicam project.

You need to be aware that there are two multicam timeline windows. The multicam angle timeline (*Figure 8.1*) shows all the tracks of the multicam, video, and separate audio if it's included. The multicam angle timeline is not magnetic.

On the other hand, the multicam project is more like a normal timeline and is magnetic. It only shows the currently active video angle and the currently active audio angle, both of which can be switched to show other angles. The switch can be made with a keyboard shortcut or a mouse click.

Think of a combined clip, which holds all the camera angles as a cylinder, where every camera angle can be spun to be visible as they are required in the edit. When you are viewing the multicam project, you should have **Show Angles** ticked, selected from the **View** menu.

The reason the combined multicam project is switched to view the different camera angles is to avoid monotonously viewing the same angle for the whole project to give life and energy to the video. The audio track is usually fixed on the highest quality track but can also be switched should the main audio be compromised at any point.

What events use multiple cameras?

Many different events are suitable for multiple-camera shoots. Let's take a look at some examples.

Feature movies

Feature movies are shot with multiple cameras for most scenes. When there are different angles available to an editor, cuts can be made to enhance the pace and creativity of the edit. The use of several cameras is a safety strategy to ensure that reshooting is not required. When several cameras are used in the same scene, it ensures that tricky maneuvers such as those involving a stunt person are captured should the main camera miss the shot.

Wedding videos

Wedding videos benefit from multiple cameras for the ceremony and the speeches at the reception. Multiple cameras used for wedding videos allow for simultaneous angles of the bride's preparations, as well as ensuring that all guests appear in edits of the ceremony. Weddings are unlike feature movies in that a scene can't be reshot. What is captured on the day is finite, so covering as many angles as possible will ensure that the important actions, such as the kiss and the vows, are captured.

Interviews

Interviews are much more interesting to view if multiple angles avoid the monotonous "talking head."

The beauty of an interview situation is that the same person can be interviewed with several cameras filming at the same time so that the scenes showing any one angle are kept short, and interest is maintained by switching to a different view as the interview progresses.

The other advantage comes when editing because sections can be cut out of the interview to avoid repetitive comments or where the person being interviewed has stopped to think about an answer. If it were just one camera filming that interview, there would be jump cuts every time something was cut out. With multicam, the cuts from one angle to another are smooth and go unnoticed as in any normal scene change.

Concerts and stadium sporting events

Depending on the size of the event, the use of multiple cameras will explode for national and international events. Smaller local concerts and even stage shows will not need as many cameras. The reasons for using multiple cameras are similar to all other categories in that the different angles can be used in the edit to ensure that the pace and creativity of the video are fresh. Multiple close-up and steady-cam cameras are important for grasping the action as well as spotting facial expressions.

Conferences and seminars

Conferences and seminars benefit from multiple angles to show close-ups of speakers and wide views of the audience. Conferences and seminars tend to be long events, so it is important to be able to choose from different angles in the edit to prevent the viewer from becoming bored of seeing the same angle for long periods. Unlike the movie and wedding categories, filming local conferences and seminars will likely only need two or, at most, three cameras filming in sync due to the extended duration of the events. Large international events will have more cameras as the events become more like concerts.

How multiple cameras are synchronized

At the filming stage, all of the cameras can make use of synchronized timecode. This is called **jam syncing** and it writes the same timecode to each camera. Jam syncing is mostly the choice of synchronization that's used on major movies or any bigger shoot where cameras can match timecode. Otherwise, for smaller shoots or where cameras don't have timecode functionality, the different cameras can all be rolling, and a clapperboard can be used in a position that all cameras can see and hear. The camera footage can then be synced with the multicam feature in Final Cut Pro as the editor can both see and hear the single frame of video. Someone clapping in view of all the cameras has the same effect.

However, with Final Cut Pro's multicam, none of these are necessary, provided all cameras record the same audio. However, it's always good to have a clapperboard or hand clap in case something goes wrong with a camera's audio. There is no harm in having something to fall back on in case of emergencies, especially if you are editing multiple cameras that have been turned on and off for short periods during the event.

The multicam feature in Final Cut Pro will match the audio for each of the cameras and external audio recorders if they are in the mix. Each camera's footage is shown as a separate track in the multicam angle timeline so that the editor can visualize and play the video and audio together to ascertain whether they are all in sync. You need to physically listen to the audio to accurately check the synchronization:

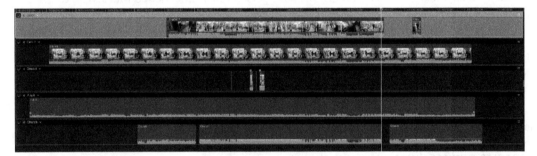

Figure 8.1 – Three cameras and two audio tracks in the multicam window

The multicam project looks similar to any normal project in a magnetic timeline. The one visible difference is the white icon with four small squares at the top left of each multicam project (see *Figure 8.2*). You can open the multicam angle timeline by double-clicking the multicam project:

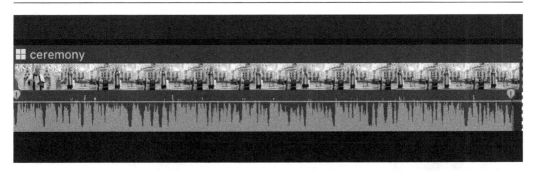

Figure 8.2 – Multicam project with a four-small-squares icon at the top left

Multiple audio sources can be displayed in the multicam project by selecting **Expand Audio Components** upon right-clicking on the timeline clip:

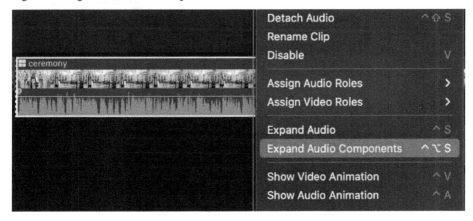

Figure 8.3 – Expand Audio Components

Figure 8.4 shows the expanded audio tracks:

Figure 8.4 – Expanded audio tracks

The multicam shoot can have many uses for different types of video styles; however, how these shoots are handled will make a big difference as to how easily you will be able to edit the multiple tracks, as you will see in the next section.

Suggestions for filming to suit multicam editing

If you are filming or can make suggestions to the shooters, the ideas described in this section will make the multicam editing process much easier for you. Multicam synchronization relies mostly on audio for non-feature-film shoots. The previous section on how cameras are synchronized discussed the timecode being used in bigger shoots. When filming with several cameras, some basic ground rules will help Final Cut Pro to be able to sync the different camera footage together. Let's see what they are.

Audio

The obvious first item to be aware of is that the same audio should be recorded on all cameras in the shoot. If you have a camera that does not record audio, make sure that a clapperboard or the like is visible on all cameras, or at least two where one has audio.

The two-minute rule

Next is to record for at least two minutes before stopping the camera. In events, it is a good rule to turn all main cameras on together and let them run for the whole session. Any **spot** cameras that are just recording specific parts of the event should follow the two-minute rule and make sure they are close to the common audio unless they are just intended to be used as B roll. Even though not every camera's audio is likely to be used in the multicam edit, it is important when synchronizing the spot camera's footage with the main camera footage.

Drones don't have audio and, for the most part, their footage is just for fillers or an intro to help with the location-establishing shots. The same applies to B roll shots: they don't need audio as they will be inserted at any point in the video.

Color balance

After the audio requirements, the next most important consideration is to match the color balance between the cameras. This is easy when you're filming with the same camera model but can become more of an issue when there is a mix of camcorder-type styles and DSLRs. It's the biggest issue with mobile phone footage. The rule here is to do the best you can to have a similar balance. Even just setting the white balance will help tremendously when you're trying to match a color in the multicam edit.

With that brief explanation about setting up the cameras for multicam, in the next section, we'll look at how multicam footage is imported and categorized in Final Cut Pro.

Settings before multicam editing

Multicam editing is more stressful on the computer's processor because several streams of video and audio need to be processed at the same time. Unless you have a very high-spec computer, it is best to set the necessary preferences/settings to ensure that optimized media is created for multicam editing.

Importing and categorizing media

Under the **Final Cut Pro** menu, select **Settings**, and click the **Playback** tab. Make sure that **Create optimized media for multicam clips** is ticked.

To describe the process of importing and categorizing the footage to be used in the multicam, I will use the footage from a wedding that I filmed. I'll use footage from the ceremony portion of their wedding day.

> **A note of thanks**
>
> Thanks to Elizabeth and Mark for their kind approval to use footage from their stylish wedding video.

A useful method of categorizing wedding footage for easy editing will be discussed in *Chapter 9*. The workflow shows suggestions for the wedding folder structure that can be set up in the **Finder** before importing the footage into Final Cut Pro. *Figure 8.5* shows how the created folders automatically appear as keyword collections in the browser sidebar after being imported:

Figure 8.5 – Keyword collections as imported from Finder folders

The objective with multicam is to assemble all of the footage from the different cameras into one keyword collection if it has not already been done in the **Finder** folders (as has been done in this case). Three cameras and two audio recorders (**Church** and **Pulpit**) are all contained in the **Ceremony** keyword collection:

Figure 8.6 – All cameras and audio in one keyword collection

The different camera clips can be recognized by the different titles that the camera automatically labels them by. In *Figure 8.6*, the **Gimbal** camera clips (outlined in yellow) are labeled by date and time.

With all of the clips from one camera selected, open the **Inspector** window by clicking the **i** (information) button. Look for **Camera Name** in the list and type a name for the camera – Gimbal, in this case:

Figure 8.7 – Camera name entered

You need to process the other cameras and the audio files in the same way. Next, select all of the clips from all cameras and audio, then right-click and select **New Multicam Clip...**:

Figure 8.8 – All clips selected to add to a new multicam clip

In the next section, we will learn how to create a new multicam clip.

Creating a new multicam clip

The first window to open (*Figure 8.9*) will show the default options. Click on **Use Custom Settings** for more control:

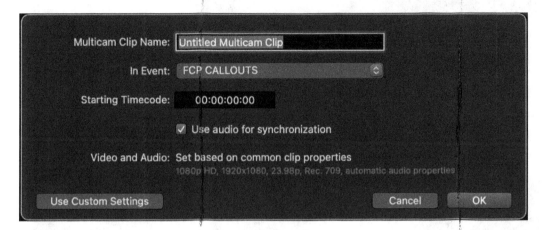

Figure 8.9 – Custom settings for more control

When the custom options window opens, make sure that **Use audio for synchronization** is ticked. Set **Angle Assembly** to **Camera Name**. Leave **Angle Clip Ordering** and **Angle Synchronization** set to **Automatic** unless the cameras have synchronized timecode. Select the **Video** format that suits your footage. Leave **Rendering** set to **Apple ProRes 422**:

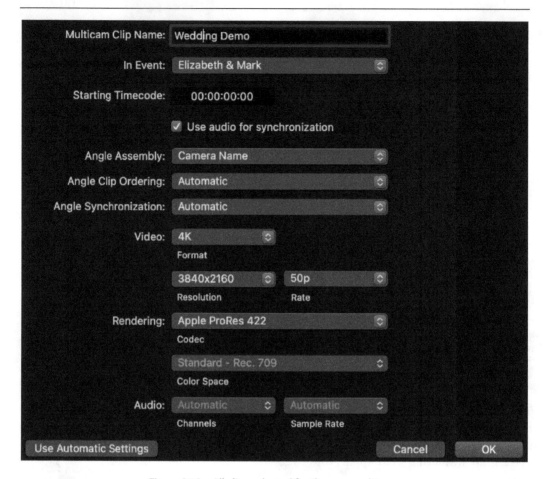

Figure 8.10 – All clips selected for the new multicam

In the majority of cases, with these settings, **audio synchronization** will work just fine. If not, there are more permutations than are in the scope of this book. There are a couple that I will mention, though.

If audio synchronization does not work for you, try **Content Created** in the **Angle Clip Ordering** and **Angle Assembly** options.

If one or more of your cameras does not have audio, you can match up the start of the first camera clip with the other clips in the multicam angle timeline (see *Figure 8.1*), as explained in the next section.

Manual multicam synchronization

Manual synchronization is best done by finding the hand clap or clapperboard clap that I mentioned in the *How multiple cameras are synchronized* section, which could come in useful in an emergency. Locate either the visual or audio on each clip and tag it with a marker at the clap (press the *M* key).

Drag each clip in the multicam angle timeline (see *Figure 8.1*) so that all the markers match up. Make sure that **Snapping** is active. Change **Angle Synchronization** to **First Marker on the Angle**. The sync may not be perfect, but it can be finessed later in the multicam angle timeline with the **Sync Angle to Monitoring Angle** command, as explained in the next section.

Multicam angle timeline adjustments

The multicam angle timeline has many adjustments that need to be explained. As mentioned in the *How multiple cameras are synchronized* section, the multicam angle timeline is not magnetic. It is track-based (the tracks are called angles) and the priority order of the angles is important when you are editing the multicam angle timeline. Ensure that the main cameras are at the top.

Independent audio angles should always be below the video angles, and the principal audio angle should be at the top of the audio group. The three-horizontal-line icons at the far right of each angle are used for reordering while ensuring that the angles stay in their current sync (see *Figure 8.11*):

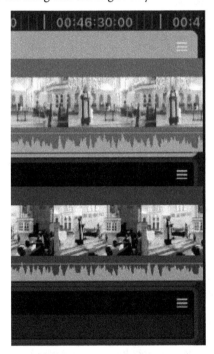

Figure 8.11 – Horizontal-line icons for reordering tracks

On the left of the timeline, any angle can be designated to be displayed in the viewer; this is termed the **monitoring angle** and shows an icon of a computer display/monitor in blue when it is activated. The monitoring angle is highlighted in a lighter gray. Only one angle can be the monitoring angle and displayed in the viewer. However, all angles can have their audio active when the speaker icon is blue. To the right of the speaker icon, the angle's name is specified (**Cam 1**, **Cam 2**, and so on):

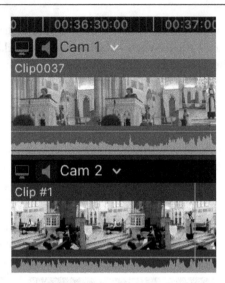

Figure 8.12 – Monitor and speaker icons

To the right of the angle's name is a chevron (drop-down arrow) that opens the following important controls:

- **Select Clips in Angle**: This control will gather all of the clips in that angle – a useful option as it means that you can zoom in for a close-up of the multicam angle timeline and still be able to select all tracks without needing to change to a wide view. This is particularly useful when you are manually syncing to the clapper, as we discussed in the *How multiple cameras are synchronized* section, where you tagged the clap with a marker.

  The **Select Clips in Angle** command ensures all clips in the track are moved in sync.

- **Sync to Monitoring Angle**: This control will move the clip to the position of the playhead in the monitoring angle. Using the clapper example, you can press *Option* and click the playhead to the clapper frame in the monitoring angle (add a marker to ensure you can return to the position again quickly). Now, select **Sync to Monitoring Angle**. The viewer will change to a two-up display. The left panel shows the position of the playhead in the monitoring angle, while the right panel shows where the skimmer is in the angle that you want to sync up.

  Hover your mouse over the frame of the clapper in the angle you want to sync up (right panel in the two-up display) and click. Once you are happy with the match, press **Done** at the bottom right of the viewer. The angle you are moving (the right panel in the two-up display) will jump to where the playhead is positioned in the monitoring angle (the left panel). If the sync is not perfect, you can use the **Sync Angle to Monitoring Angle** command.

- **Sync Angle to Monitoring Angle**: This control uses the audio synchronization method but works much more accurately when the audio to be synced is closer together on both tracks. You will use this command much more frequently than the others for fine control after the initial **Automatic** synchronization you used in *Figure 8.10*. You can use it at any time when you feel that the sync is not perfect and listen to the two tracks together (make sure both speaker icons are active and blue).

To summarize, the closer that you can manually match the audio on two angles, the easier it is for Final Cut Pro to synchronize the audio:

> **Tip**
> When you are listening to two tracks together, watch the video on the monitoring angle in the viewer where you can see lips moving while speaking. If you even suspect that the lips are out of sync, assume that they are.

Figure 8.13 – Track controls

- **Set Monitoring Angle**: Clicking **Set Monitoring Angle** is the same as selecting the speaker icon on the left of each track of the multicam angle timeline.

- **Add Angle** and **Delete Angle**: **Add Angle** will add an empty untitled angle below the current angle. Once you have an empty angle, you can drag a clip from the browser into it, cut and paste clips from other angles, and even drag a clip from another angle. If you set the empty angle as the monitoring angle, pressing the *W* key will add the highlighted clip from the browser to the playhead's position in the monitoring angle. **Delete Angle** deletes the current angle.

Multicam editing requires the original video and audio to be in good synchronization in the first place. If they are not perfectly in sync, then the next section will help you fix it.

Fixing audio and video mismatches

The most common issue with mismatched audio will be with short clips in the angle due to a camera being turned on and off during the session. Short clips may not contain enough audio for Final Cut Pro to be able to find a point to synchronize. The recovery process for this will be discussed in the *Actions in the multicam angle timeline* section.

There can be rare occasions where the audio track in the camera is out of sync with its video track. This could happen when a wireless microphone has been used and the subject is a long distance away from the camera. It's the principle that *light travels faster than sound*. Most importantly, you need to ascertain which of the video angles has the sync issue between the audio track and the video track.

The fix can't be achieved in the multicam angle timeline. You will need to manually match up the video and audio with the **Open Clip** command (see *Chapter 2*) in the browser and then start a new multicam edit.

The audio is always detached from the video in **Open Clip**, so you will be able to move the audio to sync it with the video by moving it one frame at a time compared to the video with the left and right arrow keys. Try *Command + R* to stretch the audio to bring it into sync. You could also try **Blade Speed** (*Shift + B*).

Unfortunately, **Open Clip** mode does not recognize the subframe audio level. When you have synced the audio using the **Open Clip** command, go through the whole **New Multicam Clip** process again.

If you have recorded with a separate sound recorder and there is a mismatch, it's more likely that a separate audio recorder was set at a different capture rate than the video camera's audio.

It always takes some effort to manually match audio to the video angle. The most effective way is to find a point in the video where you can cut both the video and audio tracks and treat them as separate videos. This will mean that the audio will have a shorter time to be kept in sync. Each time there is a cut, the audio and video will reset back to a new sync after you use **Sync Angle to Monitoring Angle**.

There are many options, but they will all involve an amount of manual effort. To ease your concerns, it is very unlikely that the video and audio will be out of sync on the same clip, but at least you have some ideas of how to solve the issue.

So far, the multicam angle timeline has been the focus of discussion; what hasn't been explained yet is how you can view the different angles within the viewer, which we will see in the next section.

Adjusting the angle viewer

It's one thing being able to see each angle in the multicam angle timeline but it's also important to see all angles in one viewer. At the top right of the viewer is the **SHOW** menu, where you can select the **Angles** option (*Shift + Command + 7*):

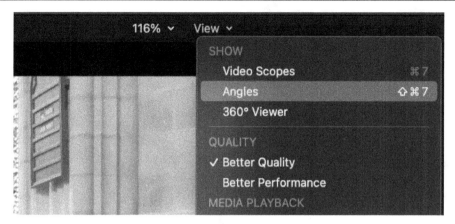

Figure 8.14 – SHOW – Angles

You will see the separate angles in the panels on the left of the main viewer window in *Figure 8.15*. The left-hand image shows the viewer: on the left are the three top panels displaying video angles; the fourth bottom panel represents the audio from the pulpit microphone. The monitoring angle is on the right of the viewer area. The right-hand image shows the position of the red playhead in the multicam angle timeline:

Figure 8.15 – Four angles with the monitoring angle in the viewer

Figure 8.16 shows a choice of four angles in four panels. You can optionally see 2, 4, 9, or 16 angles by selecting the respective settings to the left of the main viewer.

Figure 8.16 – Angle settings

You also have a choice on how the panels appear to the left of the main viewer. You can reposition the windows by hovering between them until your cursor turns into a double-sided *reposition* icon so that you can resize the windows:

Figure 8.17 – Double-sided arrow to resize window panels

Positioning the four panels differently allows you to see more of the angles and less of the viewer.

Figure 8.18 – Different layout of panels and the viewer

When you get to cutting the multicam project, you will see the same arrangement of panels on the left of the viewer as you have set in the multicam angle timeline, allowing you to click on the panel that you want to switch to. You will see how to do that in the *Editing the multicam project* section later in this chapter. In the meantime, in the next section, I will discuss the actions you need to complete before leaving the multicam angle timeline.

Actions in the multicam angle timeline

The multicam angle timeline requires several actions to be completed to ensure that all the tracks are in sync with the angle that is showing in the viewer. This is known as the monitoring angle.

Audio synchronization

The most important action is to check that the audio in all angles is in sync. This is critical because audio is the one factor that ties all of these angles together. If they are out of sync here, they will be out of sync when you are cutting, and it is time-consuming to try to match them up once the editing and cutting processes commence.

The process of checking the synchronization of the audio involves nominating a monitoring angle that has clear audio for the full length of the scene. It is ideal to have an external audio recorder that has been active for the whole session as it creates a bed to sync all the other angles. Otherwise, you can select a video angle with clear audio that runs through the whole session. You can make it the monitoring angle by activating the *monitor* icon, at which point the angle will become a lighter gray.

Activate the *speaker* icon on the monitoring angle as well as the next angle below it. Play the video and listen to ascertain that every clip in each angle is in sync with the other angle. This is best done with headphones. Do the same for each of the other angles but be sure to always use the same monitoring angle so that all angles sync to the one angle.

Synchronization is so important at this stage that I also make a habit of double-checking each angle with other angles. Make sure you check at the beginning of the footage as well as the end, watching out for audio drift.

Once all angles are in sync, the next consideration is what global adjustments can be made in the multicam angle timeline. We'll discuss this in the next section.

Global adjustments

For sure, the best workflow for multicam is to make global modifications in the multicam angle timeline. This doesn't mean you can't make modifications later in the multicam project, it's just more practical to do it first in the multicam angle timeline.

> Tip
> Adjustments made later in the multicam project are additional to those made in the multicam angle timeline.

As an example, if the volume level set in the multicam angle timeline is **+12**, when you view the multicam project, it will show as **0.0**. The actual volume will be at +12 of the recorded level but will show as **0.0** in the multicam project. Any effects added to the multicam project will be additive to any effects that were added to the multicam angle timeline.

It's important to set **keywords, favorites, and rejected** clips on the multicam project, not on the parent clips. Once you have created the multicam project, you can set the parent clips as **Rejected** clips and then set the browser to **Hide Rejected**.

Audio levels

Not all angles will require their audio to be used in the final edit, but for those that may be needed, it is important to have the levels match as well as the same audio effects added. I know the general rule is to make audio corrections after cutting, but you could save yourself a lot of time by treating the global effects while in the multicam angle timeline. If there are artifacts such as distortion or noisy backgrounds, it could be good to add those correction effects at the global stage, provided they are present in the whole angle. If the artifacts are just a certain part of the angle, then it will be better to make those corrections in the multicam project after the cutting stage, when things are being finessed. If you are not experienced or are unsure, I suggest that you don't add effects to the audio at this global stage – just balance the volume levels.

Color matching

Colors do need to be matched in the multicam angle timeline, even if there are color shifts during the session. Matching color at the global stage sets a foundation to make any necessary changes in the multicam project after cutting has been completed.

Color can be matched in the video angles by employing **Comparison Viewer** from the **Window** menu. I suggest that you white balance first by using the *magic wand* under the viewer. Make sure you change **Automatic** in the **Inspector** window to the *eyedropper* and pick white in the image. See *Chapter 14* for details.

Once the video angles have been white-balanced, you could use **Match Color** in the same *magic wand* menu, but I suggest directly using the color wheels for the less experienced, or the color curves for those more adventurous. Whichever you use, always have **Scopes** open, as you can't trust your eyes. See *Chapter 15* for details.

When you have the angles synchronized and the audio leveled and color matched, you are ready to start editing the multicam project, as you will see in the next section.

Editing the multicam project

The process of editing multicam is switching between angles that were seen as tracks in the multicam angle timeline view and that are now incorporated in the single-track multicam project view.

Right-click on the **Multicam** thumbnail with the four white squares in the left corner and select **New Project**. Give the project a title and select the **Video** format. The multicam project will open in the timeline. The angles still need to be active in the **View** menu above the viewer. The layout of the panels to the left of the viewer area will be the same as what you selected in the multicam angle timeline – four, in this case. You can change the layout anytime you wish with the **Settings** chevron.

The panels look the same as before but there is a subtle difference if you look closely. Above the panels on the left are three icons. The left-hand icon (yellow) represents both video and audio being active. The middle icon (blue) represents video and indicates that it is active in the viewer. The right-hand icon (green) represents audio, which can be from more than one source. The panels themselves now have outlines with the color of the icons, as well as the icons in the top-right corner. You will appreciate these colors when you use these panels to switch angles in the edit:

Figure 8.19 – Angles showing in the respective colors

The first action is to select the angle in the panel that has the first video footage. In *Figure 8.20*, the first video angle (blue outline) that is shown in the viewer is the **Cam 2** footage. The green outline outlines the **Pulpit** audio recorder, which started recording well before **Cam 2** was turned on. Check out *Figure 8.21* to see the project in the timeline:

Figure 8.20 – Trimming to the angle with the most visible video

You can select the panels by holding the *Option* key and clicking the panel to make that angle the active angle and visible in the **Viewer** area. The project in the timeline now shows the audio starting at **00:00** and the video from **Cam 2** starting at just after 5 minutes:

> **Tip**
> Beware! The timeline does not show an accurate representation of the start of the video. You must rely on the angles to the left of the viewer.

Figure 8.21 – The timeline with 5 minutes of audio before the video starts

Those first 5 minutes are not needed and can be deleted by pressing *Option + [.*

The steps in this next section are important to ensure that the multicam settings are correct when you start switching.

Setting up angles

You need to set which of the angles you are going to use for the start of the edit. Up to this point, for simplicity, I have used the four-panel setting. However, five angles were recorded at Mark and Elizabeth's wedding: three cameras and two audio recorders. You may not normally see this complexity of angles, but I want to show you the choices so that you understand all the possibilities. Having the five angles visible requires nine panels to be selected – four of them are empty, which takes up unnecessary space in the viewer. I'll switch back to four for convenience later:

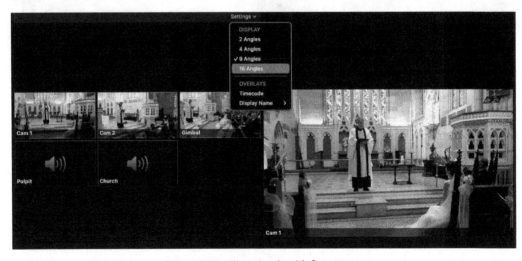

Figure 8.22 – Nine panels with four empty

Figure 8.22 shows the five angles (those with a name below them) in a nine-panel setting so that you can see the two audio-only angles. You need to establish which angles you want to start editing with. This is where the three top icons are important.

> **Note**
>
> I stress that this procedure is for setup only. Once completed, the use of the three icons will change.

For this example, let's assume that **Cam 2** will start the video with audio from the **Pulpit** and **Church** audio recorders. Click the *video filmstrip* icon, which will turn blue. Press *Option* and click the **Cam 2** panel; an outline in blue will appear. This will set **Cam 2** to be the starting video angle. Click the *audio waveform* icon, which will turn green. Press *Option* and click the **Pulpit** audio panel; the green outline will appear, and the audio will be set. If you try to select the **Church** audio panel with the same process, the **Pulpit** panel will be deactivated. To be able to select two audio sources, you need to set them up in the inspector.

Select the *speaker* icon in the inspector, open the audio configuration, and make sure both **Pulpit** and **Church** are ticked:

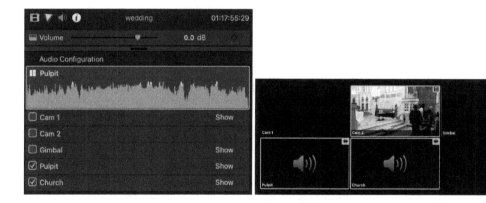

Figure 8.23 – Pulpit and Church set as audio sources

Once the sources of video and audio have been selected, the use of the three icons will change from setup to activation. In other words, the icons are now used to indicate the type of cut that is about to be made in the switch – that is, whether audio and video are switched (yellow), only video is switched (blue), or only audio is switched (green), as discussed in the next section.

Switching angles

Switching/cutting between angles is the heart of multicam editing.

The following step is supremely important: if you don't select the video icon (blue), you will switch both the video and audio every time you edit when switching angles.

Before you start to cut the multicam footage, make sure that the yellow icon (video and audio) is not highlighted (it is active by default). Click the blue *video filmstrip* icon to only switch the video angle, which leaves the audio angle always active from the same source. If you do want to switch both video and audio, select the yellow icon. If you only want to switch the audio while leaving the video from the same angle, use the green icon:

Figure 8.24 – Selecting the blue video icon to switch just the video angle

Switching/cutting can be activated by clicking on the panels to the left of the viewer when you want to switch angles. When you click on the panels, you will notice that the cursor changes to a pair of scissors to indicate you are cutting. Up until now, you will recall that I have used *Option* and clicking, which selects the panel. Directly clicking cuts the multicam project to the angle in the panel that you have just clicked on.

To summarize, click cuts and *Option* and click selects – the difference is important.

Switching can be done on the fly as the multicam project is playing or by pausing the multicam project at the switch position. If you are cutting on the fly, use the numeric keys: *1* for the first angle, *2* for the second angle, and so on up to *9*. Cutting on the fly while the multicam project is playing is neither for the faint-hearted nor newbies, but once you become proficient, it is very quick. With that said, you will likely cut just after where you need to, just because of slow reaction times. Don't be fazed by quickly switching and missing the exact frame; you can always go back to finesse the cut by trimming, as shown in the next section.

Correcting the angle

The multicam project reacts differently to a normal magnetic timeline. When the cursor is placed over the cut in a multicam project, it changes to the **Trim** tool by default:

Figure 8.25 – Trim tool by default

The viewer changes to a two-up display, which means you can drag the edit point left or right to finesse the position to the exact frame:

Figure 8.26 – Two-up display

Exactly the opposite happens to what you would expect in a normal magnetic timeline. When you press the *T* key in a multicam project, the cursor changes to the **Drag** tool to allow you to contract either side of the edit point to cut out frames. When you remove frames in the multicam project, you remove them in all angles in the project, but they remain unaffected in the multicam angle timeline:

Figure 8.27 – The Drag tool when the T key is pressed

There are more manual controls of the active video and audio angles to consider. You can right-click in the timeline on the angle you wish to manually change and select either **Active Video Angle** or **Active Audio Angle**:

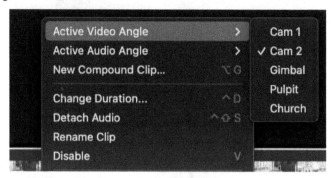

Figure 8.28 – Active Video Angle or Active Audio Angle selection

Switching angles is the prominent action of any multicam project; however, there will be a need to make corrections to the project, including fixing audio problems and stabilization, as discussed in the next section.

Stabilization

Final Cut Pro's built-in stabilization feature will not work in the multicam project. It only works in the multicam angle timeline, which is counterproductive as the multicam angle timeline tends to be a long clip of the whole event. It's a pity that the project can't be tagged with a marker that will appear in the multicam angle timeline, but there is a workaround, albeit a time-consuming and fiddly one.

Position the playhead on the edit point at the beginning of the clip to be stabilized in the multicam project and double-click the clip to the right of the edit point (see *Figure 8.29*):

> **Note**
> If the playhead's color is white, turn video and audio skimming off.

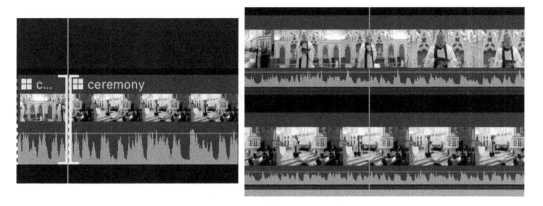

Figure 8.29 – Project on the left and angle timeline on the right

Then, when you open the multicam angle timeline, the playhead will be positioned at the frame at the angle that was visible in the multicam project (see *Figure 8.29*). Blade that frame and return to the multicam project. This time, set the playhead at the edit point at the end of the clip you want to stabilize and double-click to the left of the edit point. Again, the playhead in the multicam angle timeline will be at the appropriate frame. Blade at the playhead and you will have cut both sides of the section to be stabilized. Select the newly created clip and, in the inspector, tick **Stabilization**:

Figure 8.30 – Clip to be stabilized in the angle timeline

After checking **Stabilization**, the next step is to consider what needs to be fixed with any audio problems.

Multicam audio

Up until this point, the discussion has focused on video, with a fixed source of audio from both the **Pulpit** and **Church** audio recorders. There are times when the audio may need to be sourced from a camera, such as if a recorder fails or if something is picked up by a camera that is not heard by the recorders. Even though the camera audio has been ignored so far, it can always be activated in the inspector, as you saw earlier when both audio recorders were ticked (see *Figure 8.23*).

Every audio source that is ticked in the inspector can be shown in the timeline by right-clicking to select **Expand Audio Components**:

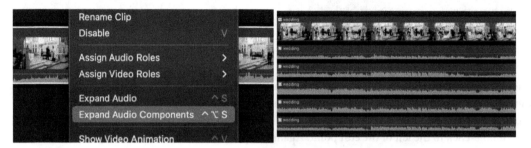

Figure 8.31 – Expand Audio Components

For some reason, the audio tracks in the timeline are not labeled with the names of the audio in the inspector but they are both shown in the same order, so the top track in the inspector is the top track in the timeline.

Multicam requires that you shoot with more than one camera… or does it? In the next section, you will see how to simulate a two-camera shoot.

Simulating a multicam shoot from one camera's footage

You can use footage from one camera to simulate a multicam shoot, which is particularly useful for interview videos. This workflow is best when using a 4k clip in a **1080p** timeline. Follow these steps:

1. Select the clip of a single-camera shoot in your browser and duplicate it from the **Edit** menu (*Command + D*).

2. Select the two clips and multicam as normal (if you are using a 4k clip, set the format to **1080p**).

3. Double-click the multicam thumbnail in your browser to open the multicam angle timeline.

4. Select one of the clips and resize the image to be at least 30% bigger than the original. There will be no quality loss, provided you are using a 4k clip in a 1080p timeline and you don't resize it by more than 50%. Use **Transform** in the viewer to resize. Because the resized clip has extra space that is bigger than the viewer area, you will be able to move the image left or right to reposition the image within the viewer frame.

5.   Right-click on the multicam thumbnail in the browser and select **New Project**:

Figure 8.32 – Two camera angles from a single-camera shoot

Multicam editing involves cutting between scenes rather than cutting out content, as you would do with a single-camera edit.

Summary

In this chapter, you learned that multicam editing is the process in Final Cut Pro that edits footage where multiple cameras have recorded the same subject or event from different angles and distances with the same audio source.

You also learned what types of events suit a multicam shoot and how those cameras can be set to film in synchronization. The settings for import and categorization were discussed, both with folders in the computer's **Finder** and as keyword collections in Final Cut Pro.

Then, you learned how to create a new multicam clip and understood the difference between the multicam angle timeline and the multicam project. You learned what modifications are best actioned globally in the multicam angle timeline compared to the piecemeal corrections in the multicam project, and that modifications made globally are additive in the multicam project.

Next, you learned about setting up the angles for switching and how the cuts can be modified after switching.

Finally, you were shown a method of simulating a multicam shoot from the footage of just one camera.

The next chapter discusses employment opportunities and how you can put your newfound Final Cut Pro knowledge to use in the workforce. You will also see the different methods of collaboration that can be achieved with other editors.

9
Project Workflows – Pace and Structure

This chapter is about the practical application of specific workflows associated with different types of video genres. There are some workflow techniques that could be applied to any type of video. The first section is a must-read for all. It's about interviews but covers numerous editing techniques that support most editing styles. The *Interviews* section describes approaches to editing videos used in the other sections, so I would suggest that you read through this section no matter what your main interests are.

In this chapter, you will learn about Final Cut Pro workflows for different genres of video, from interviews, wedding videos, and conferences to full-length movies. Other workflows will teach you skills when editing social media videos as well as home movies, with added processes for cutting to beats in music videos. Lastly, you will learn about short techniques you will use throughout your editing career, including the legal limits when exporting files and the need to retain frequently used elements that can be quickly recovered for future use.

In this chapter, we're going to cover the following main topics:

- Interviews
- Conferences and seminars
- Weddings
- Full-length movies and documentaries
- Social media videos
- Family holiday movies
- Cutting to a beat
- General techniques

By the end of this chapter, you will have learned specific workflows to suit your particular chosen editing styles, as well as become conversant with different editing styles that you may not have encountered in the past.

Interviews

Interviews and the like include any type of video that has a voice track as the main focus. That's not to say that the visuals are not important, but dialogue is the key element in this genre. Concentrating on the dialogue gives you the opportunity to cut out non-relevant words and even "ums" and "ahs". For all intents and purposes, you should treat the video as if it were an audio-only recording. This means that the visuals will also be removed where the corresponding words have been cut out, but don't worry – there are techniques to hide these missing image frames and jump cuts.

If you are the shooter as well as the editor, refer to *Chapter 3, Planning the Video Story* for details on setting up an interview shoot.

> **Tip**
> To hide the browser while editing a multicam, use *Control + Command + 1*. To show the browser again, use the same keys.

The following sections show workflows for the different stages of editing interviews.

Pre-editing

The conventional method of pre-editing is to sort the clips in the **browser** in order to find the most suitable parts of the original media and then add them to a **project**. I find that most interviews tend to be relatively short in comparison to other video types.

The following are suggestions for pre-editing methods.

First pre-editing method

The first method is to highlight the entire original interview clip in the browser, then right-click on it, and select **New Project…**, which then adds the whole interview to a project in the timeline. This is the most suitable method if you are not the shooter and don't know what content is in the interview. The other benefit is that it saves time because you are already working on the project, evaluating the material as you proceed with the removal of unwanted material. Unwanted material could be banter between the shooter and the interviewee or interrupting phone calls, which can be quickly discarded without an afterthought. Besides, working in the timeline gives you the feeling that you have already started editing, rather than just gathering the useful clips that will need to be edited later.

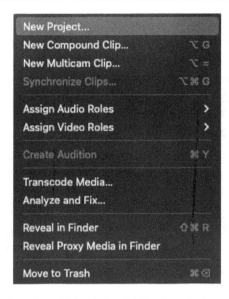

Figure 9.1 – Right-click and select New Project…

The second pre-editing method

Let's now look at the second workflow. If you were the shooter, you would have an idea of the different topics discussed in the interview. You can break up the complete footage for the different topics into **Favorites** in the browser. Then, by holding the *Command* key and clicking on the green favorite range in the clip, you can select multiple favorites.

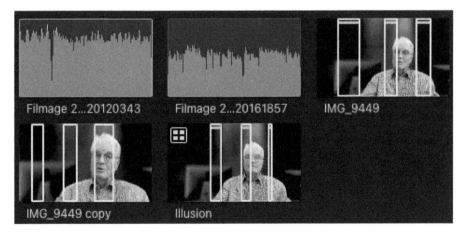

Figure 9.2 – A selection of multiple favorites in the original clip

Once the favorites are selected, as shown in *Figure 9.3*, two thumbnails are selected (the ones with yellow outlines). Right-click on each of the favorite thumbnails in the **Smart Collections** and create a new project for each. With this process, you will have a separate project for each topic.

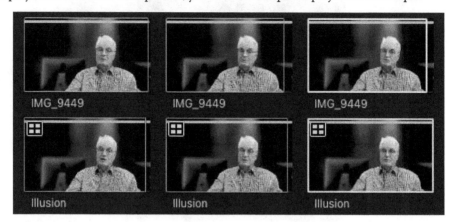

Figure 9.3 – Thumbnails showing the separated favorites, with a green bar across the top

I find that by splitting each project into smaller ones, I can focus more on the subject with less pressure, as well as get that feeling of achievement as each topic is completed, rather than having the stress of having a long project yet to be completed. When they are all finalized, you can copy and paste each topic's project into a combined project.

If the favorites are part of the same topic, then press the *E* key, and the clip will be added to the end of the current project.

If you have a multicam clip, it can just as easily be pre-edited in the browser as a standard clip. Just make sure that you set, in the multicam viewer, a video track that runs the full length of the interview.

Figure 9.4 – The multicam view

Whatever method you use, be sure to spend some time perusing the whole interview. The ultimate aim is to gather all the relevant content and arrange it into an order that makes sense, achieving your client's original brief. You may want to move parts of the interview into a different order than how it was recorded. Be careful; it always needs to make sense and be in context.

Cutting

Interviews are almost entirely edited by cutting out material. There is usually very little need to add content, other than to move words within the interview to improve the context.

There are different methods of cutting, depending on whether you are confident in deleting material with shortcuts or prefer to use the *Delete* key. We will look at the method using the *Delete* key first.

The first cutting method

Follow these steps to remove unwanted material using the *Delete* key:

1. Before you start editing, adjust the height of the audio so that you can easily see the waveforms. Use the filmstrip icon at the right-hand side of the center bar.

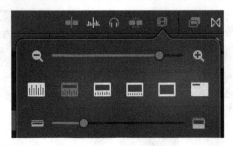

Figure 9.5 – The filmstrip in blue, third from the right, is for timeline height adjustment

2. Once the clip is in the timeline, play through it with the *L* key (double-click if you want to play at 2x speed).

3. If you have previewed the interview, know what to expect, and are feeling confident, press *Command + B* when you want to start a cut and *Command + B* to end a cut.

4. Then, move on to the next section that you want to cut out, using the same procedure.

What you now have are sections that you can remove by pressing the *Delete* key. I would suggest you wait until all the unwanted material is cut before deleting it. I'll show you, in the *Restoring removed clips* section, later in this chapter, how to restore unwanted sections should you need to retrieve what you have removed.

When working on a real project, it's unlikely, at least while you are learning this procedure, that you will be able to react quickly enough to cut anywhere near the right place. The workflow I suggest is to play through and press the *K* key, or *spacebar*, to pause, and then adjust the skimmer playhead to the exact point that you want to cut with *Command + B*. Alternatively, to save time, hold the *B* key and click at the point you want to cut. The cursor changes to a scissors icon when you drag it inside the clip in the timeline.

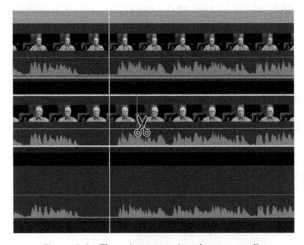

Figure 9.6 – The scissors cutting the center clip

I suggest you try both options and decide which suits you best. You can use the *Delete* key to remove any obviously unwanted material, but first, consider the procedure in the *Restoring removed media* section to retain the remaining cut-out media if you need to refer back to it.

The second cutting method

If you don't want to store the removed sections, instead of using *Command + B* twice to cut the clip in the timeline, for the second cut, use *Option +]*.

Follow the first method to where you want to make your first cut, and press *Command + B*. Hover the **skimmer** over the position where you want to end the cut. This time, press *Option +]*, and the part of the clip from the first cut to the skimmer will be deleted. This method is much quicker, especially if you cut on the fly. However, you aren't able to retain the clip so that it can be later restored.

The next section shows how to store removed media for later reference.

Restoring removed clips

If you have been given the brief to make your own decisions, you need to be able to restore removed portions of the interview should the client want to make a change. There are two methods to consider. The first involves the use of the **Roles** feature.

You will recall Roles was discussed in *Chapter 4, Pre-Editing a Rough Cut*. Here, I am going to create an audio role called Removed. The purpose is to be able to label the clips that have been cut out.

The first restoring method

This method uses the **Roles** feature to allow you to find retained media should you need to restore it:

1. Open the timeline index, select the **Roles** tab, and at the bottom of the index, click **Edit Roles...**.

Figure 9.7 – Edit Roles... at the bottom of the timeline index

2. Press the plus sign in the circle for the new audio role, and call it `Removed`.

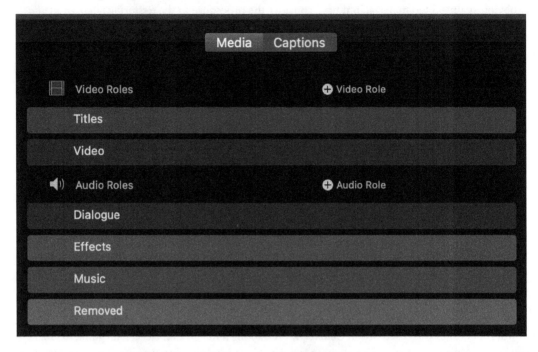

Figure 9.8 – An audio role named Removed

3. After you have completed all cuts in the first cutting method, select all of the sections that you want to remove by holding the *Command* key down, and apply the **Removed** audio role to them. They will change to the color that you set the audio role.

4. Next, duplicate the interview project using *Command + D*. The original stays in the timeline, and the duplicate project is given the same name but with 1 as the suffix. (The suffix numbers increase sequentially as you create further duplicates.) You should use the **Snapshot** option to avoid affecting multicam and compound clips that are in the project.

5. You can now remove all the unwanted clips in the timeline with the *Delete* key, and you can be confident that you can always refer back to the duplicate project should you want to recall the clips that were removed.

Figure 9.9 – The duplicate project has the removed clips. The role is in orange for easy reference

You may be wondering why I didn't suggest the previously shown method of using **markers**, as discussed in *Chapter 5, Refining the Rough Cut*. In this current example, the portion you are removing has the same clip name as the rest of the clip, so the markers would all have the same clip name. Hence, you would not be able to differentiate them from each other. However, you could record the time code position from the timeline index and insert that in the marker, as per the example in *Chapter 5, Refining the Rough Cut*.

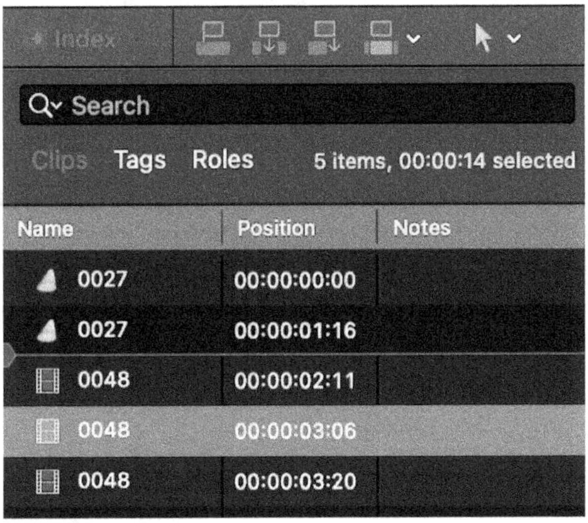

Figure 9.10 – The index showing the time code for the portion of the removed clip

The roles method allows you to keep a record of removed media. However, the next method is more hands-on and keeps unwanted media on view for you to see at any time.

The second restoring method

The second method of temporarily storing removed material, which is simpler, requires thinking outside the box. Video clips can be connected below the main storyline, which means you can simply cut (using *Command + B*) the unwanted portion of the interview and drag it below the good part of the interview in the primary storyline. Of course, the magnetic timeline snaps shut. All you then need to do is either reduce the audio in the stored clip or, better still, click on it and press the *V* key to disable the clip. It stays grayed out and ready for you to restore, if needed, by pressing the *V* key again and dragging it back into the magnetic timeline where it came from. Brilliant!

Figure 9.11 – A removed clip below the primary storyline, disabled with the V key

Whether you are confident enough in cutting and removing or feel the need to retain the media, you will next be presented with the problem of hiding the resulting jump cuts.

Hiding jump cuts

With the main unwanted material removed, it's now time to hide the jump cuts.

A word of warning, though. If the background behind the interviewee is relevant to the spoken words at the time of the cut, you will need to either keep that section or have an appropriate B roll of what is featured in the background to hide the cut.

Using the B roll

The B roll is the obvious first choice to hide jump cuts. Just drag a connected clip above the edit point – it's pretty obvious, really. However, you don't always have the appropriate B roll available, and if there are many cuts, you may end up with a video of just B roll with a voiceover and no person being interviewed. Guess you won't be paid much for that.

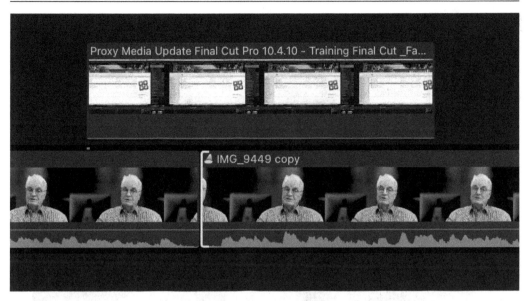

Figure 9.12 – A B roll over the cut in the interview

As with everything, a balance of B roll and some creative techniques are required to hide the edit. If you have a multi-camera shoot, then hiding jump cuts is easy – just switch to the other angle. But if there is only one camera, you need to get savvy with your ideas.

Using the Flow transition

If the interviewee does not move their head too much, then you could try the **Flow** transition from the **Transitions** browser. It's in the **Dissolves** subheading and should only be used at the default duration. Refer to *Chapter 7, Titles, Effects,, and Generators* for details.

The **Flow** transition is not a magic bullet. At best, it's a trial-and-error method, but it's well worth undertaking. The **Flow** transition is added at an edit point. Also, note the **Analyzing for optical flow…** warning in *Figure 9.13*. I recommend that you wait for this to be completed, as optical flow is, in my experience, one of those bugs that can cause an export to fail.

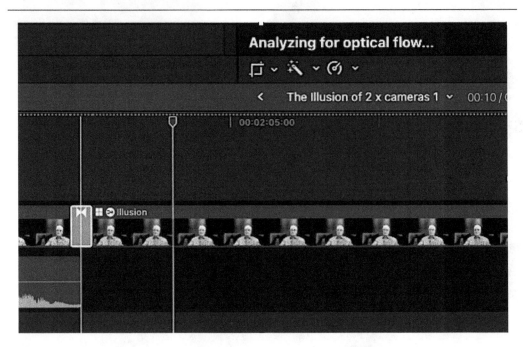

Figure 9.13 – The Flow Transition, with optical flow still analyzing

The secret is to move the **Flow** transition with the **Trim** tool until both sides of the edit point have similar head angles and looks – eyes open and the mouth open/closed. Be careful, as you shouldn't move it too far; otherwise, the lips will be out of sync with the words. Don't forget to expand the audio by double-clicking the bottom of the clip, and then the audio stays in place while you adjust the video with the **Trim** tool. The audio is still in sync, but you can see it as a separate track from the video.

The expanded audio has not been affected in any way. In *Figure 9.14*, the audio still changes at the playhead but the video switches at the **Flow** transition, and the jump is hidden. The head in the two-up display is at a similar angle.

Figure 9.14 – A two-up display, with the head and mouth in a similar position

You should be aware that the **Flow** transition is not perfect, and the jump cut can still show. Also, if you move the **Flow** transition too far away from the audio cut, the lips will be out of sync. If the **Flow** transition has not worked for you, don't try to adjust the duration; either the default works or you need to try something else.

Using 4K footage in a 1080p timeline

If you have 4K original footage, there is another option. I suggest you don't try the following with normal HD 1080p footage unless you are prepared to accept a soft image or the video will end up on a very small screen only – for example, only intended to be viewed on a mobile device.

This concept is simple and the workflow equally so, unless you are filming in front of a green screen. But even then, there is a workaround (see the *Cutting angles with a green screen* section). Think of this technique as creating a second camera angle from a single camera shoot.

Follow these steps to use 4K footage in a 1080p timeline:

1. Create a 1080p project, not 4K, even though you have 4K original footage.

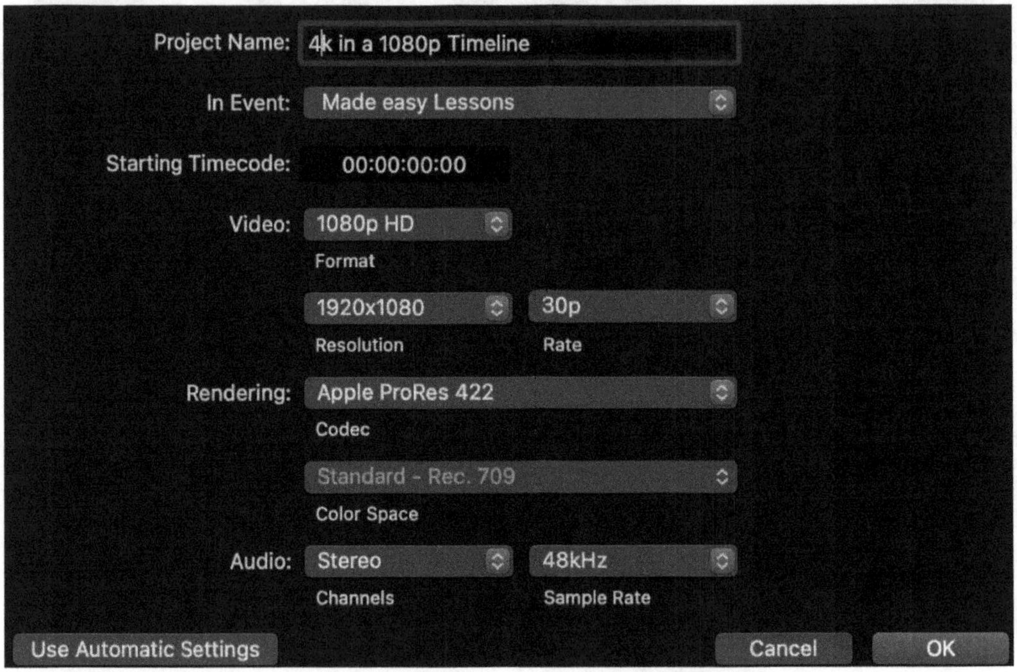

Figure 9.15 – The settings for 4K in a 1080p timeline

You can safely add the 4K footage to the timeline, and Final Cut Pro will keep the aspect ratio for you.

2. Move the playhead to the point that you want to cut, and press *Command + B* to remove the unwanted section of the clip.

3. Click on the next clip, and then open the **Inspector** window, select **Transform**, and adjust the **Scale (All)** size by entering 150%.

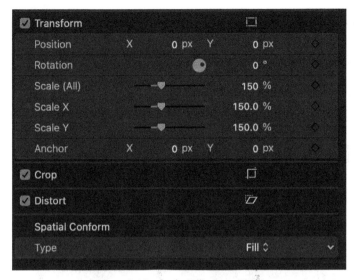

Figure 9.16 – Scale (All) set to 150%

The logic behind this is that the 4K resolution allows you to zoom into the image by an extra 50% without losing quality in the 1080p **timeline**. Now, the image is 50% larger. At the next cut, return **Scale (All)** to 100%, and repeat the change from 100% to 150% for each alternative clip by using the **Paste Attributes** command.

Figure 9.17 – 4K footage – 100% zoom on the left, and 150% zoom on the right

This method allows you to quickly change camera angles, which will avoid a jump cut. Conventionally, the change in the image size between the two shots is a variation of at least 30 degrees. You can speed up the process of changing the percentage very quickly by waiting until you have completed all the cuts, then returning to the second clip, and changing the scale to 150%:

1. Copy the clip using *Command + C*.

2. Then, select every second clip with the *Command* key held down.

3.   When they are all selected, from the **Edit** menu, select **Paste Attributes**, or press *Shift + Command + V*.

4.   Make sure **Scale** is ticked and untick all other unwanted attributes.

Now, the 150% scale will be added to every second clip.

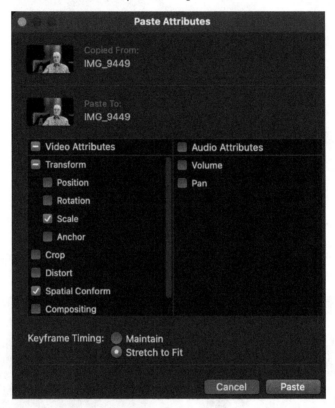

Figure 9.18 – Paste Attributes

With the unwanted material cut out and jump cuts hidden, you will want to look at the annoying vocal distractions, such as ums and ahs. These are known as fillers, and there are several ways of cutting them out, as shown in the next section.

Removing fillers

There are other minor cuts that you may want to make that will only involve a few frames of video. In these cases, the jump may not be discernible. These are, again, trial-and-error methods.

Examples of fillers you could try to remove are coughs, ums and ahs, and sniffing. (They are called fillers because when a person speaks, they may need to fill the space between words while they think.) Stuttering is hard to remove. It is also really time-consuming to try and remove blinking. The first thing you need to ask yourself is, "*Is the filler part of the character of the interviewee?*" If so, it is best to leave it in. Besides, fillers are a lot of work to remove.

If you decide to remove them all, or perhaps just the really jarring fillers, then this section describes how to do it in Final Cut Pro. Of course, other background noises can be removed with the same tools, provided they don't overlap words and are really short.

Coughs and sniffing are easy ones to remove because they occur with a good gap between words, but ums and ahs that overlap words are impossible to remove without affecting the words.

The technique here is to first select the range that the filler takes up in the clip. So, zoom in with the *Command + plus* key, and then with the *R* key held down, drag the filler over to the audio track – the filler will show as a peak in the waveform.

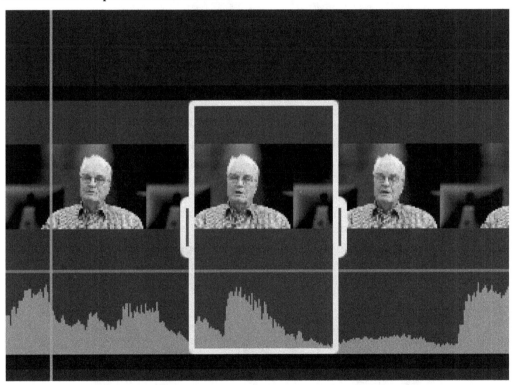

Figure 9.19 – A range selected – a yellow outline at the peak in the waveform

Drag the volume line down inside the range. If necessary, you could fill the gap with the **Speed** tool (*Figure 9.20*) but by no more than 2x. When you remove the audio, the **Range** tool creates keyframes that slightly fade the audio. You can increase the fade amount by dragging the keyframe's dots.

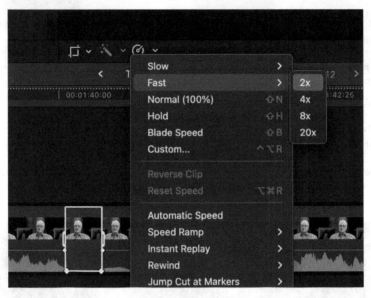

Figure 9.20 – The Speed tool showing 2x speed, with white dots on the yellow lines to fade the audio

If there is a sound gap, you may need to copy a section of the audio where there is a pause between words and paste it as a connected clip below the empty range. This will allow the ambient background noise to continue, rather than having complete silence at the gap. You will need to fade the ambient audio in the connected clip. Good shooters will likely provide you with a few minutes of empty room noise with every shoot. If you are the shooter, get into the practice of recording just the sound of the room with nobody in it; it is best to do so at the beginning of a shoot. Schedule a room sound recording as part of your setup procedure.

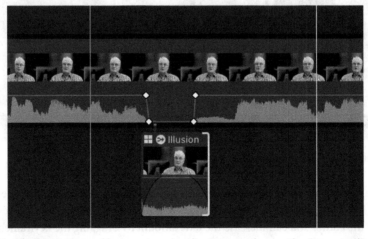

Figure 9.21 – The gap is covered by a room noise clip. You can also see the Range tool's keyframes

Interviews particularly focus on dialogue, so it's imperative to have the audio synchronized with the lips when they are visible in the video. Final Cut Pro has important techniques for keeping the audio in sync with the video. We'll revisit them here, even though they are covered in detail in *Chapter 6, Fixing and Enhancing the Audio*. There are also some traps that you should be aware of that can throw video/audio out of sync. Fortunately, the magnetic timeline does a great job of helping you stay on track. The next section is about audio sync.

Audio in sync

When you add a camera clip to the timeline that contains both video and audio, you should trust that they are both in sync. There is a chance, though unlikely, that audio recorded by a camera using a lapel mic may have a slight audio delay if recorded over a long distance. You will have to compensate for that manually, by using **Detach Audio** and moving the detached audio track one frame at a time with the arrow keys.

Also, be aware that the difference may be less than one frame of video. If that is the case, audio can be adjusted at a sub-video-frame level. Pressing *Command* and the right and left arrow keys will adjust the audio playhead to as small as 1/80th of a video frame (see *Chapter 6, Fixing and Enhancing the Audio* for details).

If the shoot was a multi-camera shoot or a single camera with an external audio recorder, you need to synchronize the tracks into one entity. I prefer to use **New Multicam Clip** for all occasions, rather than just **Synchronize Clips**. I find that there is more flexibility with the multicam viewer than there is with the **Synchronize Clips** option.

As you know, the audio appears at the bottom of the video clip. Final Cut Pro has a technique that allows you to change the edit point of the video while retaining the original edit point of the audio, and vice versa.

To ensure that the audio is kept intact, expand the audio from the video by double-clicking the audio waveforms at the bottom of the combined clip in the timeline. It will look like this:

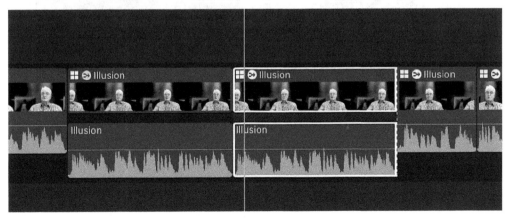

Figure 9.22 – Expanded audio

The audio is still in sync with the video, and attached, but it can be shortened or lengthened without affecting the length of the video section above. You will see how this also allows you to overlap the audio tracks in the timeline. The cuts are known as J and L cuts, as the audio can be cut at a different place than the video.

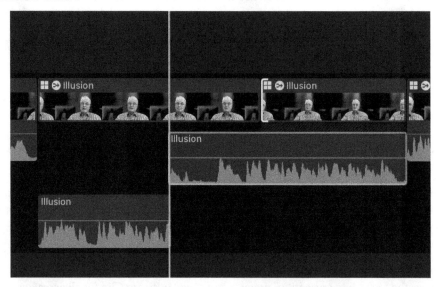

Figure 9.23 – Audio cut at a different place than the video – a J cut

This is a visual trap that you will not see coming. When the attached audio is collapsed, again, by double-clicking it, the visual that corresponds to the audio is hidden, but it still plays the sound, even though you can't see it when it is collapsed. To see the collapsed audio, double-click the separated audio track again.

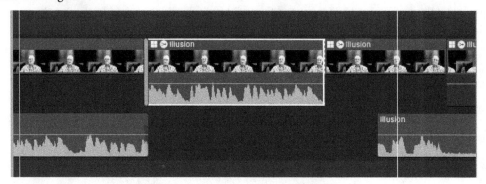

Figure 9.24 – The J cut with audio hidden

The techniques used for interview editing can also be used with other genres of editing styles. The next section explains editing techniques that are specific to conferences and seminars.

Conferences and seminars

I've included a section on conferences and seminars here, as they are very similar to interviews but with the added advantage that there is less to cut out. The content is usually retained as a snapshot in time of the whole event. You will likely have much more B roll to work with, such as audience reaction shots, which can be used in different places. Conference edits will, of course, take much longer than interviews, and you will have different types of briefs from your client as to what they would like the edits to achieve.

You can expect two types of briefs:

- Edit the whole conference as one long event
- Extract important segments and turn them into short, independent videos

Let's take a look at each of these briefs in the following sections.

One long event

One of the big advantages of this kind of brief is that your edits are only cuts between speakers with some breaks. If it's a single-camera shoot, you can select the clip in the browser and right-click to create a new project. Start playing through the clip until you see the point where the actual conference begins. Play through at normal speed for about five minutes. If the audio is fine and there are no hitches with the video, then for now, ignore the audio, and then, hover over the clip with the skimmer. I would suggest that you increase the view for more detail. You will get a feel for what you prefer regarding the amount of detail on view in the timeline. Don't be too adventurous with too wide a view. Experience will inform what is best for you.

What you are looking for is the next natural break in the conference, maybe questions, where the camera pans, or another speaker coming on stage – anything that affects the normal flow. At this stage, don't worry about the B roll or audience reaction shots. Use morning tea and lunch breaks, or any interruption as an opportunity to make an edit cut. The objective is to get through all the presentations as quickly as possible. You will go through it all again to find any glitches. With experience, you will become very quick at this rough-cut stage.

Rather than hovering, you may prefer to use the *J*, *K*, and *L* keys. Each press of *J* and *L* will speed up the play head up to eight times. The *K* key stops the playhead. The semicolon and hyphen keys will allow you to jump back and forward to your cuts should you need to refer back to anything.

Once you have the full conference roughly completed, go back to play it again, this time more slowly, listening to the words and making appropriate video and simple audio adjustments. If there are issues, leave a to-do marker using *Option + M*. You will be able to find these issues in the index later.

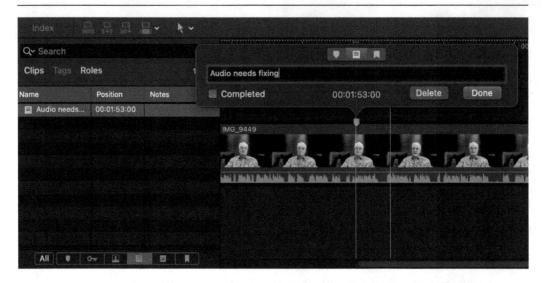

Figure 9.25 – The to-do marker

If it is a multi-camera shoot, then you need to sync your cameras first (see *Chapter 8, Setting Up and Editing Multicam* for more details). Then, follow the single-camera workflow described earlier in this section. I would go through the whole conference quickly to get the rough cut; I like to get that under my belt, so to speak. Then, at the reviewing stage, switch between angles where appropriate. You may want to switch angles as you go through the rough-cut stage. That will depend on your preference and your confidence to switch on the fly.

Short, independent videos

The rough-cut stage will be mostly the same as the one-long event described in the *One long event* section. But as you reach the end of each segment, copy all of the segments, create a new project, and paste the segment into the new project. Create a new project for each segment.

Your brief may not ask you to include the whole conference or seminar. You may have been given instructions on which parts to include. You may have been asked to make your own decisions about what to include. If so, then it perhaps a good idea to ensure the segments that you cut out can be recovered; refer to the *Restoring removed clips* section earlier in this chapter. Equally, you could complete a rough cut of the whole conference and then create separate projects. Regardless, review just one section, logically the first, and then complete that section, color-correct and audio-correct it, and move on to the next section.

By completing each section separately, you will be able to use the adjustments to audio and color in the first section and create presets, applying those to the other sections as you reach them (see *Chapter 10, The Inspector Controls* for details).

Dialogue-based video types such as interviews and conferences are quite different in look and feel from more social and family events. The most common of these is the wedding video event, which is similar to formal events such as birthdays, anniversaries, engagements, and christenings. The next section covers the formal structured type of video for weddings.

Weddings

Of all the videos that you are likely to edit, weddings have the most formality and offer the most lessons to learn. Wedding videos, unlike interviews, are edited in chronological order, much the same as for conferences and seminars. There is a set procedure for wedding videos that will save you from wondering where to start first. There are formal parts to the day – preparations, the ceremony, the photoshoot, and the reception, which has an entrance, cake cutting, speeches, and a first dance. I find it best to edit these separately and then combine them at the end.

Most of the time, there will be more than one camera to work with, so multicam syncing will be the next process after the media is organized into categories (see *Chapter 8, Setting Up and Editing Multicam* for more details). As you will see in the next section, you can organize your media into keyword collections before you start your first project (see *Chapter 2, Organizing Media* for more details).

Organizing media

My wedding video editing workflow starts with organizing media into a template.

Creating a template in Finder

There are two methods of organizing media. The first is carried out in **Finder** before importing the media into Final Cut Pro. If you frequently edit wedding videos, then you need a template. If you use the **Finder** method, you can duplicate the template for each new wedding, which is a massive time-saver (see *Chapter 2, Organizing Media* for details).

When creating a template in **Finder**, add the most important folders for the separate cameras. However, you can have as many detailed folders as you like. Don't be afraid of having folders in your **Finder** template that are rarely used. When the template is imported into the browser, only folders with content in them are added as Keyword Collections. The following sample template will give you some ideas about what you may want to add to your template. It's a good idea to label the subfolders with the title of the main folder.

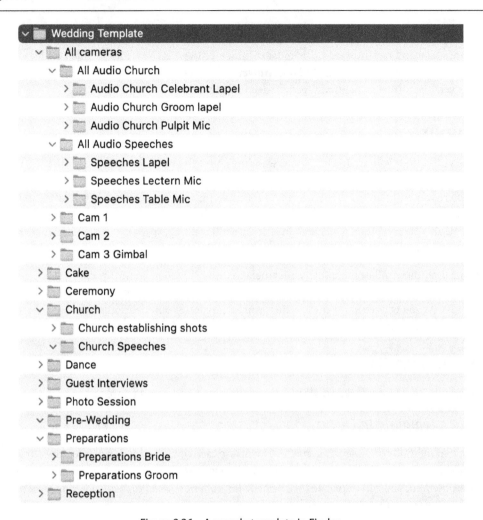

Figure 9.26 – A sample template in Finder

Figure 9.27 shows what **Finder** folders look like when they are converted into Keyword Collections in the browser's sidebar. Note that Keyword Collections lose their hierarchy. You could create folders in the browser after import to add the keywords to, but that's not the best use of time in my opinion. The reason for having the template in the first place is to save time reproducing the wedding categories over and over. The following is the **Finder** template as it appears in the browser's sidebar.

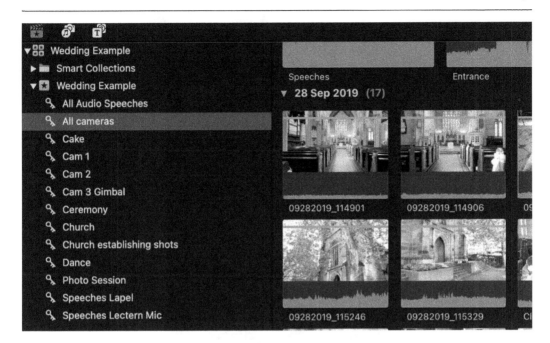

Figure 9.27 – The Keyword Collections of the Finder template

Note that not all the folders that were in **Finder** have been imported into Final Cut Pro because not all of the folders had content in them. The **All cameras** Keyword Collection has clips from all cameras, while **Cam 1**, **Cam 2**, and **Cam 3 Gimbal** have the clips from the cameras in separate folders.

As shown in *Figure 9.28*, the empty template in **Finder** can be duplicated for your next wedding video.

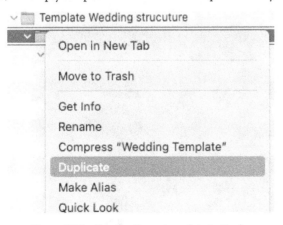

Figure 9.28 – Duplicating a template in Finder

Creating pre-set keyword collections

There is an alternative method, which I prefer, to create preset Keyword Collections. Create a new library and add folders and Keyword Collections directly in the browser's sidebar. You will notice that I have added folders, something that doesn't happen with the **Finder** template method. You can see that folders can be nested as well. As shown in *Figure 9.29*, all the audio folders are nested inside the **All Cameras** folder:

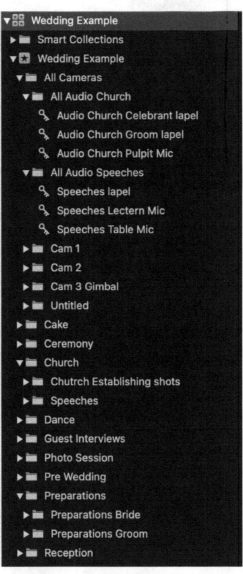

Figure 9.29 – Folders with Keyword Collections inside

You can save the empty library template to a disk, and then next time, you have a duplicate wedding edit Final Cut Pro library in **Finder**, rather than having a folder template as in the first method.

Synchronizing cameras

Most weddings have more than one camera. My preferred workflow is to edit multicam shots first. I figure the ceremony and speeches are the biggest part of the editing, so completing them first provides a good feeling of achievement.

The multicam process was explored in *Chapter 8*, *Setting Up and Editing Multicam*, so I won't go into the procedure here. Just make sure that you create a Keyword Collection that has all of the cameras and audio for the ceremony and another for the speeches. As mentioned in the previous chapter, progressively add the camera clips to the **Multicam** viewer, although no more than 10 at a time; otherwise, you run the risk of overloading the synchronization. Once synchronized, roughly color-match the video tracks in the **Multicam** view, as it will help you get a better sense of how they match when you switch the angles in the edit. You will come back to finesse the color match in the **Multicam** view after the cutting is done. Make sure you have nominated the audio track you want as the main audio and that your **Cutting** tool in the angle viewer is set to cut video only.

In most cases, an edit of the entire ceremony will have been requested by the client. I usually work on the ceremony first.

> **Note**
> Short highlight edits are done when the full edit is completed.

When producing the full ceremony video, once you have checked the audio sync, nominated the main audio source, and matched the colors of the camera angles, then right-click on the **Multicam** thumbnail in the browser and select **New Project…**. The whole multicam part of the ceremony will now be in the timeline. As mentioned earlier in this section, weddings are edited chronologically as they were filmed, so you will find that little will be cut out of the ceremony.

Most likely, you will start cutting the first camera angle as a wide shot and switch to close-ups for important happenings. Your time will be taken up with switching angles on appropriate words, hand gestures, or glances. That's all assuming that the video and audio from all sources are good, but you will have several cameras to choose from. If there is an issue with both angles filmed at the same time, add a B roll of the guests.

With the ceremony completed as a rough cut, I normally then move on to the speeches. Start a new project and follow much the same process as that for the ceremony. Sometimes, there are two sets of speeches, one before the meal and one after. I treat them as separate projects. Usually, the cake and first dance follow directly after the last set of speeches, so I include them in that project and even continue with the crowd dancing right up to the end of the event. It will depend on how much material there is to edit. There are no rules, just what suits you best when you are editing.

The cuts for other parts of the day can now be put into separate projects if you want. It goes without saying that everything is at the rough-cut stage up to now, although you will have done an early color match in the **Multicam** view.

All that is then left is sweetening the audio and the final color corrections, particularly with the photo section, which allows you the biggest creative license as far as effects and color are concerned.

I wait until the full-day video is complete, including the color correction and any effects that I decide to use, before starting the highlights edit. Before I start with the highlights, I copy a number of clips from the full day, say 10 or 20, into a new project and then cut out some to shorten the edit. The next thing I know, I'm getting right into it. Don't be afraid to switch the order of the day around, focusing on the highlights, and maybe even show a few fast shots of the day before moving on to the sequential order of events. That will give the effect of previewing the day. It's the highlight where you can get away from being adventurous, without provoking the ire of the bride's mother.

The wedding video is usually the domain of a sole editor or only small editing companies. This is different from what we will discuss in the following section, which will require multi-staffed enterprises using their own procedures. I have included the next section for smaller companies that want to be involved in creating full-length movies and documentaries.

Full-length movies and documentaries

With Final Cut Pro and other editing apps, the postproduction of full-length movies no longer necessarily needs the hordes of staff that were required in the days of film. Now, the majority of the postproduction stages can be handled by one single editor, using the techniques described in this section. That is not to say that all full-length movies are edited by just one person. It's the exact opposite in reality. It's more about splitting editing into logical sections. As you have seen in earlier chapters, editing assistants are tasked with assembling media into organized categories, and then junior editors are entrusted to add the media to an **initial assembly**. This is where the senior editor will become involved with producing the rough cut, which in turn becomes the **picture-locked** version that is then sent out to specialists for external color correction and audio improvement.

As stated, all of this could have been done by a sole editor, which is what I will cover in this section, by showing the editing techniques that they would consider.

Pacing

Perhaps the most important aspect of a full-length movie is the pace of the editing and how it matches what is on screen, or even what is not on screen, giving an overall look and feel to the movie but, most importantly, emphasizing the audience's responses to individual scenes. Pacing is simply the number of cuts in a scene, and it will vary between scenes and even within a scene. The art of pacing is a craft, not just a set of instructions, and as a general rule, a fast pace illustrates dramatic action in a scene. Slower pacing is for slower scenes, with few cuts. Something between fast and slow cutting represents normal daily life (see *Chapter 5, Refining the Rough Cut*).

Continuity editing

This cutting technique involves simply editing clips into a sequence that portrays the sense of being connected and continuous. This resembles what I talked about in the *Interview*, *Conferences and seminars*, and *Weddings* sections of this chapter. In fact, it is the same technique, and I include it here, as it is the basis of all dramatic movies that include dialogue. When it's done properly, you don't notice the editing.

When you look at it out of context, a wide establishing shot jumping to a medium shot and then to a close-up resembles a quickly cut music video. However, use all of those different shot types with the same person in the scene, or anything that is common to all scenes, and they will meld together to give an integrated flow of action, even if they are actually different shots spliced together.

There are a couple of tricks within continuity editing, known as match cutting and eye-line matching.

Match cutting

Editing is all about invisibility, so you need to hide your cuts. The match cut is the go-to way to create seamless action and movement between clips.

A match cut uses elements of one scene when cutting to the next scene. There is a visual match for scenes that don't appear to be linked, maybe different locations that mirror each other with a similar shape.

Consider transitioning from a view of Earth to a scene on Earth. The similarity of the shape ties the audience to the change in scenes.

Figure 9.30 – A transition of Earth as seen from space to a Ferris wheel
in Germany (images from Pixabay, Eikira, and Asim Bashir)

In *Figure 9.30*, both images have a circular similarity, indicating a connection when the visual transitions from the Earth as seen from space to a specific town in Germany.

Eye-line matching

Consider a scene where a person looks in one direction in the first clip. In the next clip, the audience's eyes expect to see what the person is looking at. For example, *Figure 9.31* shows a person looking at islands in the distance (left), and the next clip is a beach on those islands (right):

Figure 9.31 – (Left) a person looking at a distant island and (right) a close-up of
the island (images from SnapwireSnaps and Relaxing-Guru on Pixabay)

The visual connection between images is a powerful way of transitioning an audience from one scene to another. In the next section, you will see how cross-cutting ties a story together.

Parallel editing (cross-cutting)

This method of cutting is to tie (usually) opposing scenes and cut between them. A classic example is where the innocence of children is juxtaposed with scenes from a violent bank robbery. The intention is to help the audience see both sides of a character's personality. Most of the time, these scenes will have been filmed with this purpose in mind, rather than you having to find media that happens to fit the parallel edit. Using the children and bank robbery example, imagine scenes of a father with his children in a playground. There, you would have the perfect opportunity to cross-cut to the robbery as a thought in the father's mind. There is no reason that you can't use the bank robbery scenes twice but consider the implications of a **spoiler** by showing the robbery scenes before the actual robbery happens.

J and L cuts

Up to now, we have looked at cutting video. J and L cuts are ways of smoothing a hard video cut by cutting the audio at a different time, thus tricking the audience's perception of the hard video cut.

J and L cuts just mean that the audio cuts either before or after the video is cut. It's called a J cut, or L cut, because the audio cut in the track below the video looks like the letter *J* or *L*.

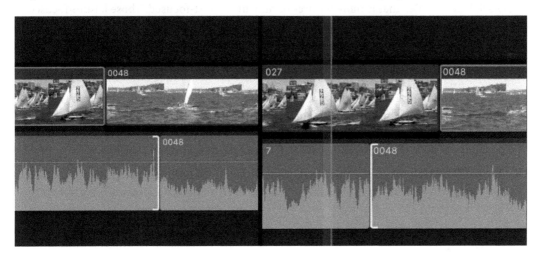

Figure 9.32 – A J cut (left) and L cut (right)

You will have seen, or more likely heard of, these types of cuts without noticing them – isn't not noticing a cut what it is all about? For example, in a scene of a rail tunnel, the train whistle might sound before you see the train in the next clip. That is a *J* cut.

Editing full-length movies and documentaries employs all of the preceding techniques, plus many more that you have looked at in different sections of this chapter. Also refer to *Chapter 5, Refining the Rough Cut*, where you will find more details about the pacing of a longer-length video. However, the techniques that you have seen in this section are thrown to the wolves in the next section, where the subtleties of pace and sophisticated cutting strategies are overlooked for the sake of portraying the most engaging information in the shortest amount of time, retaining the audience's attention before it is diverted to another video.

Social media videos

Social media videos are not just about the different vertical or square aspect ratios; the content is presented in a completely different way. You could use just one word to explain it – *fast*. But that misses the point. The cutting is done fast, but the real key to social media editing is to get the point across quickly. A social media audience is fickle, and once you understand that they will only stay to watch the video while their interest is piqued, you are on your way to knowing how to edit the material. It's easy to understand why they are so quick to switch to another video when you consider the millions of other videos at their disposal. See *Chapter 3, Planning the Video Story* about how to convert a 16x9 aspect ratio video to vertical or square and more details about the editing process.

It should be noted that the examples of social media videos in this section are marketing-focused. By marketing, I mean videos that promote a cause as well as sell ideas and products. There is a different type of social media video that is more leisure- or human-interest-focused. Those leisure-focused videos include cat and dog videos and fall into the family holiday category, which is explained later in the chapter.

There are several key elements to good social media videos:

- **Quickly producing a hook**: *Hook* is the term used for the part of the video that will grab the audience's attention and whet their appetite, causing them to stay watching longer. **Provide subtitles**, as social media is mostly used on mobile devices with the audio off or at least turned down. If you don't provide subtitles, some, if not all, of the message will be lost.

- The **call to action** should be early in the video. Don't wait until the end as you would in a conventional video, as a social media audience is likely to have stopped watching the video by then.

- **Produce templates** for the subtitles and the three-text panel format for vertical videos.

Figure 9.33 – A three-panel theme for vertical videos

- **Keep the production value low-key**. This doesn't mean making it sloppy; it's more about differentiating the video from a professionally produced TV commercial. Social media should have a flavor of the homegrown, rather than corporate money. You still need to be conscious of quality and readability, just without the razzmatazz.

Social media editing is hectic in the way that it cuts and adds wow effects to gain attention. The next section on family holiday movies also uses effects and transitions but in a much more relaxed way.

Family holiday movies

A family video should be kept low-key in terms of production value; it is about memories. The focus can be on the destination, but the real key to making the movie valuable as a future asset is to feature people. Your great-grandchildren are going to be more interested in how you dressed and reacted to situations than a long pan shot of the Tuscan valley. With this in mind, I feel it is appropriate, in this section, to talk about how the video should be filmed. If you are reading this section, then you are likely the sole editor as well as the shooter, so you need to have control over the media.

Let's look at some important points to keep in mind when shooting your travel movies.

It's easy to say that you should plan what you are going to film. Yes, you should, but you are on holiday, so what is likely to happen is that you will turn up at an interesting location and get the sudden urge to record the amazing architecture, a festival, a street scene, or any of the myriad reasons that a person picks up a camera.

An important rule to remember
Don't zoom. If you have zoomed, cut it out in the edit. Cut from the beginning of the zoom and start again at the end of the zoom.

Keep the shots of one scene relatively short, but don't cut early. Let the camera run just a little longer, after the main action, if people or animals are involved. Maybe after a troupe has ended their street acrobatics, someone from the crowd will jump out to try to reproduce the moves. Even better if it's one of your travel companions. It's those spontaneous moments that make the video compelling. However, you do need to keep the long pans of scenery to a minimum. A valley might look good to your eyes on the day, but a video will not do justice to wide-angle scenery. And did I mention, *don't zoom*!?

If you're recording your voice-over as a commentary, do a bit of research first, take your time, and don't rush the words. It's even better to interview a local; it shouldn't be intimidating to them, so *do* ask them first if you can record them.

Try not to just record the backs of your traveling companions. Position yourself in front of them before you hit the record button. Try to film them while they are unaware of the camera. Remember that you are trying to be spontaneous.

It's important to consider what you are recording in regard to audio. Think about wind noise. Try to protect the microphone with your body as a shield between it and the wind. If it's a windy day, it's a good idea to find a spot out of the wind to record a few minutes of nothing but audio. Record a voice-over at the beginning and end of the quiet audio with an explanation, saying something such as, "*ambient audio.*" Try to record ambient audio even if it's not a windy day. Finally, record close-ups, for the B roll, of items that have featured in other clips. You can never have too much B roll.

When you start editing, watch all the media in the Final Cut Pro browser. While reviewing the media in the browser, remove the bad footage, badly shaking camera footage, and shots of you walking when you forgot to hit the stop button. You can remove footage by selecting the section, then hovering and dragging with the skimmer, or by setting **in** and **out** points. When the section to be removed has a yellow outline, use the *Delete* key. The removed section is *not* deleted but in fact, stored in the **Rejected** category (see *Chapter 2, Organizing Media*).

When you reject a portion of a clip in the browser, the original clip is broken into separate sections, all with the same name as the original clip.

Figure 9.34 – After sections have been rejected in an original clip

Once you have created a new project, there are two courses of action. Either select all the media in the browser (*Command + A*) with the **Hide Rejected** filter selected and then press the *E* key or drag all the clips to the timeline.

Figure 9.35 – Hiding a rejected filter

The second method is to review all the clips in the browser before adding them to the new project. It's your decision depending on how you work best. Once the clips are all added to the timeline, edit and reorder them as usual. For family movies, you can be more adventurous with effects and transitions.

Don't forget the intro templates that ship with Final Cut Pro. There is a number under the **Bumper/ Opener** sidebar heading.

Figure 9.36 – The Bumper/Opener heading

For home movies, the most valuable title is **Date/Time** under the **Lower Third** sidebar heading – it extracts the date when the clip was filmed, so there is no need to try and find out when the video was shot.

If you want to use the date feature with another title, stack the two titles together. If you would like to use them frequently, create a **compound clip** of the two.

Figure 9.37 – Date/time in the lower third

It is best to make sure that the music that you add is royalty-free, even if the video is for personal use only. While on the subject of music, I find that most home movies have the music volume too high – just something to watch out for. This is an appropriate moment to move on to the next section, which discusses the specific editing requirements of a music video.

Cutting to a beat

Whether you are creating a music video or just want to match your cuts to a beat, there are several manual methods in Final Cut Pro. This is a useful procedure for slideshows or even short selections of similar or random video clips.

There are three different ways to mark beats, and these all involve you manually selecting the beats yourself. This is fine if you only want to create one or two projects; otherwise, I suggest that you look at software that will find the beat for you. See *Chapter 17, Supporting Software Applications for Final Cut Pro* for a review of **BeatMark Pro** (https://ulti.media/).

The first manual method is as follows:

1. Create a new project.

2. Select the music track in the browser and press the *Q* key. The music track will be added to the timeline as a connected clip, with a gray empty slug above.

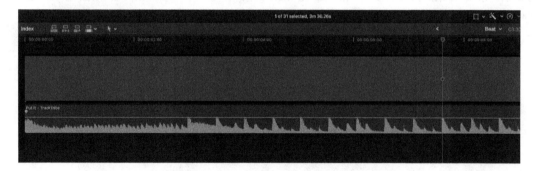

Figure 9.38 – A music track with a gray slug above

3. Zoom into the view so that you can see the beats. The first method is to add a marker, with the *M* key, to each peak of the beats you want to cut to. You can add markers by hovering over the next peak, or if you can recognize the beats quickly enough, you could play the video and press the *M* key on the fly.

4. Select the top music track to show the yellow outline. Duplicate the music track by dragging upward with the *Option* key held down. Position the top music track below the gray slug. Lower the volume level in the top music track (it's only being used as an empty track; you'll see why in a moment).

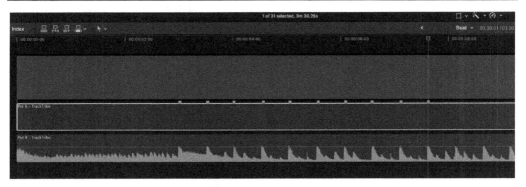

Figure 9.39 – The marker method

5. In the browser, select the first clip you want in the music video. It is best to set an in point at the frame you want the clip to start from. Make sure the empty music track is still selected. Change the filter to **Video Only**.

Figure 9.40 – Video Only selected

6. Hover over the first marker on the left. Press the *W* key. In the browser, select the in point of the second clip. Press the *W* key. The second clip cuts off the end of the first clip. Do the same for the third clip and so on. Each new clip added with the *W* key cuts the previous clip.

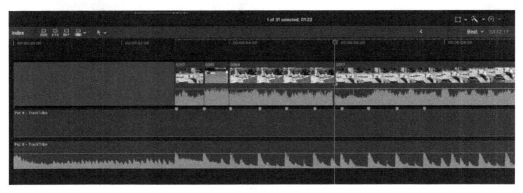

Figure 9.41 – Video added above the music track

The second method is much the same, except you don't need the two music clips and you blade the gray slug instead of adding a marker:

1. Add the music track, as in the first method (*Figure 9.38*).

2. In the browser, as in the first method, and change the filter to **Video Only** (*Figure 9.40*).

3. Select an in point and drag the clip inside the first cutout, and then select **Replace from Start**. Do the same for each of the other cutouts.

Figure 9.42 – Replace from Start

The third method takes a different approach to start with but still requires a manual input for each cut:

1. This time, add all of the video clips to the timeline first.

2. Change the filter to **Video Only**, as shown in *Figure 9.40*. You could select all in the browser and drag to the timeline or press the *E* key.

3. Next, drag the music clip below the video track or press the *Q* key. The music track will most likely be shorter than the video, but don't worry – you can add more video later or shorten the music track.

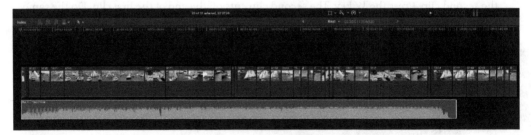

Figure 9.43 – All video clips added first before the audio

4. Zoom into the timeline and change the filter to **Video Only**, as shown in *Figure 9.40*.

5. Hover in the timeline over the first beat, and press *Option +]*. The end of the clip in the timeline will be cut and removed, even though it was not selected.

6. Move to the next beat and press *Option +]* again. If you would like the first part of the clip to be removed rather than the last, use *Option + [*.

Personally, I much prefer the third method.

The final workflows in this chapter are shorter techniques that you can use in conjunction with your general editing. Let's take a look at these general techniques in the next section.

General techniques

In this section, we will explore a range of general techniques that can complement our overall editing process.

Cutting angles with a green screen

Earlier in this chapter, in the *Interviews* section, you looked at the technique that uses 4K footage and allows you to zoom into an image by 50%, without losing quality in the 1080p timeline. With the image being 50% larger, you can, at the next cut, return **Scale (All)** to 100% and repeat the change from 100% to 150% for each alternative clip by using the **Paste Attributes** command. However, this is much more complex when the interview is filmed in front of a green screen. When a green screen is not involved, changing the angle to 150% also increases the size of the background to 150%. The same applies to the background when the cut is returned to the original size; the face and the background both return to 100%.

Figure 9.44 – 4K footage – 100% on the left and 150% on the right

The process changes dramatically when a green screen is introduced as a background, because the green screen is an individual clip positioned above a separate background clip. As shown in *Figure 9.45*, the green screen clip is the top clip in the primary storyline, so the transparent section allows the background clip below to show through. If the green screen clip is resized to 150%, the background will stay at 100%. When you cut the angle, you would also need to cut the background clip and resize that.

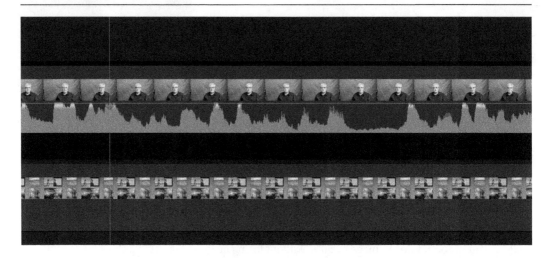

Figure 9.45 – Green screen as the top clip with a separate background clip below

I have come up with a method to duplicate the green screen and background into two clips, using the **Multicam** process to cut the angles. The procedure uses **Open Clip** in the **Clip** menu.

To explain the process, **Open Clip** allows a browser clip to be temporarily opened in the timeline. This gives you the ability to add any applicable effect or action to any clip in the timeline, including **Multicam**.

As shown in the following example, duplicate the original clip in the browser, and then, with the original clip still selected, pick **Open Clip** from the **Clip** menu. Then, drag the 100% background clip into the temporary timeline, which already has the 100% green screen clip.

Figure 9.46 – 100%-sized green screen and background clips in the temporary timeline
with a voice-over as well. The red lines represent the mask on the green screen clip

Next, select the duplicated clip in the browser and increase it in size to 150%. Then, with the resized duplicated clip still selected, pick **Open Clip** from the **Clip** menu. Then, drag the 150% background clip into the temporary timeline, which already has the 150% green screen clip.

So far, so good. The next step is to combine both the modified 100% and 150% clips into a multicam clip. In the browser, right-click on both the 100% and 150% clips as well as the separate audio and add them to a **New Multicam** clip. The two video clips line up, and the audio is synced.

Figure 9.47 shows the 100% and 150% tracks with separate audio in a multicam timeline.

Figure 9.47 – The two video clips with synced audio

Figure 9.48 shows the original 100% image (IMG_9449) on the left and the copy of IMG_9449 increased to 150% in the middle. The image on the right in the following figure is how the multicam thumbnail will appear in the browser.

Figure 9.48 – The 100% clip on the left, 150% in the middle, and a multicam of both on the right

Both 100%- and 150%-sized clips are cut as they would be with any multicam (see *Chapter 8, Setting Up and Editing Multicam*), and the background changes with the green screen at each cut.

The next technique, which is about the use of adjustment layers, is much simpler to implement.

Adding adjustment layers

Adjustment layers are added to the timeline toward the end of the edit. Their purpose is to modify or adjust any clips, including connected clips, that they cover. Mostly, they are used for color looks or themes that affect the whole video. Surprisingly, Final Cut Pro does not ship with an adjustment layer, which is similar to an empty title clip with no text. There are numerous free adjustment layers that you can download. They are all much the same. I recommend that you download this unique renamable adjustment layer from Eric Lenz: `https://ericlenz.photography/all-products/free-downloads`. The benefit is if you employ several layers with different categories of effects, they can be renamed.

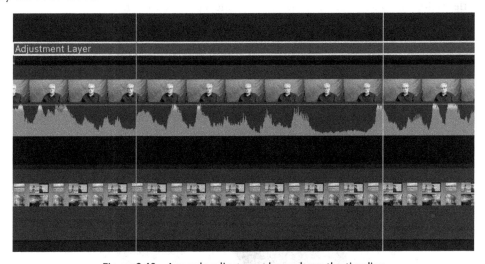

Figure 9.49 – A purple adjustment layer above the timeline

One of the main effects that you will add to an adjustment layer is the **Broadcast Safe** effect.

Broadcast Safe

Effects are added to an adjustment layer in exactly the same way as you would add them to any clip in the timeline. The **Broadcast Safe** effect is a common example of the use of an adjustment layer. It checks all clips below it to restrict the highlights luma to a level safe for broadcast.

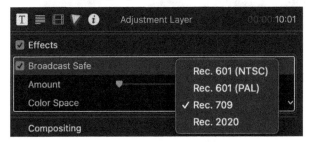

Figure 9.50 – Broadcast Safe selected for Rec. 709

Following the same theme of keeping things within legal limits, consider adding an audio limiter to an adjustment layer over the full timeline to restrict audio from peaking.

Safe zones

Other areas to keep items within legal limits are **safe zones**, which show the boundaries to keep text from running off the edge of a screen. This is not as important with digital TVs as it was previously when TV screens used analog cathode ray tubes that were subject to over-scanning. You should be aware that when words are cut off at the edge of the screen, even for a moment, they are always noticed by the audience. Conversely, actions, such as a hand being off-screen for a short time, are not noticed. **Show Title/Action Safe Zones** can be turned on from the top of the viewer.

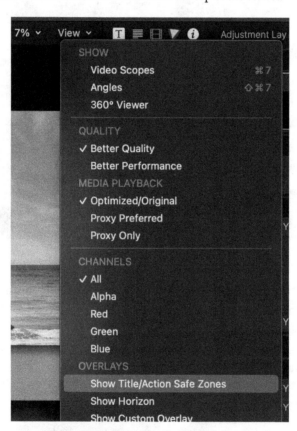

Figure 9.51 – Show Title/Action Safe Zones

The following section will give you some ideas on how to store frequently used logos, effects, graphics, titles, images, photos, and compound clips.

Storing callouts

When you are editing corporate videos, many of the elements are repeated in future videos. It is a real waste of time going back over previous work on archived disks, looking for a Final Cut Pro library with elements that you need to reuse. It is wise to store those frequently used elements so that you can easily access them. To some extent, Final Cut Pro gives you the ability to create **presets** of modified effects, such as color styles and looks, as well as standard audio adjustments, allowing you to quickly apply the adjusted effects from the **Effects** menu. The presets are created by selecting **Save Effects Preset** at the bottom of the **Inspector** window.

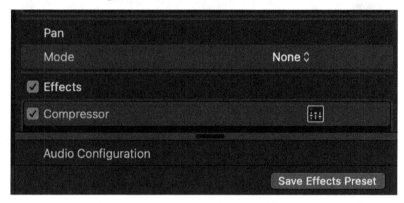

Figure 9.52 – Save Effects Preset at the bottom of the Inspector window

There are a vast number of different types of elements that can't be added to the presets that you will gather over time. You should have a mechanism to be able to store these resources quickly. Some of these elements are simple graphics for pointing out areas on the screen. These will include arrows and graphic elements. If you use these types of graphics, it's a good idea to acquire some commercially created plug-ins that include graphics. Search Google for the term `callouts` (see *Chapter 12, Using Third-Party Plug-Ins*). You could also create them yourself in Motion (see *Chapter 17, Supporting Software Applications for Final Cut Pro*).

The object of this section is not to explore what you need to store but how you store resources for easy future access. The simplest solution is to have a dedicated Final Cut Pro library that contains all the resources. Within that library, you will have separate events for the different types of elements. I've called my library `Callouts`, as that is the industry term, but it may be more useful for you to call yours `Resource Library`.

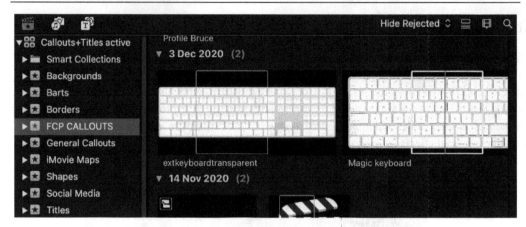

Figure 9.53 – The Callouts library for frequently used elements

Storing graphics and images in a separate library called `Callouts` keeps them available and easily accessible for future use. Even though installed titles are always available to Final Cut Pro, they contain the default fonts. The next section shows how to store modified fonts and text characteristics for future use.

Storing titles and corporate intros

A mention should be made of how you should store your frequently used titles, and compound clips that include titles. You may wonder why titles have their own event in the resource library when default titles are already available directly from the **Titles** category at the top of the browser area. The key to the difference is the word *default*. Whenever you use a title from the browser, it contains the default font and characteristics. As a corporate video editor, you will know that companies usually have a standard corporate font and even Pantone-specific colors. This is why the `Callouts` library is so important for future use because it retains the adjusted font and colors.

More importantly, when it comes to complex introduction opener titles, there will be drop zones that have been filled as well as some elements contained in compound clips. The compound clips are ideal for keeping complex graphics and titles grouped together to be viewed as a single item.

If you are a Photoshop user or have worked in Motion, you will be aware of how valuable layers are. Think of a compound clip as a single reusable container that includes layers. When used in the timeline, a compound clip is just a single clip.

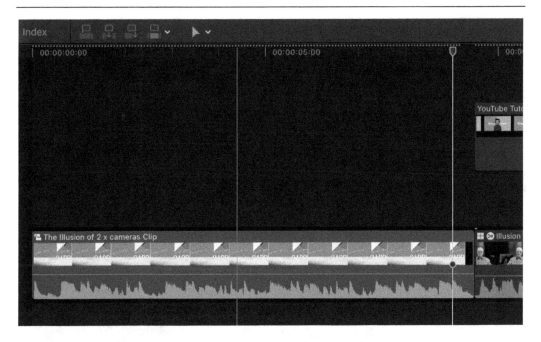

Figure 9.54 – A compound clip as a single clip in the timeline

As a bonus, every compound clip is added as an original clip in the browser, so it can be added to any other library, such as the new `Callouts` library you have just created.

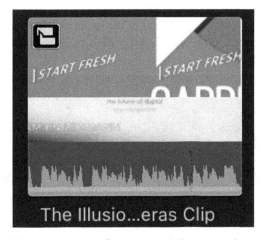

Figure 9.55 – The browser view of a compound clip icon in the top-left corner

To see the layers within a compound clip, double-click on it in the timeline. Compound clips can contain other compound clips. You can see the layers that can be reordered as needed.

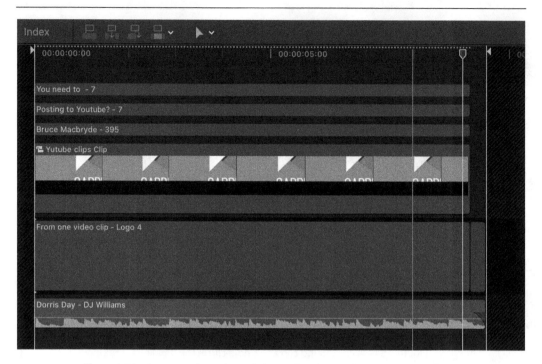

Figure 9.56 – An opened compound clip, with another compound clip inside it

As noted earlier, compound clips are designed for reuse, but to be very clear, if you make any changes within a compound clip, in all instances where that compound clip has been used or will be used, changes will be made there as well. The solution to this is simple. Only include titles within the compound clip that have fixed text elements. Any title with text elements that change should be kept separate from the compound clip.

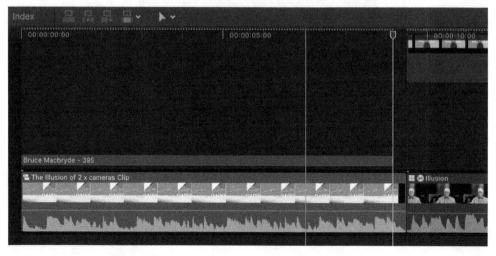

Figure 9.57 – The same compound clip used in Figure 9.54 with a separate title above

This is where the `Callouts` library is important. You can keep the compound clip along with its separate changeable title for future use.

Your resources library, whether you call it `Callouts` or otherwise, will become your go-to library, which will always be open no matter what other library you are working on in Final Cut Pro.

The next and final section in this chapter outlines the different ways of focusing on different areas of the computer screen using workspaces, helping you to see more of the Final Cut Pro interface that is important to you whenever necessary.

Using workspaces

This workflow chapter would not be complete without mention of Final Cut Pro's built-in and modifiable **workspaces**. The way you view the Final Cut Pro interface can be adjusted to feature different parts of the screen, allowing you to concentrate on a particular subject when other parts of the screen may not be as important. The edges of various panels in the interface can be dragged to increase the size of one panel while reducing the size of the neighboring panel. When you select the dividing edge, the cursor changes to a double-sided arrow, allowing you to drag to increase the size. *Figure 9.58* shows where the viewer has been increased in size at the expense of the browser:

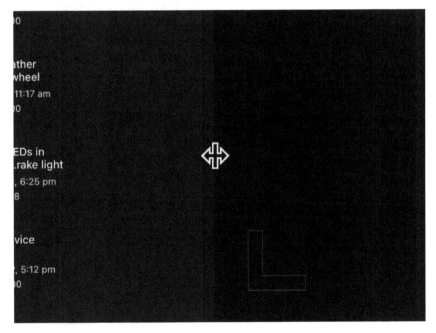

Figure 9.58 – A double-sided arrow

As well as adjusting your own sizes, you can also select default workspaces from the window menu and have the ability to save your modified workspaces as presets. *Figure 9.59* shows previously saved presets, the built-in workspaces, and the **Save Workspace as…** selection, as well as the option to open the folder that contains the saved presets and even a copy to be used on another Mac.

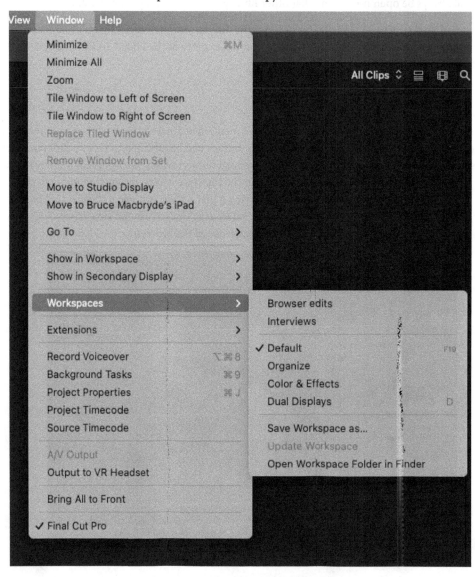

Figure 9.59 – Workspaces with Default selected

There are two other similar interface view options you should be aware of. **Show in Workspace** gives you the ability to show or remove selected panels. For instance, when you are editing a multicam in the timeline, you will not need to see the browser, so it can be removed from the screen to give more space for the angles in the viewer and timeline.

Figure 9.60 – The browser hidden

The second interface option is to place a selected panel on a second monitor. *Figure 9.60* shows the browser placed on a second monitor. When a second monitor is attached, an extra icon of overlapping screens appears above the **Inspector** window, as shown in the right-hand screenshot in *Figure 9.61*.

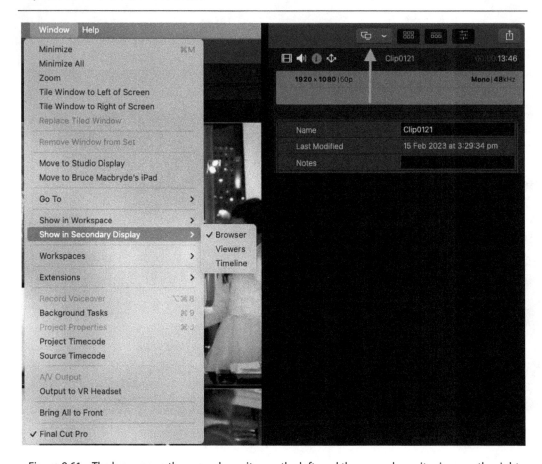

Figure 9.61 – The browser on the second monitor on the left, and the second monitor icon on the right

The use of workspaces and a second monitor will allow you to focus on the parts of the Final Cut Pro interface that are currently being used for editing.

The next section is not in itself a workflow in the strict sense of the word. It is more a method of rationalizing a complex timeline in a way that avoids the visual confusion that can arise with multitudes of connected clips.

Collapsing clips into connected storylines

A time-saver in editing complex timelines was introduced with version 10.7 of Final Cut Pro, giving you the ability to group a selection of clips connected to the main storyline, even though they might overlap and not be contiguous to each other.

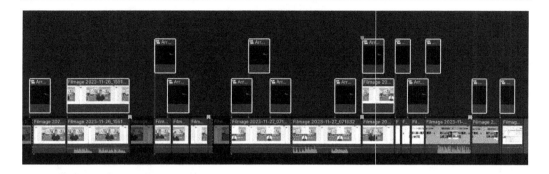

Figure 9.62 – Connected clips before collapsing

The other advantage of the **Collapse to Connected Storyline** feature is collapsing clips that are currently independent, as well as those previously grouped into a secondary storyline.

Clips grouped with the **Collapse to Connected Storyline** feature can be moved as a single item or copied and pasted elsewhere.

Prior to version 10.7, connected clips needed to be trimmed so that they did not overlap before they could be grouped. To understand the **Collapse to Connected Storyline** feature, think of it as applying a compound clip and automatically trimming the overlaps, as well as maintaining the gaps between noncontiguous clips.

Select the connected clips that you want to group, even though they might overlap with each other. Right-click and select **Collapse to Connected Storyline**. The overlaps are then trimmed, and the timeline is much tidier and easier to work with.

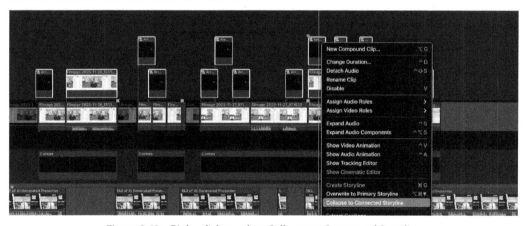

Figure 9.63 – Right-click to select Collapse to Connected Storyline

In addition to the ability to group clips that are next to each other, the **Collapse to Connected Storyline** feature also maintains any gaps between clips and includes gap clips to maintain the timing of the storyline, while maintaining the visibility of the storyline below the new connected storyline.

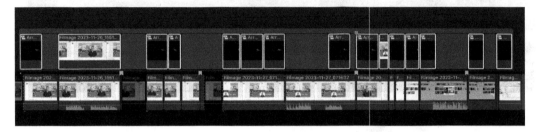

Figure 9.64 – Connected clips after collapsing, showing the gap clips

If you try to ungroup the connected storyline with the **Break Apart Clip** Items option from the **Clip** menu, any clips that previously overlapped will stay trimmed. To return to exactly how the clips were placed, you will need to use the **Undo** command (*Command + Z*).

> **Note**
> Do not include titles for a group of clips where you intend to use the **Collapse to Connected Storyline** feature. A title will be treated as a video clip and the clip below the title will be trimmed.

Summary

This has been a long chapter that I'm sure will have tested your dedication. Not all of the techniques and editing methods will be of use to you now, but many will be in later projects, so there is a good reason for you to review them all – it is very likely that you will encounter a time, in the future, where you will need to employ these techniques.

You learned the specific editing techniques for interview videos. If there is just one section that you should have read through in detail, that is the one, as it covers a broad spectrum of techniques that you will need to use in other workflows.

After you read through the *Interviews* section, you learned about specific workflows for conferences and seminars, as well as the formality of wedding videos. They are the training ground of many professional full-time editors, as the different procedures represent a microcosm of virtually all editing styles and influences. Some sections are dialogue-based, and others are music-based. These are the formal events that help build multicam expertise.

Reading through this chapter will also expose you to the experienced formal cutting styles of continuity editing, along with cross-cutting and J and L cuts, which we discussed in the *Full-length movies and documentaries* section.

Completely different from all other styles is social media editing.

You were shown how to shoot better home movies and the simple and fun ways to edit these with the whole family in mind, particularly considering how rewatching a home movie is usually done to see the people involved rather than the scenery.

Music video production, by concentrating on the beat, was covered, where you learned how to mark peaks so that the video clip matched the beat of the music.

In the *General techniques* section, you learned about some short workflow methods that will help with specific situations you may encounter. You were shown the benefits of adjustment layers and the legal limits that need to be imposed for broadcast-destined video. There was also a discussion on the benefits of creating a resources library to store frequently used callout elements for future use.

The last section covered the workspace options in Final Cut Pro, which give you the ability to focus on just certain parts of the screen.

The next chapter focuses on the **Inspector** window's controls and examines where you will make adjustments to the plug-ins and effects that have been added to the timeline.

Part 3:
Using the Inspector

Part 3 explores how the Inspector modifies the **Effects** and **Color** options for both built-in and third-party plug-ins. The Inspector is the go-to place for adjusting the default plug-ins for both video and audio, as well as all modifications to clips in the timeline. The Inspector also lists information about the source of media, as well as where libraries are located on a computer.

This part contains the following chapters:

- *Chapter 10, The Inspector Controls*
- *Chapter 11, Using Built-In Plug-ins*
- *Chapter 12, Using Third-Party Plug-ins*
- *Chapter 13, Using Keyframes to Animate Objects*
- *Chapter 14, Understanding the Principles of Color*
- *Chapter 15, Using Color Scopes for Advanced Color Correction*

The Inspector Controls

This chapter and the next go hand in hand as they both discuss plug-ins and how they are adjusted in the inspector, which is the key to defining the look and feel of the edit. If anything in the timeline or browser needs to be adjusted, you need to check out the inspector first.

Specifically, in this chapter, you will learn about the finer details of the inspector. Think of it as *inspecting the inspector*. You will learn how the inspector is divided into four main sections: **Video**, **Color**, **Audio**, and **Information**. Each of these main sections is accessed via a tab at the top of the **inspector** panel. A temporary tab will appear when needed to allow access to titles and generators.

While there is a basic view of the inspector visible all the time, you will discover that the inspector is dynamic. It changes when different effects are being adjusted and different items are selected in either the **browser** or **timeline**; this is known as context-sensitive behavior.

You will learn that there are different ways to adjust the settings in the inspector: sometimes with the use of sliders and sometimes with dials. There is always an alternative method of adjustment, which offers the most accurate control: typing in number values rather than making a freeform adjustment with a dial or slider.

In this chapter, we're going to cover the following main topics:

- The four main tabs of the inspector
- The Video inspector
- The Color inspector
- The Audio inspector
- The Information inspector
- The Titles inspector
- The Text inspector
- The Generator inspector
- The Transition inspector

By the end of this chapter, you will have a comprehensive knowledge of the regular settings in the inspector and will know how to make adjustments using the multitude of ways offered by different plug-in effects when they are viewed in the inspector.

You will understand that the inspector is not just one panel but rather an interface location for the four main panels – **Video**, **Color**, **Audio**, and **Information** – selected using their respective tabs. There are also special panels for the specific needs of titles, text, and generators that have tabs that show only when they are needed.

The four main tabs of the inspector

The four main tabs of the inspector will be visible when a clip with audio is selected in the **timeline** window. From the left, the four tabs represent video adjustments, color, audio, and information. The following figure has the **Video** tab selected for a **timeline** clip – represented as a filmstrip icon in blue.

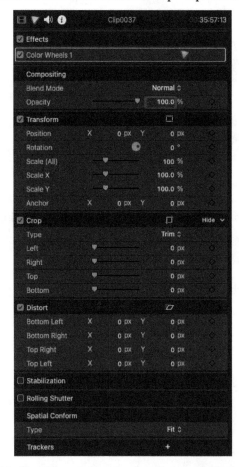

Figure 10.1 – The Video tab for a timeline clip selected in the inspector

You will see different sets of tabs when you select a clip in the **browser** as, essentially, only audio can be adjusted in a **browser** clip. When you choose a **browser** clip and select the filmstrip icon, only **Spatial Conform** shows. This will be explained later in the chapter.

Figure 10.2 – Only Spatial Conform is offered for a browser clip

The following figure shows the **Audio** tab (represented by a speaker icon in blue) when a **browser** clip is selected:

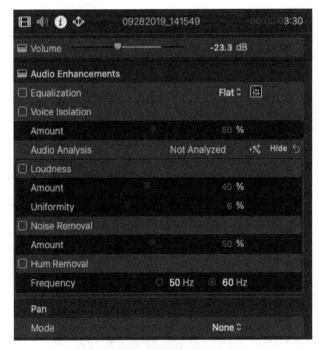

Figure 10.3 – The Audio tab selected in the inspector

The **inspector** is activated using the button at the top right of the Final Cut Pro interface, no matter which tab is selected. This is shown in blue in the following figure:

Figure 10.4 – The inspector is activated with the right-hand button

By default, the **inspector** panel will fill the top right of the Final Cut Pro interface. If you need to see more content in the inspector, you can make it fill the whole right-hand side of the interface by double-clicking the clip name at the top, and vice versa to return to normal full size. If the **inspector** panel is at full size, it pushes aside the **Effects** and **Transitions** browsers, if they are open, shortening the **timeline** view. The following figure shows the clip name (indicated with the red arrow) and the **Effects** browser shortening the **timeline** view.

Figure 10.5 – Full-sized inspector

In the next section, we will discuss the first tab, the **Video** inspector.

The Video inspector

As you can see in *Figure 10.1*, the **Video** inspector is divided into multiple sections. In this subsection, we will go over these sections and understand their uses.

Section 1 – Effects

At the top is the **Effects** heading, which displays any effects that have been added to the **timeline** clip from the **Effects** browser. I have applied the **50s TV** effect in the following figure:

Figure 10.6 – The 50s TV effect

While most of the effects will be color-based, be prepared for non -standard options to appear, such as the **Neat Video Reduce Noise** effect that has additionally been installed via a plug-in. In the following figure, you can see that **Neat Video** opens its own control panel:

Figure 10.7 – The Neat Video Reduce Noise panel

If you look back at *Figure 10.1*, you will see that **Color Wheels**, **Compositing**, and **Blend Mode** are also under the **Effects** heading. **Blend Mode** is used to merge the contents of the **Primary Storyline** clip with any clip connected below it on the timeline – for example, a **Primary Storyline** clip with a colored background below it. The following figure has the **Add** blend mode selected, visually merging the blue background with the **Primary Storyline** clip.

Figure 10.8 – Blue blend added

Below the **Blend Mode** adjustment is an **Opacity** slider to change the opacity of the selected clip so that more or less of the connected clip below will show through. In the example shown in *Figure 10.8*, the resulting image will be bluer if the **Opacity** slider is moved to the left; the more transparent the **Primary Storyline** clip becomes, the more the blue clip below shows through.

Note – Hide and Show options

If you don't see the selection you are looking for, you can try and make it visible by hovering the mouse pointer on the button to unhide the **Show** menu. The **Show** option can be seen in *Figure 10.9*.

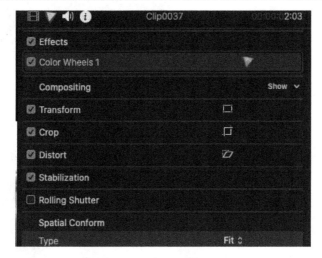

Figure 10.9 – Show/Hide sections

Section 2 – Transform

Transform has fine numerical controls for transforming a clip in the **timeline**.

Note

In the inspector, if you don't see the **Show** menu, then hovering the mouse over the position where the **Show** button should be visible will display the **Show** menu. Double-clicking on that button will open the **Show** menu.

You will be familiar with transforming an image in the viewer by selecting the blue dots at the outer edge or rotating with the center dot. Those rough-and-ready dragging adjustments are finely reproduced in the inspector by adjusting the number values next to **Position**, **Rotation**, and **Scale**:

Figure 10.10 – Image transformed and rotated

Sections 3 and 4 – Crop and Distort

These two sections share a similar type of adjustment. The **Crop** sliders allow you to make changes to the left, right, top, and bottom dimensions. In the **Distort** section, the **X** and **Y** adjustments alter the horizontal and vertical angles respectively.

All the adjustments can be keyframed for animation; see *Chapter 13*, for more details. In the following figure, all keyframes have been highlighted to show their position in the **inspector**.

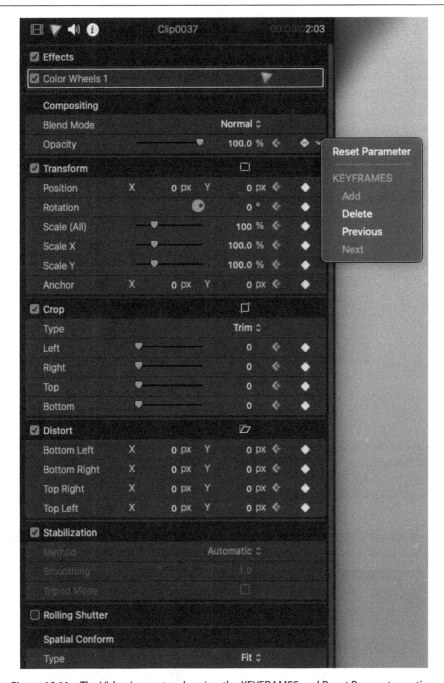

Figure 10.11 – The Video inspector showing the KEYFRAMES and Reset Parameter options

All settings can be returned to their original values by selecting the downward chevron and clicking **Reset Parameter**.

Sections 5 and 6 – Stabilization and Rolling Shutter

These sections are discussed together because they relate to camera footage. Video taken with a handheld camera will be shaky and wobbly, no matter how stable you think you have held the camera. It all comes down to whether the shaking is observable in the edit. The **Stabilization** control in the **inspector** will help reduce the shaking, but it will not remove it completely. However, it will possibly reduce it enough to be unnoticeable. **Stabilization** is not a magic bullet, though: if the shaking is too severe, the shakes will still be noticeable, and the clip will possibly look worse than the original footage if **Stabilization** is added. Even worse is what happens when there is a dramatic movement of the camera, as perhaps when filming from a boat or a car driving over a bump. **Stabilization** will cause a significant blur where the camera jumps.

Some adjustments can be made to cater to different types of shakes and shudders. Once you check the **Stabilization** checkbox, you will be warned that the dominant motion is being analyzed. It is best to wait for this to be completed before moving on:

Figure 10.12 – Analyzing for dominant motion…

> **Note**
>
> When a video is stabilized, the image will appear to have increased in size. The reason is that it is rotated to smooth the shaking, leaving blank spaces at the corners; to avoid showing these blank spaces, the image is automatically resized. The increase in size will vary depending on how much stabilization is required.

By default, **Stabilization** is not checked. When checked, it will be activated with the **Automatic** mode. The settings relate to whether the movement is vertical, horizontal, or rotational.

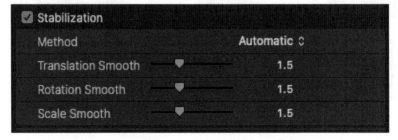

Figure 10.13 – Stabilization default setting

The type of **smoothing** to choose depends on whether the shaking motion is rotational, from left to right, or up and down. What you are looking for is to have the main subject as stable as possible without the background appearing to wobble. **Translation Smooth** corrects the amount of horizontal and vertical movement in the original image. **Rotation Smooth** is for the correction of wobbles. **Scale Smooth** allows the adjustment of the amount of resizing that has been automatically applied. You will need to try out the different options to get an optimal result.

> **Note**
>
> If the video is of a person in front of a plain background, be careful that the **Stabilization** adjustment doesn't stabilize the main subject and wobble the background. There is no ability to choose which object should be stabilized.

If there is little shaking in the video, you won't see the **Translation Smooth**, **Rotation Smooth**, and **Scale Smooth** options. There will be only a single **Smoothing** option, and if you have a very stable video, there will be the option to select **Tripod Mode**, which fixes the movement even further. If **Tripod Mode** is grayed out, it means that the image is not stable enough for it to be effective.

Figure 10.14 – Smoothing only with Tripod Mode selectable

You can select a further **Stabilization** method by clicking on the right-hand side of the window and choosing **InertiaCam** instead of **Automatic**, which can help when there is a higher motion level. You can return to the **Smoothing** options by selecting **SmoothCam**:

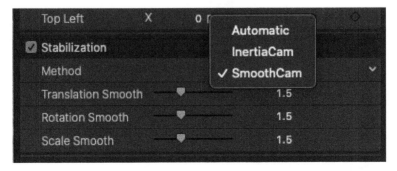

Figure 10.15 – SmoothCam selected

Stabilization is the most-used control for handheld videos; however, depending on the camera used and, to a large extent, the amount of movement in the video, **Rolling Shutter** may need to be corrected.

Rolling Shutter occurs when a camera's sensor scans an image that has different movements happening at the instant the shutter closes. In other words, not all parts of the scene are recorded at exactly the same instant and the image sensor continues to collect photons during acquisition. The result produces distortions of fast-moving objects and aliasing at the edge of the video. You can attempt to remove the resulting artifacts with a choice of strengths:

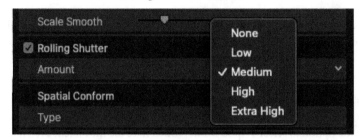

Figure 10.16 – The Rolling Shutter correction strength levels

Section 7 – Spatial Conform

This last section is principally for changing the aspect ratio of a non-conforming clip to fit the current aspect ratio of the viewer. For instance, if you add a 5 x 4 photograph to the timeline, by default, it will be set to **Fit**, meaning it will be shown in the viewer at its original aspect ratio. By using **Spatial Conform** and selecting **Fill**, the photo will fill the shape of the viewer while retaining its proportions. It will have the top and bottom cut off. In *Figure 10.17*, you can see a checkerboard background in the top image, and the bottom image fills the viewer, hiding the checkerboard, but some of the top and bottom are cut off.

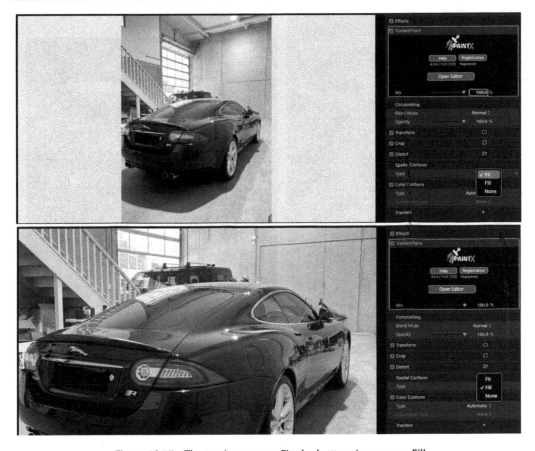

Figure 10.17 – The top image uses Fit; the bottom image uses Fill

There is one other option you will see at the bottom of the **Video** inspector, called **Trackers**. It allows objects to be tracked in the viewer. See *Chapter 12* for more details on this.

With the actions of the **Video** inspector under your belt, the next section discusses the **Color** inspector.

The Color inspector

To activate the **Color** inspector, click the triangle next to the video filmstrip. The triangle will become multicolored. When a newly added clip is selected in the **timeline**, the **Color** inspector will show the color correction preference as checked in the Final Cut Pro **Settings/Preferences** (see *Chapter 2*). The color triangle shows the color wheels, but it could optionally show the color board if that has been set in **Settings/Preferences**.

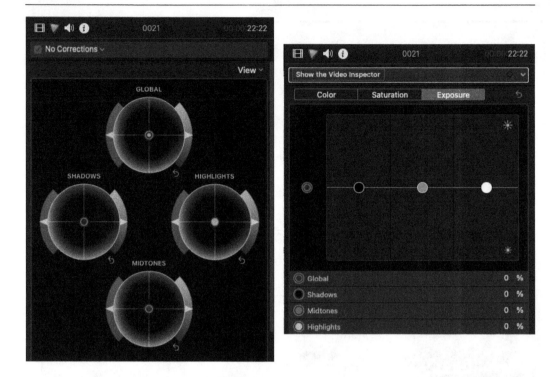

Figure 10.18 – Left: Color wheels; Right: Color board

A detailed explanation of color correction is in *Chapter 14*; however, to give you a tour of the inspector settings, I will cover the **Color** inspector controls here. As shown in *Figure 10.18*, there are two sets of basic color controls that both achieve the same results. As stated, the preferred set will show as the default when setting it up in **Settings/Preferences**. You can change the selection and select all of the color control panels from the **No Corrections** drop-down menu:

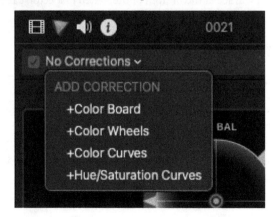

Figure 10.19 – Four sets of color control panels

The +**Color Curves** and +**Hue/Saturation Curves** options are detailed in *Chapter 15*. For now, I will only discuss the +**Color Board** and +**Color Wheels** options. **Color Board** was the original set of controls first released with Final Cut Pro X 1.0 in April 2011, and **Color Wheels** was added with version 10.4.1 in April 2018. In the next subsections, we will see how they differ and which one is more appropriate for which types of users.

Color Board

Color Board is certainly the easier to understand of the two sets and will suit an inexperienced user of Final Cut Pro, at least in the early stage of their learning. **Color Board** more clearly covers the logic of working one step at a time, following the conventional order of procedure:

- **Exposure**
- **Saturation**
- **Color**

Because each of these has its own tabs and associated panels, a new user is not tempted to mix the three steps out of order, as they could do with the **Color Wheels** combined panel.

When **Color Board** is first called up, it defaults to the **Exposure** tab, which is the correct place to start:

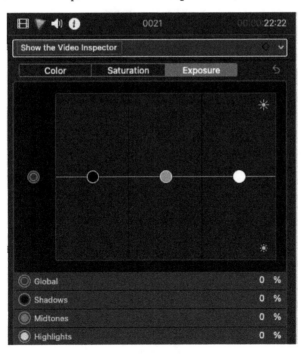

Figure 10.20 – The Exposure tab selected

There are four pucks in the center of the panel: from the right, we have **Highlights** (brightness), **Midtones**, **Shadows** (blacks), and **Global**, which controls the other three pucks. When working with **Exposure**, you should temporarily put color out of your mind and think of black and white, or more appropriately, shades of gray. **Highlights** are white, **Midtones** are gray, and **Shadows** are black.

The Exposure tab

You should look at the image and imagine it in grayscale, and then adjust the pucks by eye. Don't worry about scopes for the moment, as they will be discussed in *Chapter 15*.

If you have trouble imagining the image as grayscale, do the following until you get used to the idea. Select the **Saturation** tab and drag the **Global** puck all the way down. Return to the **Exposure** panel. Don't forget to adjust it back when you have completed the **Exposure** procedure.

> **Note**
>
> The three tonal ranges (**Highlights**, **Midtones**, and **Shadows**) overlap each other, so when you move one, you also move some of the tones in the other two.

Moving a puck up increases the associated tonal range, and moving it down decreases it. The four pucks also have numerical adjustments at the bottom of the panel; as you move a puck, the numbers will move too. The numbers are for finer control, which is extremely important with color correction.

I have a saying: "*A little bit is too much.*" I'm sure you get the idea – subtlety is the key. I would avoid using the **Global** puck in the **Exposure** panel until you are fully conversant with color correction or when you are using this panel in conjunction with color scopes, which you would typically use to measure, in a scientific way, what the eye does not see. Information about color scopes can be found in *Chapter 15*.

The following are some general rules of thumb. **Highlights** will represent the sky. **Midtones** will always affect flesh tones, no matter what the nationality. Treat **Shadows** as the word itself implies: anything that is darker and shaded from the subject.

> **Tip**
>
> The more you drag the **Shadows** puck down, the more contrast you will add to the image. Avoid dragging **Shadows** upward as that will add grain to the image.

It could be said that **Exposure** is the most important thing to get right. Think of it as the foundation for all the other settings you can make with color correction. If you don't get **Exposure** right, the others will certainly be incorrect. When you are happy with the **Exposure** settings, select the **Saturation** tab.

The Saturation tab

With **Exposure** fixed, you will find that **Saturation** will most likely need very little adjustment. What you have learned with the **Exposure** controls is replicated in the **Saturation** tab. You may consider the **Global** puck in this panel. Remember the rules set out in the previous section: subtlety is the key.

> **Tip**
> DSLR cameras tend to oversaturate an image, so you could reduce saturation for those clips.

The final tab is **Color**, and it is discussed in the next section.

The Color tab

The **Color** panel is laid out slightly differently than the other two. The pucks work the same, but the results are quite different. Yes, moving a puck up above the line increases the color, but moving a puck below the line introduces a different color. That color is, in fact, the opposing color in the color spectrum to the one above the line. This can be a little disconcerting to someone who is not aware of the principles of color. See *Chapter 14* for more information.

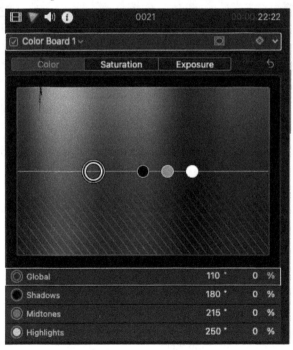

Figure 10.21 – The Color panel of Color Board

Once you have followed the procedure to adjust each panel in the sequence that I have suggested, you should now go back to each panel and balance the settings to achieve the optimal result.

I always find that if I need to make major changes in the **Color** panel, it is highly recommended to leave the edit until after a cup of tea, and then come back with fresh eyes. It's even better to leave it overnight before returning to check the color correction.

Finally, if you are having issues with trying to match a color or just feel that you have overdone your adjustments of any panels, I recommend that you scrap what you have done.

As it is not part of the inspector itself, I have not discussed the **Match Color...** option that is actioned from the magic wand icon under the viewer. This is very useful to achieve a starting point to match one clip with another. The magic wand is explained in detail in *Chapter 14*.

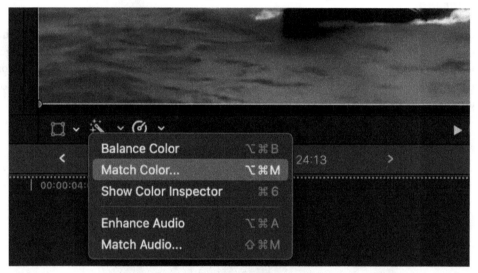

Figure 10.22 – The Match Color... magic wand option

Rather than trying to fix something that has become flawed, it's better to start again. You can use the curly arrow at the top right of each panel to reset that panel:

Figure 10.23 – Curly arrow

Color Board will do all of the color correction that you could need outside of using the color scopes and curves. The next section looks at the alternative set of controls for basic color correction: **Color Wheels**.

Color Wheels

The wheels are maybe a little harder to get started with, but they have the advantage of having all of the settings you saw in the **Color Board** section in one panel so that you can balance out the different settings without having to move between the panels as with **Color Board**. The downside is you need to be strict with yourself to work through the sequence – **Exposure**, **Saturation**, and **Color**, as outlined in the previous section – before balancing them all up.

In addition to **Color Wheels** are the **Temperature**, **Tint**, and **Hue** controls, as well as **Mix**, which combines the source image before correction with the corrected image so you can fine-tune the balance. These are all discussed in *Chapter 14*.

The major advantage that **Color Wheels** has is that the changes in all three attributes (**Exposure**, **Saturation**, and **Color**) can be keyframed so that the adjustments will appear in your video over time. This is very useful when dealing with outside footage when the sun goes behind clouds and then emerges again. This is something that is not possible with **Color Board**, where the changes you make affect the whole clip. The workaround is that you need to cut the clip with the blade tool when using **Color Board**, with the resulting jump cut from one color to another needing a B roll.

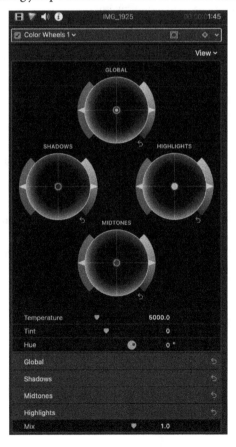

Figure 10.24 – Color Wheels

The principle of the action sequence of **Exposure** first, then **Saturation**, and finally, **Hue** is the same with **Color Wheels**. There are four wheels that each have **Exposure**, **Saturation**, and **Hue** built in. Notice that **Hue** is a different term to **Color** as used in **Color Board**. It subtly works differently in that it introduces a hue rather than adding or subtracting a color. The advantage of using **Hue** rather than adding a color is that you are changing all the colors in that particular range without introducing a single color.

In the next subsections, we will take a detailed look into these different color wheels.

The Highlights, Midtones, Shadows, and Global wheels

I will begin by explaining the **Highlights** wheel, and the details I provide will apply identically to each of the other wheels:

- The curved bar on the right of the wheel is gray. This works like the puck, and just like in **Color Board**, moving up increases the brightness, and moving down decreases it.

- To the left of the wheel, the blue curved bar increases/decreases the saturation.

- The center puck can be moved to increase the hue. Drag to the right to introduce a blue hue. Drag to the left to introduce a green hue. Drag up to introduce red. Drag down to introduce teal.

All of what you have done with the **Highlights** wheel is the same for the **Midtones**, **Shadows**, and **Global** wheels.

Color wheels have better control of what you can reset compared to **Color Board**, where the curly arrow resets everything in the panel. The color wheels let you double-click any arrow or center puck to just reset those parameters, or the curly arrow to reset the whole wheel.

Next, we will look at the different options below these color wheels and understand how they work.

Temperature, Tint, Hue, and Mix

Below the wheels are controls for **Temperature, Tint, Hue,** and **Mix**. The **Temperature** control provides colder tones when dragging to the left and warmer tones when dragging to the right. Dragging the **Tint** adjustment to the left adds green, and introduces magenta to the right.

You can add hues with the center puck to each range of tones, and the rotating **Hue** control shifts all the hues in the clip.

Finally, **Mix** uses the source clip before correction and mixes it with the correction, giving you that final balance.

Color correction is a vast area of expertise, and the specific techniques are discussed in *Chapter 14* and *Chapter 15*.

In the next section, we will look at the **Audio** inspector.

The Audio inspector

Chapter 7, discussed how to work with audio in the editing process, but it didn't focus on how audio effects are selected and adjusted in the **Audio** inspector. This section looks at the grouping of audio effects and how their position is important in the structure of the **Audio** inspector.

At first view, the **Audio** inspector appears much more complex than the other **inspector** panels. The reason for this is that there are more audio enhancements included by default. These effects must be applied to the video before the other effects are added from the **Effects** browser.

The **Audio** inspector allows adjustments to clips both from the **browser** and the **timeline**, unlike the **Video** inspector, which only works with **timeline** clips.

Figure 10.25 – Audio inspector

The big difference you will notice between the **Video** inspector and the **Audio** inspector is that the added effects are at the bottom of the **Audio** inspector, and at the top of the **Video** inspector, which emphasizes what I mentioned before: the order in which effects are added can be critical. The first heading is **Audio Enhancements**, which is discussed in the next section.

Audio Enhancements

You should adjust these enhancements only if you feel the audio in the **timeline** clip needs improvement. The same applies to any effects that you add, be they video or audio. I will discuss each option in the order in which they appear within the **Audio** inspector.

Equalization

As you would with your home hi-fi system, you can enhance certain audio frequencies to your taste. There are several presets, as well as a conventional graphic equalizer, which is selected with the small square icon to the right of **Flat**.

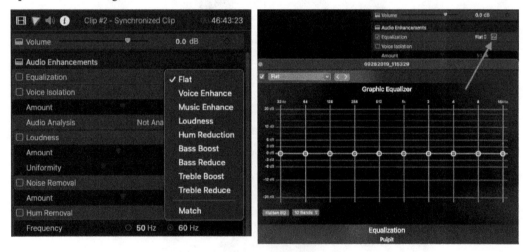

Figure 10.26 – Left: Equalization options; Right: Equalizer selector

Voice Isolation

While this is just a simple slider, if you need to remove any other sound than the human voice, it is the most effective of all the enhancements, including any external plug-ins. To say it is magic is not far from the truth. By default, the slider will be set to **50%**. It can be moved up much higher for the removal of loud noises without destroying a voiceover.

On occasion, I have had to take **Voice Isolation** to **100%** to remove the noise of an aircraft passing overhead while still allowing a reasonable-sounding voiceover. The control has mixed results for various wind noises. **Voice Isolation** seems to work on quickly changing frequencies, as opposed to the consistent noise pattern that the **Noise Removal** enhancement requires. **Noise Removal** is discussed later in this chapter.

Voice Isolation is well worth your primary consideration.

In the next section, we will discuss **Audio Analysis**, which can be set to activate automatically on import, or you can ask for audio to be analyzed after import in the **Audio** inspector.

Audio Analysis

Three categories are analyzed by **artificial intelligence** (**AI**) to give you a sound bed to work from, allowing you to add to the results of the automatic process. To set the process in motion, all it requires is to press the magic wand icon. You will see spinning wheels next to each of the sections, and after analysis, you will see either a green tick or an orange warning triangle. The required categories will be ticked, as seen in *Figure 10.27*:

Figure 10.27 – No problems detected in Audio Analysis

As a reminder, you should be aware of how to set the analysis when the video is being imported, and we will see how to do it in the next section.

Analyzing audio on import

When you open the import window, there are choices to analyze the audio in the right-hand sidebar – select **Fix audio problems**. Personally, I don't recommend using this function, but those with limited audio knowledge should be aware of the facilities for a quick fix. The **Fix audio problems** option can also be set up in **Preferences/Settings**.

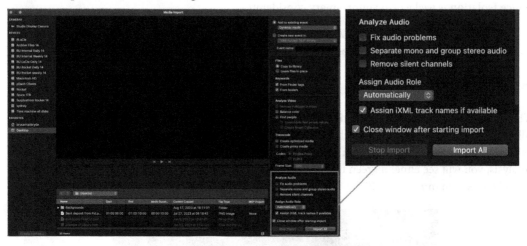

Figure 10.28 – Left: Import window; Right: Expanded view of Analyze Audio

Explanations of the three categories – **Loudness, Noise Removal**, and **Hum Removal** – follow in the next subsections.

Loudness

Loudness is different from adjusting the volume in that it adds compression to the audio. Increasing the volume just makes the audio louder without adjusting the dynamic range.

> **Note**
> Compression is where the lower levels are increased while the higher levels are normalized or decreased to give a better balance between the two.

The **Amount** slider increases or decreases the overall compression of the audio, and the **Uniformity** slider increases or decreases the dynamic range affected. When **Loudness** is ticked, the default setting is **40%** for **Amount** and **6%** for **Uniformity**.

Noise Removal

This setting gives different results for the **Voice Isolation** control in that it works best on consistent sounds and does not focus on the voice only. It is good for removing ambient room noise and a noisy microphone. The default setting is **50%**, and I suggest you lower that to 40–45% for clips with dialogue. It is best not to use it for dialogue in conjunction with **Voice Isolation** as you will likely get a helium voice effect.

Hum Removal

This control is specific to the types of sounds caused by coiled electrical cables. You won't hear them while shooting videos, but they can show up after. The hum can effectively be removed by choosing the electrical frequency in the area where the video was shot.

Pan

Think of **Pan** as the ability to increase the levels for the left or right speakers of stereo or surround-sound audio.

Figure 10.29 – Mode choices for Pan

Effects

This section is where you will see external plug-ins or effects from the **Effects** browser. *Figure 10.30* shows the **Compressor, Limiter,** and **Fat EQ** effects added. These are discussed in *Chapter 11*.

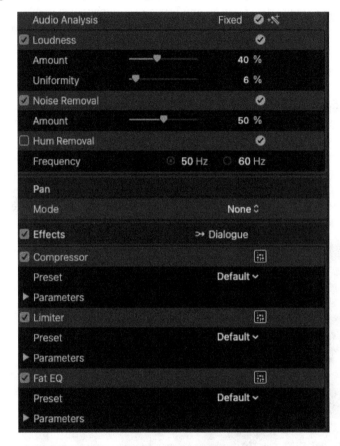

Figure 10.30 – Effects added to the Audio inspector

All the sections that have been discussed so far are about enhancing the audio or adding effects; the following section on the **Audio** inspector gives you the ability to adjust the audio tracks of the video.

Audio Configuration

The controls in the **Audio Configuration** section allow adjustments to be made to individual audio tracks as well as the ability to add effects to any track independently.

As an example, in *Figure 10.31*, there are three audio tracks – **Cam 1**, **Cam 2**, and **External Audio**. Each track has been set to dual mono. In **Cam 2**, one of those dual tracks has been disabled by unticking the checkbox.

Figure 10.31 – Individual audio tracks with a single Cam 2 track disabled

The final button in the **Audio** inspector is **Save Audio Effects Preset**, which we will discuss in the next section.

Save Audio Effects Preset

After you have spent time adding all the enhancements and effects to the **Audio** inspector, you can save the specific mix of effects for use on other clips in the future.

Press the **Save Audio Effects Preset** button, and you will be presented with the following pop-up window:

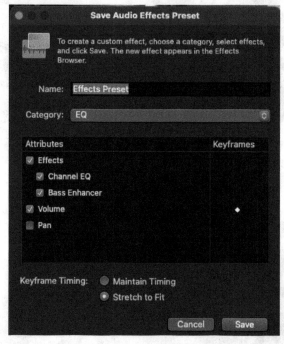

Figure 10.32 – Save Audio Effects Preset

Give it a name and add it to a category in the **Effects** browser. You can include or disable any effects. The presets are stored in the `Effects Presets` folder on the system disk and can be shared with other users if you wish. *Figure 10.33* shows the path where the `Effects Presets` folder is located:

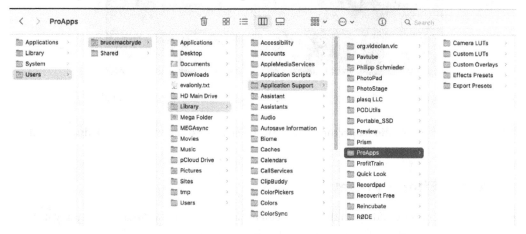

Figure 10.33 – Path to the Effects Presets folder

The next section discusses the fourth of the permanent inspector tabs: the **Information** inspector.

The Information inspector

The **Information** inspector is accessed via the ▣ tab, and it gives individual metadata information about clips and projects in the **browser**, or clips, titles, or generators in the **timeline**.

There are several different ways of viewing the information, from **Basic** to specific metadata.

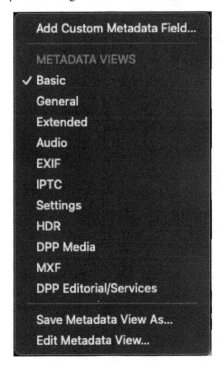

Figure 10.34 – Different ways of viewing the metadata

The **General** view gives most of what you will need to know on a daily basis:

Figure 10.35 – The general view of the Information inspector

At the bottom of the **Information** inspector, you will be shown the status of the **Original**, **Optimized**, and **Proxy** media, as well as another place to transcode media.

Project information

When you select a project to view in the **Information** inspector, you are given the option to modify the settings of the project:

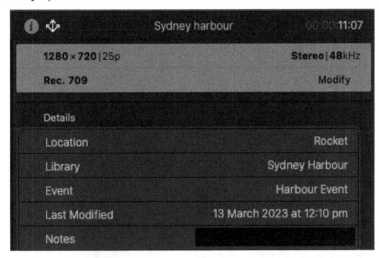

Figure 10.36 – Modifying a project

You can change the **Format** and **Resolution** settings but the frame rate is fixed at the original rate:

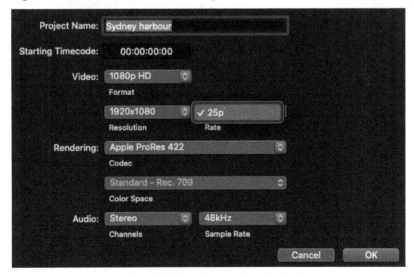

Figure 10.37 – Frame rate is fixed

If you need to change the frame rate, open the old project in the timeline and then choose **Select All** and **Copy** and create a new project with a new frame rate chosen. Lastly, paste it into the new empty project.

Library information

When you select a library to view in the **Information** inspector, you will be given data about where the library is stored and the size of the **Original**, **Optimized**, and **Proxy** media.

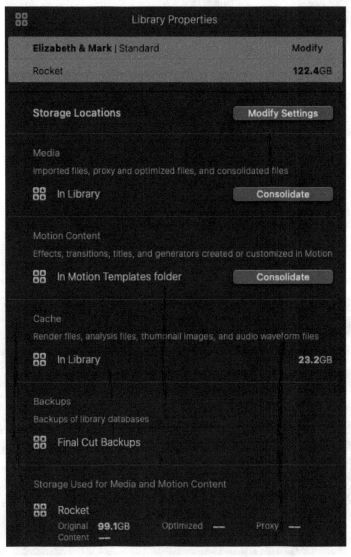

Figure 10.38 – Library information

Export information

There is another tab that appears for **browser** clips and projects, which is most useful for projects that have been previously shared/exported. The tab is a trident shape and shows the dates the project was exported and where to locate it in the Finder. The following figure shows the trident icon at the top and the dates at the bottom.

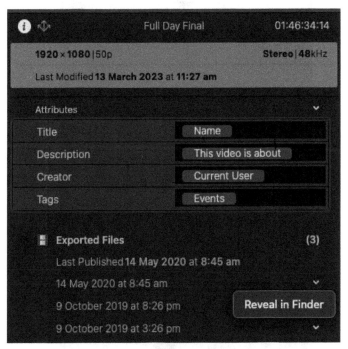

Figure 10.39 – Dates and locations of exported projects

The four main **inspector** tabs open panels for you to make adjustments as well as get information about the library, clips, and projects. The next section shows you how to modify titles, text, and generators.

The Titles inspector

You should think of Final Cut Pro titles as little video clips that contain animated text and, in some cases, dropzones. The terms *titles* and *text* are different, and are not interchangeable. Titles are receptacles that contain textual items. Titles, with their associated text, are usually added to the **timeline** as connected clips. You can find more details about titles in *Chapter 7*.

When a title is added to a project in the timeline, a new tab for the **Text** inspector appears at the top left of the **inspector** panel.

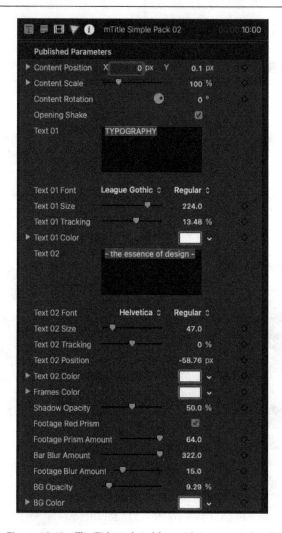

Figure 10.40 – The Titles tab in blue with inspector details

The **inspector** panel for a title will show specific choices for that title. Every title will show different settings.

As stated before, a title is a container for you to add text, and since every title is different, the way that text can be added will sometimes be different as well.

Some titles will allow you to add text and others may not. Usually, if the text is added within the **Titles** panel, there will be some restrictions as to how it can be modified.

In most cases, text can be added when the separate **Text** tab is selected to reveal the **Text** inspector panel. You will sometimes find with some purchased title plug-ins that you will only be able to enter text in the plug-in and not in the **Text** inspector. The **Text** inspector is discussed in the next section.

The Text inspector

The **Text** inspector has more adjustability than any other entity, so much so that the mind boggles at times, especially when venturing into the aspects of 3D text.

> **Important note**
>
> Note that text needs a Final Cut Pro title. Text cannot exist without having a title or generator as its container.

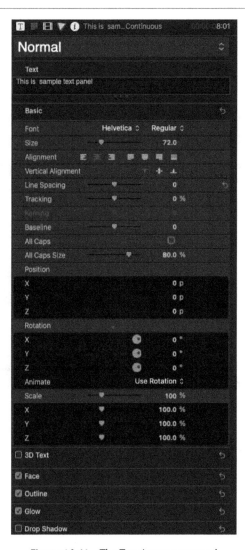

Figure 10.41 – The Text inspector panel

As noted in the previous section, every title is different, and so the way that text is handled will likely be different as well. I mention this here not to disturb you, but more to warn you that things may not always be as you would have expected. It's this diversity that makes titling and adding text in Final Cut Pro so refreshingly unique.

I am not going to cover every little detail of the **Text** inspector panel, as a good proportion of it is what you would find in any word-processing app. However, there are sections in the panel that are specific to Final Cut Pro.

Text division

At the top of the inspector is an input field called **Text**. This is where you type the text, and in most cases, you will also be able to add and modify text directly within the viewer. In *Figure 10.42*, the word text is highlighted in the viewer as well as in the input field in the inspector. Clicking and dragging the dot with the circle in the viewer lets you move the text around the viewer.

Figure 10.42 – Text entered in the viewer and the inspector

The **Text** field in the inspector can be increased in size with the three dots at the bottom of the field. Text in the **Text** field is very small and cannot be increased in size, so increasing the space to type in is critical. Compare *Figure 10.41* to *Figure 10.43* and notice the double arrow that shows when you adjust the size.

Figure 10.43 – Text division expanded

I'll skip all of the **Basic** word processor-style division and move to the **Position** division in the next section.

Position division

In the **Position** division, you can move the text horizontally with **X** and vertically with **Y**. You can rotate as well as scale on the same **X** and **Y** basis. Usually, you can do the same directly in the viewer, but as noted previously, don't be surprised if the viewer is locked to you. Again, due to the diversity of title plug-ins, the **Position** subdivision in the **Text** inspector may not be available.

Figure 10.44 – Text inspector without the Position division

At the bottom of the **Text** inspector, there are five checkboxes. I am skipping the **3D Text** checkbox as, in my mind, it's a bit of a novelty that quickly wears thin with audiences, but I will cover **Face** in the next section.

The Face checkbox

Face is the color of the font used in the text. It can contain a texture as well as a gradient. One trap you should be aware of is that the checkbox may be hidden. If it is, hover to the right of **Face** and select **Show**:

Figure 10.45 – If Face is hidden, select Show

It seems somewhat counterproductive that the color of the font used in the text should be all the way at the bottom of the **Text** inspector, but *it is what it is*.

Click on the **Color** rectangle to open the color wheel. Also, you can adjust the **Opacity** setting of **Color**, along with **Blur**:

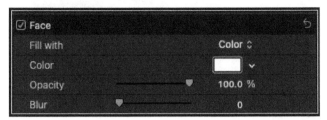

Figure 10.46 – The Color rectangle, Opacity, and Blur

To the right of **Color**, you can select **Texture** and **Gradient**. In the following figure, **Texture** is grayed out as the particular title does not allow it:

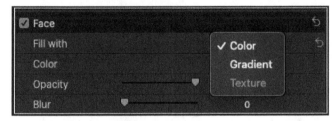

Figure 10.47 – The Color, Gradient, and Texture options

The **Outline**, **Glow**, and **Drop Shadow** checkbox options are adjusted in a similar way as with **Face**.

Titles and text go hand in hand. The next section covers how the **Generator** inspector is different.

The Generator inspector

Chapter 7 showed how generators are like titles in the way they are little animated video clips. The tab for the **Generator** inspector is in the same location at the top left of the **inspector** window as the **Titles** tab is positioned.

Figure 10.48 – The Generator tab in blue

By default, the content of the **Generator** inspector will look much more complex due to the inherent complexity of the generator itself. As with titles, each generator is unique and more likely to include dropzones as well as the ability to enter text.

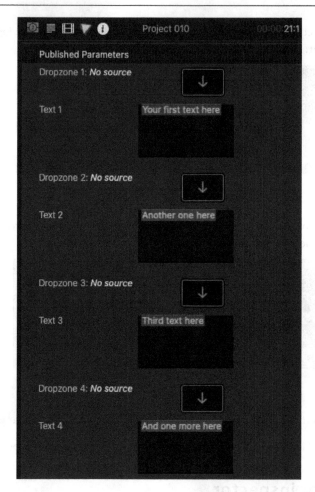

Figure 10.49 – Generator with dropzones and Text panels

The key to working in the **Generator** inspector is to expect the unexpected. It pushes the boundaries of what can be achieved with a plug-in, so will be complex by nature.

The next tab that I will cover is a temporary tab that will only appear when a transition is selected in the timeline.

The Transition inspector

The tab for the **Transition** inspector is located in the same position as the **Titles** and **Generator** tabs. When a transition is selected in the timeline, the tab is automatically activated to show the **Transition** inspector. In most cases, the sole adjustments will be for the **Fade In** and **Fade Out** settings of the audio related to the transition. A few transitions have **Text** and even **Dropzone** options, as in the Crypto Pop transition shown in *Figure 10.50*.

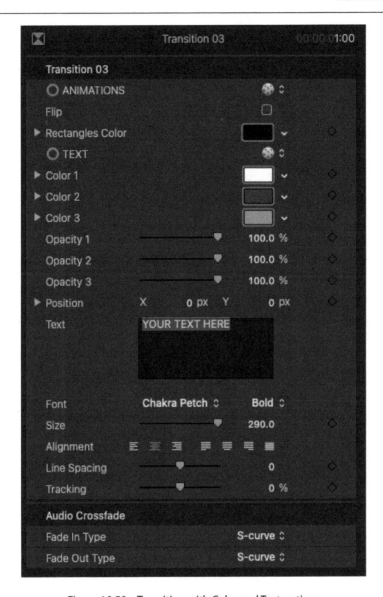

Figure 10.50 – Transition with Color and Text options

Summary

At first glance, the inspector is a single panel; it's not until you look a little deeper that you see it is, in fact, several different inspectors that vary depending on whether you are inspecting a video clip from the **browser** or the **timeline**. The view of the inspector will be different when inspecting a project or a library.

In this chapter, you learned about the different panels for the **Video** inspector where built-in and purchased effects are added from the **Effects** browser. You saw how to transform and crop images in the viewer by using the numerical controls in the inspector. You were shown details of how the stabilization of shaky footage can make an unusable clip functional.

You were shown how the **Color** inspector enhances clips with either the **Color Board** approach or with **Color Wheels**. There was a discussion of the advantages of each and how inexperienced users should build up from using **Color Board** to become proficient with **Color Wheels**, mainly due to the ability to add keyframe changes within a clip with the **Color Wheels** approach.

You learned how the **Information** inspector showed the disk space taken up by different transcoded media, as well as where the library is located on the computer. You also learned how titles and text are interconnected but are separate terms, and how the **Titles** and **Generator** inspectors are almost the same in their use. Finally, you saw how transitions have their own panel in the inspector, with a unique tab to access that panel with sometimes surprising options.

In the next chapter, which is about plug-ins, you will be able to make use of your newly acquired knowledge of the inspector from this current chapter, as plug-ins also rely heavily on the inspector.

11

Using Built-In Plug-Ins

In *Chapter 10, The Inspector Controls*, you learned everything about the inspector's controls and settings using the various inspector panels. This chapter will show you how to put that knowledge to good use when you add effects to timeline clips. You will learn about the built-in titles, generators, effects, and transitions, with several examples featured to show you the full gamut of settings. I use the term *built-in* to refer to all the effects, sometimes known as plug-ins, that are supplied as part of the purchase of Final Cut Pro.

The main topics covered in the chapter are as follows:

- An explanation of plug-in terminology
- Plug-ins – general knowledge
- Using built-in plug-ins
- Creating custom plug-ins from built-in plug-ins

In this chapter, you will learn how plug-ins are added to clips in the timeline. Previously, in *Chapter 10, The Inspector Controls*, you saw where these plug-ins appeared in the inspector. In this chapter, you will have a chance to see what results can be produced with a selected number of plug-ins.

You will learn about plug-ins for color and audio correction issues, video noise and grain, and the stabilization of shaky footage.

By the end of the chapter, you will know how to produce startling effects with Final Cut Pro's built-in plug-ins.

An explanation of plug-in terminology

Throughout the time you have been using Final Cut Pro, it's likely you will have heard of a number of different terms such as third-party plug-ins, default plug-ins, built-in plug-ins, plug-in developers, and effects. Now is a good point to explain what all of these terms mean.

Final Cut Pro ships with a number of what it generally refers to as **effects**. Effects can be categorized as **Titles**, **Generators**, **Effects**, and **Transitions**. Now, you can already see the problem with the term *effects*. First, the main category is known as **Effects**, but it also has a section inside called **Effects**, which is most confusing. To avoid replication in the terminology, Final Cut Pro sometimes uses the alternative term **Plug-ins** for the main **Effects** category.

This would be much more logical, except that the term *plug-in* tends to indicate something that is added. However, as Final Cut Pro has titles, generators, transitions, and effects that are built-in, how can they be plugged in if they are built-in?

My suggestion, to avoid confusion, is to call all effects *plug-ins*, whether they ship with Final Cut Pro or are added later. This way, effects can just be thought of as only the items that are in the **Effects** browser.

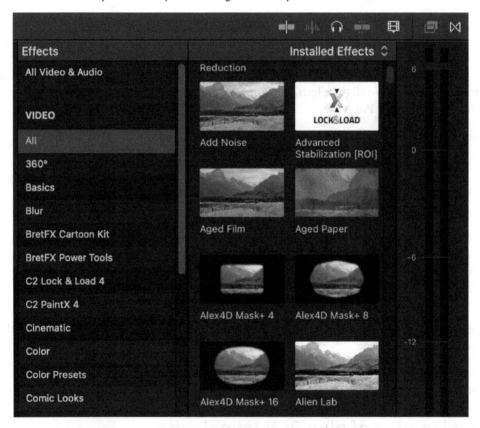

Figure 11.1 – The Effects browser

That covers just one confusing term, but what about *third-party plug-ins*, *default plug-ins*, *built-in plug-ins*, and *plug-in developers*?

An explanation of all these terms is as follows:

- *Default plug-ins* and *built-in plug-ins* are exactly the same thing; they are plug-ins that have shipped as part of your Final Cut Pro purchase

- *Third-party plug-ins* are plug-ins that are not part of the Final Cut Pro package; they are add-ons

- *Plug-in developers* are the individuals and companies that make plug-ins

Now that you understand the terminology, let's look at some general knowledge about plug-ins in the next section.

Plug-ins – general knowledge

The two specific features that many plug-ins use relate to entering text and adding video and stills to portals on the screen; these areas are called a **drop zone** or, in some cases, a **media well**.

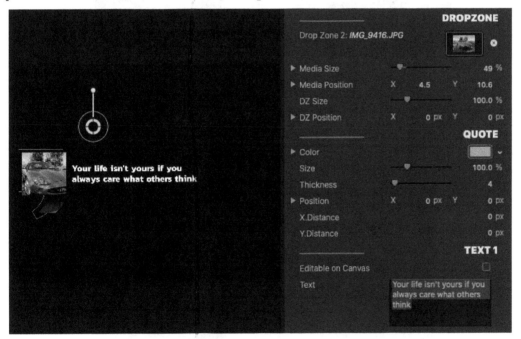

Figure 11.2 – A Drop Zone and text panel in the inspector, with the viewer also shown

Text can be typed directly into a plug-in; however, for multiple words, it pays to prepare the text in a text editor, such as Apple's **TextEdit** app, and then copy and paste it into the plug-in. The reasons for this being a good approach are, first, you have more time and space to think precisely about what words you want to construct, and second, the size of the **Text** area in the Final Cut Pro inspector is very small and text can be hard to see, so it's better to not have to worry about editing in a restrictive area, as shown in *Figure 11.3*.

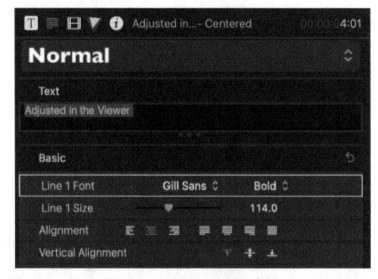

Figure 11.3 – A very small Text field

Using a text editor will mean the words will be quicker and easier to type and error-free when they are pasted into the plug-in.

The second specific plug-in feature is the use of a drop zone. A drop zone is a panel in the inspector that will allow you to add video and stills inside the plug-in.

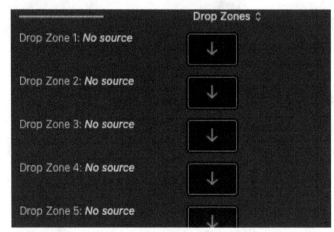

Figure 11.4 – A drop zone is represented by a blue rectangle

When you use a drop zone, both video and still images are selected in the same way. However, you need to be aware that the video that you select needs to have at least the same duration as the time that is displayed visibly in the title in the timeline. If the video is shorter, it will freeze before the text's full duration is shown in the timeline. For instance, if the title is set to play for 10 seconds and the video is only 5 seconds in duration, the image shown in the drop zone will freeze and be shown as a still frame for the last 5 seconds that the title plays. With this information in mind, you also need to be aware that it's critical at what point you click in the video clip; the clip needs to be long enough from the point that you click on it for the available content to play to the end of the title's duration.

As for adding text to a plug-in, it is useful to be proactive and preselect the video or stills you intend to use before rushing in, willy-nilly, looking for suitable items on a whim. It is characteristic of a drop zone that once an image is added to it, it can't be modified without removing it and replacing it with a new image. So, you need to make any modifications to the image first before adding it to the drop zone. You could create a compound clip if you wanted to include stacked timeline clips.

Now that you understand what plug-ins are, let's look at the different types of plug-ins, starting with the built-in plug-ins, explained in the next section.

Built-in plug-ins

I intend to discuss the built-in plug-ins by category. First, I'll cover **Titles**, starting with the **Build In/ Out** category of basic animated titles, followed by **Lower Thirds** and **Bumper/Opener**.

Then, I'll cover three subcategories of **Generators**, starting with **Elements** and **Solids**.

After **Titles** and **Generators**, I will first cover effects in the **Effects** browser, specifically those that are related to color and looks. Then, I will cover effects that make dramatic changes to a clip in the timeline. These include **Keyer** for a green screen effect and **Masks**, which allows you to hide parts of an image or cut out objects.

I will then cover two representative categories of **Transitions**, including the morphing **Flow** transition and **Wipes**, which are suitable for introducing new sections of a video.

Because all editors using Final Cut Pro have access to built-in plug-ins, effects added with these plug-ins tend to be recognizable and may not look fresh. In this chapter, you will see how to make effects that are unique to your style.

Using built-in titles

There are two distinct ways of using titles: either as a means of providing information with plain words (let's call these titles *informational*) or as a complex animation that may introduce your video, such as the titles of a feature movie.

Informational titles

Informational titles are often used in two different ways. They can be used as a way of telling the viewer something, with an emphasis on one or two words, or they can show the name of the person talking on screen, known as a **lower third**.

A simple one- or two-word title can quickly be added to the timeline with the *Ctrl + T* shortcut. A **Basic** title can be added as a connected clip above the magnetic timeline.

Figure 11.5 – A Basic title

Basic Title and other titles can be accessed from the **Titles** and **Generators** tabs above the **Media** browser.

Figure 11.6 – The Titles and Generators tabs

Expand the drop-down menu from the arrow to the left of **Titles** to show the list of **Titles** categories. Select the **Build In/Out** category, and look at the **Centered** title as an example. Drag the **Centered** title as a connected clip above the primary storyline in the timeline. *Figure 11.7* shows the timeline and the viewer, with the **Titles** tab selected. The words **Title** and **Subtitle** are automatically entered at the center of the viewer.

Figure 11.7 – A centered title added to the timeline

As you saw in *Chapter 10, The Inspector Controls*, when working with titles, both the **T** tab and the **Text** tab allow you to add text to a title.

> **Note**
> You will find that most of the information in the subsections that follow will apply to all titles, both built-in and purchased.

In the following section, I will discuss how to adjust the settings under the **T** tab when it shows as blue, which is the indicator of when a tab is active.

Using 3D text

3D text is not something that you will want to use every day of the week, so I will mention it only briefly here and refer you to Apple's Final Cut Pro help for the finer details, which can be found at `https://support.apple.com/en-gb/guide/final-cut-pro/ver41f467778/mac`:

You can also select **Help** from the main menu bar to find out how to use 3D text.

3D Text controls in Final Cut Pro
In Final Cut Pro, use the 3D Text controls in the Text inspector to adjust the depth, thickness, and edge attributes of 3D text.

Add 3D text glows or shadows in Final Cut Pro
In Final Cut Pro, apply glow and drop shadow effects to 3D text.

Add a light-emitting material to 3D text in Final Cut Pro
In Final Cut Pro, add a light-emitting material layer to 3D text so that it appears lit from within.

Add materials to 3D text facets in Final Cut Pro
In Final Cut Pro, apply different materials to different facets of 3D text.

Add preset materials to 3D text in Final Cut Pro
In Final Cut Pro, add preset materials to 3D text to define its color, reflectivity, and other visual attributes.

Adjust 3D text lighting in Final Cut Pro
In Final Cut Pro, choose a lighting style for 3D text and control the appearance of shadows.

Adjust basic 3D text settings in Final Cut Pro
In Final Cut Pro, modify the attributes of 3D text, including font, size, tracking, line spacing, and capitalization.

Change the 3D text lighting environment in Final Cut Pro
In Final Cut Pro, create reflections on the surface of 3D text using environment lighting.

Intro to 3D text lighting in Final Cut Pro
In Final Cut Pro, you can add lighting and reflectivity to 3D text to create natural-looking 3D titles.

Intro to 3D text materials in Final Cut Pro
In Final Cut Pro, you can apply materials (layers that mimic a substance or finish) to the surface of 3D text to give it a realistic appearance.

Modify 3D text depth and edges in Final Cut Pro
In Final Cut Pro, modify the depth and thickness of 3D text. Set the style of corners and the size and style of the edges between facets.

Work with 3D text material layers in Final Cut Pro
In Final Cut Pro, add material layers to 3D text, rearrange the order of layers to create different looks, and remove layers.

Convert text to 3D text in Final Cut Pro
In Final Cut Pro, convert titles back and forth between 2D and 3D.

Modify 3D text materials in Final Cut Pro
In Final Cut Pro, modify preset materials to create custom materials. Restore a modified preset material to its original settings.

Save modified 3D text materials in Final Cut Pro
In Final Cut Pro, save custom materials as presets so that you can reuse them.

Figure 11.8 – Help material for 3D text

The basic 3D controls let you adjust the depth, weight, and edges, as shown in the top section of the **3D Text** dialog box in *Figure 11.9*:

The second section (**Lighting**) allows you to adjust the way that each of the edges are lit (**Intensity**) and the ways that shadows are affected by lighting.

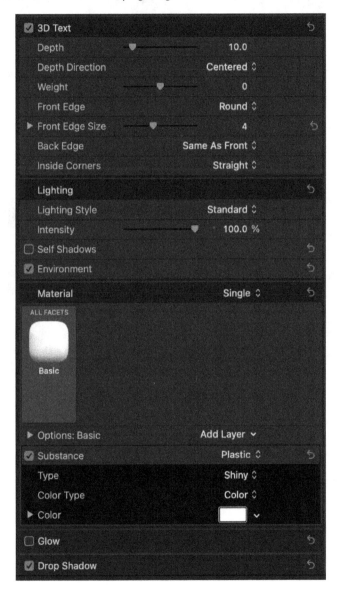

Figure 11.9 – 3D Text options

The third section (**Material**) covers the type of materials that can wrap the 3D text, and the last section (**Substance**) covers the substance of those wrapping materials, including **Shiny**, **Matte**, and **Textured**. *Figure 11.10* shows the options for **Stone**:

Figure 11.10 – The 3D options for Stone

The next section includes **Face**, which is where the text color is selected. When the **3D Text** checkbox is unchecked, the **Face** checkbox becomes visible, as shown in *Figure 11.11*.

Using the Face settings

Face is the term for the 2D or 3D outer face of text. It can be filled with a color, a gradient, or a texture. The **Opacity** level can be adjusted, as can **Blur**. *Figure 11.11* shows the options:

Figure 11.11 – Face controls

The previous sections mainly focused on the texture and color of the text; the next section will focus more on the use of the style of the words themselves.

Using Outline, Glow, and Drop Shadow

The settings in each of the **Outline**, **Glow**, and **Drop Shadow** sections are similar to the **Face** controls, except for **Drop Shadow**, which gives us the choice of the distance a shadow is from the text and the angle, as shown in *Figure 11.12*:

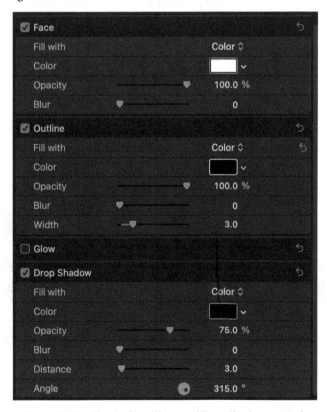

Figure 11.12 – The Outline, Glow, and Drop Shadow controls

Note that the settings in *Figures 11.9* to *11.12* (except for *Figure 11.10*) all refer to the **Centered** title, which illustrates how some titles will have different settings adjusted by default. If you refer back to *Figure 11.12*, you will see that **Face** is white, **Outline** is black with a width of 3 . 0, and **Drop Shadow** is set to a distance of 3 . 0.

Simple titles aim at providing the video's audience with information, and no area is more important than the one providing the name of a person on screen. This type of title is called a **lower third**, as you will see in the next section.

Using Lower Thirds

Everything you have seen so far can be replicated for all titles, including **Lower Thirds**. These have a fancy name but are, in fact, the same as the simple titles shown in the *Using Outline, Glow, and Drop Shadow* section, except for the default area in which they are located in the viewer. They also usually have two lines to accommodate a person's name and their job title or rank.

Most lower thirds are animated by default, as the next example shows. Previously, you saw an exception with the **Basic** title, which can be added to the timeline with a shortcut, and there is also a shortcut to add a **Basic** lower third – *Shift + Ctrl + T*.

Using the Left lower third

For this exercise, I will use a lower third from the **Documentary** section of **Lower Thirds** called **Left**. I picked this lower third not because it is particularly attractive but because it demonstrates that there are subsections in the **Lower Thirds** category – in this case, we will use **Documentary**. The **Left** lower third has some usual features missing, and it is different from the normal lower third in that there is only one line, whereas most lower thirds have two lines. Also, the **Left** lower third, in addition to being animated, has a built-in set of background shapes that can be modified.

Figure 11.13 – Lower Thirds selected in the side bar

Add **Left** as a connected clip to the timeline. The **T** tab in the inspector shows the options to change the *background* of the lower third, but it does not offer an option to change the *text*.

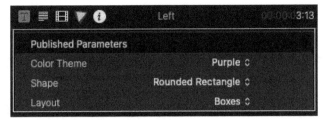

Figure 11.14 – The T tab for Left

You can change the words directly inside the viewer; double-clicking the words will highlight them.

> **Note**
> By double-clicking an animated title in the timeline, you can automatically position the playhead to when the entire text is visible in the viewer after animation.

The **Left** lower third only has one line; if you need two, just press the *Enter* key after the forward-slash for the second line to appear below.

Figure 11.15 – Words modified directly in the viewer

While the **T** tab is still selected, you can change the background shapes, the color scheme, and the layout.

Figure 11.16 – The Color Theme, Shape, and Layout options

As you saw in the **Lower Thirds** section, you can also change the words with the **Text** tab's inspector panel selected.

Figure 11.17 – NAME/DESCRIPTION pre-selected in the Text inspector

The words in the viewer, **NAME/DESCRIPTION**, are highlighted in the **Text** inspector, ready for you to change.

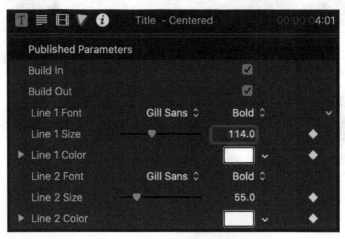

Figure 11.18 – The T tab selected

The **Centered** title has been selected as an example because it contains two lines of text, whereas the **Basic** title contains just one line of text.

The first options in the **Centered** title are **Build In** and **Build Out**, which are related to the animation that has been programmed into this particular title. **Build In** refers to the beginning animation, and **Build Out** refers to the end animation of the title. This means that you can have animation turned on or off at the beginning and/or at the end.

Line 1 Font speaks for itself. The downward chevron to the far right will appear when you hover the mouse over it, and it will give you the choice to reset any changes you make to the **Font** selection.

The orange keyframe diamonds are visible in *Figure 11.18*; I have shown them only for reference so that you can see where they are located. They will not show unless you set keyframes (for more details, see *Chapter 13, Using Keyframes to Animate Objects in Final Cut Pro*).

All other settings will be familiar to you as a current user of Final Cut Pro. As stated previously, every title will have varying settings. The **Centered** title is a basic example.

When you are adjusting text in the **T** tab, all available lines of text can be adjusted in the same inspector panel.

In many cases, text can be adjusted directly in the viewer itself. In this case, the **Centered** title does allow direct adjustments in the viewer. If you refer to *Figure 11.7*, you can see that the default word, **Title**, in the viewer was changed to **Adjusted** by typing directly into the viewer, as also shown in *Figure 11.19*:

Figure 11.19 – Text typed directly into the viewer

Some complex third-party titles will have a checkbox option to turn on **Editable on Canvas**. In this case, the word *Canvas* is an alternative term for the *viewer*.

Figure 11.20 – The Editable on Canvas option

Whether the text is editable in the viewer or not, usually, any text selections that you see when the **T** tab is highlighted are also adjustable by selecting the **Text** inspector tab to the right of the **T** tab. The downside to using the **Text** inspector panel is that each line needs to be adjusted independently, but to offset that, you have much more word processor control and flexibility, as you can see in *Figure 11.21*:

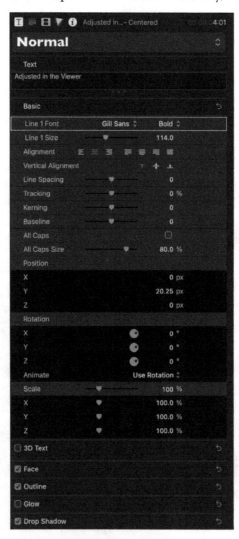

Figure 11.21 – More options with the Text inspector

I won't explain the word processor extras, as we covered the five bottom checkboxes in the *Informational titles* section. Now, let's move on to dynamic titles.

Using Dynamic Titles

Dynamic Titles was a new addition to version 10.6.6 of Final Cut Pro; it contains a mix of basic titles and animated groups, with matching effects for opening, closing, and lower third use. They have limited control in the inspector and are ideal for editors not wanting to spend time modifying an effect. Be careful about overuse, as they are likely to be used by other people because of their simplicity. However, a copy can be opened in **Motion** to add functionality (for more details, see *Chapter 17, Supporting Software Apps for Final Cut Pro.*

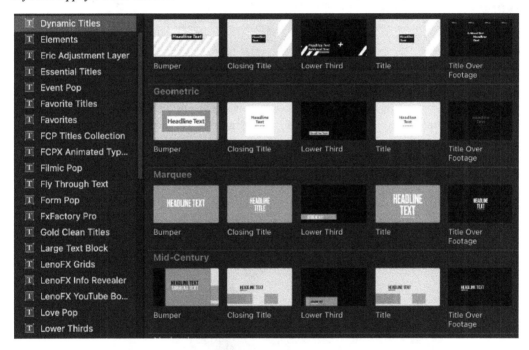

Figure 11.22 – Dynamic Titles

Dynamic Titles is useful for quick edits; however, to appear professional, it's better to use more unique title effects, as you will see in the next section.

Using Bumper/Opener

The **Bumper/Opener** category adds to what you have seen with **Dynamic Titles** while keeping the basic similarities of text selection. This category has a drop zone included and a built-in background that can be disabled. The example in the following subsection uses the **Point** title.

The Point title

The example I am using is the **Point** title in the **Bumper/Opener** category. If you do not know where **Point** is located in the **Titles** browser, you can search for it. Select the **Titles** main category, and type `Point` in the search field (the magnifying glass) on the right, as shown in *Figure 11.23*:

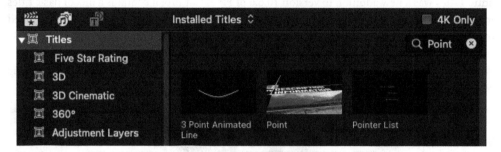

Figure 11.23 – Searching for Point in the Titles heading

When you double-click on the title, it will be added at the playhead position as a connected clip in the timeline. I suggest that this title is held in the timeline for an extended duration to allow the viewer to read the text – try 10 seconds. Then, check the **T** tab in the inspector, as shown in *Figure 11.24*:

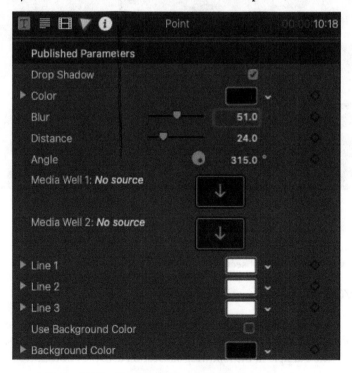

Figure 11.24 – The Point title selected in the inspector

The **Point** title has three text lines and two drop zones, which are collectively called a **media well**. Follow these steps to activate the drop zone and add the clip to it:

1. To activate a drop zone, in the inspector, make sure the **T** tab is selected. Then, click on the downward white arrow in the **Media Well** section to select the drop zone. When the drop zone is selected, the downward arrow will turn blue with the message **Selecting source clip…**, indicating that the drop zone is selected. Both the blue and white arrows are shown in *Figure 11.25*, with the blue arrow showing **Selecting source clip…** and the white arrow showing **No source**.

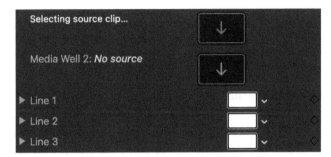

Figure 11.25 – Drop zones showing the blue and white arrows

2. Move the cursor to the browser, and click on the video or still that you want to use in the drop zone (remember to allow enough length for the video to fill the title's duration).

    The viewer will split into two panels, and the left panel will show the frame of the video or still that you selected to fill the drop zone. The drop zone that previously had the blue arrow in the inspector will also show the same frame (see *Figure 11.26*).

Figure 11.26 – The split panels showing the media in the inspector

3. If you are happy with the selection, click **Apply Clip**.

The words in the **Point** title need to be selected directly by first clicking on them in the viewer (make sure that the transform option is disabled) and then making the changes in the inspector, with the **T** tab selected.

Most of the information in the section on simple informational titles can be replicated in any title and, in many cases, in generators, where text options are included, as you will see in the next section.

Using built-in generators

You will be forgiven for thinking that generators have all the same features as titles. In many ways, they have, and that is why they are located in the same place as titles. However, there are some finer details you should be aware of. In this section, I will show you generators in the **Elements** and **Solids** categories.

The Elements category

There are four generators in the **Elements** category – **Counting**, **Placeholders**, **Shapes**, and **Timecode**. **Placeholders** are discussed in detail in *Chapter 4*, *Pre-Editing a Rough Cut*.

Generators are added to the timeline in the same way as titles – they are dragged in as a connected clip. Let's look at the other three generators, starting with **Counting** in the next section.

Using the Counting generator

Counting can be used for **Number**, **Currency**, **Percent**, **Scientific**, **Spell Out**, **Binary**, and **Hexadecimal**. You would use this generator with selected start and end times, but be aware that **Counting** does not relate to the playing time of the video. As an example, you could have the count start at number **1** and finish at number **5** but take 2 minutes to do so. If you want to count the time taken of the video itself, use the **Timecode** generator. The big missing feature with the **Counting** generator is that it only counts upward; it can't count down.

Figure 11.27 – The Counting generator

The next generator in the **Elements** category that I will show you is **Shapes**.

Using the Shapes generator

When you want to add graphics to Final Cut Pro, it is best to draw them in a drawing application such as Pixelmator or Photoshop. However, you can create some basic shapes with the **Shapes** generator directly in the timeline. See *Figure 11.28* for the options:

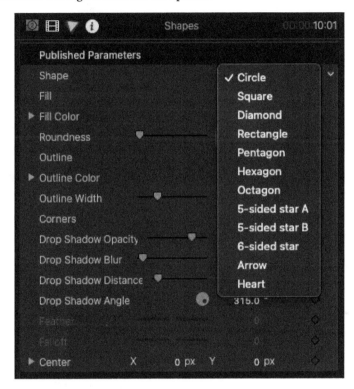

Figure 11.28 – The options in the Shapes generator

Here, **Outline** can be turned on/off. The edges of the outline can have their corners changed to round, square, or beveled. You can have multiple **Shape** generators stacked in the timeline to give different shapes. The shapes can be resized by selecting **Transform** and using the blue corner dots:

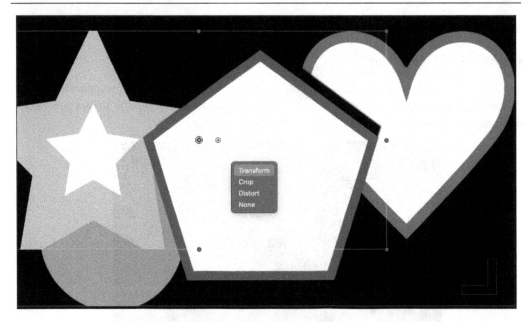

Figure 11.29 – Choices of shapes

The last of the **Elements** category that I will show you is the **Timecode** generator.

Using the Timecode generator

When you need to send a draft of your video to a client, I suggest that you always add the **Timecode** generator. There are two reasons. The first is the most obvious, in that your client can refer you to the exact timecode that they want to make changes to. That's what you want them to think is the reason that you included the timecode.

However, the real benefit to you is that the timecode acts like a watermark. The client can't run off with your video without paying until you remove the timecode. The downside to **Timecode** is that you can't remove the hours and minutes in the readout if they are not needed. You can move the position of the timecode on the screen by adjusting **Center – X** for the horizontal axis and **Y** for the vertical axis.

Figure 11.30 – Timecode

The next category of generators that I will show you is **Solids**. These will give you the ability to draw lines.

The Solids category

When you select **Solids** in the **Elements** category, you only need to consider the **Custom** solid, as this can be made into any color:

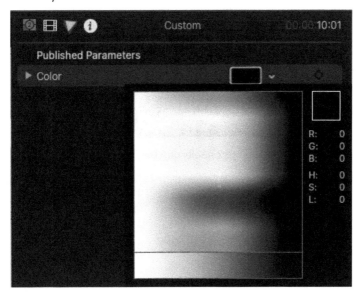

Figure 11.31 – Color choices for the Custom solid

A major use of **Solids** is to provide a background for titles that are transparent apart from the text itself. Because of this, unlike any title or generator we have looked at so far, the solid will be added to the timeline below the transparent clip, which will most likely be below the primary storyline.

Note

If you are using backgrounds in this way, I suggest you also look at the options in the **Textures** category of **Generators**.

When added to the timeline, the **Custom** solid, by default, will fill the whole screen. However, it can be cropped and moved within the viewer with **Transform**.

Follow the following steps to customize the **Solids** generator:

1. Drag the **Custom** solid generator below the primary storyline but not as a connected clip.

2. Select the solid in the timeline.

3. With the **Option** key held down, drag a copy of the solid below the original in the timeline, and then select the lower copy of the solid in the inspector.

4. Change the color to white (you will still be seeing black).

5. Select the top copy of the solid in the timeline.

6. Right-click in the viewer and select **Transform**:

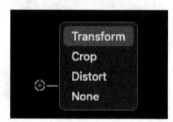

Figure 11.32 – Selecting Transform

7. With the top copy still selected, click in the viewer and drag down; you will see the appear:

Figure 11.33 – The white background appears

8. With the top copy still selected, right-click in the viewer again and select **Crop**.

9. Drag one of the dotted lines to crop the image.

10. Select the **Filmstrip** tab in the inspector.

11. In the **Crop** section, drag the top and bottom sliders until you have a thin black line.

12. In the **Scale** section, move **X** and **Y** to position the line.

13. **Scale All** and **Rotation** will change both the **X** and **Y** values and the rotation of the solid.

Congratulations! You have created a line in Final Cut Pro. You can stack further lines on top of each other to build different shapes and change colors. Try it out for yourself, and try the same with the **Textures** generators. As I said earlier, it's much easier to create graphics with Pixelmator or Photoshop, but it's useful to know how to create a quick line without leaving Final Cut Pro.

It's time to leave generators and look at the effects in the next section.

Using built-in effects

You can activate an effect by either dragging it inside a clip in the timeline or by double-clicking the effect when a clip is selected in the timeline. If you hover the cursor over an effect in the **Effects** browser, you will see a representation of how the effect will look in the clip in the timeline.

After **Titles** plug-ins, **Effects** plug-ins will be the most frequently used, and they fall into two loose groups.

- **Color-affiliated effects**: These are mostly about color and quick ways of adjusting it with a preset color effect
- **Non-color-affiliated effects**: These are for making major changes to the clip in the timeline

Let's start with color-affiliated effects.

Color-affiliated effects

The use of color-affiliated effects is a quick way to customize the feel of images.

In the first section, we will look at the **Basics, Light,** and **Looks** categories. The following are examples of the subtle differences in the **Basics** effects category.

The Basics effects category

The following figure shows quick ways to customize the feel of an image:

Figure 11.34 – Basic effects – Crisp Contrast (left), Hard Light (center), and Vibrancy (right)

The controls in the inspector are simple, and the idea behind these effects in the **Basic** categories is to make quick adjustments without needing to spend too much time tweaking them. The **Vibrancy** effect does have the option to protect skin tones. **Crisp Contrast** and **Hard Light** just have a slider to adjust the amount.

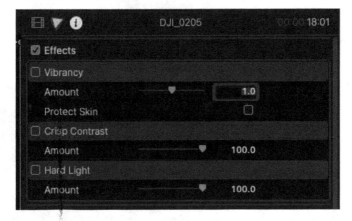

Figure 11.35 – Controls in the inspector for the Basic category

The next category that I will show you is the **Light** effects grouping. These all affect how light is used in the clip.

Light effects categories

There are 15 **Light** effects built in. I will show you **Bokeh Random**, **Highlights**, and **Shadows**. The three effects in the inspector are shown in *Figure 11.34*:

Figure 11.36 – Controls in the inspector for the Light category

Bokeh Random gives you the **Circles** and **Hexagons** options, along with the ability to control their size, number, pattern, and the speed at which they move. **Blend Mode** affects how they merge into the clip.

The **Highlights** effect gives you control over the temperature, from **Cool** (the default) to **Warm** or **Neutral**. **Offset** allows the effect to be positioned in different places using the **X** and **Y** coordinates

The **Shadows** effect simulates blinds or windowpanes:

Figure 11.37 – The Window-Leaves Shadow Type option

The feel of the image can also be customized by using the **Looks** effects, as you will see in the next section.

The Looks effects category

Looks provide more of a color change than the **Exposure** controls that are part of the color wheels or color board in the inspector's built-in **Color** controls (see *Chapter 14, Understanding the Principles of Color*).

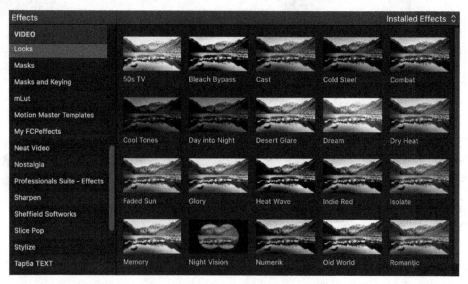

Figure 11.38 – The Looks category

There are 26 **Looks** options. Rather than the subtle differences you saw in the **Basic** category, these effects can make a dramatic difference and reproduce conventional color styles. I will show you three of those: **Bleach Bypass**, **Teal & Orange**, and **Day into Night**.

Figure 11.39 – Looks – Bleach Bypass (left), Teal & Orange (center), and Day into Night (right)

The options are similar to previous effects that I have shown.

The **Looks** controls can be significantly improved by using the **Color Grading Presets** controls discussed in the next section.

Color Grading Presets

Color Grading Presets were introduced in version 10.6.6 of Final Cut Pro, and they not only offer presets for color grading but also extensive slider controls in the inspector to modify the color grading.

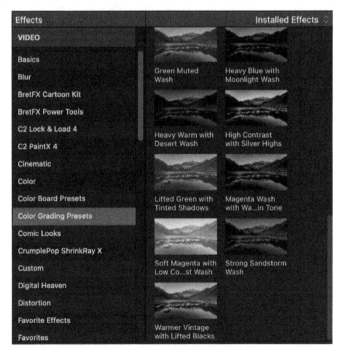

Figure 11.40 – Color Grading Presets

The titles of these grading controls give a clue as to what the color effect will look like when applied to a clip.

The color adjustments give you a way of trialing different color effects. The **Exposure** and **Contrast** settings will make the biggest difference. As with all color adjustments, only make small changes, and refer back after a period of time so that your eye has had time to adjust. You can use the blue check mark to see the before and after results.

Figure 11.41 – The inspector controls for Color Grading Presets

The second group of effects that make non-color-related adjustments to clips are discussed in the next section.

Non-color-affiliated effects

The effects in this group will completely change a clip. In this section, I will show you the **Scene Removal Mask**, **Green Screen Keyer**, and **Mask**, which allows you to hide parts of an image or cut out objects. The three are under one category in the **Effects** sidebar: **Masks and Keying**.

The Scene Removal Mask effect

This effect will attempt to remove backgrounds from video clips. The effect does require some specific things to be present in the clip, and that includes a clear image of the background by itself without the object that you want to retain.

In the inspector, select the frame that has the background without the image to be retained. It can be the first frame, the first frame + 1 second, the last frame – 1 second, or the last frame.

Figure 11.42 – The Scene Removal Mask removes backgrounds

Let's make a comparison of images without and with the **Scene Removal Mask** effect added. This is what the image without the effect looks like:

Figure 11.43 – Without Scene Removal Mask

And this is how it will look after applying the effect:

Figure 11.44 – With Scene Removal Mask

Scene removal is a way of correcting already recorded images in a video. However, the use of a green screen for recording will make an image much more realistic.

The Green Screen Keyer effect

This effect gets its name from its ability to create a green screen, in which you key out the color green.

Green screen is simply the term for when a video is shot in front of a green-colored screen so that when the **Green Screen Keyer** effect is added, the green color is extracted, leaving a transparent background that allows any clip connected below the keyed clip to show through.

Figure 11.45 – The Green Screen Keyer effect – original (left), with the
effect added (center), and the timeline view (right)

The Final Cut Pro **Green Screen Keyer** effect is very good at removing the green color, perhaps the best to automatically achieve a good key, but it's not a magic bullet. There is an art to green screening, and it's beyond the scope of this book to cover the intricate details. However, what I show you here will show you how to work with **Green Screen Keyer**, provided the original image has a good *key* – the term for a solid, well-lit, and even green color.

Drag **Green Screen Keyer** to the clip that has been shot by employing a green screen. It is ideal that **Green Screen Keyer** is always the topmost effect in the inspector because the order of the effects will change the look of the effects below, and the green screen effect needs to be dominant.

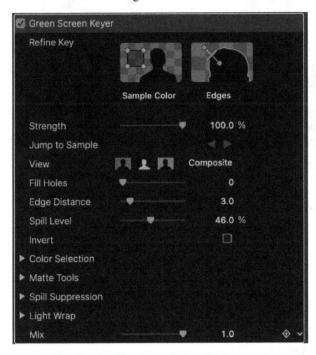

Figure 11.46 – The Green Screen Keyer controls

If the clip has a good key, the green will be removed instantly. Otherwise, click **Sample Color** in the inspector and draw over any background that has not been keyed out.

Figure 11.47 – A sample color drawn in the viewer

If there is still some background showing, reduce the **Strength** slider to 0, and then draw sample color squares over the green areas.

You can review the changes with the three **View** buttons: **Composite**, **Matte**, and **Original**.

Figure 11.48 – Three View buttons – Composite (left), Matte (center), and Original (right)

Below the **View** buttons in the inspector window are the **Fill Holes**, **Edge Distance**, and **Spill Level** sliders.

To improve the key, we will now concentrate from now on on the **Matte** view, as shown in *Figure 11.48*. The **Matte** view needs to be only black and white, with no black holes inside the white. You need to balance the following controls until you have the best key.

Draw **Sample Color** squares, and adjust the **Strength** and **Edge Distance** sliders. If you have black inside the white of the person, use **Fill Holes**. The **Spill Level** slider controls the green that was reflected onto the subject when the video was shot. This can be caused by the poor lighting of the subject when the video was taken.

If you find that you almost have the key and then it goes astray, use *Command + Z*. If that still doesn't help, right-click on the chevron to the right to reset.

Figure 11.49 – A sample color drawn in the viewer

I won't go into the other settings. Further information is provided by Apple support at https://support.apple.com/en-gb/guide/final-cut-pro/ver40b003bc/mac:

One of the secrets of keying is to reduce the amount of green in the image being keyed, as some areas may not have been lit well or the fabric of the green screen may have been creased.

The next section covers the **Mask** effect, which can cut out those nuisance areas.

The Mask effect

If you need to remove something from a clip in the timeline, then masking is the place to start. You can see a number of **Mask** presets in **Masks and Keying** in the sidebar of the **Effects** browser. Some of these are just designed for a quick mask, but I believe you really only need to consider one **Mask** style, **Draw Mask**, as it can do most of what the other masks can, and it is really suitable for the current job in hand – to remove as much of the green color as possible from the original clip we are working with.

Drag **Draw Mask** inside the clip in the timeline, and make sure that **Transform** is not active. The viewer will display the following message – **Click to Add a Control Point**; if you don't see the message, check whether the **Transform** tool is not active.

With **Click to Add a Control Point** visible, click in the viewer at the bottom left. Continue to click as you work your way around the image you want to retain. A red dot will be placed each time you click. Bear in mind that whatever you are masking may move throughout the length of the video, so you must always be outside of the image. Remember that heads can move significantly. Finally, click at the top of the first dot that you entered, which will close off the mask. You can select any dot and adjust its position. If you need to add a dot to the mix, hold the **Option** key and click on the red line. Now, when you try to key this image, there is less green to remove, as shown in *Figure 11.50*:

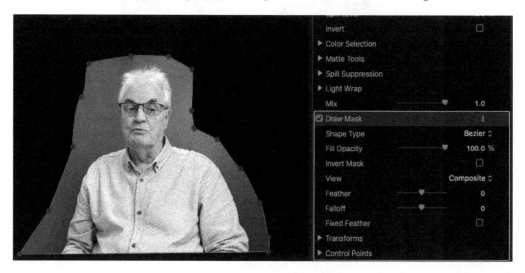

Figure 11.50 – The background removed with Draw Mask

This method of masking removes the background, but what if you want to cut something out of an image?

The process is just the same, except that you need to tick **Invert Mask** in the inspector, which reverses the mask.

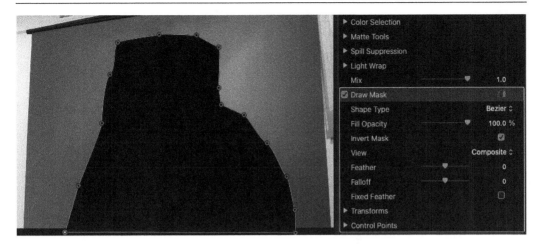

Figure 11.51 – The image removed with Draw Mask

Be aware that any clip below the one being masked will show through the cutout. You can use the **Feather** slider to soften the edges of the two clips to hide any sharp, unnatural-looking blending between the two images. You can animate the mask so that it moves with the subject image by using keyframes (for more details, see *Chapter 13, Using Keyframes to Animate Objects in Final Cut Pro*). In the next section, we will introduce you to the final plug-in group, **Transitions**. Transitions help you smooth the jarring of a jump cut between two clips. A jump cut occurs when a segment in the middle of a clip is removed, causing a jump from one scene to another. Jump cuts are most noticeable in interview videos, where the position of the subject's head appears to jump from one orientation to another.

Using built-in transitions

There are two styles of transition – those that hide the cut between two clips and those that announce the change from one clip to the next. My opinion of transitions is that they are to be avoided. However, with that said, there are occasions when some transitions are useful. I will leave this discussion here by saying that it's the editor's choice, and it depends on the audience.

Transitions that hide a jump cut are found in the **Dissolve** category; pretty much all other categories have transitions that emphasize a cut.

In this section about built-in transitions, I will feature the **Dissolve** category and give special mention to the **Flow** transition. For the announcement type of transition, I will cover the **Wipes** category.

The Dissolve category of Transitions

A common transition is **Cross Dissolve**, which merges the end of one clip with the beginning of the following clip. It tries to soften the jarring jump between two clips.

Cross Dissolve

In most cases, **Cross Dissolve** is to be avoided for commercial videos. Certainly, it should not be used frequently. In my mind, it is better to have matched cuts that are planned and filmed by the cameraperson. I agree that, as an editor, you don't always have that luxury, so you may have to provide some form of softening transition. The redeeming feature of the **Cross Dissolve** transition is the ability to shorten its duration, so it is barely noticeable but still softens the jump cut – three to five frames will do the job.

Fade to Black

Final Cut Pro calls the **Fade** transition **Fade to Color**. It defaults to black, which provides the conventional fade for TV shows. We are so conditioned to seeing a fade to black that our eyes may see it but our brain does not register it. Despite this, don't overuse it. Treat a **Fade to Color** transition as a "get out of jail card."

The transition in the next section is similar to **Cross Dissolve**, except it morphs between two clips. Morphing is defined as changing smoothly from one image to another in small increments, using computer AI.

Flow

If you are editing interviews or dialogue scenes, the **Flow** transition can be lifesaving, but, as I have said several times about other features of Final Cut Pro, it's not a magic bullet. The secret to the **Flow** transition is ensuring that head angles and the position of the lips and eyes are in a similar position. You can tell immediately when the **Flow** transition is not going to be effective, by placing the playhead in the middle of the transition and still seeing a soft dissolve after the **Optical** flow has been analyzed.

Figure 11.52 – An unusable Flow effect

The **Flow** transition can be repositioned by dragging the transition at the edit point with the **Trim** tool to a slightly different position and matching the head, eyes, and lips as much as possible. Before you drag the video, make sure that the audio is expanded so that when you drag the **Flow** transition, the audio stays in place. When you drag the transition in the timeline, a two-up display shows in the viewer, so you can match angles as much as possible.

> **Note**
> The Flow transition should only be used at the default duration.

Figure 11.53 – A two-up display showing matched frames for the Flow transition

A completely different style of transition is covered in the **Wipes** category in the section that follows.

Wipes

The announcement type of transition is well represented by the **Wipes** category of **Transitions**. There are 12 **Wipes** effects, and they all give a feeling of ending one story and starting another, which is exactly what the announcement of a new scene should do.

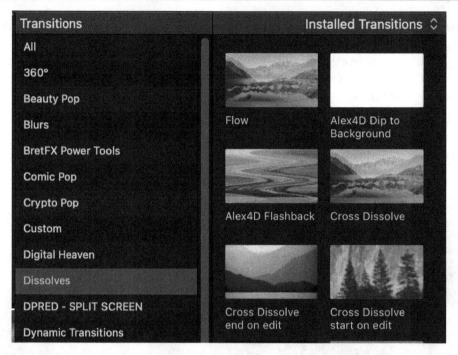

Figure 11.54 – The Wipes transitions

In general, the built-in transitions do not require many adjustments, so I will show an example with the **Checker** transition that does have a number of adjustment options.

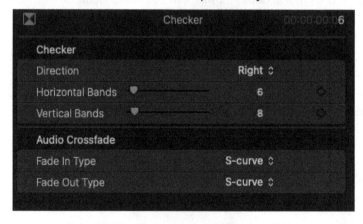

Figure 11.55 – Controls in the Checker transition

You are able to adjust the number of bands as well as modify the style of fading in and out.

The adjustments discussed so far are modifications of the default plug-ins. However, it is better to create your own unique look, as you will see in the next section.

Creating custom plug-ins from built-in plug-ins

All editors using Final Cut Pro have access to and use the built-in plug-ins, so the effects added using them may become recognizable.

To achieve a fresh, unique look, a simple solution is to combine the different effects to give them your own distinctive identity.

The **Simple** title icon on the left of *Figure 11.56* is the built-in **Centered** title. It can be transformed by using a **Dynamic** background and the **Social** lower third, with a logo (as shown on the right of *Figure 11.56*) – all effects that are supplied as part of Final Cut Pro.

Figure 11.56 – Built-in Centered (left) and the transformed (right) titles

The built-in effects will give you a good start with plug-ins, but you will need more as your editing skills progress. The vast number of available free plug-ins is the next place for you to look, which will be discussed in *Chapter 12, Using Third-Party Plug-Ins*.

Summary

This chapter covered many diverse styles of plug-ins. You now know that it's the add-ons that make Final Cut Pro the powerhouse that it is. You learned that a number of plug-ins are supplied with the software when it is first installed.

You were shown the built-in **Titles** plug-ins, leading with the **Build In/Out** category of basic animated titles, **Lower Thirds**, and **Bumper/Opener**.

You learned that **Titles** plug-ins allow you to both enter text and add video and stills to portals on the screen, using a drop zone.

You were introduced to **Elements**, **Solids** generators, and then effects in the **Effects** browser. You saw two representative categories of **Transitions**, including the morphing **Flow** transition and **Wipes**.

You learned that **Effects** plug-ins are not just about color manipulation and have diverse options to produce results, such as green screen videos and cutouts using **Masks**.

You were introduced to the concept of combining built-in plug-ins to create unique effects that are no longer recognizable as the standard plug-ins supplied with Final Cut Pro.

The next chapter is a logical extension of what you have learned in this chapter, as it explores free and purchasable third-party plug-ins.

12
Using Third-Party Plug-Ins

In *Chapter 11,Using Built-In Plug-Ins*, you learned about the built-in plug-ins that are supplied with Final Cut Pro. You were introduced to the terminology of the plug-in infrastructure, and you saw how to use the built-in titles and effects, as well as generators and transition effects.

In this chapter, you will learn about the multitude of third-party plug-ins that can be added to Final Cut Pro. Some are free and mostly very simple to use, while others can be purchased. You will learn how to control the settings in the different types of plug-ins, from text manipulation to adding stills and video into drop zones.

The third-party purchasable plug-ins are listed by the developer. A number of these have been provided to me by the developers as evaluation copies, while I have purchased others for my own use.

The main headings in the chapter are as follows:

- Free plug-ins
- Purchasable plug-ins
- Title plug-ins
- Audio correction plug-ins
- Workflow extensions
- LUTs
- Uninstalling plug-ins

In this chapter, you will learn how third-party plug-ins are treated the same as the built-in plug-ins, as explained in *Chapter 11, Using Built-In Plug-Ins*. You saw where they appeared in the inspector in *Chapter 10, The Inspector Controls*.

You will learn about plug-ins for color and audio correction issues, as well as for video noise and grain, the stabilization of shaky footage, and even extracting people from the background without requiring a green screen.

At the end of the chapter, you will see how to produce captions from a voiceover as speech-to-text and the use of workflow extensions. Finally, I will explain the use of LUTs.

Let's get started!

Free plug-ins

The main reason that developers provide free plug-ins is to promote their paid versions. However, some developers only offer free plug-ins. I have found that some of the free plug-ins are surprisingly good.

In this section, I will show you packages from two developers, one who only supplies free versions and another who is promoting his paid versions with an excellent package of simple power tools. The next section covers what I refer to as one of the *gem categories* of the Final Cut Pro plug-ins, and it's free.

Andy's plug-ins

Andy Mees offers all of his plug-ins for free; they are simple, single-focus effects. I'm going to show you one of them: **Andy's Elastic Aspect**.

Andy's Elastic Aspect

You will be aware of the different size ratios of older standard definition videos, which have a ratio of 5 x 4 compared to today's 16 x 9 video formats. It is a bit like trying to put a circle in a square hole. Either black bars are needed or something needs to be left out or cut off. *Figure 12.1* presents a 5 x 4 image on the left and a 16 x 9 image on the right in a 1080p timeline:

Figure 12.1 – A 5 x 4 image on the left and a 16 x 9 image on the right in a 1080p timeline

You will see from the 5 x 4 image that black bars, known as letterbox and pillarbox, are needed to fill the 1080p timeline that has a 16 x 9 aspect ratio. To fit the left image into the timeline's ratio, you would normally use the **Spatial Conform** option at the bottom of the *filmstrip* inspector's window, setting it to **Fill**.

Spatial Conform will fill the 16 x 9 screen but it will cut off the top and bottom of the image. This is not ideal, but it works as a quick fix. A problem occurs when the parts to be cut off have something that needs to be shown in the video.

It would appear to be against the laws of physics to be able to fit the almost square image into a rectangle. This is where **Andy's Elastic Aspect** can help by stretching parts of the image while being able to retain the aspect for objects that wouldn't handle being out of shape.

There are two images in *Figure 12.2*: the one on the left is after setting **Spatial Conform** to **Fill**, (note how the groom's hand is missing) and the one on the right is the stretched image using **Andy's Elastic Aspect**. The yellow area shows the part of the image that is not stretched:

Figure 12.2 – A 5 x 4 image on the left after using Spatial Conform Fill
and a 16 x 9 image on the right using Andy's Elastic Aspect

Andy's plug-ins can be downloaded from `https://fxfactory.com/products/andymees/`:

There are so many free effects to choose from. Next, I'll show a package that is well worth adding to Final Cut Pro: **BretFX Power Tools Lite**.

BretFX Power Tools Lite

As with most free plug-ins, this package is a teaser for the paid version, but it does include valuable tools. If nothing else, the **Border** and **Emboss** effects are well worth having. The next section shows how they are used.

Border

Still images added to a video can look out of place. You could try to hide the fact they are not video by using the **Ken Burns** effect or you can feature them as an integral part of the video. One of the effective ways of featuring a still is to add a border to the edge. The **PT Border** effect gives quick access to border color and width options and also lets you adjust the border to suit a cropped image, something the built-in **Simple** border can't do. *Figure 12.3* shows the still with a border color from the video on a cropped image; the original image before cropping is represented by the white lines:

Figure 12.3 – Picture-in-picture with PT Border

The next effect is **Emboss**.

Emboss

The **Emboss** effect is something out of the ordinary to grab attention. The controls are simple to adjust to give an oil painting effect, as shown in the image on the left in the following figure:

Figure 12.4 – Emboss added to the image on the left

BretFX Power Tools Lite can be downloaded from `https://bit.ly/3MXcQOM`:

The plug-ins discussed previously are just a sample of the free effects that you can download. The most useful plug-ins that add major benefits to Final Cut Pro will need to be purchased. I will show some examples in the next section. The vast number of purchasable plug-ins are titles and transitions. Since both of these categories were extensively explained earlier in *Chapter 11, Using Built-In Plug-Ins*, I will only briefly cover them in the next section.

Purchasable plug-ins

On the whole, plug-ins fall into two categories: those that correct issues with your clips and those that add benefits to your clips. I will show you plug-ins for color and audio correction issues as well as for video noise and grain. I will also show you some for the stabilization of shaky footage and for extracting people from backgrounds without the need for a green screen.

First, I will explain CoreMelt's **Lock & Load Stabilize** plug-in, which is a fast stabilizer for shaky video footage that has the major advantage of being able to stabilize multicam footage, something the built-in Final Cut Pro stabilizer can't do without a workaround.

Lock & Load Stabilize

Lock & Load Stabilize Only is significantly faster than the built-in stabilizer and has much more control. The effect appears in the **Effects** sidebar under the **C2 Lock & Load** category.

As normal, you drag **Lock & Load** to the clip in the timeline. If you check the inspector, you will see the following message in red: **No Tracking Data**. When you click the **Track Motion** button, the tracking percentage will count down. *Figure 12.5* shows **Stabilize Only** about to stabilize a multicam clip:

Figure 12.5 – Lock & Load Stabilize Only

When tracking is completed, the red message will turn green and will say **Tracking Data Ok**:

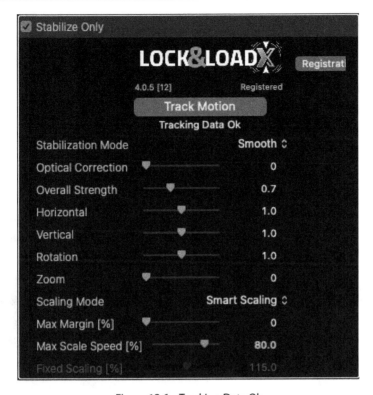

Figure 12.6 – Tracking Data Ok

In most cases, the default settings will give an excellent result, provided there is not too much camera shake or particularly jerky camera movement. The default **Lock & Load Stabilization Mode** option is **Smooth**; if you select **Lock Down**, the image will be more stable but will be significantly zoomed in. You can purchase **Lock & Load** at `https://tinyurl.com/2ywdbcs4`:

PaintX

The second plug-in that I will show you to help fix video issues is CoreMelt's **PaintX**. You can use this to remove skin blemishes, paint out power lines or antennas, apply digital makeup, warp, stretch, and repair damaged video. You can simply draw a stroke by pressing just one button and the stroke will track the movement in your video.

The tools provided include a color brush and tools to adjust color, blur, smear, sharpen, warp, shrink/expand, clone, reduce noise, heal, and erase.

PaintX is good for both repairing images and adding effects such as adjusting makeup or enhancing facial features, as well as providing a bit of painless nip-and-tuck cosmetic surgery.

For this example, I will remove the logo on a yacht's sail and have it track for the whole video clip. In *Figure 12.7*, the **PaintX** effect is in the inspector and the center yacht has an **M** logo that will be removed using the **Heal Brush** option:

Figure 12.7 – PaintX in the inspector

When the **Open Editor** button is pressed, the editor window appears, as in *Figure 12.8*. Now, follow these steps to remove the logo:

1. Position the playhead at the beginning – play through the clip to make sure that the item being actioned is visible for the whole clip.

2. Return the playhead to the beginning of the clip.

3. Select **Heal Brush** at the top of the window (three buttons to the left of **Animate**).

4. Draw over the logo until it is removed by mixing the white of the sail, as in *Figure 12.8*:

Figure 12.8 – PaintX window

5. With the logo removed, press the tracking button, and the clip will play with the logo removed.

6. When you are happy with the result, press **Save Changes** and play the clip in the timeline.

As you can see, PaintX is a much cleaner way of tracking than the built-in Final Cut Pro tracker.

> Tip
>
> Some fashion model agencies like to show their models with thin arms. You could use PaintX with the built-in **Mocha** effect to make arms thinner in your fashion videos.

PaintX is CPU-intensive. I find it is best to temporarily disable the plug-in if you need to process several trackings on one project. You may also need to temporarily disable the plug-in if it is being used in other projects in the library. PaintX can be purchased from `https://tinyurl.com/ykr97w3j`:

The next plug-in we will cover is **Keyper**, an AI-powered way of instantly cutting out people from their backgrounds.

Keyper

Some plug-ins appear to be magic and just do what they say instantly. Keyper is such an example. It doesn't require any green screen as the built-in **Keyer** effect does.

Figures 12.9, *12.10*, and *12.11* show the differences between the built-in **Keyer** effect and the **Keyper** plug-in. The results speak for themselves. The first image is the original:

Figure 12.9 – Original image by Irina Gromovataya from Pixabay

The second image uses **Keyper** with a little thinning added; it could handle a little red added to match it to the original. The controls are intuitive and offer the choice of **Matte**, **Composite**, and **Original** views:

Figure 12.10 – Keyper plug-in

The third image uses Final Cut Pro's built-in **Keyer** effect; there is no way any adjustment with this background will give a good key!

Figure 12.11 – Built-in Keyer effect

Keyper is available at `https://tinyurl.com/ysfdfsya`:

The fourth plug-in that is used to fix video issues is explained in the next section: **Neat Video noise reduction**.

Neat Video noise reduction

Noise in a video is a term to describe something that shows up as grain and is caused by not enough lighting when the scene is filmed. When the video plays, the grain shows a shimmering effect. Final Cut Pro has a built-in noise reduction effect as part of the **Basics** category in the **Effects** sidebar, but **Neat Video** can remove noise that the built-in effect will only reduce.

You should be aware that because it is so intensive, Neat Video really stresses the computer's processor to the point that Final Cut Pro will slow down significantly while **noise reduction** is active. The same applies to the built-in noise reduction effect as well but to a lesser extent. Only activate Neat Video after all the other edits are complete, or disable noise reduction in the inspector while you continue to edit, remembering to enable them again before export.

Exporting will also take longer while noise reduction is being rendered, but it will completely transform your video, so the downside of slower rendering is well worth the wait.

To use Neat Video noise reduction, drag the **Reduce Noise** effect inside the clip in the timeline. The inspector will only show a small section with a button called **Options Window…**:

Figure 12.12 – The Options Window… button in the inspector

After the button is pressed, a separate window appears with the clip and three smaller windows, **Y Enhanced**, **Cr Enhanced**, and **Cb Enhanced**. This plug-in has many controls; to take full advantage of these controls, you will need to spend time learning about and understanding them, starting with **Beginner Mode**. The following explanation will achieve a default result but it just scratches the surface.

The objective is to select an area in the window that contains just noise. Draw a green shape over the plainest area you can find; before you release the mouse, wait for the shape to indicate **Size: Good**. Try different areas to find the highest **Noise Level** value. *Figure 12.13* gives a noise level of **8.4**, which is a reasonable result considering that the image has no completely uniform areas. At the bottom of the window are small images that represent frames. You can try for a better noise level on either side of the blue outlined frame you have selected.

Figure 12.13 – Green outline for selection of the area of noise

When you have the highest noise level, click the **Build Profile** button. The green outline will turn blue. You could use the **Adjust** and **Preview** buttons, but to keep things simple here, just press **Apply**.

What has been shown here is just a preview of the capability of Neat Video noise reduction. Even if this is all that you do, you will see a significant improvement. The plug-in can be purchased from `https://tinyurl.com/558d3mxx`:

Another style of plug-in that you will most frequently use comes under the **Titles** category. Many developers produce excellent examples of simple **Titles** and **Lower Thirds** plug-ins; the following section shows some examples.

Titles plug-ins

There are myriads of developers of **Titles** plug-ins. Here are just some examples of the ones that I use.

PremiumVFX InfoBars

PremiumVFX has an enormous collection of **Titles** and **Presentation** templates that will save you hundreds of hours if you try to produce them yourself. The animations are smooth, and there is something for every need. I will show just one **Titles** group called **Infobars**; this has an optional way of splitting the video to introduce the title, which then slides back out of the way as the video continues to play.

Figure 12.14 – The clip split on the left; no split on the right

PremiumVFX InfoBars is in the **Titles** browser's sidebar:

Figure 12.15 – PremiumVFX InfoBars with 25 Infobar options

All the **Infobar** titles have similar controls. Here, I will demonstrate **Infobar 03**:

Figure 12.16 – The inspector window for the Infobar

You will be familiar with some of the following controls from reading *Chapter 11, Using Built-In Plug-Ins* about the built-in titles. The **Build In** and **Build Out** checkboxes control the start and ending animations. The **Split Media** checkbox controls whether the vertical title separates the video to show the title without hiding any of the clip. **X Position** moves the whole title horizontally and, along with **Texts Size**, controls the first **Text** section. The controls are reproduced for each block of text. PremiumVFX InfoBars is available at `https://www.toolfarm.com/store/cart/referral/referrer/VTUTOR/url/premiumvfx_infobars_for_fcpx/target/buy`:

The next developer is LenoFX, which has similar offerings to PremiumVFX with over 7,000 elements in their collection. Here, I'll show two groups of plug-ins: the **Grids** package and the **YouTube Booster** collection.

LenoFX Grids

The **LenoFX Grids** collection includes 170+ titles and 32 transitions. Think of grids as a split screen on steroids:

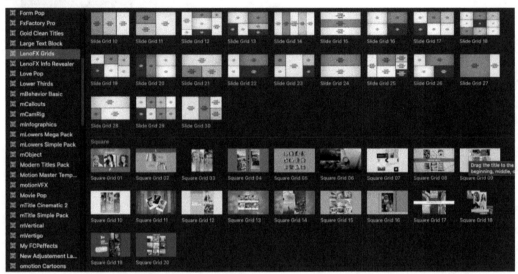

Figure 12.17 – Selection of Grids titles

The concept is that each of the grids can hold either a still or video clip, while there is an option for the clip in the timeline to show when the grid is on display. Then, when the playhead is past the grid in the timeline, the video smoothly moves up to fill the screen. **LenoFX Grids** is a brilliant way of introducing corporate or documentary videos by previewing short segments of what will be in the video's main body:

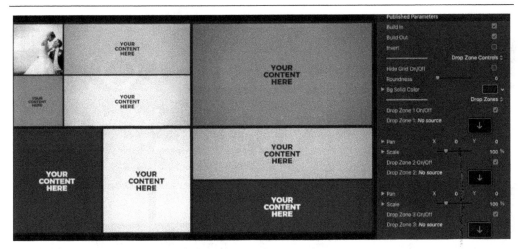

Figure 12.18 – Grids in the viewer and inspector

Grid transitions are also part of the package and provide a similar experience to introducing each section of a documentary.

LenoFX Grids is available from `https://tinyurl.com/2ahetu82`:

Another useful LenoFX plug-in is the **YouTube Booster** package, as discussed in the next section.

LenoFX YouTube Booster

The **LenoFX YouTube Booster** package is ideal for any editor involved with social media to give over 260 different social media elements to keep vertical, horizontal, and square video aspects fresh.

I find that **LenoFX YouTube Booster** offers far more than titles for YouTube, and with some modifications, when opened in **Motion**, the titles can be used for corporate introduction animations (see *Chapter 17, Supporting Software Applications for Final Cut Pro*).

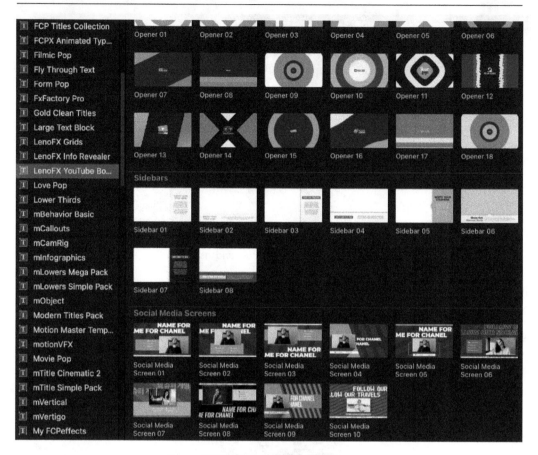

Figure 12.19 – Openers in YouTube Booster

All LenoFX plug-ins are available from `https://www.lenofx.com/`:

The set of titles I will feature in the next section is the **mLowers** pack from **MotionVFX**.

MotionVFX

One of the issues I have with many lower-third templates for titles is that many of them only have the text showing. So, the colors in the background of any video can compete with the words in the title, making the text hard to read against the multicolored video. With 130 + titles, the majority of this package has colored backgrounds behind the text. I'm continually looking for titles that have detailed controls built in. The **mLowers** pack from MotionVFX has more controls than I have seen from any other developer:

Figure 12.20 – Detailed controls and 131 titles from MotionVFX

mLowers is available from `https://tinyurl.com/95xjv2bv`:

As well as individual developers, third-party plug-ins can also be acquired from suppliers who provide a platform for smaller developers to promote their plug-ins. The following section discusses some plug-ins provided by TOOLFARM.

TOOLFARM

TOOLFARM is a platform for third-party developers of plug-ins for both video and audio. TOOLFARM supplies not only titles but the whole gamut of plug-ins for Final Cut Pro. It's the go-to shop for plug-ins and even includes the full catalog from FxFactory. In the next section, I will cover an outstanding **Titles** plug-in from the TOOLFARM catalog: **Yanobox Motype 2**.

Yanobox Motype 2

Many **Titles** plug-ins have extensive controls, but nothing comes close to **Motype 2**. There are hundreds of settings for each of the 260+ plug-ins in the **Motype 2** package. This package verges on being its own title graphics platform. It's like a separate graphics application within the Final Cut Pro interface. *Figure 12.21* shows the options in the inspector. Each of the expansion arrows can contain 10–20 settings. *Figure 12.21* shows the list of headings and the settings that are under just one heading – **Motion Mixer**:

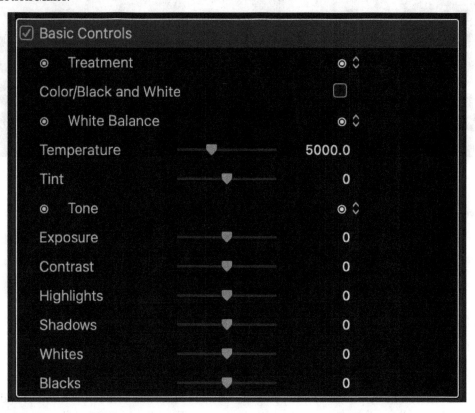

Figure 12.21 – Settings headings (left) and Motion Mixer settings (right)

The unique look and feel of Motype 2 is shown in the way that color trails are animated as part of the text. They are sometimes over the top in the WOW factor but can be dialed back if necessary for a more subtle effect:

Figure 12.22 – Motype 2 color trails

A unique part of this plug-in is that the controls are also accessible in the viewer and the text can be edited in a separate editor, which is a welcome difference from the cramped Final Cut Pro panel for editing text.

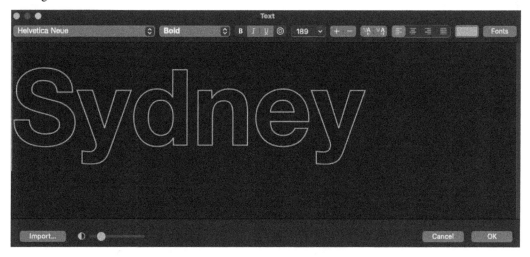

Figure 12.23 – Motype 2 text editor

Motype is available from TOOLFARM at `https://www.toolfarm.com/store/cart/referral/referrer/VTUTOR/url/yanobox_motype/target/buy`:

The plug-ins that have been discussed so far are all video-related. Audio plug-ins are available from specific developers. The next section discusses some of the many audio plug-ins.

Audio correction plug-ins

Audio plug-ins tend to be supplied by specialized developers such as Boris FX and iZotope. Audio is hard to describe in a written form such as this book. I will attempt to do so by showing you the change in waveforms and explaining what I can hear. I have chosen to discuss the **Boris FX CrumplePop** package of audio plug-ins in the next section as an example of those available. I suggest you visit the websites of the main contenders as mentioned previously; most have a trial version for you to try.

Boris FX CrumplePop Complete

The **Boris FX CrumplePop Complete** package of audio plug-ins will quickly remove common issues, even using the default settings, with a myriad of settings that you can adjust:

Figure 12.24 – Adjustments for CrumplePop's EchoRemover dialog

The package includes tools to remove clips, echoes, pops, rustling, traffic, and wind. Let's look at **EchoRemover** in detail in the next section.

EchoRemover

Final Cut Pro does not have a suitable built-in solution for echo removal. I use **EchoRemover** by CrumplePop, which employs AI to remove echo from your audio. *Figure 12.25* shows the waveform with room echo at the troughs:

Figure 12.25 – Waveforms with room echo

Figure 12.26 has **EchoRemover** added. You can see the room echo waveform at the troughs has been reduced and the peaks, which feature the voice, have been increased:

Figure 12.26 – Echo removed with CrumplePop's EchoRemover

The next CrumplePop plug-in is **ClipRemover**.

ClipRemover

This plug-in automatically restores clipped and distorted audio. **ClipRemover** can intelligently identify the clipped areas, restore them, and reconstruct the missing audio. *Figure 12.27* shows the peaks clipped in red on the audio meters:

Figure 12.27 – Clipped audio red peaks before using CrumplePop's ClipRemover

When there is no data above 0 dB, the waveform usually shows as a flat line at the top, and after using **ClipRemover**, the flat line has gone, leaving natural-looking peaks. *Figure 12.28* has had **ClipRemover** added, with the output level adjusted from the default now peaking at -6 in the audio meters:

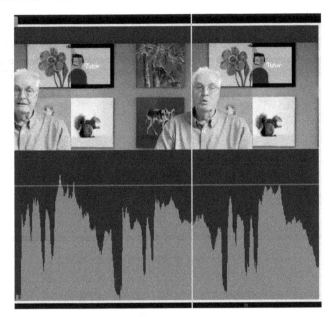

Figure 12.28 – ClipRemover added, peaking at -6

The next CrumplePop plug-in is **WindRemover**.

WindRemover

One of the most common issues when filming outside is wind noise. There are many audio frequencies represented in the sounds produced by the wind, so it is time-consuming to attempt to remove wind with the audio pass or **Limiter** controls built into Final Cut Pro. **WindRemover** intelligently targets and removes only wind noise, leaving the voice intact. *Figure 12.29* shows the waveforms with very strong wind noise:

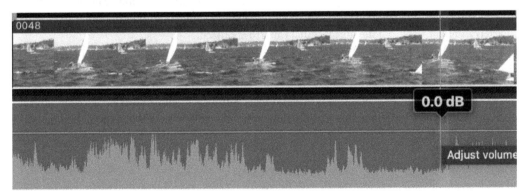

Figure 12.29 – Waveform with strong wind noise before adding the plug-in

The majority of wind noise has been removed from *Figure 12.30* using **WindRemover**. Be careful, as very strong wind noise could also contain the frequencies of the voices you are trying to isolate:

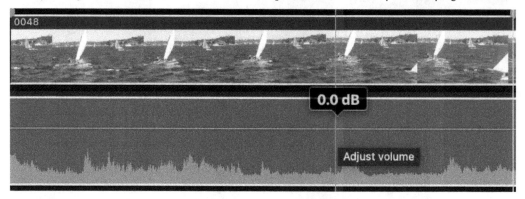

Figure 12.30 – Waveform with WindRemover added

CrumplePop plug-ins are available from `https://tinyurl.com/mrx5n89z`:

The plug-ins covered so far in this chapter follow Final Cut Pro conventions. The next two plug-ins are outside of what I normally expect of a plug-in. The next developer is Eric Lenz, and he has approached Final Cut Pro color management from the point of view of a Lightroom photographer to offer a completely different way from the normal Final Cut Pro approach.

Eric Lenz

The lead item in the Eric Lenz collection is **Professionals' Suite for Final Cut Pro X**. The suite covers the complete gamut of functions that a professional photographer versed with Adobe Lightroom controls would seek.

Professionals' Suite of effects

These are the individual functions offered in the Professionals' Suite, which all use sliders rather than the color wheels approach that is normal in Final Cut Pro: **Adjustment Layer**, **HSL Color View** and **HSL View**, **Vibrance Saturation**, **Black and White Mix**, **Channel Mixer**, **Color Balance**, **Contrast**, **Exposure/Gamma**, **Exposure Check Layer**, **False Colors**, **LUT Loader**, **LUT Mixer**, **Selective Color**, **White Balance**, **Basic Controls**, **Camera Calibration**, **Clone Stamp**, **Effects** (**Vignette** and **Grain**), **Presence** (**Dehaze**, **Texture**, and **Clarity**), **Sharpening**, **Spot Healing Brush**, **Upright**, **Channel Blur**, and **Grade Cleaner**.

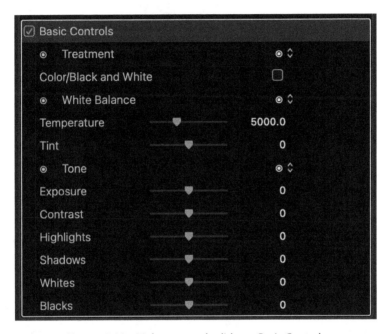

Figure 12.31 – Lightroom-style sliders – Basic Controls

The Professionals' Suite is available from `https://tinyurl.com/yc6ssyh8`:

The second of the non-conventional plug-ins creates captions as well as burnt-in subtitles – it's called **Captionator**.

Captionator

Captions and burnt-in titles are different ways to have text in a video. **Captionator** provides both of these methods of displaying text. Captions can be turned on or off by the person viewing the video, depending on the device. Captions always appear at the bottom of the video, usually as white text on a strip of black. Burnt-in titles are essentially titles added to your video that are always visible; they are not user-selectable.

Captionator is a plug-in that exports to a separate app, which converts a voiceover in the video to text and automatically imports that back into Final Cut Pro as a separate project named **Generated Captions**. The new project contains the text, both as captions available in **iTT**, **CEA-608**, and **SRT** formats, as well as titles with the font of your choosing.

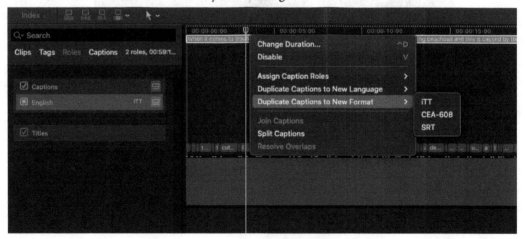

Figure 12.32 – Captions and Titles – speech to text

The titles and/or captions can be copied and pasted into the video that has the voiceover, and you can use the **Roles** tab to select either **Titles** or **Captions**. The titles can be repositioned, as well as lengthened or shortened in the timeline. They can be corrected for spelling mistakes or even completely retyped.

The real advantage of the low-cost **Captionator** app is to provide titles quickly from a voiceover without needing to use a keyboard. The results are particularly suitable for vertical and square social media videos to give information to the viewer, who is likely to have the sound turned off.

Figure 12.33 – Captions and titles from a voiceover

Captionator is available from the Apple App Store by selecting **App Store** under the **Apple** menu on your Mac.

The next two sections are not strictly plug-ins but they serve a similar role as add-ons to Final Cut Pro. The first is the most underused feature of Final Cut Pro, known as **workflow extensions**, and we will follow this with an explanation of **LUTs**.

Workflow extensions

Workflow extensions are third-party applications that can be actioned in a separate window directly inside the Final Cut Pro interface. The apps include stock media, so you can access images without leaving Final Cut Pro, as well as places to access plug-ins and work on asset management. Particularly useful is the access to collaboration tools without leaving the Final Cut Pro interface. *Figure 12.34* shows the button to open the installed workflow extensions:

Figure 12.34 – Installed workflow extensions

The next section is about **lookup tables** (**LUTs**). These are color presets that allow you to quickly change the color attributes of a clip in the browser.

LUTs

Most high-end cameras shoot in a **Log** (**logarithmic**) profile, which preserves a wide color gamut and dynamic range. Current video formats don't support the information captured by a higher-end camera's sensor, which means that the higher dynamic range would not be available in Final Cut Pro. Footage shot with a **Log** profile looks washed out when imported into a **Rec. 709** timeline, so Final Cut Pro uses LUTs to convert the extra dynamic range into an image that fits the **Rec. 709** standard for video.

There are built-in LUTs for common camera formats, and additional LUTs can be installed by scrolling to the bottom of the **CUSTOM CAMERA** section and selecting **Add Custom Camera LUT….** There is a vast range of LUTs available to download from camera manufacturers as free downloads.

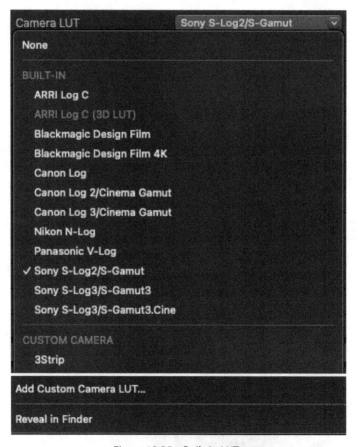

Figure 12.35 – Built-in LUTs

To convert a clip with a **Log** profile using a LUT, select the clip in the browser, then in the inspector's **i** (**info**) tab in the **General** mode, change the **Camera LUT** setting:

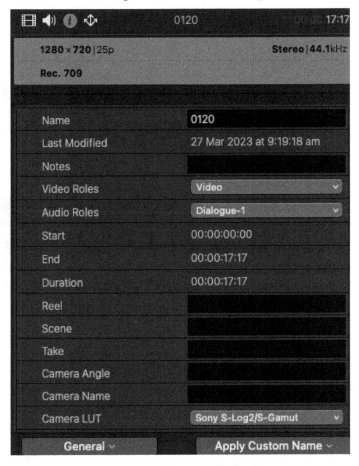

Figure 12.36 – Camera LUT selection

> **Note**
> LUTs work differently than other methods of color correction. It's most important to recognize that a LUT changes the whole clip in the browser as if it were imported in that form. This means that the LUT needs to be always available; otherwise, the clip will display a red error warning.

All third-party plug-ins are installed in library folders on the system's disk. As with LUTs, if plug-ins are removed, a red warning will show in Final Cut Pro.

Built-in effects included with Final Cut Pro don't appear in library folders and can't be removed manually. The following section shows how to remove third-party plug-ins.

Uninstalling plug-ins

When Final Cut Pro is launched, it automatically checks the compatibility of third-party plug-ins. If they aren't compatible, you will see a message, as in *Figure 12.37*:

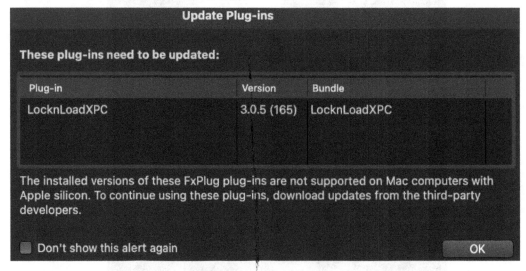

Figure 12.37 – Plug-in warning

If updates aren't available, you can uninstall the incompatible plug-ins until compatible versions are provided by the developer.

Manually uninstalling plug-ins

Developers of third-party plug-ins usually provide uninstallers to remove their plug-ins. Otherwise, you can uninstall them by quitting Final Cut Pro and then manually removing the plug-ins from one of the following locations on your Mac. I suggest you move them to another folder, at least temporarily, rather than trashing them immediately.

Check the following folders first:

- `Users/Movies/Motion Templates/Effects`
- `Users/Movies/Motion Templates/Generators`
- `Users/Movies/Motion Templates/Titles`
- `Users/Movies/Motion Templates/Transitions`

(To locate `Users`, click **Go** in the **Finder** menu bar and press **Home**.)

If the plug-ins are not in these folders, they could be in many locations. It is best to check with the developer, or try the following System library folders:

- `/Library/Plug-Ins/FxPlug/`
- `/Library/Audio/Plugins`
- `/Library/Application Support/Final Cut Pro`
- `/Library/Application Support/ProApps`
- `/Library/Application Support/*Name of developer or plugin*`

If the plug-ins are not in the System library, try the folders with the same names in the Home library.

Audio unit plug-ins for Final Cut Pro appear as individual components in either the System or Home library folders on your Mac.

To access the System library, click **Go** in the **Finder** menu bar, select **Go to Folder**, enter `/Library/Audio/Plug-Ins/Components` in the **Go to Folder** field, and then click **Go**.

To access the Home library, click **Go** in the **Finder** menu bar, select **Go to Folder**, enter `~/Library/Audio/Plug-Ins/Components` in the **Go to Folder** field, and then click **Go**.

Summary

This chapter has covered many diverse styles of plug-ins. You will now realize that it's the add-ons that make Final Cut Pro the powerhouse that it is. You have learned that many plug-ins are supplied with the software when it is first installed. You have seen that to achieve the full editing benefits, you should consider the range of purchasable titles and effects.

You have learned about a few suggested plug-ins from third-party developers that will assist you in editing in Final Cut Pro, including Lock & Load Stabilize Only, PaintX, Keyper, Neat Video noise reduction, PremiumVFX, TOOLFARM, and Boris FX CrumplePop.

You have seen that audio correction is easy to achieve, even with the default settings when audio plug-ins are added to suspect clips.

You have seen how captions and titles can be created as speech-to-text with the low-cost Captionator application.

Finally, you have learned about the locations of third-party plug-ins and how to uninstall them.

The next chapter is a logical extension of what you have learned in this chapter, as it shows how keyframes can be used in the plug-ins outlined in this chapter. The chapter on keyframing continues the hands-on aspect of learning how to use Final Cut Pro by explaining the process of animation using keyframes. You will learn how to change the levels of audio over time, as well as about color shifts due to exposure drifts in the camera footage.

13

Using Keyframes to Animate Objects in Final Cut Pro

In *Chapter 11* and *Chapter 12*, you learned about built-in and third-party plug-ins and how they add powerhouse effects to Final Cut Pro. In this chapter, you will learn how to manipulate the settings in these plug-ins to change the view of the clip as the video plays. As a simple example, think of a clip that starts with a red color as it opens in the project, but by the time it has finished playing, the color has changed to green. Equally, an object can be moved across the screen to give the impression of animation.

You will learn that you can define the start and end points of any change with the use of markers called **keyframes** to anchor the start and end action points.

The term *keyframe* is used because, at an individual frame in the video, you can enter a keyframe that locks that frame with a setting at that time in the video, and then when a new keyframe is set at a later time in the video, there is a gradual change as the video plays from the first keyframe to the last keyframe. During this process, keyframes can be added between the original start and end keyframes to change the action in between.

In this chapter, you will learn how to set keyframes for both audio and video, as well as for color changes. You will be shown how to set keyframes for plug-ins in the inspector as well as in the **viewer**, and even the timeline itself.

You will also learn that a keyframe is represented, before it is set, by a diamond shape with a plus sign inside it, at the current position of the playhead. When the keyframe is set, the diamond with the plus sign will change to orange to confirm that it is set. When the playhead moves back to that frame in the video, orange will appear again.

The sections in this chapter are as follows:

- What is a keyframe?
- Audio keyframing
- Keyframing in the inspector

- Keyframing in the viewer
- Viewer keyframe controls
- Video animation keyframing
- Ken Burns on steroids

By the end of this chapter, you will have learned that keyframes can be used throughout Final Cut Pro, both with audio and video. Keyframes allow changes in position, color, volume, rotation, transformation, cropping, exposure – the list goes on.

You will understand that keyframing is concerned with setting a starting point for an animation and then setting another keyframe as an ending point. But it's not just about the start and end points – once the beginning and end points have been set, Final Cut Pro takes over and adjusts each frame of video between the start and end points to create a smooth motion.

What is a keyframe?

Visually, a keyframe appears as a white dot in the audio track in the timeline, yellow when selected (see *Figure 13.3*), and as an orange diamond in the inspector (see *Figure 13.6*). A keyframe can also be a white dot in the opacity setting of a video track (*Figure 13.1*):

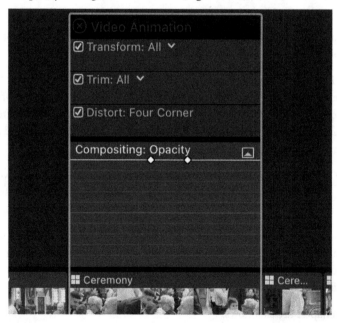

Figure 13.1: White keyframe dots showing in the video opacity setting

A keyframe can also show as white dots or an orange diamond on a red line when displayed in the viewer, as shown in *Figure 13.2*:

Figure 13.2: White keyframe dot on a red line in the viewer

Keyframes all look slightly different and react a little differently, but all represent the same concept. The common factor is that a keyframe is needed to start a change and another keyframe is needed to indicate the end of the change. If you add another keyframe in between, then the added keyframe becomes both the new end point for the original start keyframe and the new start point for the original end keyframe.

Whenever I talk to new students about keyframes, their eyes start to glaze over. It's not an easy concept to grasp, but it is the key – pun intended – to an amazing way to transform your videos.

Understanding keyframing is not a wasted exercise as it is a concept that is used by all video editing apps, as well as all animation applications. Apple's Motion works without keyframes by providing preset gestures but still allows access to keyframes once a gesture is applied. My advice is to get comfortable with using keyframes as soon as you can. You won't look back once you have the concept under your belt.

To start understanding keyframes, let's look at the different places they appear in the Final Cut Pro interface. The simplest form of a keyframe is for audio as it only does one thing: it changes the volume level. The next section looks at audio keyframing.

Audio keyframing

As you are aware, video clips in the timeline can contain both video and audio. Audio keyframing allows you to change the volume within the clip – not just as a volume level for the whole clip but with varying volume levels throughout the clip.

Let's start our first exercise:

1. Add a clip containing audio to the timeline. It can be a video clip with audio or an audio-only clip – both work the same. I have added a video clip containing audio. For better visibility, you can expand the audio by double-clicking on the audio waveform of the clip or using the *Control + S* shortcut.

   As you know, the faint horizontal white line allows the volume to be changed for the whole clip, but for this exercise, I'll add keyframes to lower the volume for the second half of the clip.

2. With the *Option* key held down, click on the horizontal white line; a white dot will appear.

3. Click a little further along the clip and do the same with the *Option* key while clicking on the line to produce another white dot.

4. Select the second dot – it will turn yellow to indicate it is active – and drag it down a little:

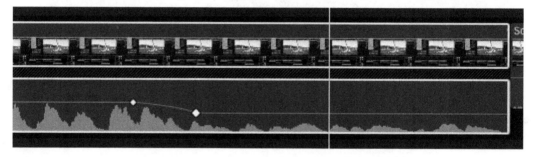

Figure 13.3: Two keyframe dots to lower the volume

This is a really simple example, but it underscores the concept that any change needs to have a start and an end. You need to be clear on this as it is the principal basis that makes keyframing work.

The preceding simple example is just one aspect of how an audio clip would normally need to be changed in volume. The levels will most likely need changing up and down as the audio track progresses. So, let's take this exercise to the next level:

1. This time, create four dots with the *Option* key held down.

2. Then, drag the line between the two center dots down. They will both turn yellow as they are now active:

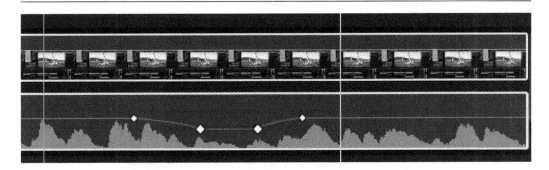

Figure 13.4: Four keyframe dots to lower the volume in the middle of the clip

Using the process of holding the *Option* key is one way of changing the volume, but there is a much quicker and more intuitive way to do this. Let's take a look:

1. Position the playhead in the audio portion of the clip in the timeline. While holding the *R* key (the shortcut key for range selection) and dragging from left to right, a range will be selected:

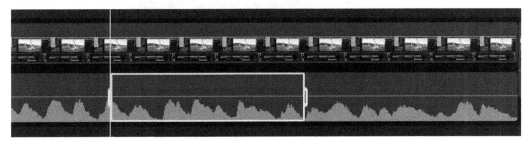

Figure 13.5: Range selected

2. Drag the horizontal white line down.
3. Click away; you will see the four dots as in the previous exercise.

The fades have been put in for you; you can adjust them to suit your needs:

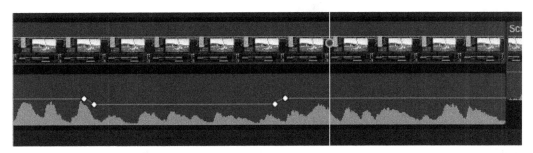

Figure 13.6: Four keyframe dots produced by the range option

Keyframing can be actioned in the timeline, inspector, and viewer. It is not a commonly used feature of the browser, but you should be aware that you can adjust audio in the browser with keyframes. The keyframes are added with the volume slider at the top of the inspector. Let's provide an introduction to keyframing in the inspector, which is the most common place you will use keyframes:

1. Set the playhead in the clip in the browser.

2. In the inspector, click the keyframe diamond with the plus sign in it to the right of the **Volume** slider:

Figure 13.7: Diamond with a plus sign

3. Once you've clicked the diamond with the plus sign, it will change to orange:

Figure 13.8: The diamond has turned orange

4. Back in the browser, move the playhead further along the clip.

5. Change the volume level with the slider in the inspector; a new keyframe will be added for you. A gray left-hand facing arrow will signify that there is a previous keyframe:

Figure 13.9: The second keyframe indicated by a gray left-facing arrow

6. Move the playhead further along the clip and change the volume with the slider in the inspector again. You will see an orange diamond and will still see a left-facing arrow, which will take you back to the previous keyframe.

7. Click the gray arrow. You will see that the previous keyframe is orange, but now, there are two gray arrows – one that will take you to the first (starting) keyframe and one that will take you to the third (ending) keyframe.

Let's review what has happened. There was an initial keyframe. It was set by clicking the diamond with the plus sign. The diamond turned orange to indicate that a keyframe had been set. Two other keyframes were added at different positions in the clip. When there are two or more keyframes, gray arrows will indicate the previous and next keyframes.

However, there are two more things to learn. How do you remove a keyframe that's already set and how do you remove all keyframes?

First, let's look at single keyframe removal. Whenever the playhead is parked on a keyframe, the diamond will show as orange. But when you hover over the orange diamond and it turns to a white diamond with a minus sign in it, you can simply click to remove that keyframe:

Figure 13.10: A white diamond with a minus sign

To remove all the keyframes in a clip, click the downward chevron to the far right of the volume slider and select **Reset Parameter**:

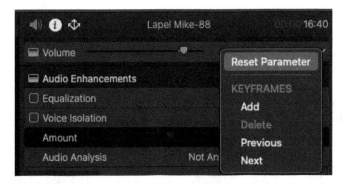

Figure 13.11: Removing all keyframes – Reset Parameter

Congratulations! You have just learned how to set keyframes in any plug-in in the inspector. In the next section, I will show you, with different plug-ins, the conventions of keyframing in the inspector.

Keyframing in the inspector

As you saw in *Chapters 11* and *12*, keyframes are available for just about any setting that can be adjusted in the inspector.

In this section, I will use the built-in **Comic Looks** plug-in in **Comic Basic**. Normally, if there are sliders for **Position** and **Rotation** adjustments, both will be able to be keyframed.

Keyframes only show in a plug-in when you hover over the diamond, unless a keyframe has already been set. In *Figure 13.12*, I have set keyframes so that you can see diamonds for all the adjustments that have keyframes available. The keyframes will only appear as orange if keyframes have previously been set:

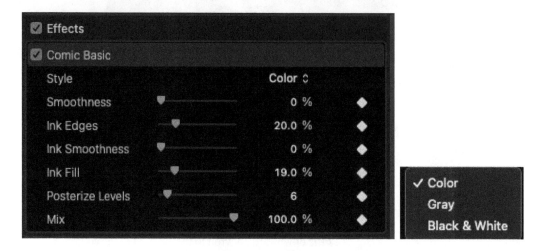

Figure 13.12 – The Comic Basic plug-in with the expanded Color option

You will notice that the **Color** option does not have a keyframe because it's a dropdown. That is the convention, but not always so. As an exception, the **Drop Shadow** plug-in *does* have a keyframe option in its dropdown. This means you always need to check the different plug-ins for different options:

Figure 13.13 – Drop Shadow does have a keyframe for dropdowns

The next section explains the conventions as to where multiple keyframes are set.

Keyframe conventions

There are certain conventions about the use of keyframes in the inspector, relating to when multiple different adjustments are keyframed. The common practice is that when you have different items being keyframed, any changes are set on the same video frame so that they all occur at the same time when the video plays. It's not a hard and fast rule, but it is worth following unless there is a good reason not to. In *Figure 13.14*, I have highlighted all the adjustments that can be keyframed in the standard **Transform**, **Crop**, and **Distort** options. You will see that **Stabilization**, **Rolling Shutter**, and **Spatial Conform** can't be keyframed:

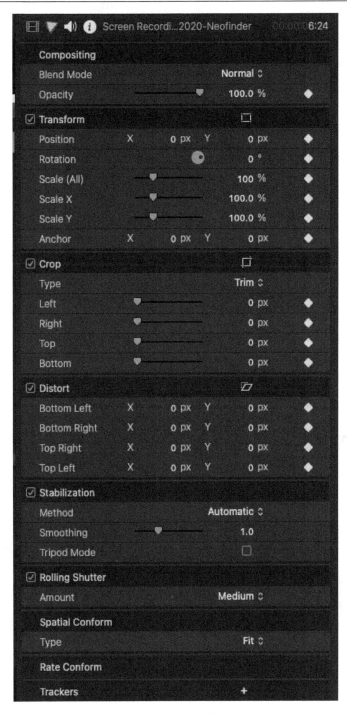

Figure 13.14 – Standard position options

In the next exercise, I'll show how an image with a transparent background can be moved across a video, giving the impression that it is part of the video. We'll use an image of an F16 and fly it over Sydney Harbor. This can be achieved by reducing the size of the F16 so that it's in keeping with the proportions of the Sydney Harbor video.

First, let's reduce the percentage size of the viewer so that we can see some of the black surround – in this case, let's set it to 50%.

> **Note**
>
> When you change the size in the viewer, the size change is only visual so that you can see more details. The size change in the viewer does not change the size of the clip in the timeline or affect the size that is exported.

Next, drag the F16 image into the timeline as a connected clip. At the first position (*Figure 13.15*), right-click in the viewer and select **Transform** to resize the F16 to an appropriate size. Then, drag the F16 offscreen to the left. In the inspector, click the diamond with the plus sign for **Position** and **Scale (All)**, as shown in *Figure 13.15*:

> **Note**
>
> **Scale (All)** also sets keyframes for **Scale X** and **Scale Y**.

Figure 13.15: Position and Scale (All)

Move the playhead in the timeline to later in the clip, to the second position (*Figure 13.16*):

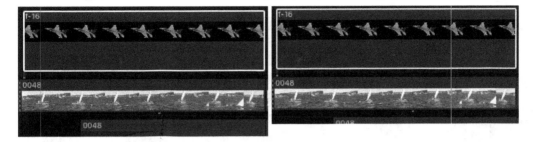

Figure 13.16: Playhead at the first (left) and second (right) positions

Drag the F16 in the viewer to the right and offscreen. A red line will appear, showing the path that the F16 traveled, with new position numbers displayed in the inspector:

Figure 13.17: F16 in the viewer, right and offscreen, shown with the red line

When the clip is played, the F16 will travel across the screen while following the red line. You can reproduce this by dragging the playhead over the clip in the timeline.

The straight flight path is somewhat unnatural; you would expect the path to be a curve as the plane flew over. I will simulate the curve by moving the playhead in the timeline to the center of the clip and then dragging the image down a little.

Since a position keyframe has already been added, the new image position will automatically add a new keyframe for just that position setting.

Move the playhead to the middle of the clip and drag the F16 slightly lower so that it appears to be dipping lower toward the water – once you release the mouse, a new keyframe will be added:

Figure 13.18: F16 dipping at the center of the viewer

I want you to ponder on this for a moment as this is a really important aspect of keyframing, and if you are not careful, it can get completely out of control.

> **Note**
> Let me repeat, *once a keyframe has been added, every repositioning of the image will automatically add another keyframe.*

You need to be careful about how you handle the changes to the image. As I mentioned previously, as soon as you release the mouse, a new keyframe is added. It is really useful for adding different directions to the red motion path but needs to be thoroughly thought through.

The next important aspect to consider is when you want to make changes to other settings than just the dip in the middle of the path. What if you need to flip the angle of the wings to make the dip more realistic?

It's easy to quickly flip the wings with **Scale Y**, but you must do it at the correct time. As I mentioned earlier, the convention is that multiple changes are made to common video frames. This example of the wing flip will clearly show you why.

For example, in the *Audio keyframing* section, you saw gray arrows that are used to move to the previous and next keyframes. Let's revisit that concept with this keyframing of the F16. As shown in *Figure 13.18*, in the inspector, regarding the **Transform** and **Position** settings, there are two gray arrows – X is 32.4 and Y is 244.7.

The flip that uses **Scale Y** needs to be done at that position. But as the playhead has been moved so that we can see the video play, it will not be where X is 32.4 and Y is 244.7 anymore.

This is how we can get the flip back to that exact middle position. So far, there are keyframes at the **Position** setting in the three locations: left offscreen, the middle of the screen, and right offscreen. **Scale (All)** only has keyframes for left offscreen and the middle of the screen. I need to set a keyframe for **Scale (All)** for right offscreen. Click the right arrow until the F16 is at the right offscreen position. Now, set the keyframe for **Scale (All)**. As mentioned previously, **Scale X** and **Scale Y** will also be set for you.

Click the **Position** left arrow until the F16 reaches X at 32.4 and Y at 244.7. Now, **Scale Y** can be adjusted to produce a flip at the center of the flight path.

A lot of details were covered in this section. I have added the extra keyframes to show you the possibilities. You mustn't get overwhelmed. So, I will review what has happened with just the basic movement without the dip and flip actions at the center:

1. The playhead was positioned at the beginning of the clip in the timeline.
2. The F16 was positioned left offscreen in the viewer.
3. A keyframe was set for the position in the inspector.
4. The playhead was moved later in the clip in the timeline.
5. The F16 was dragged to right offscreen, at which point a keyframe was automatically added for you.

Once a keyframe has been added, any further change will automatically add another keyframe each time you release the mouse. You need to be clear on this as it's easy to start making adjustments you don't want to be recorded as keyframes. If this happens, it is best to reset the keyframes.

Keyframing will require practice before you become proficient. Don't be afraid to make mistakes. At worst, you can reset and start again.

As you have seen, keyframes can be activated both in the inspector and the viewer. Up to now, I have set them in the inspector; the next section shows how you modify keyframes and keyframe paths directly in the viewer.

Keyframing in the viewer

You will start keyframing videos in the inspector and then adjust them directly in the viewer. Let's use the example of the F16, including the dip and flip at the center, and add another keyframe.

Adding new keyframes

With the *Option* key held down, click on the red path in the viewer. Several things will happen. First, the playhead in the timeline will jump to a new position that represents where you clicked in the path.

Then, a yellow diamond will appear on the red line where you clicked. The diamond can be dragged to a new position. On either side of the yellow diamond, you will see Bezier adjustment handles, as shown in *Figure 13.19*:

Figure 13.19: New keyframe added with the Option key held

With that, you have seen how to add keyframes. Now, let's look at how to make them appear as more realistic movements.

Selecting linear or smooth curves

The Bezier adjustment handles can be used to rotate the image, but more importantly, when you right-click on the yellow diamond, you have options to select **Linear** or **Smooth** curves from the previous and next keyframes. You can choose **Delete Point** or **Lock Point** so that it can't be accidentally moved or disabled and it doesn't affect the curve but is left there in case you need to reactivate it later:

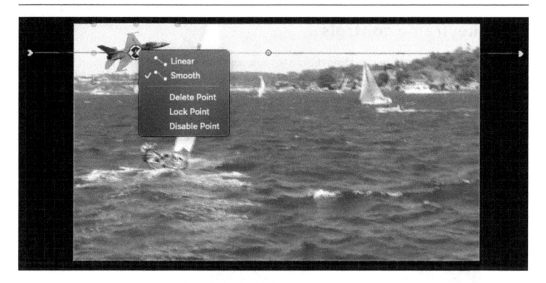

Figure 13.20: Choosing Linear or Smooth curves

Whenever you click on a diamond on the red path, the image will jump to that position in both the timeline and the viewer:

Figure 13.21: Multiple keyframes

You can use the direct controls in the viewer popup or, as you will see in the next section, use the **Transform** or **Crop** control.

Viewer keyframe controls

When you select **Transform**, **Crop**, or **Distort** from the onscreen buttons located at the bottom left-hand corner of the viewer, future changes can be keyframed by selecting the diamond in the top-left corner:

Figure 13.22: Diamond before (left) and after (right) setting

The principle is the same as setting keyframes in the inspector. They are set when the diamond has a plus sign, but with a slight difference: rather than changing to orange as it does in the inspector, the diamond has a small **x** when a keyframe has been set. Changes that are made in the viewer are also shown in the inspector.

The viewer controls are very useful for making minor alterations in the cropping of an image where a clip has temporary intrusions at the edges of the clip, such as a logo that is not wanted onscreen or where a handheld camera's framing of the shot has a doorframe that protrudes into the edge of a scene.

After a keyframe has been set, each time the clip is cropped, the removed portion will stay out of the scene until the cropping is changed. This means that you can continually change the cropping of the clip if there's an object that you don't want in view, such as a doorjamb, transforming the clip back to full size as the door goes out of shot. Each time you crop, a new keyframe is automatically entered for you. Just be careful not to pixelate the images with changes that are too large. The other issue to watch out for is that the linear change in an image may be slower than any quick camera movements, so the door may still be in view at times. It's a trial-and-error exercise, but it's still much better than having to reshoot the scene.

The inspector and viewer are the most common places where you will set keyframes. You have seen that audio can be keyframed in the timeline, as can opacity and other plug-ins that have been added to the clip, as I'll explain in the next section.

Keyframing video animation

The **Video Animation** window allows you to control the built-in plug-ins that have been added to the timeline clip. This is an alternative to making adjustments in the inspector. The feature is best used to quickly change the opacity directly in the timeline rather than moving to the inspector. **Video Animation** can be activated from the **Clip** menu, but as it is generally used as an opacity quick fix, the shortcut is worth remembering: *Control + V*. To activate any of the options, click the arrow in the square on the right. *Figure 13.23* shows **Opacity** exposed, with keyframes added:

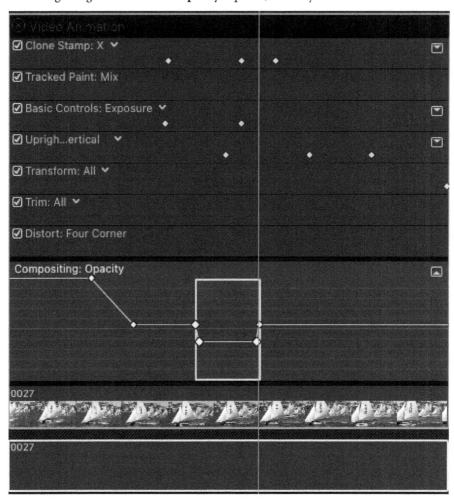

Figure 13.23 – The Video Animation window

Keyframes are added in the same way as audio keyframes – by either pressing *Option* and clicking or holding down the *R* key to create a range.

When a dropdown collapses, any keyframes that have been added will show up as dots on the collapsed lines, as shown in *Figure 13.23*.

As you have seen, even though keyframing can provide complex animations, there is a much simpler way of changing the size of images in the viewer. You might be familiar with the *Ken Burns effect*, which does not use keyframes. In the next section, you will learn how to set the Ken Burns effect to feature more than one zoom.

Ken Burns on steroids

The **Ken Burns** effect is a simple way of animating a zoom-in effect when you want to smoothly move from a wide view of a scene to a close-up or vice versa.

You will be familiar with the use of the Ken Burns effect and how the green outline represents the starting point of the change in size and the red outline shows the ending size:

Figure 13.24: Ken Burns green to red

The *Ken Burns* effect is certainly a quick alternative to keyframing a change of angle. However, you need to be careful that the original image has a high enough resolution, avoiding the zoomed-in portion pixelating. If you have filmed in 4k and have the clip in a 1080p timeline, you will be able to zoom in 2x (or 100%) of the screen size.

You can achieve this by starting the project at 1080p and dragging in the 4k clip. Final Cut Pro will fit the 4k clip into the 1080p timeline. *Figure 13.25* shows a 1080p project on the left and a 4k clip added to the 1080p timeline on the right:

Figure 13.25: A 1080p project (left) and a 4k clip in a 1080p project (right)

Because the Ken Burns effect is designed as a quick fix, there is no further flexibility than the linear change in size. It starts at one size and ends at another. There is no opportunity to slow the action or even freeze it in the middle before moving to a different part of the video. *Figure 13.26* shows the resizing from wide to zoomed-in on the bride and groom. I will show you a workflow where the zoom on the bride and groom will pause, then switch to a zoom of the two bridesmaids, then pause on them.

To achieve this animation without keyframes, I need to break the clip into four sections. The first will zoom on the bride and groom, the second with hold on the bride and groom, the third will zoom on the bridesmaids, and the fourth will hold on the bridesmaids:

Figure 13.26: Clip split into four sections

The first section has the same settings as in *Figure 13.26*, with wide zooming on the bride and groom. The second section will use the switch button control to switch to the end size of *Figure 13.26*. The second section uses the same start size as the end size of the first section. The second section will be the same size at the end as at the beginning so that there is no change:

Figure 13.27: Section two has no change in size

Then, the third section will use the switch button to set the green start to the same size as the end of the second section. The third section will end with a zoom of the two bridesmaids:

Figure 13.28: Section three starts with the bride and groom and moves to the bridesmaids

The last section will hold the end size of the third section, by having both green and red at the same size:

Figure 13.29: Section four has no change in size

The Ken Burns effect can be modified by splitting the clip, but in my mind, it is much better to become familiar with adding keyframes as the flexibility is worth the time spent learning to become proficient with keyframes.

Summary

This may have been a short chapter, but it had thought-provoking content. You have learned everything you need to know about keyframing. I would like to stress that adding keyframes is not complex once you get your head around it. The principles are simple, but you need to plan ahead as to how you approach it.

You should keep this basic concept in mind: every change needs two keyframes – one to start the change and the other to end the change. The green and red rectangles in the Ken Burns effect are a good example to keep in mind.

I recommend that you get to understand keyframing as soon as you can. You will be able to use the knowledge in all NLEs once you have the concept under your belt.

You learned that once a keyframe has been added, any further change will automatically add another keyframe each time you release the mouse. You need to be clear on this as it's easy to start making adjustments that you don't want to be recorded as keyframes. If this happens, it is best to reset the keyframes and start again.

The next chapter takes a tangential turn and looks at the principles of color.

Summary

14

Understanding the Principles of Color

This chapter is more theory than practice, but you will need the knowledge provided here as a foundation for when you move on to *Chapter 15, Using Color Scopes for Advanced Color Correction.*

In this chapter, you will learn the principles of color theory and how to use color to hold or divert attention from characters and locations in your videos. You will learn to recognize that colors have different meanings in different cultures and how color can not only change the mood of your whole video but also signify to the audience different locations, or even different times when there are flashback scenes in your video.

The possibilities are numerous when you consider that a color palette can, for example, indicate a dream sequence to the audience or transition to a childhood scene to explain why a character is behaving badly in the present.

You will understand that color theory is essential in video production as it enables video professionals to create accurate and consistent colors across different displays and devices to assist in color grading and correction.

After that, you will learn how the **color wheel** is your reference for formal and traditional color correction. You will learn the theory behind color combinations and how to reproduce them with free online color calculators. You will learn how the **color value** is the lightness or darkness of a color and the **intensity** is the strength of a color.

You will learn that color is seen in different ways depending on the light source. Color on a printed page has a different tone to color in a video. You will understand that there are different ways of mixing color depending on the light source, be it natural light reflecting off a page or artificial light being transmitted to produce colors. Digital colors are represented by **Red, Green, and Blue (RGB)** and printed colors by **Cyan, Magenta, Yellow, and Black (CMYK)**.

You will learn that digital colors may be mixed with RGB, and also about the **Hue, Saturation, and Lightness (HSL)** method, which increases the number of colors at your disposal to eight (red, orange, yellow, green, cyan, blue, purple, and magenta), allowing fine-tuning with precision.

Blue and red produce purple, blue and yellow produce green, and yellow and red produce orange. You will learn about monitoring color accuracy and color calibration. Finally, you will learn about color correction and grading and will be shown some automatic color-matching tools in Final Cut Pro.

The main sections in this chapter are as follows:

- Color theory
- Color wheels in Final Cut Pro
- Color harmony
- Monitoring color accuracy
- Color correction and grading

By the end of this chapter, you will have learned about the theory of color along with techniques for implementing the concepts when editing in Final Cut Pro. You will understand that selecting appropriate colors will not only make your video more visually appealing but also help to instill your message in the minds of your audience. Mismatched colors will make your video less appealing and increase the chance that your audience will stop watching more quickly, particularly if the video is on social media. Mismatched colors simply won't be attractive to the eye.

You will have learned that there is more to picking colors than simply matching your client's logo or, for example, randomly selecting a blue tone because you have been told blue is the color to use. You will also have learned that the secret is to know what other colors will match well with the color that you have picked.

You will understand that you don't need a diploma in design to be able to choose appropriate colors for video when you understand the basics of how colors are mixed in color theory.

Color theory

The theory of color for video is based on the understanding that colors can be created through the mixing of different primary colors. This has been understood since the Renaissance. Leonardo da Vinci was one of the first to configure our understanding of color. But the modern system of color theory, which is based on HSL, was not developed until just over 100 years ago.

Color influences the audience's perception of a video just as much as music, though in a more subtle way. Music stands out and is immediately noticeable. The color scheme of a video is just as important to set the mood but is less noticeable. As an extreme example, consider the movie *The Wizard of Oz*. Think of the bright colors when Dorothy landed in Oz and the euphoria you felt when you first watched the scene, which was emphasized further by the switch from black and white.

Color is also a powerful communication tool that can evoke various moods, emotions, and meanings across different cultures and contexts. The way people interpret and respond to colors can be influenced by their cultural background, their personal experiences, and even their physiological responses.

In Western cultures, black is often associated with mourning, formality, or sophistication, while in some Eastern cultures, such as Japan, it can symbolize mystery or fear. Similarly, white is often seen as a symbol of purity or innocence in Western cultures, but in some Eastern cultures, such as China, it can symbolize mourning or death.

Colors can also have different meanings and associations in the commercial world. Blue is often associated with trust, reliability, and calmness in the corporate world, while in the healthcare industry, it can symbolize cleanliness, hygiene, and professionalism.

Color is not only important in the look and feel of dramatic videos but also in corporate and commercial videos that rely on text and colors to make text stand out without being garish. The secret is to make your videos attractive but also look professional. Colors help to reinforce branding. If your brand colors are yellow and blue, use these colors throughout your video to create a sense of consistency and familiarity.

When it comes to marketing videos for businesses, it's important to keep the audience and message in mind. While bright, stylized colors and designs can be visually appealing, they may not always be the best choice for marketing videos, as they can distract from the message and make the video less effective. Just as the choice of font needs to be representative of the product, so do the color decisions.

Instead, it's generally a good idea to choose colors that are consistent with the brand's identity. If the brand is focused on sustainability, using green or earthy tones is a good choice. Similarly, if your target audience is mostly professionals, using neutral or muted colors would be more appropriate.

Now, let's take a look at the classification of colors based on color theory.

Color classification

In video production, the primary colors (red, green, and blue) are based on the additive color theory, where the primary colors are combined in equal amounts to produce white light. So, when all the pixels on a video display are illuminated with red, green, and blue light, they appear as white.

Mixing two of the colors creates a third color; so, when different amounts of red, green, and blue light are combined, they can produce a wide range of colors. Red and green will produce yellow, while combining equal amounts of red and blue light creates magenta.

Warm colors such as red, orange, and yellow are often associated with energy, excitement, and enthusiasm. They can be used to create a sense of urgency, draw attention to important information, or evoke a feeling of warmth and comfort. In contrast, cool colors such as blue, green, and purple are often associated with calmness, relaxation, and trust. They can be used to create a sense of professionalism, stability, or serenity.

In addition to warm and cool colors, there are also neutral colors, such as black, white, gray, and brown, which can be used to create a sense of balance, simplicity, or sophistication. These colors can be used as a background to highlight other colors, or to create a minimalist or elegant design.

In addition to the RGB color model, there is also the CMYK color model, which is based on the subtractive color theory, which will be discussed later in this chapter, in the *Subtractive model of color mixing (CMYK model)* section. This model is used in printing and the process is the subtraction of colors from white light. The primary colors in the CMY color model are cyan, magenta, and yellow. When combined in equal amounts, they produce black, which is why the model is also known as the CMYK model, with the *K* standing for black.

Primary colors

For video, the **primary colors** are red, green, and blue. They are called primary because they cannot be created by mixing other colors; they are the base colors used to create all other colors in a video.

Figure 14.1 – Primary colors: red, green, and blue

These are also known as **additive** colors, as opposed to the **subtractive** process of **CMYK**, which you will learn more about later in this chapter, in the *Subtractive model of color mixing (CMYK model)* section.

The *additive color model* is a method of color mixing where colors are created by adding light together. This model is used in electronic displays, such as computer monitors, televisions, and projectors.

The *RGB* color model is the most common type of additive color model used in video production. When all three primary colors are combined in equal proportions, white light is produced. When no light is emitted, the result is black.

Colors are created by varying the intensity of each of the three primary colors. For example, a bright red color can be created by combining high levels of red light and low levels of green and blue light. Similarly, a yellow color can be created by combining high levels of red and green light and low levels of blue light.

The additive color model and RGB color model are important concepts in video production because they help to explain how colors are created and mixed on electronic displays.

Final Cut Pro has two color correction tools, allowing you to adjust the balance of red, green, and blue in your video. You can use either **Color Board** or the **color wheels** to adjust the balance of red, green, and blue until you achieve the desired color balance (see the *Color wheels in Final Cut Pro* section for details). If your video appears too warm (yellowish), you can increase the amount of blue in the video to balance it out.

Equally, if you want to make a specific object in your video redder, you can increase the red value of that object while leaving the green and blue values unchanged. You can initially work with primary colors to adjust the balance of red, green, and blue and then use color grading to fine-tune the overall color balance of the video.

Primary colors are not just important for mixing colors; they are also important markers to help the audience recognize certain scenes, people, or even brands in a video.

There are special reasons to use primary colors to single out a main character in a video. It's a technique that has been used in many films to draw the audience's attention to a particular character or object on screen.

For example, green is used in The Matrix to establish and reinforce character traits and story themes. The dark green jacket worn by Neo is a visual element that helps to set him apart from the other characters in the film and emphasizes his role as the hero. Green is a color that is often associated with growth, renewal, and transformation.

The use of the secondary color yellow in Kill Bill is another example of how color can be used to establish and reinforce a character's traits and personality. The bright yellow jumpsuit worn by The Bride is a striking and memorable visual element that helps to immediately draw the audience's attention to her.

Yellow is a color that is often associated with energy, optimism, and confidence. These are all traits that are embodied by The Bride's character, who is a fierce and determined fighter on a mission of revenge. By dressing her in yellow, the filmmakers were able to visually reinforce these traits and establish her as a powerful and central character in the story.

As the video editor, you may not have the opportunity to dress the characters, but you can help emphasize the colors that the production team has chosen to dress the main characters in.

A further example of the use of primary colors is the characters played by John Wayne in his movies. The colors associated with his characters helped establish him as a heroic and larger-than-life figure. John Wayne was known for playing tough characters. In many of his films, the costumes and sets around him were often designed with bold primary colors such as red and blue, along with white. These are common colors in a number of countries' national flags, giving a strong sense of loyalty.

Now that you have seen the importance of primary colors, let's look at the next level of mixing primary colors to create secondary colors in the next section.

Secondary colors

Secondary colors refer to the colors created by mixing the primary colors: (red + blue = purple), (red + green = yellow), and (blue + green = cyan). Combining all three primary colors gives white.

Figure 14.2 – Secondary colors: Red, green, and blue overlapping creates purple, yellow, cyan, and white

Here are some uses of secondary colors for you to consider:

- By using secondary colors, you can create contrast in your video. For example, if your subject is wearing a blue outfit, you can use a contrasting yellow background.

- If you have too much of a single color in your video, you can use secondary colors to balance it out. For example, if your video is primarily red, you can add green or cyan elements for balance.

- Using secondary colors that are adjacent in the color wheel can create a sense of harmony in your video. For example, using both blue and purple together can create a calming, relaxing mood.

The process of mixing the three primary colors is much more intuitively controlled with a plug-in called **Channel Mixer**, which is part of the Professionals suite from Eric Lenz (`https://ericlenz.photography/244012-bruce-macbryde-diy-video`).

The full package is discussed in *Chapter 17, Supporting Software Applications for Final Cut Pro*.

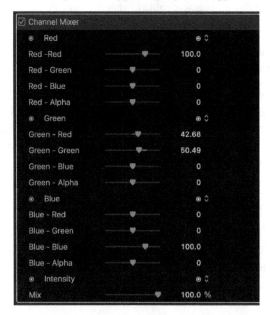

Figure 14.3 – Channel Mixer plug-in

You can create further color combinations by mixing primary and secondary colors into tertiary colors, which is discussed in the next section.

Tertiary colors

You produce tertiary colors when you mix any primary and secondary colors. Intermediate colors can be produced when the full saturation of one primary color is mixed with half saturation of another primary color without any third primary color. The six tertiary colors are amber, vermilion, magenta, violet, teal, and chartreuse.

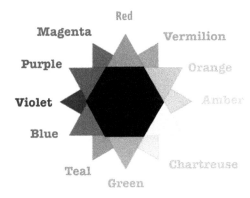

Figure 14.4 – Tertiary colors for subtle color grading

If you only use primary and secondary colors, the color range in your videos will be limited. Tertiary colors open up much more variance in the resulting video.

Here are a few ways tertiary colors can be used in your videos:

- Tertiary colors create subtle color grading effects. For example, adding a small amount of chartreuse to a shot can create a more natural and organic look.
- By adding tertiary colors, you can create a more complex and layered color palette. This can add depth and visual interest to your video and help it stand out from others.
- Tertiary colors can be used to fine-tune the color balance of your video. For example, if your video is too red, you can add a small amount of teal to balance it out.
- Tertiary colors add depth and complexity to the color palette and allow for more nuanced color grading.

Tertiary colors are the last of the major color mixes. The following combinations are much more subtle.

Warm colors

Using warm colors in video production can have several benefits. Warm colors such as red, orange, and yellow are known to evoke emotions such as excitement, enthusiasm, and passion. By using these colors in your video, you can create a sense of energy and excitement in the viewer, which can help keep them engaged.

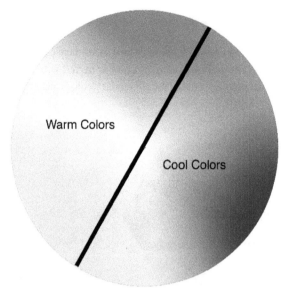

Figure 14.5 – Cool and warm colors

Warm colors are associated with sunlight and fire. By using these colors, you create a sense of warmth and comfort, which can be particularly effective in creating a cozy and inviting atmosphere.

Warm colors are often more attention-grabbing than cool colors such as blue and green. By using warm colors in key areas of your video, you can draw the viewer's eye to specific elements and create a sense of focus.

Warm colors can also enhance skin tones, making them appear more vibrant and healthier. You should remember this for videos that feature people, such as interviews or vlogs.

You can establish a theme with warm colors by using shades of orange and yellow, for example, to create a warm and inviting atmosphere for a cooking video. In contrast, using shades of red and black can create a dramatic and intense atmosphere for an action video.

Warm colors are the reds and yellows of the color wheel, while cool colors are the greens and blues, as you will see in the next section.

Cool colors

The main difference between using cool colors and warm colors in a video is the emotional and psychological effects they have on the viewer.

Cool colors such as blue, green, and purple are associated with calmness, relaxation, and tranquility. Using cool colors in a video where the goal is to convey calmness and serenity can be particularly effective in creating a peaceful and relaxing atmosphere. Cool colors can also be used to create a sense of depth and distance, making them effective for landscape or outdoor shots.

Overall, the choice between using cool or warm colors in a video depends on the emotional and psychological effects that you want to create. Cool colors are effective in creating a calming and peaceful atmosphere, while warm colors are effective in creating a dynamic and exciting atmosphere.

Now that we have learned about the different classes of colors based on color theory, let's consider the lightness and darkness of the color hues in the next section, on color values.

Color values

The term **color values** refers to the brightness or darkness of a color, not the amount of black or white in a color. The value of a color is determined by the amount of light or darkness it contains. A high color value means a light color, while a low color value results in a dark color. Color value, also known as *hue value*, refers to the intrinsic darkness or lightness of a color, regardless of its brightness or saturation.

A bright red and a dark red may have the same brightness and saturation, but their hue value is different. Similarly, a light blue and a dark blue may have the same brightness and saturation, but their hue value is different.

A color value is determined by the color's position on the gray scale, with white being the lightest value and black being the darkest value. A light blue would have a higher value than a dark blue because it is closer to white on the gray scale.

Adding black or white to a color modifies its brightness or lightness but not its value. This is known as tinting or shading.

In summary, a color value is actually a shade of lightness, or more specifically, shades of color. In the next section, you will learn about the color wheel.

The color wheel

The **color wheel** is an essential visual tool used to adjust and manipulate color grading and your digital reference to formal color relationships. You will see how further mixing of colors and their positioning on the color wheel gives tertiary colors, analogous colors, color triads, tetradic colors, complementary colors, warm colors, and cool colors. They all have a relationship to each other on the color wheel.

Sir Isaac Newton created the first circular diagram for colors in 1666. That diagram is still the standard for understanding color today.

The color wheel on the right of *Figure 14.6* is divided into 12 sections, each representing a different color. The three primary colors, red, blue, and yellow, as in the left-hand wheel in the same figure, are represented by the four primary sections of the 12-section wheel, while the secondary colors, green, orange, and purple (shown in the middle wheel), are located in between the primary colors. The remaining six sections represent tertiary colors, which are created by mixing a primary and a secondary color.

Figure 14.6 – Color wheels representing primary (left), secondary (middle), and tertiary (right) colors

It's one thing to understand the theory of color, but you also need to know how to apply the knowledge, which is why the following section explains how the concept is used in Final Cut Pro.

Color wheels in Final Cut Pro

The color wheel is one of the mainstays of selecting color on the Mac (*Figure 14.7*). Final Cut Pro uses a representation of the color wheel when you adjust **Highlights**, **Midtones**, and **Shadows** (*Figure 14.7*):

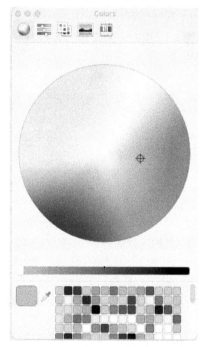

Figure 14.7 – Final Cut Pro color wheel with saved colors

In addition to adjusting color, you can use the Final Cut Pro color wheels to adjust the saturation and brightness of a scene. By adjusting the saturation, you can make colors more vibrant or more muted. By adjusting the brightness, you can make a scene brighter or darker.

As previously explained in *Chapter 10, The Inspector Controls*, there are two sets of basic color tools in Final Cut Pro. You can set your preferred selection as the default in **Settings | Preferences**. You can change the choice and select all of the color control panels from the **No Corrections** chevron at the top left.

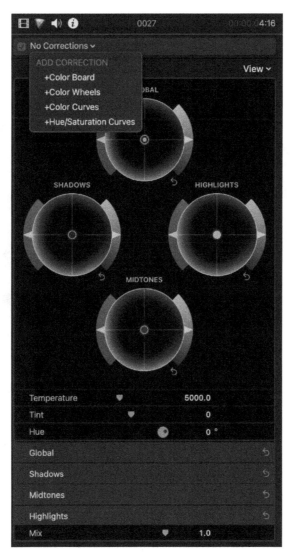

Figure 14.8 – Final Cut Pro color wheel controls

The Final Cut Pro wheels have the advantage of being able to be keyframed, as well as all of the settings being in one panel so that you can balance out the different settings without having to move between the panels, as is the case with the **Color Board** option, which we will discuss first in the next section.

Color Board

Color Board helps you to follow a logical workflow following the conventional order of correction:

1. **Exposure**
2. **Saturation**
3. **Color**

Figure 14.9 shows the three Final Cut Pro Color Board controls:

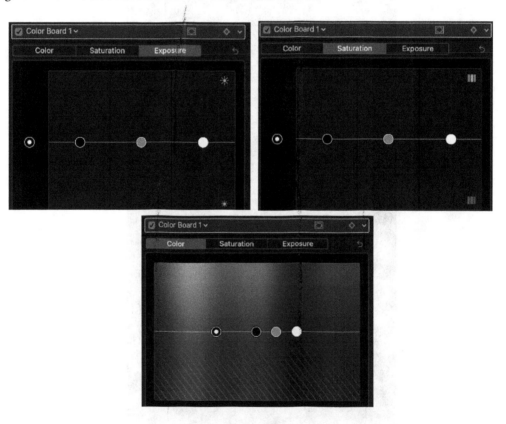

Figure 14.9 – The three Final Cut Pro Color Board controls

Let's take a look at each of these controls in detail in the following subsections.

Exposure

When the **Color Board** is first called up, it defaults to the **Exposure** tab, which is the correct place to start:

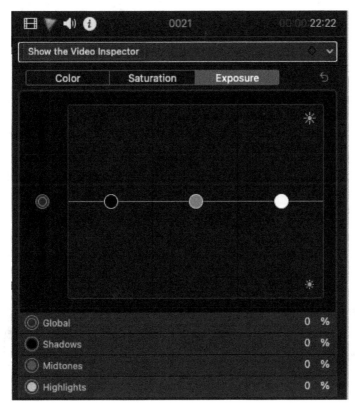

Figure 14.10 – Exposure tab selected

There are four pucks in the center of the panel: from the right, **Highlights** (brightness), **Midtones**, **Shadows** (blacks), and **Global**; the far-left puck, **Global**, controls the other three pucks. When working with **Exposure**, you should temporarily put color out of your mind and think in terms of black and white, or more appropriately, shades of gray. **Highlights** are white, **midtones** are gray, and **shadows** are black.

You should look at the image and imagine it as a grayscale image, then adjust the pucks by eye. Don't worry about scopes for the moment; they provide methods of measuring color information without relying on the eye. Scopes are discussed in *Chapter 15, Using Color Scopes for Advanced Color Correction*.

If you have trouble imagining the image as grayscale, do the following until you get used to the idea: select the **Saturation** tab and drag the **Global** puck all the way down. Return to the **Exposure** panel. Don't forget to adjust the puck back when you have completed the **Exposure** procedure.

> **Note**
>
> The three tones, **Highlights**, **Midtones**, and **Shadows**, overlap each other, so when you adjust one, you move some of the tones in the other two.

Moving a puck up increases the associated tones, while moving it down decreases them. The four pucks also have numerical adjustments at the bottom of the panel. As you move a puck, the values will move too. The numbers are for finer control, which is extremely important with color correction.

These are some general rules of thumb. **Highlights** is used to adjust the brightness of the sky. **Midtones** always affects flesh tones, no matter the skin color. Treat **Shadows** as the word itself implies – anything that is darker and obscurses the subject. A good rule of thumb is to always add a couple of points to **Shadows** to pop the contrast in an image.

It could be said that **Exposure** is the most important thing to get right. Think of it as the foundation for all the other settings you configure when working with color correction. If you don't get **Exposure** right, the others will certainly not follow. The curly arrow at the bottom right (*Figure 14.11*) resets all the changes in each panel separately:

Figure 14.11 – Curly arrow

When you are happy with the **Exposure** settings, next select the **Saturation** tab.

Saturation

With **Exposure** fixed, you will find that **Saturation** will usually not need much adjustment. What you have learned with the **Exposure** controls is replicated in the **Saturation** panel. You may consider the **Global** puck in this panel. Remember: subtlety is key.

The final tab is **Color**, and it is discussed in the next section.

Color

The **Color** panel is laid out slightly differently than the other two – presumably so you recognize that it is different than the other two panels. The pucks work the same, but the results are quite dissimilar. Yes, moving a puck above the line increases the amount of that color, but moving a puck below the line introduces a different color. That color is, in fact, the opposing color to the one above the line in the color spectrum, known as the **complementary** color, as you will see later in this chapter, in the *Color harmony* section.

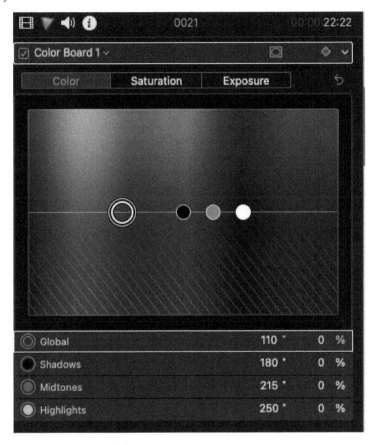

Figure 14.12 – Color panel of the Color Board

The **Color Board** will handle all of the color correction that you need outside of using the **color scopes and curves**. The next section looks at an alternative set of controls for basic color correction in Final Cut Pro, **color wheels**.

Color wheels

The wheels have all the settings you saw in the **Color Board** section, but all on a single panel so that you can balance out the different settings without having to move between the panels, as with the **Color Board**. But you still follow the workflow sequence of **Exposure**, **Saturation**, and **Color**, as outlined in the *Color Board* section, before balancing them all.

The major advantage that the **color wheels** (refer to *Figure 14.8*) have is that the changes in all three attributes can be keyframed so that the adjustments will appear in your video over time. This is very useful when dealing with outside footage, where the sun goes behind clouds and comes out again, which ends up changing the exposure on cameras that have been set at manual exposure. This is something that is not possible with the **Color Board**, where the changes you make affect the whole clip. With the **Color Board**, you would need to blade the clip with the resulting jump cut from one color to another, requiring a B roll.

There are four wheels, which have **Exposure**, **Saturation**, and **Hue** built into them. Notice that **Hue** and **Color** are separate terms in **the Color Board** and the **color wheels**. It has a subtle difference in how it works in that it introduces a hue rather than adding or subtracting a color. The advantage of using hue rather than adding a color is that you are changing all the colors in the given range without introducing a single color.

Highlights wheel

The **Highlights** wheel's controls are the same as in each of the other wheels:

- The curved bar on the right of the wheel is gray. This works like the puck in the **Color Board**; moving up increases the **brightness**, while moving down decreases it.
- On the left of the wheel, the blue curved bar increases/decreases the **saturation**.
- The central puck can be moved to increase the hue. Dragging to the right introduces a blue hue and dragging to the left introduces a green hue. Dragging up introduces red and dragging down introduces teal.

Everything we have mentioned regarding **Highlights** works the same for **Midtones** and **Shadows** as well as for **Global**.

Color wheels have better control of what you can set, compared to the **Color Board**, where the curly arrow resets everything in that panel. The **color wheels** let you double-click any arrow or center puck to reset just those parameters, or the curly arrow to reset the whole wheel.

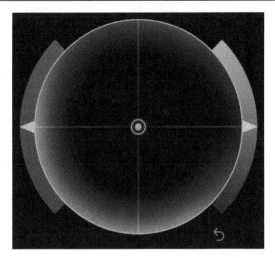

Figure 14.13 – Left curve: saturation; right curve: lightness; curly arrow bottom right

With this knowledge of color wheels, let's now see how to mix colors for harmonious combinations in Final Cut Pro.

Color harmony

Harmonious color combinations are the foundation for creatively appealing videos. The choice of colors can greatly affect the overall aesthetic and impact of the content. It's important to consider the color scheme carefully to ensure that it is harmonious and visually appealing.

One way to achieve a harmonious color combination is to use **complementary** colors (opposite colors on the color wheel) or **analogous** colors (colors next to each other on the color wheel) to create a cohesive and balanced look. It's a good idea to avoid bright and oversaturated colors; they can detract from a corporate message and are hard on the eyes for entertainment videos.

Additionally, you can also use contrast to make your text or images stand out against the background. For example, using a dark font on a light background or a light font on a dark background can create a clear and legible contrast. With these principles under our belt, let's learn about some common color schemes.

Common color schemes

While it may feel daunting to create combinations of harmonious colors, if you follow the steps, the combinations will fall into place.

Now that you have an understanding of color harmony, let's look at some more subtle color types that still reference the color wheel, starting in the next section, which is about *monochromatic* colors, where different shades of a single color are used.

Monochromatic colors

A *monochromatic* color type refers to a color scheme that uses variations of a single hue or color. This means that different shades, tints, and tones of the same color are used to create a harmonious and unified look.

Principally, you think of various tones of gray, but tones of any color will fit the category. Sepia tones relay a sense of older times.

A monochromatic color scheme in a video could be created by using various shades of blue, such as navy blue, sky blue, and baby blue. These different shades of blue would be used throughout the video to create a unified and cohesive look.

Monochromatic color schemes give a sense of harmony and simplicity. They are also easy to work with and can be used to create a clean and polished look.

However, it's important to note that using a monochromatic color scheme exclusively can result in a lack of visual interest and variety. It's usually a good idea to incorporate some other colors, such as complementary or analogous colors, to add depth and complexity to the video.

Moving away from the possibly monotonous color palette of the monochromatic color type, the next section on complementary colors will help you provide much more interesting effects for your video.

Complementary colors

For a good method of attracting attention to important parts of your video, consider using pairs of colors that are opposite each other on the color wheel. These are known as complementary colors.

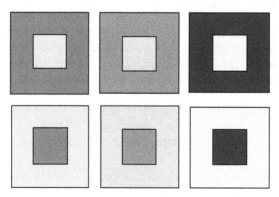

Figure 14.14 – A selection of complementary colors

Here are some ways to use complementary colors in video editing:

- Using complementary colors will create contrast in the video. For example, using a blue background with an orange subject in the foreground can create a strong visual contrast that draws the viewer's eye to the subject.

- Complementary colors create a visually interesting and dynamic look to emphasize a sense of tension and excitement that helps keep the viewer engaged.

- Using complementary colors can also enhance skin tones. For example, using a green background can make skin tones appear more vibrant and healthy, while using a purple background can make skin tones appear more natural and subtle.

- Complementary colors can also be used to establish a mood or tone for the video. Using shades of red and green can create a festive and celebratory atmosphere (Christmas themes). Using shades of blue and orange, on the other hand, can create a calming and peaceful atmosphere.

While using complementary colors in video editing can create contrast and visual interest, enhance skin tones, and establish a mood or tone for the video, even more variance can be achieved with analogous colors, as shown in the next section.

Analogous colors

An **analogous** color type is a color scheme that uses colors that are adjacent to each other on the color wheel. These colors share a similar hue and create a sense of harmony and unity when used together.

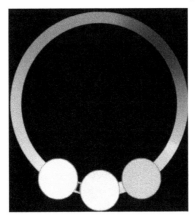

Figure 14.15 – Analogous color for subtle color grading

Here are a few ideas of how to use analogous colors in your videos:

- Analogous color schemes can be used to create a specific mood or atmosphere in a video. Warm analogous colors using shades of orange, yellow, and red can create a cozy and inviting feeling, while a cool color scheme using shades of blue and green can create a calm and peaceful mood.

- Analogous color schemes can be used to establish a theme or tone for the video. Analogous color schemes with shades of pink and purple can create a romantic or feminine theme, while a color scheme using shades of green and brown could be used for a natural or outdoor theme.

- Analogous colors can be used to highlight key elements in a video. If the main subject of the video is wearing a red shirt, using colors such as orange and yellow in the background can help draw attention to the subject.

- Analogous colors can add depth and dimension by using colors with varying shades and tones. Using a light shade of yellow, a medium shade of orange, and a dark shade of red can create a sense of depth and complexity.

Further variations still referencing the color wheel are the *triadic* and *tetradic* color palettes, which are discussed in the following sections. Tetradic and triadic colors are both color schemes that are commonly used in video production. The difference between the two is the number of colors used in each scheme.

Triadic colors

Triadic colors involve using three colors that are evenly spaced around the color wheel. A triadic color scheme might involve using red, yellow, and blue, or green, orange, and purple:

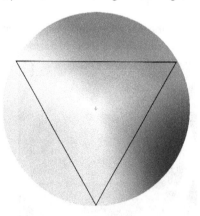

Figure 14.16 – Triads are three colors evenly spaced around the color wheel

If you are using colors for text, you should use one of the three colors as the background, another color for the text, and the third for any highlights.

The benefit of using color triads is the sense of balance in the video for a visually appealing and harmonious look. Using three different colors in a color triad allows for a variety of colors in the video while still maintaining a cohesive look. The three colors used can be adjusted in their shade, tone, and intensity to create even more variety and interest. By using different combinations of colors, you can create contrast in different areas of the video to draw the viewer's eye to specific elements.

Tetradic colors

Tetradic colors involve using four colors that are evenly spaced around the color wheel. Instead of making a triangle on the color wheel, they can form a square or a rectangle.

Square tetradic colors

A square color scheme consists of four colors in a square spaced evenly around the color wheel. Choose a base color to stand out and use the remaining three colors to attract the eye to parts of your video.

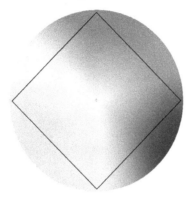

Figure 14.17 – Four colors in a square spaced evenly around the color wheel

Because of the contrast it produces, even a desaturated square tetrad will look dynamic and feel playful and vibrant.

Use these examples of square tetradic colors as primary, secondary, or tertiary colors:

- Red, green-yellow, cyan, and blue-magenta (purple) (as in *Figure 14.17*)
- Green, blue cyan (azure), magenta, and orange
- Blue, green, yellow, and red magenta (rose)

You can use the square pattern in any position on the color wheel to create a selection of colors that have some relationship to each other. Choose between a warm or cool tone as your predominant color and see what results you get.

Rectangle tetradic colors

Using the shape of the rectangle on a color wheel is another way of generating selections of four different color tetrads.

A rectangle tetradic color scheme might involve using red, yellow, blue, and green or orange, purple, yellow, and blue. Tetradic color schemes are often used because they provide even more contrast and visual interest than triadic schemes but can also be more challenging to balance and harmonize effectively.

The rectangle tetradic color scheme is very specific, as in these examples:

- Red, yellow, blue, and cyan, as shown in *Figure 14.18*

- Green, blue, yellow, and magenta (primary and secondary colors)

- Red-magenta, orange, green, and blue cyan

- Green-cyan, green-yellow, red-magenta, and blue-magenta

While the color combinations will look vibrant, cheerful, and colorful, be careful of the tetradic color scheme; they can look overly aggressive if applied by an inexperienced hand.

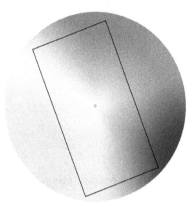

Figure 14.18 – Tetradic colors evenly spaced in a rectangle around the color wheel

Overall, the choice between using a tetradic or triadic color scheme in your video depends on the specific needs and goals of the project. Triadic schemes can create a sense of balance and harmony, while tetradic schemes can provide even more contrast and visual interest. However, both schemes can be effective when used appropriately.

Color schemes for non-designers

It's all well and good knowing the theory but it's another thing remembering it all. It's good that you have studied the theory, but now for the cheat sheet!

Take note of the following color schemes. There are three options – a high level of contrast with a dynamic and energetic look; a contrasting look that's bold and eye-catching; or a harmonious, calming, and relaxing design:

- Stick with the triadic color scheme, including red, yellow, and blue, or purple, green, and orange. This color scheme provides a high level of contrast and can create a dynamic and energetic design.

- A complementary color scheme involving two colors that are opposite each other on the color wheel, such as blue and orange, or red and green. This color scheme provides a high level of contrast and can create a bold and eye-catching design.

- An analogous color scheme involving three colors that are next to each other on the color wheel, such as yellow, orange, and red, or blue, green, and yellow. This color scheme provides a harmonious and cohesive look and can create a calming and relaxing design.

If you find the manual selection a chore or prone to errors, there is a quick way to calculate the combinations online with free color calculators.

Online color calculators

A number of free color calculators are available online. Try the **Canva** calculator (https://www.canva.com/colors/color-wheel/) by entering your base color and watch it pick the combinations for you.

Then, you can enter those hex values into the macOS **Color Picker**. In *Figure 14.19*, I've used the yellow Pantone color, shown later in this chapter, as the base, using the hex value #F9D948. You can also pick a color directly from the wheel that's on the Canva calculator site.

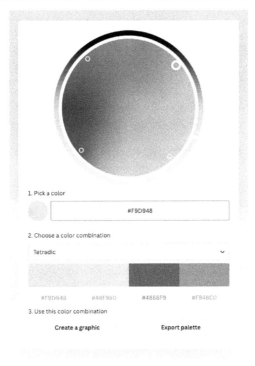

Figure 14.19 – Canva color calculator

To be able to see colors accurately, it is important to have a color-accurate monitor and to calibrate that monitor on a regular basis. Accurate monitors and their calibration are discussed in the next section.

Monitoring color accuracy

Color accuracy is a crucial aspect of monitoring performance, particularly for professional video editors, photographers, and graphic designers who require accurate color representation for their work. Inaccurate colors can result in images and videos that appear unnatural, washed out, or overly saturated, which can compromise the quality of the final product.

Color accuracy is typically measured using industry-standard metrics such as **Delta E**, which calculates the difference between the intended color and the color displayed on the monitor. A Delta E value of less than 2 is considered excellent, while a Delta E value of 3-4 is considered acceptable for most users.

You can read more about colors at. `https://colorwiki.com/wiki/Maxwell_Metrics`

Color-accurate monitors

A color-accurate monitor will reproduce colors and shades with minimal deviation from their intended values, resulting in more lifelike and vibrant images that closely match the original content.

The way videos are displayed on screen can vary greatly from device to device depending on factors such as screen brightness, color temperature, and color accuracy. Many monitors ship with default color settings that may not accurately represent the colors in a video, leading to inconsistencies in color reproduction, so you need to set your monitor to a known standard, such as Rec. 709 or sRGB.

Take a look at this article about color spaces: `https://www.videomaker.com/how-to/technology/what-is-color-space-and-why-does-it-matter/`

A color-calibrated monitor is essential for digital creative work as it ensures that the colors you see on your screen are accurate and consistent with the original content.

Monitor calibration

Color calibration involves adjusting the monitor's color settings to match a standard color space, such as sRGB or Adobe RGB. This can be done manually using software tools and calibration devices or automatically using built-in calibration features available on some monitors.

It's important to regularly calibrate your monitor to maintain accurate color representation, as the display can drift over time due to factors such as age, temperature, and humidity. By calibrating your monitor regularly, you can ensure that your work is represented accurately and consistently across different devices and platforms and avoid issues with color matching and inaccuracy.

Fortunately, there are various tools and techniques available for calibrating monitors to ensure accurate color reproduction, which are explained in the following subsections.

Hardware calibration

To correctly calibrate a monitor, you typically need a device called a colorimeter or spectrophotometer, which is a small puck-like device that sits on your screen and measures the colors being displayed. These devices work by analyzing the light emitted by the monitor and comparing it to a standard color profile, allowing them to determine how accurate the monitor's colors are.

Online calibration

Online calibration is a simple way of establishing the best performance that your monitor can handle. There are a number of sites that you could try; for instance, `www.photofriday.com/info/calibrate` and `http://www.lagom.nl/lcd-test/` let you look at your screen's contrast, resolution, sharpness, gamma, and more. The websites show patterns that will help you adjust your monitor by comparing the images with what you see on your monitor.

Software calibration

macOS has built-in calibration controls; go to **System Settings | Preferences** and click **Displays** to calibrate your screen.

Figure 14.20 – Built-in calibration controls in macOS Sonoma

Select the **Preset** dropdown, choose the appropriate display profile, and click **Calibrate Display....**

Now that you have your monitor in the best color-accurate state, let's look at some color schemes for non-designers.

Color correction and grading

Color correction forms the basis for color grading. Color correction aims to produce realistic colors, as close as possible to how they look in real life. Color grading is when the editor creates a color styling with a look and feel that represents the theme of the video.

Adjusting temperature, tint, and hue

Temperature, tint, and *hue* are three terms used in video editing to describe different aspects of color correction and grading:

- **Temperature** refers to the color temperature and is measured in **Kelvin (K)**. A lower color temperature, such as 2,800K, will give an image a warmer, yellow-orange tone, while a higher color temperature, such as 6,500K, will give a cooler, blue tone. Adjusting the temperature of an image can be used to create a specific mood or correct unwanted color casts caused by lighting or camera settings.

- **Tint** refers to the balance between the green and magenta hues in an image. A green tint is caused by an excess of green in the image, while a magenta tint is caused by an excess of magenta. Adjusting the tint can be used to correct unwanted color casts or to create a specific aesthetic.

- **Hue** refers to the actual color of an image, such as red, blue, or green. Adjusting the hue can be used to change the color of an object or to create a specific color scheme for the entire image.

Temperature, tint, and hue are often adjusted together as part of the overall color-grading process to create a specific mood or look that enhances the visual storytelling of the project.

Now, let's look at how to adjust the temperature, tint, and hue in Final Cut Pro.

Adjusting the temperature, tint, and hue in Final Cut Pro

As shown in *Figure 14.21*, below the wheels are controls for **Temperature**, which add cooler tones when dragged to the left and warmer tones when dragged to the right.

Sliding the **Tint** adjustment to the left adds green and sliding to the right introduces magenta.

You can add hues with the center puck in the color wheel itself to each range of tones; rotating the **Hue** control shifts all hues in the clip.

Finally, **Mix** uses the source clip before correction and mixes it with the correction after correction, giving you that final subtle balance.

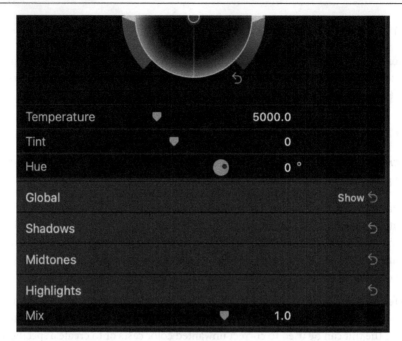

Figure 14.21 – Temperature, Tint, and Hue in Final Cut Pro

The selection of the color palette is critical in portraying the emotions that are best suited to the video. Choose colors that align with the message and tone of your video, as well as the target audience. For example, a video for a children's product might use bright and playful colors, while a video for a luxury product might use more sophisticated and muted colors.

An emotional video will have stronger styling color effects, with darker colors for drama and brighter colors for children's movies.

Marketing and corporate videos will have less styling and will use more realistic color choices.

Sticking to tried and tested color schemes can be a good option if you're unsure about your color choices. It's also worth noting that the specific shade or tone of a color can have a big impact on how it interacts with other colors and the overall mood of the video.

It's important to consider the context of the video and the message you're trying to convey when choosing a color scheme. Additionally, experimenting with different color combinations and getting feedback from others can help you find the right balance of colors for your video.

When you are working on interviews or corporate profiles, the choice of background is very important. Consider the person being videoed, such as their skin tone or clothing that might clash with the background.

Beige backgrounds can be boring, but vibrant colors such as yellow and red will distract from the people in the video. Consider darker shades of blues and greens, which offer a professional touch while maintaining the balance of vibrancy. If you are uncertain about the color scheme that you've picked, then you can stick with conservative schemes and consider the choice of cooler colors.

Don't force two colors together that just don't work; stick to tertiary or analogous color choices. You will increase the appeal of your video if you choose colors that match the theme of your video.

Once you understand the color palettes available you will be on your way to getting a feel for the psychology of colors and the moods specific colors normally generate, especially in marketing.

Colors are important in setting the scene for your video, but the mix of colors is nowhere more important than when it comes to marketing videos and ensuring the colors used for text and graphics are appropriate. This is the area where your knowledge of color mixing and the relationships that you saw earlier in this chapter will come to the fore.

Up to this point, I have concentrated on the **RGB** methods of mixing color using the color wheel. There are two other processes to learn about. They are the use of **HSL** tuning using sliders and producing a wider mix of colors than the **RGB** color wheel method with **CMYK, called the subtractive model**. First, we will discuss the **subtractive** model for color mixing and then the **HSL** method.

Subtractive model of color mixing (CMYK model)

The subtractive color model, also known as the **CMYK** model, is used in printing and is based on the concept of subtracting colors from white light to create different colors. Colors are created by subtracting or absorbing varying amounts of cyan, magenta, yellow, and black ink from white paper. The more ink that is applied, the more colors are absorbed and the darker the resulting color appears.

The CMYK model is not the color process for digital displays or video production, but there are benefits to using the subtractive color model in postproduction. It's also important for your overall understanding of color to be aware of the way that the model mixes colors.

The CMYK color model is useful in postproduction to ensure that the colors in the final print product accurately match the colors in the video. This is especially important when producing video content that will be printed or displayed in print media, such as promotional materials or packaging.

Additionally, the CMYK color model can be useful in color grading and correcting for print materials. For example, if a video has colors that are too vibrant or intense for print, they can be adjusted using the CMYK color model to ensure that the final printed product looks accurate and visually appealing.

While the CMYK color model is not commonly used in video production for electronic displays, don't underestimate its importance for ensuring accurate color reproduction in print materials.

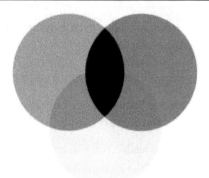

Figure 14.22 – CMYK color wheel

The recognized standard for CMYK is the Pantone color system.

Pantone

One of the mainstays of the CMYK world is the **Pantone** color system. It has become the industry standard for picking colors. Corporations choose a particular Pantone color number so that printing and digital images can be matched to the Pantone color bridge.

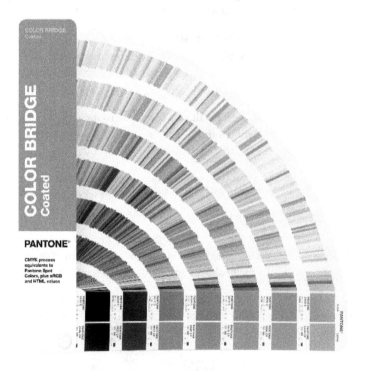

Figure 14.23 – Pantone color bridge swatches

Pantone's color bridge provides both physical references and digital values needed to effectively apply color across all printed and digital media. The Pantone color bridge also includes values for RGB, HTML/hex, and CMYK.

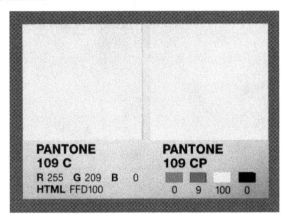

Figure 14.24 – Pantone color with RGB, CMYK, and hex values

These values can then be entered into the **CMYK** or **RGB** sliders in the macOS **Color Picker** for a digital match.

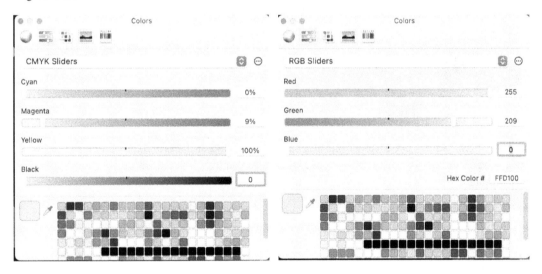

Figure 14.25 – macOS Color Picker showing CMYK, RGB, and Hex values

The colors can be adjusted for your monitor by selecting your monitor in the macOS **Color Picker**.

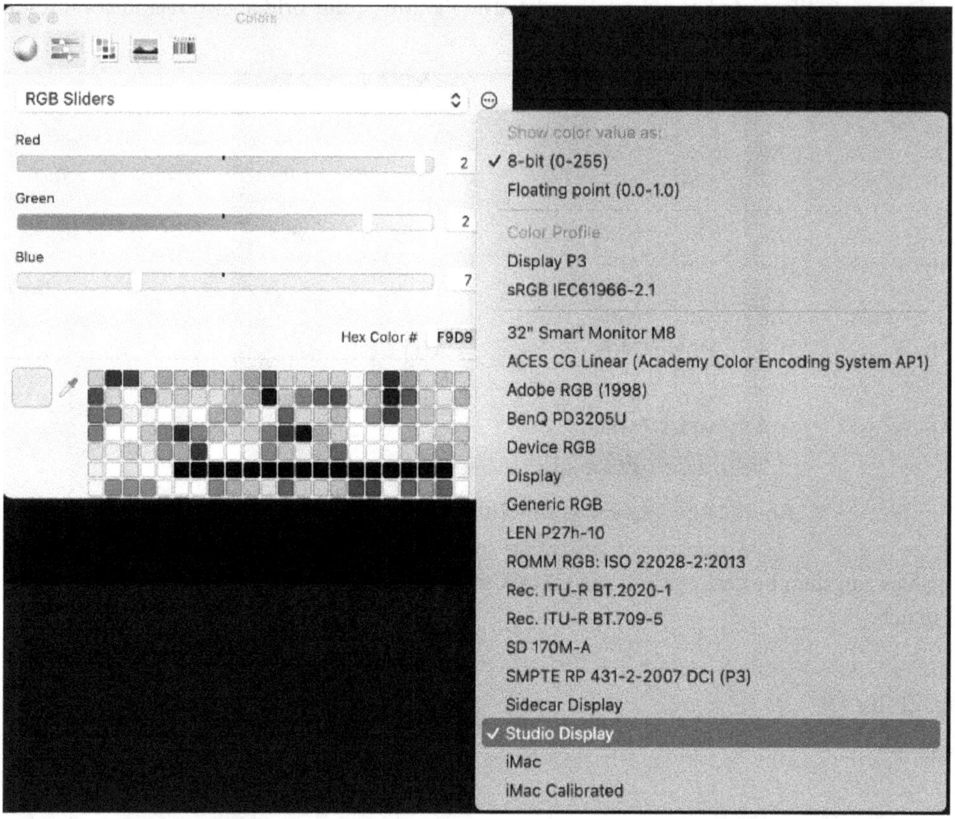

Figure 14.26 – RGB Sliders with Studio Display selected

The Pantone charts show two formats, one for coated or gloss-like surfaces and the other for uncoated or matte-type surfaces. There are two options as the amount of light reflection gives the same Pantone color number a different look depending on whether the color is used on a shiny or flat surface.

The Pantone system was developed for printed material using the subtractive model of mixing color, but since most design is now produced digitally, the system has been adapted for the additive process to closely match the colors between the two systems.

The next section, on HSL grading, is aimed directly at video postproduction.

Using HSL tuning for color grading

While the **RGB** color model is commonly used in video production for **additive** color mixing, it is not the best choice for color grading. **HSL** tuning can be a more effective method for color grading because it allows for greater control and precision over the final color grading results. **HSL** is known on macOS as **HSB**:

- **Hue** refers to the actual color of the image, such as red, green, or blue
- **Saturation** refers to the intensity or purity of the color
- **Brightness** refers to the brightness or darkness of the color

In contrast, **RGB** tuning involves adjusting the intensity of each of the three primary colors (red, green, and blue) separately. While **RGB** tuning can be effective for adjusting the overall color balance, it can be more difficult to achieve precise adjustments to specific colors. The independent control over the lightness of the hue and saturation makes it easier to achieve a specific contrast and brightness in the video.

Using **HSB** tuning for color grading provides several benefits over using **RGB** color grading. It's easier to adjust the hue and saturation of specific colors in the video. **HSB** tuning provides a more consistent color grading result across different displays than **RGB** color grading. This is because **HSB** tuning is based on perceptual color space rather than **RGB** color space.

When using **HSL** tuning for color grading, you can adjust each of these three parameters independently, allowing you to make subtle and precise adjustments to the color balance and tone of the image. You can adjust the hue of a specific color without changing the saturation or lightness or adjust the saturation of a color without changing the hue or lightness.

In *Figure 14.27*, the macOS color wheel is replaced by the slider tab to show **HSB Sliders**:

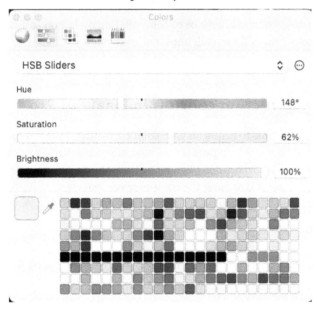

Figure 14.27 – HSB Sliders in Final Cut Pro

Let's take a look of each of these controls in detail:

- **Hue**: The **Hue** color grading slider is a powerful tool for adjusting the colors in a video. By shifting colors toward analogous hues, you can create a more cohesive and harmonious color scheme. This can be particularly useful when trying to enhance the mood of a scene or draw attention to a specific object or element in the video. The ability to personalize color palettes can also be beneficial for branding purposes, helping to create a consistent visual identity across multiple videos.

- **Saturation**: The **Saturation** color grading slider can be a powerful tool for adjusting the intensity of colors. By increasing the saturation of certain colors and decreasing it for others, you can create a selective color effect that draws attention to parts of the video. This can be particularly useful in marketing or promotional videos where you want to emphasize certain products or features. The ability to adjust the saturation of colors also allows for highly customizable color grading, helping you achieve the desired look and feel for your video project.

- **Brightness**: **Brightness** or the amount of white in a color, is an important aspect of color in a video. The **Brightness** color grading control can be a useful tool for adjusting the brightness or darkness of colors, which can be particularly helpful in correcting overexposure or underexposure in a scene. By adjusting the lightness of colors, you can also change the overall mood or atmosphere of a scene, which can be useful in creating the desired emotional response from your audience.

These controls can help ensure that the colors in your video are well balanced and suited to the tone and mood of the content. If you need to make more dramatic changes, revert to the color wheel controls, which allow you to adjust colors beyond what **HSB Sliders** permits.

By experimenting with different combinations of color grading tools, you can create a unique and cohesive visual style that enhances the overall impact of your video.

In the next section, we'll take a look at how we can correct color in Final Cut Pro.

Automatic color correction controls in Final Cut Pro

Final Cut Pro has built-in controls to help with your color correction. I suggest that you don't ignore these automatic options as they can help produce a foundation for you to work on with the manual controls. The following sections discuss these automatic controls, starting by looking at the **Balance Color** option and then looking at **matching the color** between two clips.

Balance Color

The **Balance Color** controls are located at the bottom of the viewer and will help you not only with quick fixes but also function as a foundation to base your manual controls on. Click the magic wand at the bottom left of the viewer.

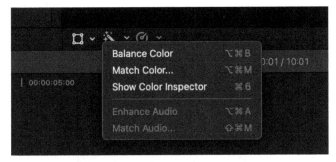

Figure 14.28 – Balance Color and Match Color... options

There is more to it than just selecting **Balance Color**. You need to open the inspector's **Film Strip** tab, select the default value of **Automatic** in the **Balance Color** effect, and change it to **White Balance**.

Figure 14.29 – The Automatic and White Balance options

Look in the viewer with **Transform** turned off. You will see an eyedropper with a message to click or drag over an area of the image with pure white to set **White Balance**.

Figure 14.30 – Click on white with Transform turned off

Setting **White Balance** is the first step; if you need to make further changes to match the color, the next step is to use the **Match Color** automatic setting.

Match Color

Match Color is an AI-assisted option to bring one clip in line with the color in another clip. You first need to choose a clip that you want to match to another's color context.

The button is in the same location as **Balance Color**, below the viewer to the left, as shown in *Figure 14.31*:

Figure 14.31 – Match Color below the viewer

Click on **Match Color** while the clip you want to change is selected. A two-up display will show inside the viewer with the clip you are changing on the right and the clip you want to match it to on the left. When you have the correct clip showing in the left panel, click on that clip in the timeline. **Apply Match** will appear in the viewer:

Figure 14.32 – Clip on the right is matching the color information of the left clip

As you have seen, color correction, grading, and balancing will raise the quality of your video from normal to outstanding.

Summary

There has been a lot of theory in this chapter, with some practical elements to show you how to implement the theory in Final Cut Pro.

You learned the principles of color theory, with specific mention of the primary, secondary, and tertiary models and how they can be built on, from combining the primary colors to get secondary colors and then mixing primary and secondary colors to create tertiary colors.

You saw how colors can affect the mood of a video as well as help to make characters stand out, particularly with the use of primary colors.

You were shown how the combinations of monochromatic, complementary, analogous, and triadic/tetradic color types further add to the variance of color schemes available to you. You were also shown how to mix the colors with a free online color calculator, as well as using preset color combinations to assist you directly.

Then, you learned the value of having a color-accurate monitor and how a monitor needs calibration on a regular basis.

You learned about color corrections using temperature, tint, and hue adjustments as well as HSL tuning.

Finally, you looked at the automatic processes that Final Cut Pro offers to build a foundation for you to manually add your own color correction with the Balance Color and Match Color features.

The next chapter follows on from this one, with detailed explanations of how the color scopes introduce a graphical way of measuring how color appears in Final Cut Pro.

15

Using Color Scopes for Advanced Color Correction

This chapter is a direct follow-on from the last one, where color theory was explained, along with methods for taking color grading and correction to the next level so you are not just trusting your eyes.

In this chapter, you will learn how to read the settings supplied with **color scopes**. You will see how scopes provide a precise way of viewing color mixes and corrections as you make them. Scopes are displayed as either graphs or waveforms so that you are not just relying on your eyes to adjust color.

You will learn how scopes allow you to visualize the conventional process of changing exposure first, then adjusting the saturation with specific scopes, and finally, correcting color with scopes such as **RGB Parade**.

You will learn about terms such as histogram, vectorscope, and waveform. These are the forms of graphic display shown in the color scopes. You will also be presented with information about separate controls for **color curves** and **hue/saturation curves**. There are different methods of viewing the curves depending on your needs.

You will learn about the eyedropper method of selecting a specific color tone and manipulating that tone without affecting other colors in the image.

You will then learn about the importance of knowing how to select a specific portion of an image and apply secondary color correction to either the inside or the outside of the shape that you draw on the image, allowing you to adjust the portion of the image on either side of the shape.

In this chapter, we're going to cover the following topics:

- Waveformmonitor
- RGB Parade
- Vectorscope
- Histogram
- The **Video Scopes** menu
- Scopes workflow in Final Cut Pro
- Color curves
- Hue and saturation curves
- Color shapes and masks

By the end of this chapter, you will have an understanding of color scopes and both the color and hue/saturation sets of curves for color grading and correction.

You will have learned exactly what scopes do and seen how they are used to selectively adjust the color grade.

You will understand that when you're color correcting, you need to be able to accurately display the video's exposure, saturation, and color. You will understand that your eyes adapt to the light in the room in which you are editing, and hence they can't be trusted to produce accurate results, which is why we need to use video scopes.

Even though they may seem intimidating, you will learn how to interpret and trust video scopes, because they never lie.

Displaying the scopes

To show video scopes in Final Cut Pro X, go to **View** | **Show in Viewer** | **Video Scopes**, or go to the smaller **View** menu above the viewer and select **Video Scopes**. The video scopes will now be displayed in the viewer.

To change the video scope, click the small square graph icon, then select **Waveform**, **Vectorscope**, or **Histogram**.

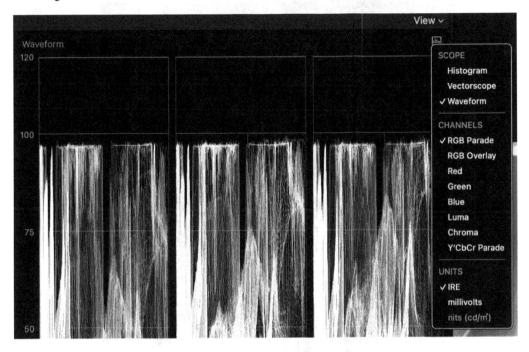

Figure 15.1 – Graph icon selected with an RGB Parade waveform

To select a combination of scopes, click on **View**.

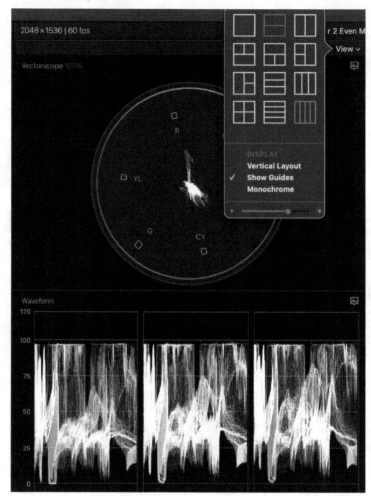

Figure 15.2 – Different options when selecting View

Waveformmonitor

The Waveformmonitor describes an image by its brightness, not its content.

It shows the relative levels of luma or chroma by displaying peaks and troughs that depict the brightness and darkness of an image, respectively. Peaks represent the brighter areas; troughs represent the darker regions.

When you open the Waveformmonitor, it will display **RGB Parade** by default. I suggest you change it to **Luma**, which displays grayscale values, for the first color grading of the exposure.

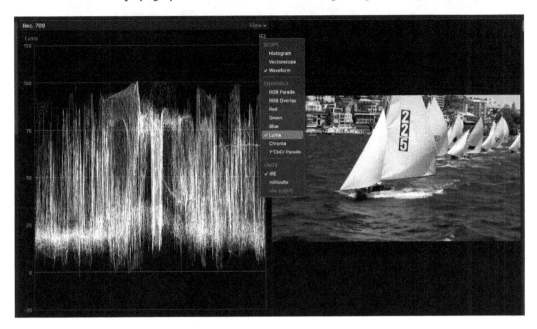

Figure 15.3 – Luma Waveform

When working with the Waveform monitor, the top is the brightest and the bottom is the darkest.

The peaks are not to exceed 100 IRE, the maximum allowable brightness (the top white line marked **100**); dark values should not go below 0 IRE, as this is the maximum allowable darkness (the bottom white line marked **0**).

When the Waveform monitor is set to **RGB Parade**, the perfect color balance will have all three colors showing a similar Waveform shape with bright and dark peaks within the boundaries of 0 to 100 IRE. All three channels should be equal horizontally, showing equal amounts of red, green, and blue to produce white.

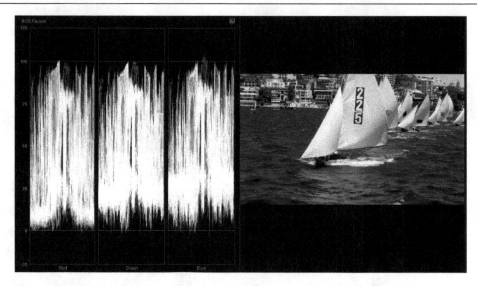

Figure 15.4 – Waveform– RGB Parade creating waveforms with similar shapes

Vectorscope

The vectorscope is just a color wheel, showing hue and saturation. Inside the wheel are cyan, green, and yellow. The center of the circle has the least saturation, whereas the outer edge shows 100% saturation. The saturation is lowest at the center of the circle, whereas it is at its maximum (100%) at the outer edge. The hue varies around the edge of the vectorscope; the line between yellow and red is called the **skin tone line**, and it is where skin tones should be in a correctly color-balanced image.

Figure 15.5 – Skin tone line at 11 o'clock

The vectorscope displays the color values of every pixel displayed in the viewer. Gray is in the center. The vectorscope is used in tandem with the Waveform monitor, which shows values in grayscale with the vectorscope showing color values.

In the following figure, the vectorscope shows strong green pointing to the yellow and green hue edge of the vectorscope. The red and blue pointers show the amount of saturation at the red and blue edges of the circle.

Figure 15.6 – Vectorscope

Histogram

A histogram is a graphical representation of the number of pixels of each color or luma level as you would have seen in a camera or image editor such as Photoshop. The histogram displays the range or color change from dark on the left to light on the right, as shown in *Figure 15.7*. Each increment represents a percentage, while the height of each segment indicates the number of pixels relating to the percentage.

The small square graph icon in the upper-right corner of the histogram provides either just the **Luma** component of the video or **RGB Parade**. The following figure shows a histogram with the **RGB Parade** function:

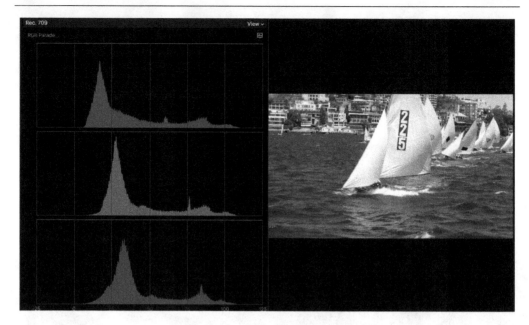

Figure 15.7 – RGB Parade histogram

RGB Overlay combines waveforms for the red, green, and blue colors into one graph. If the image has equal amounts of different colors, you will be shown the combined colors. Green and blue will show as cyan, green and red as yellow, and red and blue as magenta. Red, green, and blue appear as gray.

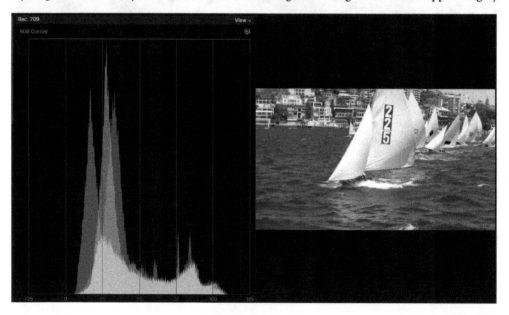

Figure 15.8 – RGB Overlay histogram

The Video Scope menu

You can combine the different scopes in one display. You can have a single type of scope or combine up to four different scopes, horizontally or vertically.

Figure 15.9 – Multiple scopes

The **View** menu in the center of the display allows you to choose the arrangement of the scopes. I have found that a side-by-side, vertical layout of a **Luma** waveform, **RGB Parade**, and **Vectorscope** is a good choice for a large monitor and even better for a second monitor, as in *Figure 15.10*.

Figure 15.10 – Luma waveform, RGB Parade, and Vectorscope

Now that you know what the color scopes show you, let's put them to use with the three stages of color grading – exposure, saturation, and color.

Scopes workflow in Final Cut Pro

In *Chapter 14, Understanding the Principles of Color*, you saw how to follow the three stages of color grading, starting with exposure, moving on to saturation, and, finally, color. Now that you know about the color scopes, it's time to combine the three stages to show how the scopes give you more accuracy by offering graphs, rather than relying on your eyes, to assist with the adjustments made in the color board or color wheels.

Step 1 – exposure correction

As explained in the previous chapter, when adjusting the exposure, in your mind, think of it as grayscale rather than color. This is where the **Luma** Waveform monitor is most useful. The following is the **Luma** Waveform of the image to be corrected before any changes:

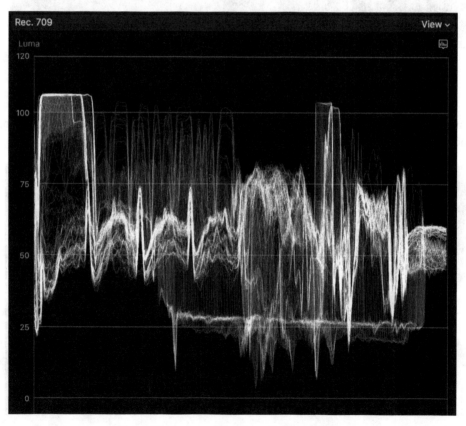

Figure 15.11 – Luma Waveform before changes

The brightness is too high, above 100, and the dark values are well above the 0 mark. You should always remain within the 0 to 100 IRE range, called the **dynamic range**; otherwise, you risk colors bleeding and blacks and whites washing out.

Refer to *Figure 15.3* to set the Waveform monitor to **Luma**. Select the color wheels and adjust the **Highlights** right-hand curve down in the inspector, to bring the bright peaks that are currently above 100 IRE down to 100, as shown in the following figure:

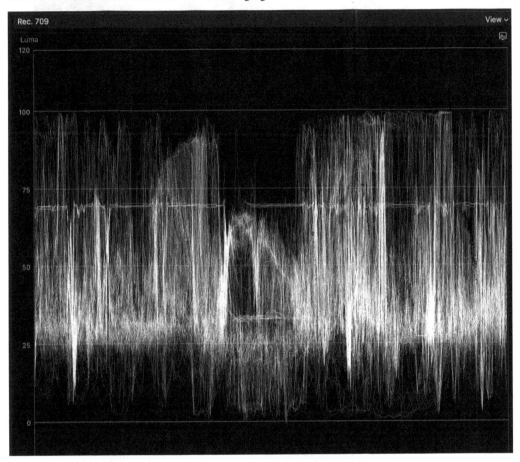

Figure 15.12 – Bright values at 100; dark values at 0

Next, to move the blacks to the **0** mark, drag the right-hand curve down in the **Shadows** wheel until it reaches **0**. Now, to set **Midtones**, which should be between 60 and 70 IRE, drag the right-hand slider in the **Midtones** wheel depending on your needs. You may find that this changes your **Highlights** and **Shadows** settings, so you will need to balance out the three wheels. **Midtones** is the trickiest of the three to get right; use your judgment to settle on the final result. Getting these correct will give a great contrast to the image.

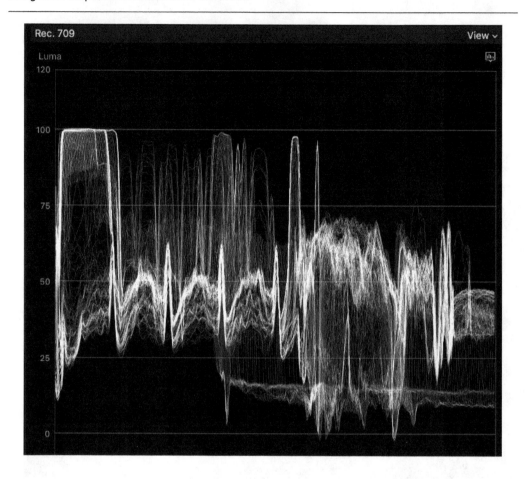

Figure 15.13 – Luma Waveform corrected to be within the 0 to 100 IRE range

Correcting the exposure on a normal camera image is done differently when the footage has been filmed with a LOG setting, as you will see in the next section.

Manual correction of LOG footage

LOG is a video format produced by higher-end cameras, as discussed in *Chapter 1: It's All About the Media*

The reason that cameras shoot in LOG is to retain the high dynamic range that the camera sensor is capable of. The compressed formats that Final Cut Pro uses are not able to retain the camera's high dynamic range. The end result is that when you import the clip into Final Cut Pro, the image shows as washed out and requires color correction. The quickest solution to restore the color is to use a **lookup table (LUT)**, as shown in *Chapter 1: It's All About the Media*. If an appropriate LUT is not available, the **Luma** Waveform provides a simple manual correction for LOG footage. Make sure **Shadows** is at **0** and **Highlights** is at **100** while adjusting **Midtones** by eye, as in *Figure 15.13*.

Once you have a suitable color correction, it is a good idea to create a preset and save the color correction settings to the color grading presets using the **Save Color Effects Preset** option at the bottom of the inspector.

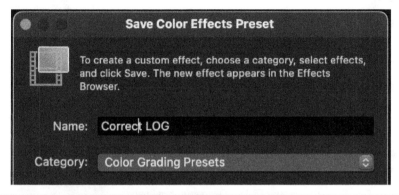

Figure 15.14 – Save as Color Grading Presets

Once the exposure is set, we will move on to the next step, which is saturation control.

Step 2 – saturation control

The vectorscope is ideal for correcting saturation as the circle is neutral at the center and saturated at the outer edge, so the scopes will easily show oversaturation, as in the following screenshot:

Figure 15.15 – Oversaturated image

Most of the image sits in the **MIDTONES** range, so more saturation should be removed from **MIDTONES** as well as a little from **HIGHLIGHTS** and **SHADOWS**.

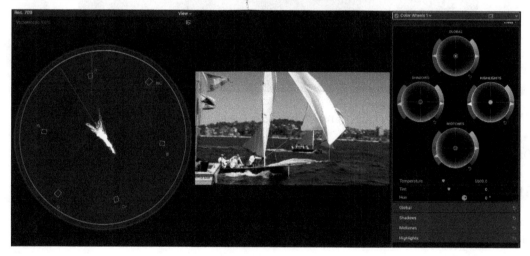

Figure 15.16 – Saturation reduced but color is muted

When you remove saturation, be careful that the color is not also reduced. In the following figure, blue is added for the sky in both **HIGHLIGHTS** and **MIDTONES**, and some green is added to **SHADOWS** to differentiate the water from the sky.

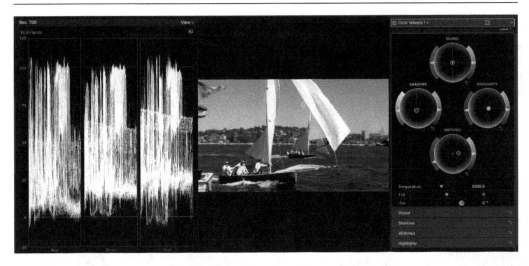

Figure 15.17 – Saturation balanced out

With the exposure correct and the saturation fixed, we will move on to the balancing of color.

Step 3 – color balance

The objective of balancing color is to neutralize any color casts.

> **Note**
>
> A color cast is an undesirable color that affects the whole image, usually from an unfavorable light source such as a sunset or sunrise.

Set the Waveform monitor to **RGB Parade** to control an over-prominent color. The center puck in each of the color wheels will let you adjust the color along with **Temperature**, **Tint**, and **Hue** controls.

RGB Parade helps determine the cause of a color cast in shadow or highlight areas. Such casts can be caused by clipping (overexposure or underexposure) in one of the color channels. It's almost impossible to fix this issue without **RGB Parade**.

In the following figure, the red channel is dominant. First, the exposure needs to be set.

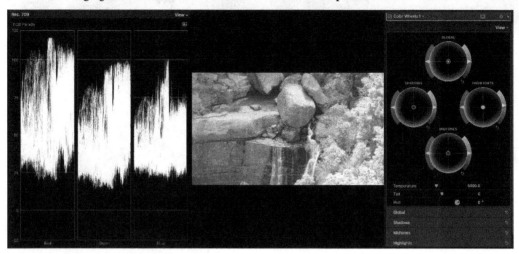

Figure 15.18 – Red color cast

Correcting the exposure helps, but green and blue need to be added to the color wheels or color board in the inspector.

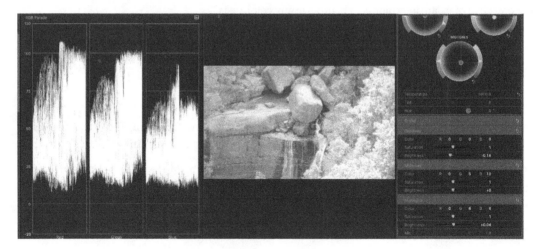

Figure 15.19 – Color cast removed

The scopes are used for measuring color without relying on just your eyes. The next section discusses color curves. You will still use scopes to verify the changes that you make with the curves just as you do with the color board and color wheel methods of correction.

To summarize, curves and color boards/wheels are ways of adjusting the exposure, saturation, and color. Scopes are graphical tools for monitoring the changes made.

Color curves

While you should always try to capture the best image you can with the camera, color curves give you the ability to produce almost as good an image as should have been captured by the camera and fulfill the director's promise to be able to "fix it in post."

Color curves were not initially offered with Final Cut Pro; they only became available in late 2017 with version 10.4. They are now a well-used alternative to the color board and the color wheel. Color curves should definitely be part of your color correction arsenal.

The following section looks at the different curves in detail.

Luma curve

All color curves are displayed as graphs; the horizontal axis is at the bottom and the vertical axis is on the left side. I'm going to start by showing the Luma curve, which represents black and white and grayscale, from **0** (black) to **255** (white), with the bottom-left corner being black and the top-right corner being white. There is a 45-degree line from the bottom left to the top right. The image in the following figure is uncorrected:

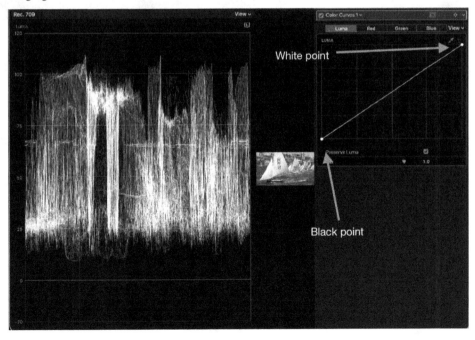

Figure 15.20 – Luma curve uncorrected image

Earlier in this chapter, *Figure 15.11* was corrected with the color wheels for exposure; the same can be done with the color curves, as shown in the following figure, where the black point (bottom left) has been moved to the right and the white point (top right) has been moved down so that the Waveform is between 0 and 100 IRE:

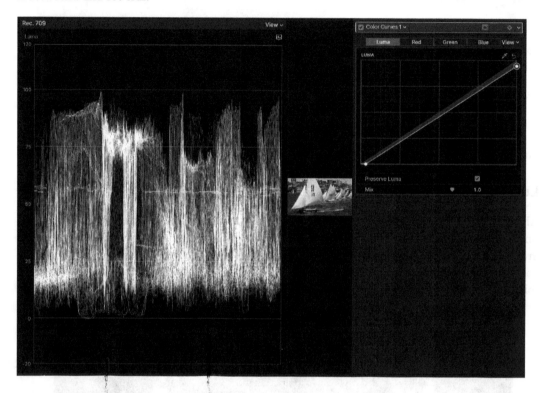

Figure 15.21 – Luma curve with points moved for exposure correction

To fully explain the principle, let me explain what the left and right default points will do at their extremes. If you drag the black point (left dot) all the way up, the image will be completely white:

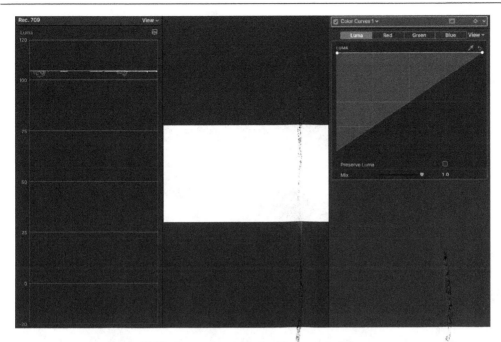

Figure 15.22 – Luma curve with the black point all the way up

By moving the black point (the left dot in the following figure), halfway across the bottom, the black takes over more of the image:

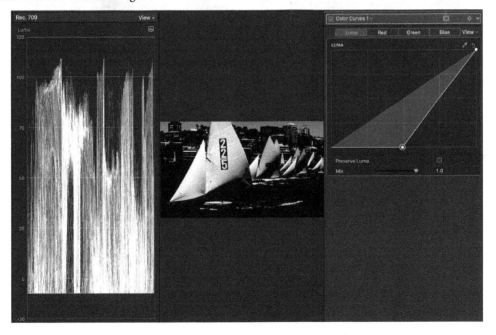

Figure 15.23 – Luma curve with the black point halfway right

On the other hand, if the white point (right dot) is moved all the way down, the image will be completely black:

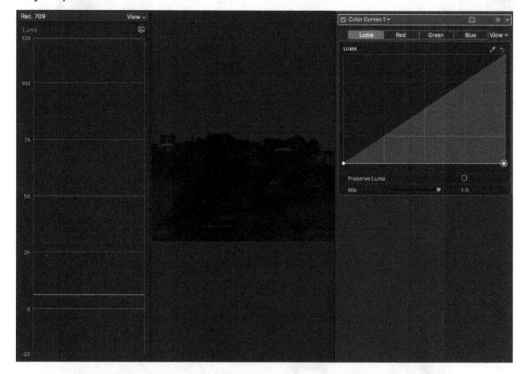

Figure 15.24 – Luma curve with the white point all the way down

Now, let's take the exercise to the next level by adding control points (dots) on the line to create a mix of midtones that protect the positions of the black and white points, and only adjust the midtones at the location where the new points have been moved.

In the following figure, the black points are locked onto **0** and the white points onto **100**, with the midtones positioned at the center of the image. The dot with the circle around it is the active dot and can be moved or deleted while the circle is around it.

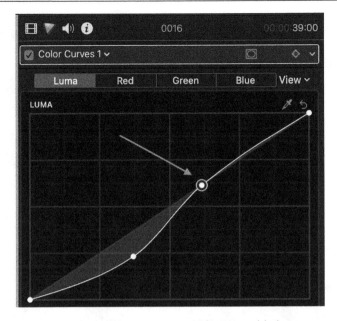

Figure 15.25 – Luma curve with points added

This is where color curves offer a significant advantage. If you were adjusting with color board, you would be moving back and forth between panels, balancing the changes made in **Exposure** with the adjustments in **Midtones**. The advantage is even more evident when you work with the full range of curves, as you will see in the following section.

All color curves – RGB

Up to now, you have been viewing **Luma** as a single curve. It can be viewed with RGB curves as well.

Figure 15.26 – Single Curves or All Curves

I'll be using the red curve as an example, and the same things can be done as we did with the **Luma** curve. The same applies to all the other colors. Now, drag the left red dot all the way up.

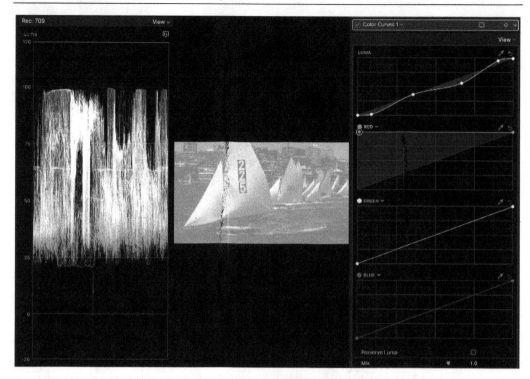

Figure 15.27 – The red left dot is dragged all the way up

Color curves can manipulate color in a way that can't be done with color wheels or color board. In both of those color methods, all of a selected color is corrected, not just a range that you want. With color curves, you have much finer control over the tone of color being corrected because you can tell the color curves the actual color that you want to change.

Select **All Curves**, as in *Figure 15.26*. You will see four diagonal lines, as in *Figure 15.27*: white, red, green, and blue. The checkbox at the bottom, **Preserve Luma**, retains the brightness of the image as you make adjustments.

The eyedropper

Color curves has a special tool called the eyedropper, which allows you to sample the color at the point on which you click on an image. When the eyedropper is colored blue, it is active.

To remove a color cast from an image, click the eyedropper at the top of one of the color curves; then, in the viewer, click or drag over an area of the image that is white, such as the sail in the following figure:

Figure 15.28 – Color cast

You will see a gray line appear on the color curve. Click a control point (dot) on the line, then drag the dot down. Clicking either side of the original control point will add dots, which can narrow the range of the color change:

Figure 15.29 – Side dots narrow the range of the color

To change the color of a line, bring up the color wheel by clicking on the chevron on the left:

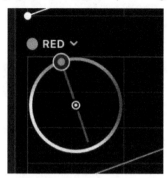

Figure 15.30 – Color wheel selected by clicking the chevron

To prevent any changes to the brightness or darkness, click control points to pin the curve to the diagonal line. Select the **Preserve Luma** checkbox to maintain the brightness.

Now that you have an understanding of the methods of manipulating the diagonal lines in **Color Curves**, the hue and saturation curves covered in the next section will extend that knowledge. The same principles you saw for color curves apply to hue and saturation curves, including the use of the eyedropper.

Hue and saturation curves

There are six hue and saturation curves for color-grading clips. You can adjust the hue, saturation, and brightness of any color. You can adjust the saturation for a range of brightness or saturation values in a clip. You can also adjust the saturation of a specific color at any point in its range of brightness. It sounds complicated, but it is not so difficult once you understand it.

When you first see the window with the six curves, it looks quite intimidating. That's because the headings don't explain what the curves actually do.

This list will help:

- **HUE vs HUE**: Changes a color (hue) in the image
- **HUE vs SAT**: Changes the saturation of a color in the image
- **HUE vs LUMA**: Adjusts the brightness of a color in the image
- **LUMA vs SAT**: Reduces oversaturation
- **SAT vs SAT**: Changes the range of saturation within the video clip's original saturation
- **ORANGE vs SAT**: Maintains skin tones

You can view them as single curves or all six together:

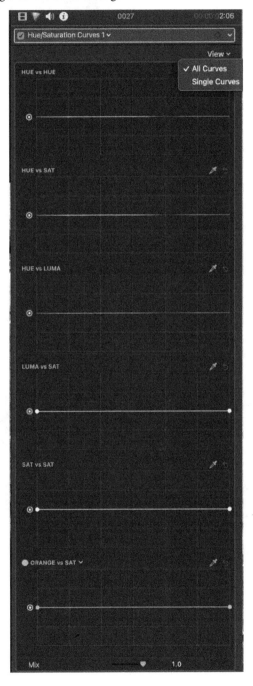

Figure 15.31 – Single Curves or All Curves option

The original control point (dot) is usually added by using the eyedropper as in the color curves. The color wheel, as shown in *Figure 15.30*, can be used to add a color. Dots can be added to the line by clicking on the dots on either side of the original control point (dot). Selecting the two outer dots will introduce a range of that color between those dots. To adjust the range, drag the two outer dots to the left or right. An active dot has a halo around it; when active, the dot can be moved or deleted.

You can make fine adjustments by holding the *Option* key and dragging. Holding the *Shift* key will constrain the control point (dot) to vertical or horizontal movements only. Use both the *Shift* and *Option* keys for fine adjustments as well as constraining.

HUE vs HUE

This curve is used to change the image's color. Use the eyedropper to add a gray line, and click on the gray line to create a control point (dot). It is best to isolate the color by clicking on the dot on either side of the gray line, as close as possible to the control point.

The left and right dots control the range of the color, while the middle dot is adjusted vertically for corrections. The left and right dots are adjusted horizontally.

Figure 15.32 – Original image with red on the spinnaker

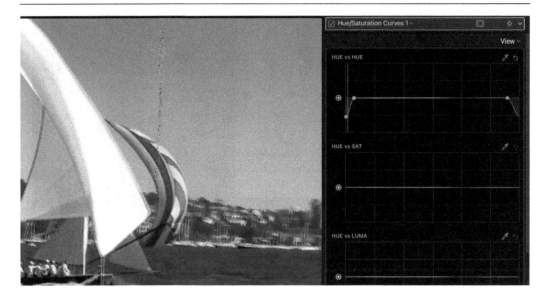

Figure 15.33 – Red becomes green without affecting any other colors

HUE vs SAT

This curve is used to change the saturation of a color in the image. Drag the middle dot up to increase the saturation or down to decrease. Add or adjust dots as needed. The original image shown in the following screenshot has an over-bright yellow, which we can reduce without reducing the red. Remember the name of the game is to be subtle with color adjustments.

Figure 15.34 – Original bright yellow (image by Yerson Retamal from Pixabay)

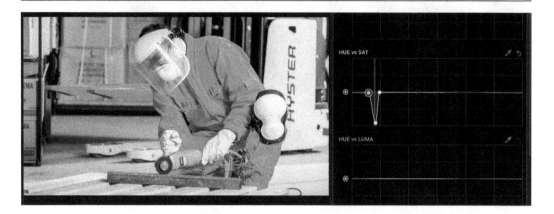

Figure 15.35 – Yellow reduced without affecting the red

HUE vs LUMA

This curve is used to adjust the luminance of a color in the image. Drag the middle dot up to increase the luminance or down to decrease it.

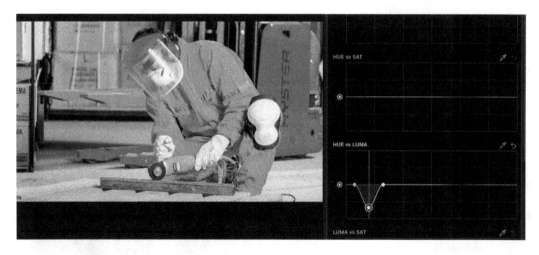

Figure 15.36 – Luminance decreased

LUMA vs SAT

This curve selects the brightness and changes its saturation, as opposed to reducing the saturation of the color as **HUE vs SAT** does or reducing the luminance as with **HUE vs LUMA**.

It's a subtle difference. After all, that is what color grading is all about, small adjustments that provide a look and feel and not a dramatic change in tone. In the following figure, the overalls have been reduced in brightness:

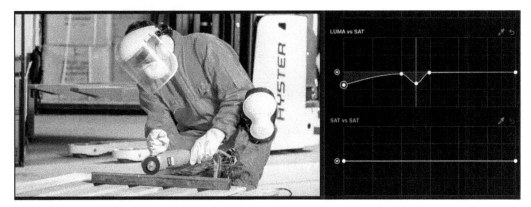

Figure 15.37 – Overalls reduced in brightness

SAT vs SAT

This curve lets you modify the range of saturation within an image's original saturation. Notice, in the following figure, how the tones of the boxes in the background have been reduced:

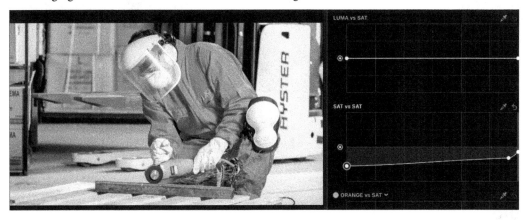

Figure 15.38 – Background box tones reduced

ORANGE vs SAT

This curve is named *orange* because that is the color aligned with skin tones. Use this curve to adjust skin tones without affecting the rest of the image too much. The top part of the image in the following figure has too much red in the skin:

Figure 15.39 – Face flushed with red

The following figure has the red cast removed from the face:

Figure 15.40 – Red in the face reduced

The next section discusses color shapes and masks that can be used with the color wheels, color board, color curves, and hue and saturation curve methods of correction. Color shapes and masks should also use the scopes to ensure a level of accuracy that you may not manage with just your eyes.

Color and shape masks

Scopes show you how exposure and color should look, but you need tools to be able to make those adjustments. As you have seen, color wheels and color boards are basic tools and, along with the curves, color shapes, and masks, allow you to change the color within a part of a clip. This means that you can change part of a single color or a shape that you can draw in the clip without changing the color of the entire clip.

You have the choice of two masks: a shape mask and a color mask. I'll explain the shape mask as it has a specific use of its own. You saw the hue and saturation curves earlier in this chapter. It is much better to use them rather than the color mask.

Figure 15.41 – Shape and color masks

The shape mask lets you select a physical portion of the image so that you can adjust the color aspects inside or outside the shape. This can be used as a secondary color correction as you could have corrected the whole image. You can change both the inside and outside and have the choice of resetting either. The following figure has blue added to the inside:

Figure 15.42 – Blue added to a shape mask

The shape mask is fixed as a circle or rectangle shape, but be aware that you can add any number of masks to cover an irregular shape. The following is the same image with five masks added to cover more of the sail and less of the water:

Figure 15.43 – Blue with five shape masks

The color mask has an eyedropper that allows you to select a color from the image. Unlike the shape mask, you can only have one color mask, as the eyedropper selects the range of color when you drag over.

Pick the color mask, as in *Figure 15.41* and click the blue eyedropper; drag it over the color you want to select – the white of the sail in *Figure 15.42*. The color mask works best for solid colors. The following figure shows a lot of color bleed, which is why the hue and saturation curves do a much better job.

Figure 15.44 – Color bleed

In my mind, color masks are not the best way of changing the color of a portion of an image; it is much more intuitive and flexible to use the hue and saturation curves, as you saw earlier.

Summary

In this chapter, you have seen that color scopes are used as a reference to check the technical parameters of color grading.

You saw that color curves and color boards/wheels are ways to process the order of color grading by adjusting the exposure, saturation, and color. Scopes are graphical tools for monitoring the changes made.

You saw that there are three main scopes: waveform, vectorscope, and histogram. Each has its use.

You learned that scopes provide more accuracy than your eyes can enable. Scopes are used alongside all of the correction tools: color board, color wheels, color curves, and hue/saturation curves.

You saw the value of the eyedropper selection method in color curves as well as the extensive use of the eyedropper in hue/saturation curves.

With the knowledge gained in the chapters so far, you will be now well equipped to understand, in the next chapter, how to use that knowledge in your job role, particularly when collaborating with other editors.

Part 4:
Outside Final Cut Pro

Part 4 details options that are not part of the Final Cut application that add that extra wow factor to edits as well as offer functionality for captioning, object tracking, color enhancements, and media organization. There is a discussion about your workspace as well as how you can jointly edit projects with other editors. Part 4 provides a proven workflow of techniques for troubleshooting, as well as a discussion on suggestions for archiving.

This part contains the following chapters:

- *Chapter 16, Your Job Role – Collaboration*
- *Chapter 17, Supporting Software Applications for Final Cut Pro*
- *Chapter 18, Troubleshooting Final Cut Pro*
- *Chapter 19, Backing Up and Archiving Libraries*

16

Your Job Role – Collaboration

Video is becoming, if it's not already, a part of every administrative job role. This chapter will show how any job role requires some knowledge to at least evaluate and critique video productions.

In this chapter, you will learn what specific jobs require the ability to edit a video. You will learn which roles in your organization edit videos, along with the specific job titles within a video production team.

The chapter also covers the vast area of collaboration between Final Cut Pro editors, both at a local level and collaborating globally.

You will learn techniques for collaboration as well as the actual setup and use of the various services and software applications designed for video collaboration. By the end of this chapter, you will have learned about the various job roles in a video production team as well as roles in the industry where video editing forms a major part. You will also be aware of the benefits and disadvantages of freelance editing.

The main topics covered in this chapter are as follows:

- Understanding the job roles in video production
- Exploring the industries that require video editors
- Should you be a freelancer?
- Collaboration between remote video editors

Understanding the job roles in video production

The various roles in a video production team require not only capable people to fill them but also people who know how and where they fit in the pecking order.

The hierarchy of roles is likely to be the same in different-sized organizations, but smaller teams will have people taking on several roles, ultimately to the point that sole proprietors will be responsible for all the roles. Even in the sole proprietor's case, it is important to know the roles and how they fit into the postproduction process.

In a full postproduction environment, there are two distinct teams that need to work together. The communication between these teams is usually between the producer and the senior video editor, each being the head of their respective team and the glue that binds the whole production together.

Since this is about teams, there will be a number of people involved in small-to-medium-sized organizations who will be responsible for several roles. However, larger establishments will have several people in each of the minor roles supporting the leaders.

To ensure that you understand your position within the hierarchy, I'll cover all the roles, starting with the producer as the top dog, that is, the most senior position in the organization.

The production team

The production team is responsible for what takes place prior to and during filming and is separate from the postproduction team. The production team is headed by the producer and assisted by the director, and they will both need to liaise with the video editor from the postproduction team.

Producer

The producer is the overall head of the enterprise. They need to understand the complete operation, from preproduction and shooting to postproduction, while balancing the creative, financial, and logistical needs of the team.

Director

The director has a more hands-on role in the projects themselves, as opposed to the producer's more administrative and budgeting role. The director is more involved in the day-to-day running of projects, deciding on the selection of locations, recommending casting, and even deciding on wardrobe and dialogue. Overall, the director is responsible for shooting schedules and staying within the budget set by the producer.

The director is responsible for assembling the production team and hiring and firing. When you are considering your value and position in the team, look to the director as your *adviser*.

Director of photography (DOP)

For most organizations or even one-off productions, the DOP will also be one of the cinematographers or videographers. The DOP works closely with the director when searching for locations, arranging camera equipment, and hiring camera operators, gaffers, and grips.

The producer, director, and DOP are the major stakeholders in a full production house. The shoot itself includes specialist technicians such as the digital imaging technician, audio technician, gaffer and key grip, camera operators, set/hair/makeup/wardrobe crew, and production assistants.

After the shoot, it is time for the postproduction team to take over. This team will operate mostly as a separate entity, reporting to the producer and director via the senior video editor. Let us now learn more about this team.

The postproduction editing team

This team is headed by the senior video editor who liaises with the producer and director from the production team. The postproduction team has a broad range of skills, both technical and aesthetic. The core function of a video editor is to cut, trim, and sequence video clips into a structure that eventually becomes the final video. To make use of all the skills, there can be a number of different roles in the postproduction team.

The senior video editor

To fulfill this role, a video editor needs to be aware of all of the techniques and workflows of editing. The secret to success in this role is collaboration – being able to work well with others. The senior video editor is responsible for the whole postproduction team. Larger organizations will have separate postproduction teams headed by video editors and assistant editors. TV series in particular will have many editors collaborating on Final Cut Pro projects, as you will see later in this chapter in the *Collaboration between remote video editors* section.

The assistant editor

The assistant editor can be known by several different titles that mostly boil down to the same thing. Different employers will use various terms: junior editor, runner, deputy editor, sidekick, and so on. While the assistant editor may not primarily be involved in actual editing, the role is principally involved with the logging of footage and setting up keyword collections for the video editor.

There can also be a number of assistant editors, splitting the tasks of asset organization, creating proxies, adding metadata, and hunting for extra media. Assistant editors mainly exist in larger production houses, as the organizational workflow is now so integrated within Final Cut Pro that it is easily handled by the video editor in a smaller enterprise, as you have already seen in *Chapter 2*, where media organization in Final Cut Pro was discussed.

The assembler

The assembler is a separate role from the assistant or junior editor. They are often found in a corporate environment, where they produce templated and routine edits most likely for social media use. The assembler can produce large volumes of videos without the experience of a long-term editor.

The freelance editor

The freelance editor is a combination of producer and editor in one role, working as an independent contractor and as an individual operator. Because they take on the whole of the postproduction, they have a wide skill set and can be considered a jack of all trades. They need to have the skills of the director, producer, and assembler to be able to get the job done without being an expert in every detail. The freelance editor is unique in that they can envisage the whole production from beginning to end and foresee the client's needs, right throughout the postproduction process.

The postproduction team must work as a unit, with a shared understanding of the team's organization of keyword collections, workflows, title and effects usage, and, ultimately, the editing style. Every member of the team should be able to continue with Final Cut Pro projects already created by other members of the team.

With this knowledge of the roles available in a video editing career, let's move on to the next section, which covers the different industries that employ video editors.

Exploring the industries that require video editors

There are various industries that require video editors: corporate, social media, feature films, documentaries, commercials, TV, trailers, music videos, and weddings.

You will be surprised at how many different types of video editing jobs you can specialize in, and each industry has its advantages and disadvantages. Hopefully, the following list will help you decide which industry type will suit you the best by explaining the differences between them.

Corporate

The corporate realm is not an area that you would immediately think of as the most common employer of individuals who edit videos. However, it is probably the biggest employer of people editing videos. The video work can be repetitive, but it is well paid, the positions are permanent, and video is usually only part of the job role, which will also incorporate administration, marketing, and even financial aspects of the corporate job requirements.

There is still a tendency for corporate organizations to be conservative with their video content. However, the rise of social media is changing that, and there are organizations searching for ways to increase their social media presence, thus offering good opportunities for capable video editors.

As mentioned, corporate video editing may not be your complete role. You may find that you work in corporate administration and promote material for your company. With the ease of use of Final Cut Pro, it only takes a short time to become proficient enough to produce simple videos about the products or services within your sector of the company.

Video editing in the corporate environment will suit those who are looking for a 9-to-5 job, where they can depend on a secure wage and work with familiar material, while still having some space for creativity to make each day different.

Social media

Editing for social media is also covered in the corporate environment, so what we will discuss here will apply to the corporate realm as well. The turnaround of videos for social media is quick, and the quality tends to be simple on purpose, due to the need to publish content when there is a time-sensitivity factor. The general look and feel of social media videos adheres to the philosophy *content is king*, with quality coming second. Social media editing is dominated by freelance editors, both for clients and their own social media online presence.

The *assembler* editor thrives in this field, as the use of templated formats and similar themes is the key to publishing as much material as possible in a short timeframe.

The social media field is a great training ground for new and inexperienced editors to practice their skills while still getting paid.

Movies and TV

Movies, or in fact any scripted narrative videos, from the public's point of view are at the top of the tree. It would be the ultimate accolade for any editor to be recognized with an Oscar. However, you are more likely to win the lottery than for that to happen. There's no harm in dreaming and aiming high, though.

Overall, there is less work in the movie and TV industries than in all the other avenues that offer work for editors. The competition is high, with few roles available, so only the best will rise to the top.

Reality TV offers opportunities for assistant editors because of the many hours of footage to log and organize, allowing the editor to consider the most suitable footage.

Movie and TV editors tend to be employed by studios rather than contracted freelancers, so this is regular employment. The downside is that the employment is usually per project. Movies can run for a year, but TV series and reality TV can run for several years.

Documentary

Documentary editing is storytelling at its purest, and from an editor's point of view, the dramatization of material is the most rewarding of all the editing experiences. The documentary is where the editor is able to be the storyteller, rather than simply editing someone else's story or script.

Documentary work can be edited by both freelance and employed editors. It is a niche skill and experienced documentary editors are in demand.

Commercials

There is a special skill associated with commercials to get the whole story told in 15 or 30 seconds. Admittedly, the scriptwriter sets the tone, but the editor needs to present the images and have them planted in the audience's brain in the shortest time possible. It usually needs to be done with a sense of humor.

It is often the case that feature editors want to edit commercials and commercial editors want to edit features. They are both at opposite ends of the editing spectrum in terms of time and creative freedom.

It must be noted, however, that the burnout rate is high with editors of commercials, as the tension and pressure are not the easiest thing to manage.

Trailers

Trailer editing is similar to commercials and involves less creativity. You could describe it as social media editing on steroids. Possessing the ability to condense the essence of a story into a short timeframe is imperative. Trailers tend to be formulaic, which can be helpful to the editor initially but tends to become boring for audiences over time. There is a skill in promoting the spirit of the story without giving away the plot while whetting the audience's appetite to go and watch the movie.

Now that you know the industry groups and where you fit in that structure, the next section looks at the differences between freelance and full-time employment.

Should you be a freelancer?

As a reader of this book, you are likely employed in some type of video editing enterprise, either on a full-time or freelance basis. Starting out as a freelancer is a big risk and can be expensive to set up. Most people who are new to the video editing field are already in some employment related to video editing, and they may have progressed from assistant editor status to being a video editor.

The question is, should you continue to work as a full-time employee or are you better off venturing into freelancing?

It's great to have the stability of a full-time job, but you may feel that the company you work for puts their own interests ahead of yours.

On the other hand, to become a freelancer, there is a considerable investment in equipment and the risk of an erratic workflow from many clients. The decision is much easier when there is one main client that you can focus on. However, don't be dragged into a scenario where one client fills too big a portion of your total clients. You need a mix of major and drop-in clients, but what is the percentage of each?

Some freelancers deal with one or two clients; others can have a large number of clients on their books. Every client demands a varying size of workload; you should set an objective for the number of clients you want to deal with. While thinking about whether or not to be a freelancer, you might want to consider the factors described in the subsequent sections that will affect your client load.

How much work from a client

One client could take up a couple of hours per week; others could require 10 or more hours. Make sure you discuss the potential workload before taking on a regular client. Don't overload yourself; what's worse than not having enough clients is if you can't service the ones you have committed to.

There is always a temptation to, at first, take on all the work that is offered to you. That may be fine initially for one-off clients but don't take on regular clients if you can't be sure that you will be able to meet their needs on a timely basis. Video is an industry that is time-sensitive, so late deliveries will lead to you losing clients.

Type of work

You need to evaluate your priorities and consider the reasons that you decided to become a freelancer. If it was money, be careful not to burn out by taking on too many clients. It's all about the work/life balance.

After you have become established, you can pick the types of projects that you enjoy. When you are starting out, however, you should take on whatever you are capable of fulfilling, which will help you decide which projects you prefer. Unless you enjoy taking it on, beware of clients who want you to do all the admin tasks, such as phone calls and paperwork. You will need to be clear on how you itemize these tasks in your billing.

The schedule

You need to plan ahead as to how many hours you want to work in a week. Of course, there will be special projects that last longer than a week, but don't make a habit of overworking.

Balancing time

It's not all about video editing; you also need to allocate time for admin, banking, marketing, networking, updating your website, and posting on social media. Establish a balance and split your editing to 80-90% of your week. So, for a 40-hour week, allow 3-4 hours for non-editing roles.

Intensity of work

Freelancing is not just about time but also about your energy levels. Check your schedule to ensure that you don't start feeling exhausted. Burning the candle at both ends will lead to bad decisions and sloppy editing.

Financial reward

You need to establish an hourly rate that is attractive to clients but rewarding to you. Different regions have varying average hourly rates. Establish the rate for your locality. Use Facebook or social media forums to ask what others are charging. Establish an hourly rate for yourself, but ensure it amounts to a daily rate that you are happy with. Be careful that discount levels for larger clients ensure you receive an adequate daily return.

The risk/comfort factor

Income and workload will vary each week when working as a freelancer. It comes down to all the factors that have been discussed so far. What daily rate do you want? What are the schedules you will need to comply with? How intense is the work? How many clients will you need to deal with? One or two long-term clients usually account for the highest percentage of your income, and losing one client isn't such a big deal when you have a number of clients.

Freelancing is more than just freedom; it's taking control of your future and establishing your self-worth.

Whether you are working full-time for a company or freelancing, you will be confronted with the need to collaborate with other editors on a Final Cut Pro project. It may be with editors in the same office or across the world. The next section will discuss the varying ways to collaborate either on a temporary basis or for large-scale permanent workflows.

Collaboration between remote video editors

"No man is an island," so the saying goes, and this is no truer than when you consider the need to collaborate on a Final Cut Pro project.

The number one rule of working with two computers or more in a collaboration environment is that they must all have the same plug-ins, which includes any presets you have created for effects. Refer to the *Save effects preset* section in *Chapter 10, The Inspector Controls*. To a lesser degree, you need to have the same fonts on each computer; other fonts can be substituted without the red warning filling the viewer, as shown in *Figure 16.1*.

Figure 16.1 – A red warning in the viewer notifying about a missing effect

> **Note**
> Don't forget, if you use them, you need to have the same camera **lookup tables** (**LUTs**) on all computers.

In whatever way you decide to collaborate on your Final Cut Pro projects, you will need shared storage devices, whether they are on one local site, in the cloud, or synced devices in several locations.

With that said, there are some occasions where you can, on a temporary basis, remotely collaborate on a project without shared storage. The old way, when collaborating occasionally, was the swapping of a disk when editors were on a single site. Even shipping hard disks from location to location was a historical option. Thankfully, shipping is no longer needed, as there are much quicker options using cloud services. While swapping projects over the web is not recommended, it does offer a temporary solution for one-off occasions, as in the scenarios discussed in the following sections.

Sending proxy and XML files

This involves sending just the smaller proxy files from the shooter to the editor, who imports the proxies into a Final Cut Pro library and exports the project as an XML file that can be emailed back to the shooter, which is synced with the full-sized original media when the XML is received.

The process starts on the shooter's computer. They create a Final Cut Pro library, import the footage, and create proxy media, as the **Import** window shows in *Figure 16.2*.

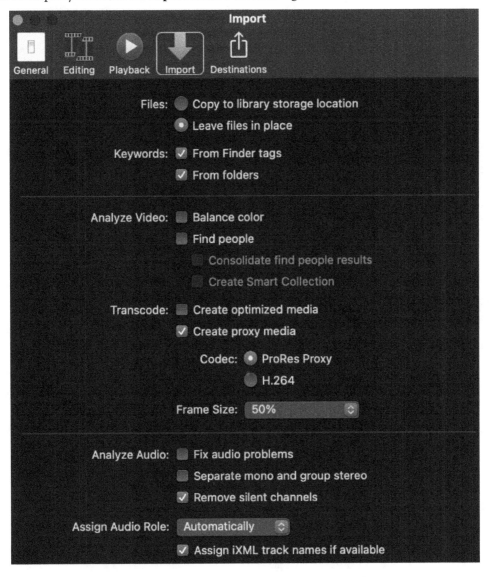

Figure 16.2 – Import and transcoding to proxy media

I suggest choosing a **ProRes Proxy** codec with a frame size of 25-50%. You can use **H.264**, which is more compressed but of a slightly lower quality. If you want a smaller file size, you can go lower, but H.264 with a frame at anything less than 25% is very hard to edit, as you can see in *Figure 16.6*.

Figure 16.3 – Full-sized media

Figure 16.4 – Proxy media at 50% and ProRes

Figure 16.5 – Proxy media at 25% and H.264

Figure 16.6 – Proxy media at 12.5% and H.264

When the proxies are transcoded, check in the inspector with the **i** tab selected to see whether they have been created, as shown in *Figure 16.7*.

Figure 16.7 – Checking whether the proxy media has been created

> **Note**
>
> During proxy creation, clicking on the **Show or Hide Background Task** window button will display the background task processes in progress.

The process of creating a new library with only proxy media involves selecting all the proxy clips. From the **File** menu, select **Copy Clips to Library | New Library….** Name the new library, and select a location on a disk, as seen in *Figure 16.8*.

> **Note**
>
> Events can be sent to the new library in a similar way.

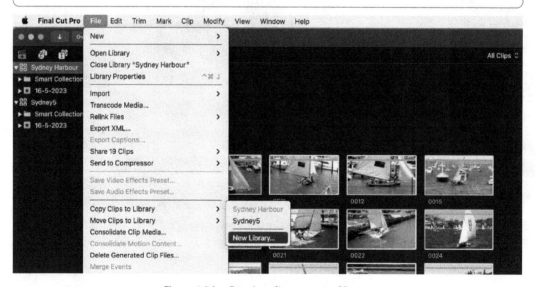

Figure 16.8 – Copying clips to a new library

The next window has the **Include | Media** option; just select **Proxy media** and untick everything else. By not ticking **Original media**, only proxy media will be in the new library. This is important, as the choice will significantly affect the size of the Final Cut Pro library. You can mirror the settings shown in *Figure 16.9*.

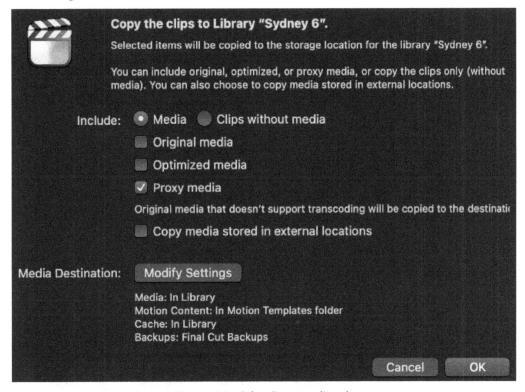

Figure 16.9 – Select Proxy media only

The size of the library will be about half the size because the proxy media was created at 50% the size of the original.

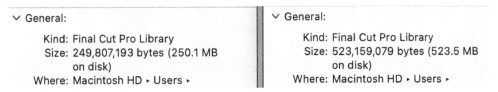

Figure 16.10 – 50% proxy media only versus the original full-sized media

Upload the new library to Dropbox or IDrive, and then send the link to the editor. The library will be relatively quick to download.

> **Tip**
>
> Not all cloud services will keep a Final Cut Pro library intact. Most cloud storage will break the library package into separate files. Use Dropbox or IDrive to be safe.

Once the proxy library is received, double-click the purple library icon, and edit as normal. Once the edit is completed, select the library in the **Browser** sidebar, go to the **File** menu, and then click **Export XML…**:

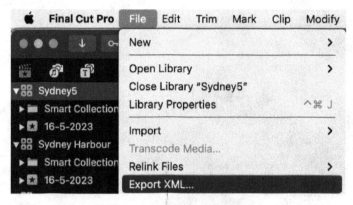

Figure 16.11 – Export XML…

Then, select the current version, as shown in *Figure 16.12*:

Figure 16.12 – Choose the current version

The XML is so small that it can be sent to the shooter in an email (45 KB compared to the library with the proxy media, which is 249.8 MB), as it is only a text file with just the editing instructions. The following figure shows the size of an XML file at 45 KB compared to a library at 249.8 MB:

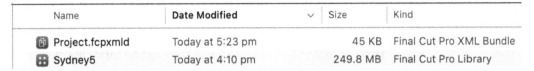

Figure 16.13 – The XML file and the library it came from

When the XML file is received by the shooter, they can import it via **File | Import | XML…** into the first original library that they created with the full-sized media, not the new library they created with the proxy media. The XML file will link to the original footage, allowing the shooter to finish editing, and then they can share/export the video.

Figure 16.14 – File | Import | XML…

If your collaboration requirements are more permanent, transferring XML files will soon become tedious. The next section looks at better alternatives, starting with if you are working at shared premises and then moving on to the case of remote access.

Collaborating at the same premises

A single shared storage device can be used to hold a Final Cut Pro library and allows multiple editors to access it.

> **Note**
>
> Single shared storage comes with a proviso. Final Cut Pro has no facility to stop two editors from accessing the same library at the same time, and this is something that could cause a Final Cut Pro library to become corrupted.

You could set up a traffic light system that indicates when a library is being accessed by another editor. You can also use a folder structure with one folder for each editor and one accessible folder for everyone to access. When an editor wants to access the library in the accessible folder, they would move the library to their folder. No one else should access it until it is returned to the accessible folder. Both the folder and traffic light systems are manual operations, so editors would need to be conscientious. The user should always remember to return the library to the accessible folder when they finish editing. Neither system physically stops other people from accessing the library; it's just a way of knowing who has the library open.

There are software applications that control access to the library and lock other users out. They will be discussed later in the chapter in the sections about PostLab, SNS EVO, and Frame.io.

The process to set up a library on a shared server requires the media and cache to be located on the shared server. Set the **Motion Templates** option to **Copy to library** so that everyone has access to the motion effects that you create. Don't forget to select **Consolidate Motion Content…** from the **File** menu, as you create effects with Apple's Motion app.

Select the library in the browser's sidebar, and press the blue **Modify** button in the inspector:

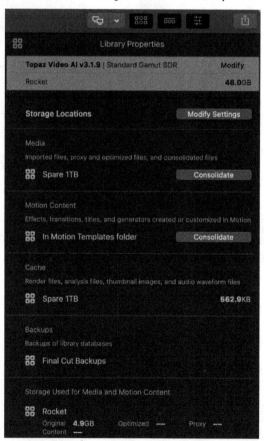

Figure 16.15 – The Modify Settings button

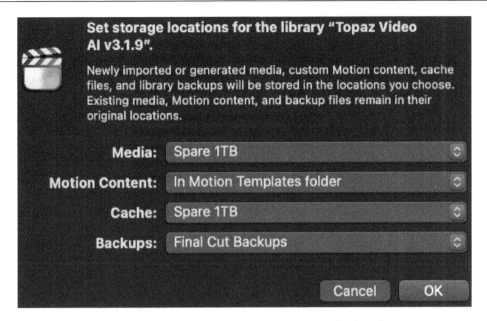

Figure 16.16 – Media, Cache, and Motion Content on the shared server

It's also a good idea to set the **Music iTunes** and **Photos** apps in a common location on the shared storage and ask all users to point to it. This will allow the users to access the same music and photo libraries.

In this chapter, we will discuss, starting with Dropbox, the remote storage options for shared projects between editors in remote locations in comparison with on-premises storage. The next section shows you how to use Dropbox to share Final Cut Pro libraries being accessed by separate editors, with the library being kept in sync on the platform.

Collaborating on Dropbox

On first impression, using Dropbox appears to be seamless, but care needs to be taken in how libraries and media are organized.

From a practical point of view, there are a couple of things that Dropbox does that are not provided by all cloud services:

- The Final Cut Pro library is kept intact by Dropbox, rather than as separate files that are contained in the Final Cut Pro.fcpbundle package.

- Files on Dropbox can be available offline or online only. Files labeled as *available offline* are stored on a user's local computer. Files labeled as *online-only* are no longer available on the local computer, remaining on Dropbox, but they can be resynced as required. Each user can control what is on their local disk by setting it as available offline (on the local disk) or online only (only on Dropbox). *Figure 16.17* shows the options:

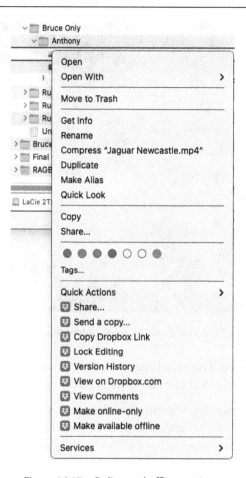

Figure 16.17 – Online and offline options

Final Cut Pro libraries

A Final Cut Pro library is a special type of folder (Final Cut Pro.fcpbundle) that acts as both an application and a folder. The Final Cut Pro.fcpbundle can be double-clicked to launch the application, but it also includes all the files needed by the application, including media or links to external media.

The media types contained in the Final Cut Pro library can be the original media, optimized media, proxy media, or links to external media outside of the Final Cut Pro.fcpbundle. At least one of the three media types or a link to the external media must be present in the Final Cut Pro.fcpbundle for the media to be recognized; otherwise, a red error message will be displayed.

Many cloud services will not keep the Final Cut Pro.fcpbundle intact and will break it into the separate files it contains. If the Final Cut Pro.fcpbundle is not kept intact, it can't be used as an application. In my experience, Dropbox and IDrive are the only common cloud services that retain the Final Cut Pro.fcpbundle structure.

Online only and available offline

It's important to note that Dropbox files that are not online only take up the equivalent space on a local disk that they would take up on Dropbox. It takes considerable time for large-sized files to be synced between the Dropbox cloud storage and the local disk. Because Dropbox creates a folder on your computer's internal system disk, you need to be aware that it can significantly fill up your system's disk space. If you need more space for the Dropbox folder, there is an option to relocate the Dropbox folder to a local external disk. Instructions can be found in the Dropbox FAQs at the following link; make sure you use a fast SSD so that the media will transfer at a workable rate (`https://www.dropboxforum.com/t5/Apps-and-Installations/Syncing-Dropbox-folder-to-external-hard-drive-Mac/td-p/221957`).

> **Important note**
>
> When the Dropbox folder is on an external disk, each time the computer boots, Dropbox may not launch, as it looks for its folder on the system disk. You may need to open Dropbox manually on each boot. There's nothing wrong with this – it's just something you need to remember to do.

On the surface, using Dropbox seems like a very good option, but in practice, it can be a time-consuming process, as once a library has been made online only, to get access to it, you need to wait for it to sync with the local storage again. As with the initial download, the sync can take a considerable amount of time with large file sizes. A library of several GB can take hours to sync up, depending on your internet speed. The workaround is to be better organized and know when a library is not active. Then, move it to another folder on Dropbox (perhaps calling it `Archives`) before making it online only. Once you have decided to archive it, hopefully there is less chance you will need to sync it up again. The best option is to download the libraries to be archived onto cheap spinning HDDs on your premises. You will learn more about this in *Chapter 19, Backing Up and Archiving the Project*.

Dropbox has indication icons to signify the status of files, as shown in *Figure 16.18*. A green tick means available offline, a gray cloud means online only, and a blue recycle icon indicates that a file is being synced.

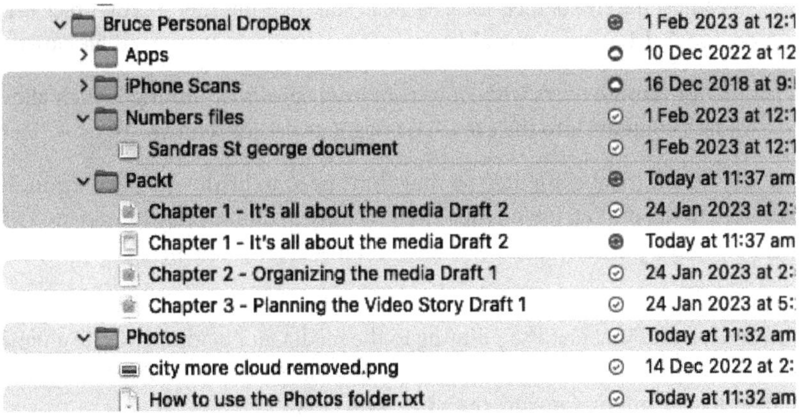

Figure 16.18 – Dropbox indicators

When using Final Cut Pro, you will not notice anything different when a library is accessed from Dropbox, provided you have the Dropbox folder on the system disk or a fast SSD. In fact, everything happens on the local disk; Dropbox just syncs the changes to the cloud behind the scenes.

This is all quite seamless while the internet is up and running. However, be prepared for minor glitches when renaming projects in Final Cut Pro, as this can cause the application to quit. This happens when the project name is recorded in the online database but is not actually present in the browser. When this happens, you will get a warning that the Final Cut Pro library is damaged. You can ignore the warning; it will eventually disappear when the internal database catches up with the projects that are being synced to Dropbox.

Dropbox is suitable for remote editors working anywhere in the world with reasonable internet access. It's easy to use, but don't forget that you need a manual system to prevent two editors using the same library at the same time. There are safer collaborative editing methods, as you will see in the sections about PostLab, SNS EVO, and Frame.io.

To get the full benefit of the Dropbox experience, you need its business version, which costs around $200.00 per year for three users and offers up to 5 TB of storage. You can learn more about this on this web page: `https://help.Dropbox.com/plans/standard-plan`.

For those who have outgrown the functionality of Dropbox but still want the convenience it offers, the next step up would be to look at LucidLink, which is discussed in the next section.

Collaborating with LucidLink

LucidLink sets a folder in the finder sidebar that looks and acts like any Mac folder. New libraries can be created, or existing libraries opened, just as they would be from any local disk. However, you need to check your preference settings for imports and existing libraries. You are only required to do this once.

LucidLink uses a cache file, which is like a warehouse that manages data and serves it to the remote user. Files are downloaded as small packages into the online cache ready for Final Cut Pro to access them.

Each remote user can adjust the size of their local cache to suit their internet speeds. Once the allocated cache on the remote user's drive is full, the oldest or, more accurately, least-used files are deleted.

An important feature for remote users with slower internet speeds is pinning, which allows you to fully download a folder's contents into the cache and flag it as do not remove.

The pinned files stay on the local computer, so they don't need to be downloaded again. If another user uploads new files to the pinned folder, those new files are automatically downloaded to the local cache of the user who has it pinned. The local cache of other users is not affected.

A workflow example for LucidLink and Final Cut Pro is to create a Final Cut Pro library in the LucidLink cloud drive, with Final Cut Pro pointing to the media on LucidLink. Once a remote editor opens the library in Final Cut Pro, the appropriate media is streamed in small packets to that editor and cached on their local computer during the editing process.

LucidLink manages the Final Cut Pro library, keeping it in sync for all editors. Individual editors can adjust the cache on their local computers to suit their internet issues, and they also have the option to pin files in the local cache if there are internet slowdowns.

To avoid conflicts of more than one editor accessing the library at the same time, each editor should have their own folder on LucidLink. They can move the library from the open folder to their own folder while editing and return the library to the open folder when finished.

The system administrator should set up permissions so that standard users only have access to their own folders. This means that the Final Cut Pro library is only accessible by the owner of that folder and not by other standard users. Users set as administrators should have access to all folders.

Knowing how LucidLink functions is important, but before you can use it, you need to set it up, as shown in the next section.

Setting up LucidLink

When you set up LucidLink, you create a **Filespace**, which is a similar concept to the production space that is part of PostLab (which you will learn about in the *PostLab* section later in this chapter). Further, Filespaces can be set up with the desktop app.

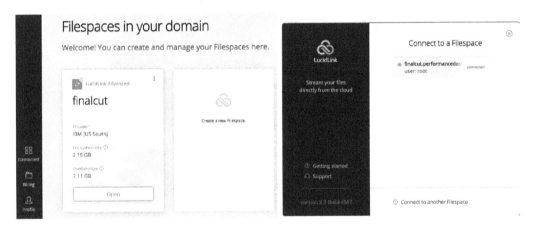

Figure 16.19 – Connect to a Filespace on the web or desktop app

Once you have connected the Filespace, a drive with the same name as the Filespace will appear in the finder sidebar.

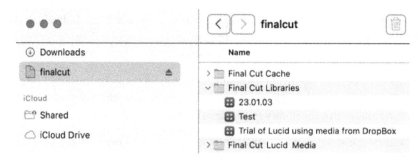

Figure 16.20 – The Filespace drive in the finder sidebar

You should create three folders in Filespace – the Final Cut Cache folder, the **Final Cut Libraries** folder, and the Final Cut Lucid Media folder. These folders will keep the files in the correct locations for LucidLink to operate optimally.

When you create a new library in Final Cut Pro or copy an existing library, select the library in the browser sidebar, and in the inspector, change the storage locations for **Media** to **Final Cut Lucid Media** and **Cache** to **Final Cut Lucid Cache** in the LucidLink drive folder.

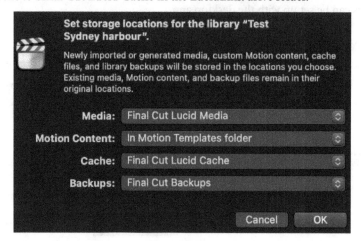

Figure 16.21 – Setting the storage location

Don't forget to change the locations for any libraries that you drag (and copy) to the LucidLink drive. It is important not to have the Final Cut Pro import media settings as **Copy to library**; you need to change the setting to **Leave files in place**. If the files are in the library, they will take up extra storage space on LucidLink.

If you are creating libraries for use outside the LucidLink workspace, then remember to change the media and cache locations back to **Copy to library storage location**. The settings shown in *Figure 16.21* can be used as a reference for the next library you create.

When a shooter uploads media to LucidLink, ensure that they use the **Final Cut Lucid Media** folder. This will allow LucidLink to operate optimally.

Figure 16.22 – Leave files in place

Now, just use the Final Cut Pro library in the **LucidLink Libraries** folder, as with any other library.

The **Advanced LucidLink** license allows five users, either on a month-by-month subscription or a negotiated contract. Users are added by the root user, as explained in the next section.

Adding new users

The original administrator, known as the root in LucidLink, can add new users to Filespace. To do this, open the LucidLink desktop app. There are three tabs: **Status**, **Snapshots**, and **Control panel**.

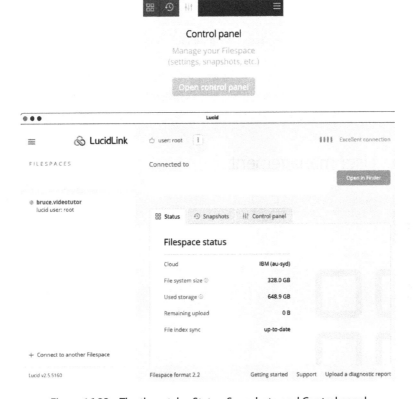

Figure 16.23 – The three tabs: Status, Snapshots, and Control panel

Select the right-hand tab at the top, which is Control panel:

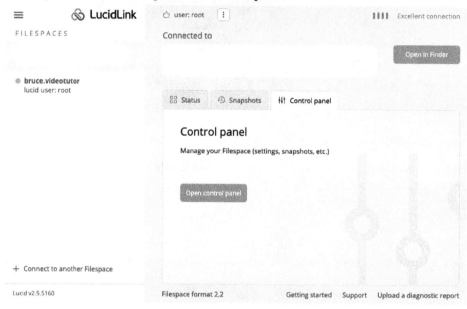

Figure 16.24 – Select the third tab, Control panel

Select the **Users** tab, create a username, and add a temporary password that the new user will be able to change. As the root user, you can set up groups and permissions for access in the same window.

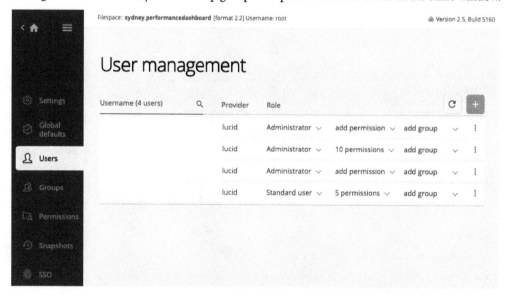

Figure 16.25 – Set up and administer users when the Users tab is selected

There are two categories of user – **standard** and **administrator**. It's important to set standard user permissions for users; otherwise, they will just see an empty folder. A user set as administrator will have access to all folders.

Ask the new user to download the desktop app and give them the name of the domain and Filespace, as well as their username and temporary password.

You can download a free trial of LucidLink from this web page: `https://www.lucidlink.com/`.

If you prefer not to use the cloud and would rather have local storage for collaboration, there are a number of choices. The first option is to have VPN access to a centralized server attached to a large storage device, as discussed in the next section.

VPN access to a centralized local server

How does this method work? The storage and server are on one site, and the remote editors will have VPN access to the server. With this method, using Final Cut Pro is as seamless as using Dropbox or even a local disk. It just means that the library is in a remote location. The only real consideration is that internet speeds need to be very fast. This is not an option for users with slow internet, and even with the best speeds, there could be some lag.

There is no real need for each editor to have large local storage, as required by the Dropbox folder, although it would be good practice to copy active libraries to a local disk, allowing for any internet outages.

There is not a lot to be added here because this is a simple system that relies on the local hardware and, I stress, fast internet. The storage size is a matter for you to evaluate with your future needs in mind. The server computer does not need much horsepower, so a basic Mac mini will do the job. The real downside, as with Dropbox, is there is no built-in safeguard to stop concurrent access to libraries by more than one editor. You will need the same manual process discussed previously in the Collaborating on Dropbox section. You could consider the PostLab solution, as discussed in this chapter. PostLab has its own cloud server, which is a more practical solution than adding its collaborative controls to a local server.

A more robust alternative to one local server with VPN access is to have a local server at each editor's location, allowing them to be kept in sync.

The ideal solution is to have a local server with collaborative controls; the next section discusses such a solution, from SNS EVO.

Using SNS EVO with Final Cut Pro

SNS (which stands for **Studio Network Solutions**) EVO is a shared storage system designed for video workflows, with software called ShareBrowser that lets you control shared libraries, which is designed for use with Final Cut Pro and other editing and audio production software. EVO is also supplied with the **Nomad** software, which transfers media or Final Cut Pro libraries from the EVO server to a remote computer.

Unlimited software licenses are included in Nomad as well as ShareBrowser, which integrates directly with Final Cut Pro as a workflow extension, as discussed in the *ShareBrowser workflow extension* section.

The workflow with EVO is ideal for assistant editors, and they can use the supplied Nomad software to either ingest the media on the EVO server and tag it or use the search functionality to remotely preview files on the server. From there, they can be further tagged for the project at hand and placed in bins, where proxy files are created for the editor to view from the unique Final Cut Pro workflow extension.

An alternative workflow is for a remote editor to use ShareBrowser over a VPN to mount the **Share** folder that has the required media. Once the **Share** folder is mounted, Nomad will bring the proxy files to the local drive for you to use in your Final Cut Pro library. If there are no proxy files, then the original files will be transferred. The next section discusses shared libraries using EVO.

Currently, there is no way to stop two editors, when they are using Final Cut Pro, from opening the same library over a network. To stop more than one editor from accessing a library at the same time, EVO automatically locks Final Cut Pro libraries when they are in use.

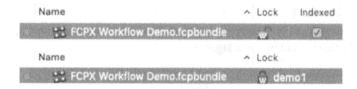

Figure 16.26 – Locked libraries

When a library is open, ShareBrowser will display a lock with the username next to the file. When you need to access an in-use library, you can use ShareBrowser to send a message to that user and request access to the library. This method of library sharing is unique to EVO and a safe way to handle Final Cut Pro libraries with network storage.

ShareBrowser workflow extension

ShareBrowser is also available as a workflow extension that can be used directly inside Final Cut Pro to browse, search, organize, and import media and metadata into a project without ever leaving it.

Workflow extensions are third-party apps that integrate into the Final Cut Pro user experience. You will learn more about them in *Chapter 12, Using Third-Party Plug-Ins*.

With the ShareBrowser workflow extension, you can do the following:

- Drag and drop media from shared storage directly into your media library
- Organize media with custom tags and comments
- Import Final Cut Pro keyword collections and notes from ShareBrowser
- Quickly find and preview clips, audio files, graphics, and other media files

To learn more about the ShareBrowser workflow, read this: `https://www.snsftp.com/guest/workflow/FCPX-Shared-Workflow-Guide-July-2019-Web.pdf`.

To use the EVO server, you need to have at least 30 TB of storage, and you can attach via USB your own storage to archive files no longer needed as active files on the EVO server.

More information on SNS EVO can be found at `https://www.studionetworksolutions.com/how-to-buy/`.

The EVO server storage and software is a turnkey solution but comes at a cost, requiring the purchase of new hardware as part of the integrated package of free unlimited software. If you already own your storage, you can combine that with a software solution that doesn't break the bank, as discussed in the next section about collaboration software.

Collaboration software

While the server solution from EVO provides collaboration software to control file locking and communication between editors, there are software solutions available that offer locking and communication facilities.

First, there is PostLab, which controls file locking at the library level as well as keeping track of version changes and comments. The second software package, Frame.io, allows much better communication notifications in the Final Cut Pro interface, as it is a workflow extension. However, it does not offer any file locking control. The next section discusses PostLab in more detail.

PostLab

PostLab was designed specifically for Final Cut Pro. It controls the collaboration of Final Cut Pro libraries in the cloud. The key advantages of PostLab are its core principles of locking, versioning, and activity logging. PostLab adds an extra layer to the hierarchy of Final Cut Pro. The top tier is a PostLab production container, which can accommodate a number of Final Cut Pro libraries.

The libraries and media can exist on a local server at an editor's location or on a special PostLab drive in the cloud. The PostLab drive uses a cache on the remote user's drive in a similar way to LucidLink, as you saw in the *Collaborating with LucidLink* section. The difference with PostLab is its file locking facilities, as well as workflows, Drop Off, a built-in sync client, and workspaces.

PostLab has the same pinned feature as LucidLink for remote users with slower internet speeds, allowing you to fully download a folder's contents into the cache by using the pinning feature, which flags the folder as not to be removed.

The pinned files stay on the local computer, so they don't need to be downloaded again. If another user uploads new files to the pinned folder, those new files are automatically downloaded to the local cache, but not the global cache on the PostLab drive.

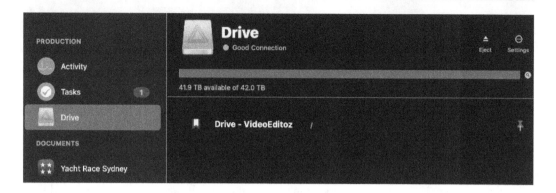

Figure 16.27 – Pinned – the pinned folder

PostLab refers to users as team members, who are able to access a Final Cut Pro library in the PostLab production container, while other team members are locked out but still able to open a read-only copy to view. The process of setting up PostLab does require providing specific access in the privacy and security settings in macOS, but that's just a one-off exercise.

Setting up PostLab requires you to first create a team, and then once a team member is added, you can start a PostLab production container, which can contain a number of Final Cut Pro libraries. Select **Production**, as shown in *Figure 16.28*.

Figure 16.28 – Selecting Production

Figure 16.29 – Naming a team member

Once team members are added, they can select **Production** and start a new Final Cut Pro library, by filling out the name and location, as shown in *Figure 16.30*.

Figure 16.30 – Starting a production and a Final Cut Pro library

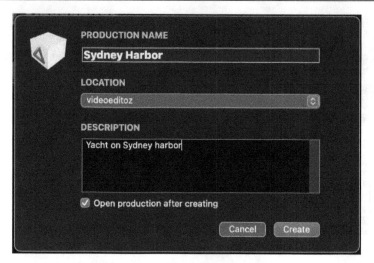

Figure 16.31 – The production name

Then, the next step is choosing between **Individual** or **Shared** for the media location, as shown in *Figure 16.32*. **Individual** allows each team member to store the media in a location of their choice. **Shared** means the media is stored in a central location for all members to access.

Figure 16.32 – Selecting Individual or Shared

In the **TEMPLATE LIBRARY** field, you can choose templates of Final Cut Pro libraries that you may have previously set up. When you click **Save**, the Final Cut Pro library becomes a document in the PostLab production.

Figure 16.33 – The Final Cut Pro library is now a document in the production

Now, select the Final Cut Pro library in the center panel, and it's ready to be opened.

Figure 16.34 – The open Final Cut Pro library

To access the Final Cut Pro library, click **Start Editing**. Since this library has not been opened before, Final Cut Pro will ask where the media and cache should be stored. This is an important step, and once completed, you will not be prompted again unless you wish to change the locations, which can be done in the Final Cut Pro inspector.

Select a fast SSD rather than the PostLab drive for both the media and the cache, as shown in *Figure 16.35*. Use these settings:

- **Media**: Your fast, local SSD
- **Motion Content: In Motion Templates folder**
- **Cache**: Your fast, local SSD
- **Backups**: The **Final Cut Backups** folder

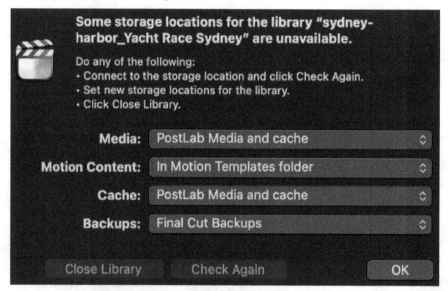

Figure 16.35 – Media and cache on a fast, local SSD

When you click **Save**, the Final Cut Pro library will open, awaiting the import of media. It is best to set **Leave files in place** in the import settings, as well as setting the **Create proxy media** option.

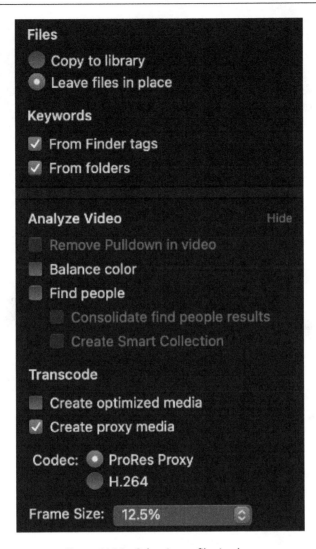

Figure 16.36 – Select Leave files in place

When you have completed editing, go back to the **PostLab** app, and upload your changes under **UPLOAD YOUR WORK**.

You will be required to enter the details of any changes you have made to the Final Cut Pro library before PostLab continues. This is a security measure to ensure that records are kept of the changes as well as the team member who made the changes. Even if you close the Final Cut Pro library in the Final Cut Pro app, PostLab will still find it on your disk when you select **UPLOAD YOUR WORK**.

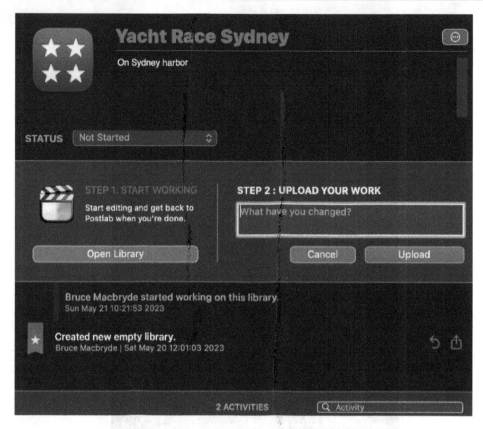

Figure 16.37 – Uploading your work

Other team members who try to access a library currently opened by another team member will see that the library is locked. They can, however, open a copy of the last saved version. They can edit that copy, and when the original becomes available again, they can transfer their work to the original copy with the **Copy to Library** command in Final Cut Pro's **File** menu.

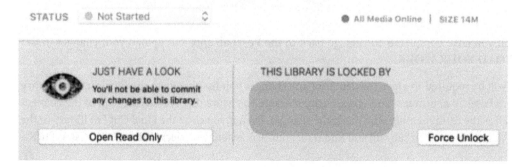

Figure 16.38 – Opening a copy and the locked original

> **Note**
>
> In 2024, the next generation of PostLab will be released. It will feature the same principles of file locking, versioning, and activity logging for Final Cut Pro, while also making that functionality available for any other creative app.

Final Cut Pro collaboration will not only be provided with the current library locking but will also add the new feature of event locking. Once the Final Cut Pro library is imported into PostLab, all events across all libraries will be available for team members to add to their library of choice. If a team member is working on an event in a library, that event will be locked to others. If another team member needs to access that event in their library, they can do so, but the event will be read-only. PostLab will report the locked state of the event in use, and Final Cut Pro will display a padlock emoji in the event name. Projects in a read-only event can be duplicated, and changes can be made in the duplicated project. The duplicated projects can be added to the original event once it is unlocked.

The next generation of PostLab will not necessarily require the use of cloud infrastructure; it will run on local and shared storage, which will improve the speed with no ongoing costs. Storing your work in PostLab will be simpler, as you'll be able to work – solo or in a team – from local storage, shared storage, or remote storage, such as a LucidLink Filespace.

A free trial of PostLab is available here: `https://hedge.video/postlab`.

If you are looking for alternative ways to manage and communicate during the production process, then the next section on Frame.io will be of interest to you.

Frame.io

Frame.io is a video collaboration platform that supports the Final Cut Pro workflow with time-stamped comments, annotations, hashtags, and enhanced communication for collaborative editors. Frame.io also offers a streamlined process to share video drafts and obtain approvals with customizable approval workflows, version control, and automated notifications.

Frame.io is further enhanced for use with Final Cut Pro, as it is a workflow extension that allows Frame.io to open directly inside the Final Cut Pro interface. Clips can be dragged to the workflow window to share with other editors.

Frame.io offers a free account for two users and 2 GB of storage. The first paid plan is $13.00 per month for up to five users, offering 2 TB of storage.

The workflow extension for Final Cut Pro is available from the Mac App Store. After you install it from the App Store, it automatically appears as an extension in Final Cut Pro.

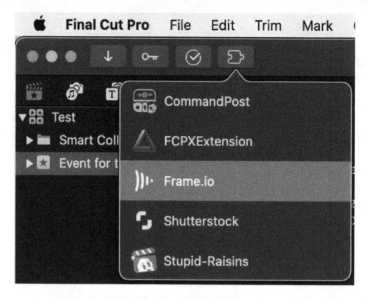

Figure 16.39 – The Frame.io workflow extension

The **Frame.io** window will appear in Final Cut Pro, and you can drag clips to projects. Frame.io takes only a little time to sync, meaning the window inside Final Cut Pro appears inactive until the sync is complete. After syncing, the clips can be dragged from the open Final Cut Pro event to a project in Frame.io, and any clips from Frame.io can be dragged to the event open in Final Cut Pro.

Figure 16.40 – Clips shown in the Frame.io window

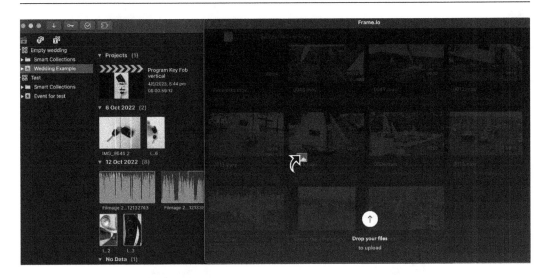

Figure 16.41 – Dragging a clip to and from Frame.io

The benefits of Frame.io, outside of using it to share content, are its organizational features, where you can comment and draw on the frames to make your comment clearer. Editors can review and approve frames, as well as receive automatic alerts for actions, such as when new media is added, which alleviates the tracking of emails. Also useful is the feature that allows clients to review and leave comments.

Direct transfer of Final Cut Pro libraries

As I have previously noted, many internet options do not recognize the Final Cut Pro.fcpbundle structure, so direct transfer of Final Cut Pro libraries from one computer to another was impossible without a **virtual private network** (**VPN**), until the arrival of a simple app that runs on all platforms – Mac, Windows, Linux, Android, iPhone, and iPad.

The app, called **Blip**, allows a Final Cut Pro library to be transferred directly from one computer to another without the upload and download process required by internet storage drives, such as Dropbox or IDrive.

The process of transfer is similar to what you use with AirDrop between Apple devices; however, Blip works over the internet and is not limited to sending to nearby devices only (like AirDrop). The sender can select a Final Cut Pro library, right-click, and select **Blip…** from the services menu.

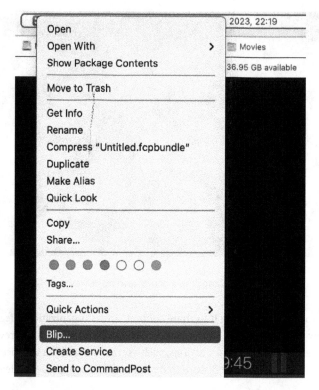

Figure 16.42 – Select Blip… by right-clicking on the library file

The sender is then presented with a window, asking for the email address of the intended receiver. Start typing the receiver's email address and Blip will search for a user with that email address registered on the app.

Figure 16.43 – The email address of the receiver

The received is then notified on their app that a Final Cut Pro library is waiting to be accepted.

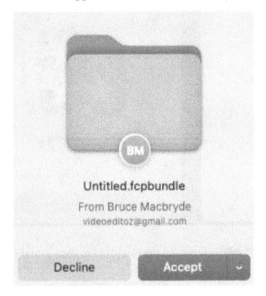

Figure 16.44 – A library awaiting acceptance

The sender's computer shows that the library is waiting to be accepted by the intended receiver.

Figure 16.45 – The sender's computer shows a "waiting to accept" message

Once the library has been received, it will appear on the receiver's desktop with confirmation of who it was sent from. The sender's computer receives confirmation that it has been sent.

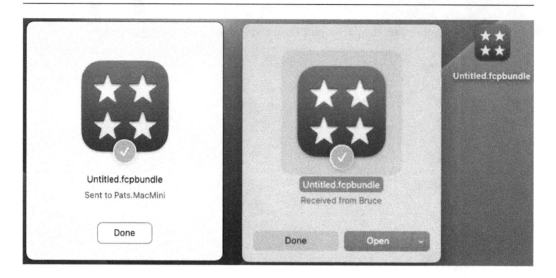

Figure 16.46 – Confirmations and the Final Cut Pro library on the desktop

Double-clicking the library on the desktop will open it in Final Cut Pro on the receiver's computer.

It is important that the library being sent by Blip has had the media originally imported using **Copy to library** to ensure all media is enclosed. It is also advisable that the library is consolidated prior to transfer by Blip.

Changes can be made to the library on the receiver's computer and then returned to the original sender using the same process. For speedier returns, the changed library could be exported as XML, which would ensure a faster transfer back to the original computer's version of Final Cut Pro, as the media is still stored with the original.

Blip transfers take half the time as would be the case with an internet drive solution such as Dropbox or IDrive, where the file is stored on the internet. This is because the receiver does not need to wait for the file to be uploaded before they can start downloading it. However, internet drive storage works out to be an advantage for files sent to people in different time zones because with the Blip solution, the receiving computer's operator needs to accept the transfer.

The Blip solution has some other major advantages. You do not need to pay for storage as you do with internet drive solutions because there is no size limit to Blip transfers. Blip compresses the files for you to make sure transfers are as fast as possible. Compression is also lossless, which means you won't lose any quality.

Blip has auto-resume. If you're sending a large project and suddenly lose a connection, your transfer will pause and resume when you're back online.

Here's a tip – if you have control of both the sending and receiving devices, you should sign in with the same email address, which will process the transfer without the receiver having to accept. This is really handy for transferring between different time zones, meaning the receiver does not have to be active for the file to be received, provided the computer is turned on.

Blip is not just for Final Cut Pro libraries; in fact, any application file's structure is recognized and will open on the receiver's computer, providing the application is present. Folders of files can also be sent without the need for them to be combined in a ZIP file.

The Blip solution may be the last in the list of options discussed in this chapter, but in many cases, it will be the collaboration solution of choice for editors in similar time zones with infrequent collaboration needs. At the time of writing, the Blip solution is offered free of charge but is expected to become chargeable for commercial use.

Blip is available from `https://blip.net/`, and Frame.io has a free trial option here: `https://accounts.frame.io/welcome`.

Summary

In this chapter, you have seen the different roles within a video postproduction team and other organizations dedicated to video production. You learned which specific job roles require you to edit videos, as well as an evaluation of the job roles in your organization that may need to edit videos.

The chapter also compared different forms of collaboration between Final Cut Pro editors, both at a local level as well as for those collaborating globally.

You learned different techniques of collaboration as well as the processes that require proxy media and XML transfers. We also looked at the use of Dropbox and LucidLink as web-based solutions.

You saw server-based collaboration as well as mixed server/software solutions from PostLab and Frame.io that allow version control, along with commenting and review functionalities.

Finally, you looked at Blip direct file transfer collaboration, which has the advantage of being simpler and available as a free service (at least for private use).

The next chapter looks at the different software applications that support Final Cut Pro, both for editing and color correction, as well as animation and archiving.

Supporting Software Applications for Final Cut Pro

This chapter follows on from the last, where software for collaboration was discussed. This chapter talks about applications and utilities that are not directly involved in the editing of clips in Final Cut Pro but, instead, provide better-prepared clips for Final Cut Pro to use.

You will see applications that provide facilities for backing up files, archiving, and transcribing text. You will also learn about applications that help prepare media for Final Cut Pro, including image-editing applications as well as transcription, organization, and conversion applications.

The chapter is split into two sections – applications from Apple and those from other developers.

The main topics we'll be covering in this chapter are as follows:

- Motion 5
- Compressor
- QuickTime
- Preview
- Keynote
- Photos and iTunes
- Final Cut Library Manager
- CommandPost
- VLC
- Handbrake
- Audacity
- Pixelmator Pro

By the end of this chapter, you will have an idea about the software applications that can assist you in your use of Final Cut Pro.

The software that we will discuss in this chapter will add functionality to Final Cut Pro, as well as make using Final Cut Pro easier and more productive.

You will learn that Final Cut Pro's effects are all produced in its sister application, **Apple Motion 5**. You will also learn how to modify and personalize built-in and third-party plug-ins in a way that is tailor-made for the project you're editing.

You will see how the default Apple applications supplied with Mac computers can be integrated with and assist in the use of Final Cut Pro. You will also examine software applications that are produced by third-party developers, some that are free and others that you will need to purchase.

There are certainly many applications that can support Final Cut Pro, but I have included the applications that I consider the most useful when editing in Final Cut Pro.

Apple applications that support Final Cut Pro

This section will show you applications that are developed by Apple that have features that are useful to Final Cut Pro editors.

Motion 5

Motion 5 is a motion graphics application that creates 2D, 3D, and 360° titles and transitions in real-time. As an indication of the integration of Motion 5 and Final Cut Pro, all effects that are part of Final Cut Pro, both default and third-party, have been created with Motion 5.

The Motion 5 application is so fully integrated into Final Cut Pro that all of the third-party plug-ins that you use with Final Cut Pro are contained in a folder on your system hard disk, called `Motion Templates`. The folder exists when you use third-party plug-ins, even if you don't own the Motion 5 application.

I strongly urge you to purchase Motion 5. As you will see in this section, it allows you to personalize plug-ins and provides the opportunity to create your own digital animations, which can be used within and independently of Final Cut Pro.

If you want to follow along with this section, you will need to own a copy of Motion 5, which, unlike Final Cut Pro, does not have a trial version. However, for $49.00, it is the best-value software I know.

To be clear, this section about Motion 5 will only discuss how the application integrates with Final Cut Pro to modify plug-ins. It is outside the scope of this chapter to teach the full usage of Motion 5, other than how it relates to modifying Final Cut Pro plug-ins.

Since Motion 5 is so integrated into Final Cut Pro effects, you should be aware of how plug-ins work within Final Cut Pro. We discussed plug-ins in previous chapters, so I will not cover here what they are and how they are used with Final Cut Pro. The objective of this chapter is to show you how to modify your plug-ins with Motion 5 so that they look different than they would appear normally. Why, you may ask, is it necessary to modify an already good-looking plug-in? The answer is simple – so that you can personalize plug-ins to make them look like your own handiwork, rather than something that has been created for you by someone else.

There is a minor difference between plug-ins provided as part of Final Cut Pro – known as default plug-ins – and third-party plug-ins that have been added to Final Cut Pro after the purchase of the application. Motion 5 will allow you to modify purchased plug-ins unless developers have locked them. However, default plug-ins can't be modified with Motion 5, but copies of the originals can be modified. Default plug-ins are embedded in the Final Cut Pro application, and third-party plug-ins are in a separate folder on your system that you have access to (see *Chapter 12, Using Third-Party Plug-Ins*). There are both free and purchasable third-party plug-ins.

Modifying default plug-ins

Most of the default plug-ins provided as part of the purchase of Final Cut Pro only have the ability to change colors and fonts and other basic functionality. However, purchased plug-ins do offer the ability for much more modification.

As an example, I will show you how to modify the default **Dramatic** title plug-in from its standard three text animations and add a fourth text animation, with an optional colored background that can be disabled, as well as a fade out of the new fourth animated word. The **Dramatic** title can be accessed from the **Titles** tab at the top left of the Final Cut Pro interface, under the **Build In/Out category** heading.

The following figure shows the options. Only the font color and reflection can be changed:

Figure 17.1 – The basic options of a default title

The default **Dramatic** title plug-in is locked by Final Cut Pro, so you can't modify the published parameters, but you can change a copy. The default title is shown in the title's browser:

Figure 17.2 – The default Dramatic title showing in the title browser

You start the process of modifying the **Dramatic** title by right-clicking on the title in the title browser and selecting **Open a copy in Motion**.

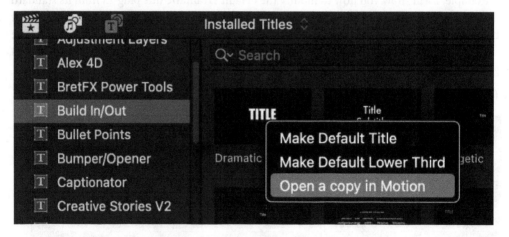

Figure 17.3 – Right-clicking on the default Dramatic title to open a copy

Now, if you own Motion 5, it will be launched with the **Dramatic** title, opening in the **Project** panel on the right:

Figure 17.4 – The default Dramatic title opening in the Motion 5 interface

The Motion 5 interface has a similar color theme to Final Cut Pro. The default view has five panels (in the preceding figure, I have labeled the panels in red):

- **Library and Inspector**: The **Library** panel contains media and objects that can be used in Motion 5.

- **Project**: This contains **objects** dragged from the **Library** panel or added behaviors. **Behaviors** are actions that can be added to objects to cause them to animate.

- **Timing**: This duplicates everything that is in the **Project** panel, purely for convenient access when working in the **timeline**, which is the panel to the right of the **timeline sidebar**.

- **Timeline**: The timeline is similar in concept to the Final Cut Pro timeline – it is where actions can be adjusted.

- **Viewer**: The **Viewer** is also similar in concept to the Final Cut Pro viewer, where all results are shown when exported.

With the **Dramatic** title open in Motion 5, let's concentrate on the **Project** panel. As you have seen, the **Dramatic** title contains three animated words. In this exercise, we are going to add a fourth word with the same animations as the original three.

One of the main concepts of Motion 5 is that all objects are contained in groups. When an action is added to a group, it affects all the objects in the group. When an action is added to an individual object, only that object is affected. This is similar in concept to a compound clip in Final Cut Pro.

There must be at least one group, irrespective of whether you have one object or more. With the **Dramatic** title, there is only one group. This is unusual because plug-ins in Motion 5 tend to have several groups. You will see how to add more groups as we progress.

The group in the **Dramatic** title is called **Main**. All objects in the **Project** panel can be renamed to suit your needs:

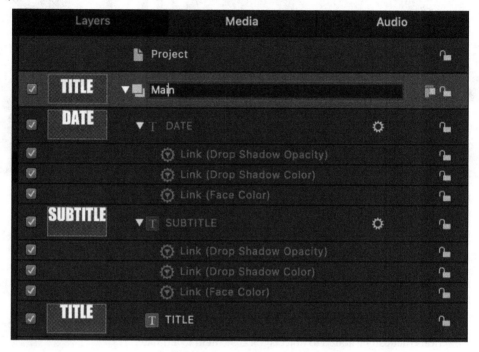

Figure 17.5 – Objects and groups can be renamed

Groups can be opened or exposed with the arrow:

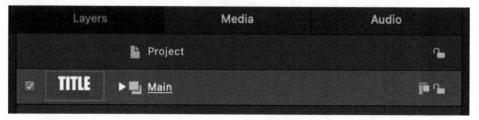

Figure 17.6 – A group closed

In *Figure 17.5*, you can see the three words that are in the **Dramatic** title – **DATE, SUBTITLE**, and **TITLE**. They can be changed in the **Project** panel or the **Inspector** window to the right. In the following figure, the word **DATE** is selected in the **Project** panel, and it can also be changed at the bottom left of the **Inspector** window when the **Text** tab at the top of the **Inspector** window is selected:

Figure 17.7 – Changing text contents

When you change any text attributes in Motion 5, they become the default text when you save the plug-in for Final Cut Pro to use.

One of the key things to remember about Motion 5 plug-ins for use in Final Cut Pro is that in order to be able to modify the plug-in when it is used by Final Cut Pro, you need to *publish* the option; otherwise, it is fixed at what you set it in Motion 5, and you will not be able to modify it within the Final Cut Pro interface.

There is an exception to that rule – you're allowed to modify text with Final Cut Pro. The option to modify text is turned on by default and can be disabled in Motion 5.

The following figure shows the disabling option. When **Editable in FCP** is unticked, text options will not be modifiable in Final Cut Pro.

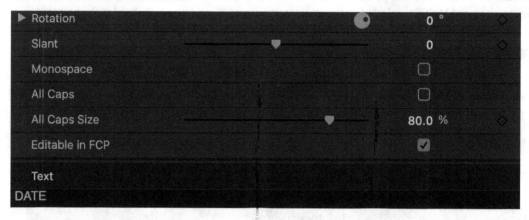

Figure 17.8 – When Editable in FCP is ticked, any text is modifiable in Final Cut Pro

Since this exercise involves adding a fourth text animation, replace the **DATE** text with 3rd text to see the change take place:

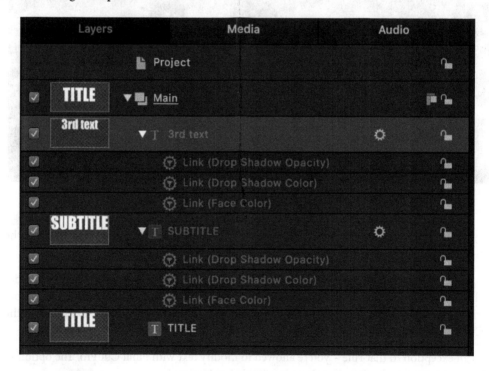

Figure 17.9 – Text changed to 3rd text

To provide space for the fourth text animation, the duration of the project needs to be increased. The **Dramatic** title has a default of 9 seconds. You can see that by selecting the **Edit** menu and selecting **Project Properties….**

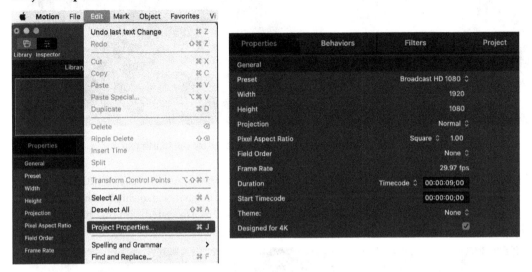

Figure 17.10 – Project Properties… in the Edit menu

Change the duration to 12 seconds. The timecode duration view can be changed to seconds:

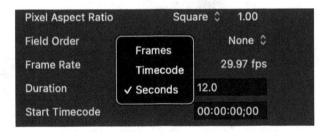

Figure 17.11 – The timecode changed to seconds

To view the whole project in the timeline, press *Shift + Z* to fit it in the window. You will recall that this is the same command used in Final Cut Pro.

To allow space for the fourth text animation, you will need to shorten the duration of **3rd text** by moving the top **3rd text** track away from the white end triangle at the 12-second mark to the 9-second mark. Be careful not to drag the main track, as that will shorten the project duration.

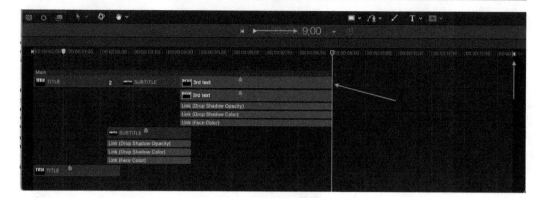

Figure 17.12 – Shortening 3rd text to give space for the fourth text

Select and highlight the **3rd text** in the **Project** panel (it will turn blue), and then copy it with *Command + C*. When you copy the **3rd text** heading, you also copy all the behaviors associated with it. The gear logo within the heading line enables or disables all the behaviors associated with that heading. The blue checkmarks enable and disable each line in the **Project** panel.

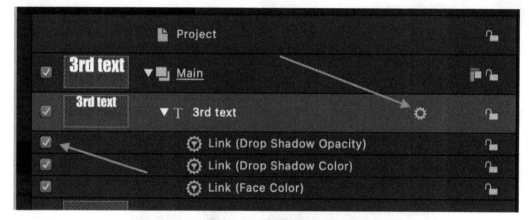

Figure 17.13 – Enable and disable lines and behaviors

In the timeline, place the playhead at the 8-second mark and paste with *Command + V*. Change the **3rd text** copy type to 4th text in both the **Project** heading and the **Inspector** window.

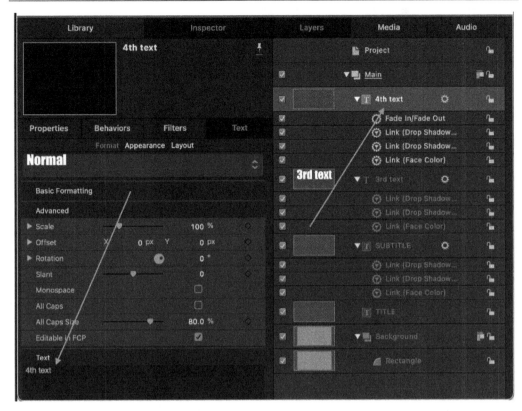

Figure 17.14 – Changing the name in both the Inspector window and the Project panel

You may need to extend the length of the lighter-blue **4th text** top track in the timeline to the white end triangle.

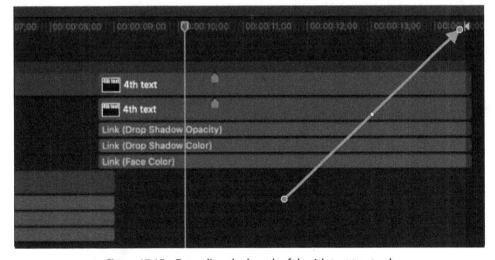

Figure 17.15 – Extending the length of the 4th text top track

> **Note**
>
> Whenever you paste or insert an object into the timeline, it will always be inserted at the position of the playhead.

That is all you need to do for the fourth animation, but let's add a couple of extra features so that you can familiarize yourself with other features of Motion 5. I'll add a fade-out on the **4th text** word with a behavior, and I'll also add a background color to the title that can be disabled in Final Cut Pro if needed.

To add the fade-out behavior, select the **4th text** heading, and from the behavior gear logo button at the top of the screen, select **Basic Motion | Fade In/Fade Out**.

Figure 17.16 – The behavior gear | Basic Motion | Fade In/Fade Out

You will see the **Fade In/Fade Out** behavior added to the **Project** panel. The **Inspector** window should open, with the blue **Behaviors** tab showing the **Fade In/Fade Out** controls. Slide **Fade In Time** to **0**, and leave **Fade Out Time** at **12**.

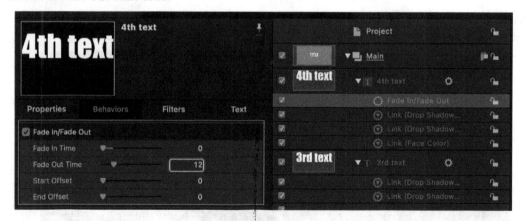

Figure 17.17 – The Fade In/Fade Out Inspector controls

It would be good to be able to control the length or disable the fade-out when using the plug-in within the Final Cut Pro interface. To enable that functionality, Motion 5 provides the option to publish the controls so that they will show in the Final Cut Pro **Inspector** window. To the far right of the line labeled **Fade Out Time** is a drop-down arrow that, when clicked, shows the **Publish** option.

Figure 17.18 – The Fade Out Time | Publish option

Another option for this example is to provide a background that can be disabled in the Final Cut Pro **Inspector** window. Move the playhead in the timeline to the beginning of the project. From the **Object** menu, select **New Group**.

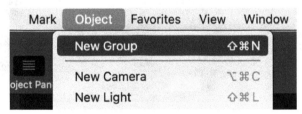

Figure 17.19 – New Group

New objects are added at the top of the **Project** panel under the **Main group** heading. Drag the new group down to below the title heading, and change the name to background. With the **background** group highlighted, select the **Rectangle** tool in the center of the screen (the tool icon will turn blue when selected).

Figure 17.20 – The blue Rectangle tool

Draw a rectangle to fill the viewer. In the **Inspector** window, with the **Shape** tab selected and highlighted in blue, change the **Fill Color** color. To the right of the **Fill** heading, select the drop-down arrow (next to **Hide**) and select **Publish**:

Figure 17.21 – The drop-down arrow in the Fill heading

To the right of both **Fill Color** and **Fill Opacity**, select the downward chevron and then **Publish**:

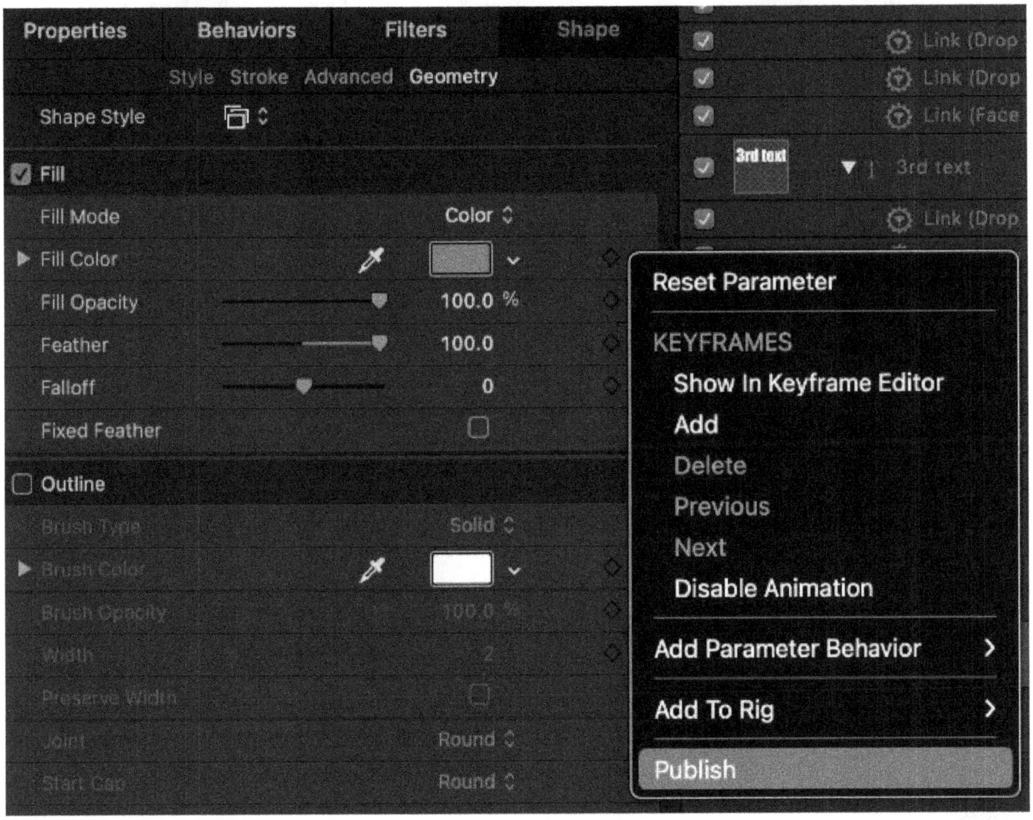

Figure 17.22 – Publishing the Fill mode

The plug-in is just about ready to save, but first, you need to check which controls you want to display in Final Cut Pro's **Inspector** window. Select the **Project** heading at the top of the **Project** panel. With the **Project** tab selected in the **Inspector** window., you will see how the controls will appear in Final Cut Pro. If there are controls that you don't want to be in Final Cut Pro, you can **unpublish** them by selecting the arrow to the right, or if controls are missing, you will need to go back and check that you published them earlier. Unpublish **Graphics HDR**. You can reorder and change the names of the options. Change the name of **Fade Out Time** to Fade Out 4th text. Drag **Fill Color** above **Fill**, and change the name of **Fill** to Fill On/off.

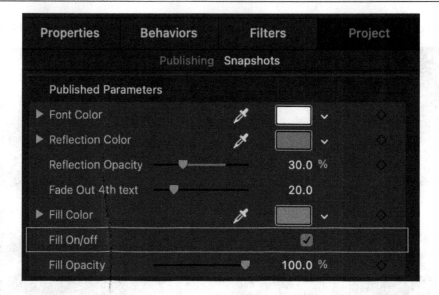

Figure 17.23 – Check the project for options that have been published

All that is left to do now is to save the project. At the very top and middle of the screen, you will see that the project is titled Dramatic.copy.moti. It is a copy because, as previously mentioned, you are not able to change the default plug-ins that ship with Final Cut Pro. This is a blessing in disguise, as it stops you from overwriting the original plug-in. However, you will see later in this section that third-party plug-ins can be overwritten, so you need to be careful with them.

Select the **File** menu and select **Save**; alternatively, if you want to save under a different name, select **Save as**.

Give the plug-in a name under **Template Name**, and select the category where the original was located (don't worry about the theme). If you are modifying an existing title, it's a good idea to keep the original name and add any different text at the end. Tick **Include unused media** if you used photos or videos in the project. Then, select **Publish**.

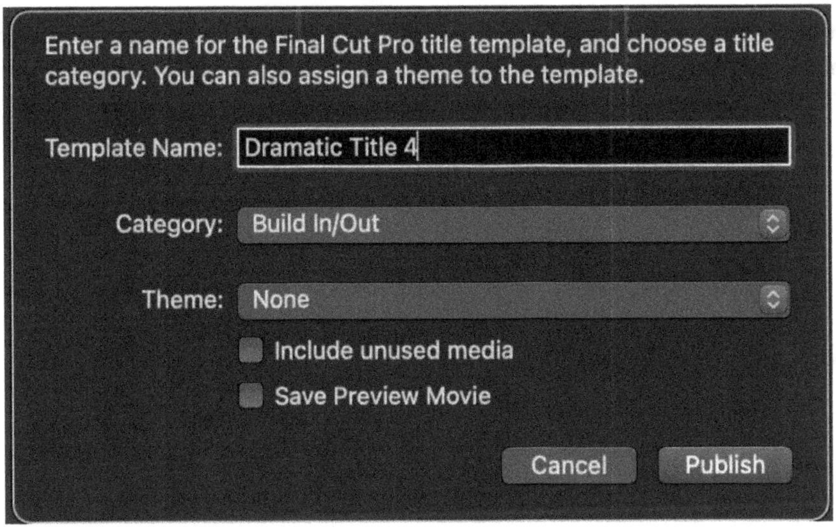

Enter a name for the Final Cut Pro title template, and choose a title category. You can also assign a theme to the template.
Template Name:
Dramatic Title 4
Category:
Build In/Out
Theme:
None
Include unused media
Save Preview Movie
Cancel
Publish

Figure 17.24 – Saving the project

In Final Cut Pro, you will see the modified plug-in when you open the title category you saved it in.

Installed Titles
3D Cinematic
360°
Adjustment Layers
Alex 4D
BretFX Power Tools
BretFX Quick List
Build In/Out
Bullet Points
Bumper/Opener
Captionator
Search
Assembler
Blur
TITLE
TITLE
Dramatic
Dramatic Title 4

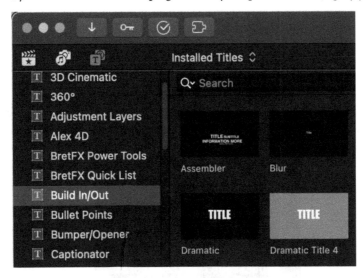

Figure 17.25 – The original Dramatic title and the new Dramatic Title 4 title

Drag the new title into a timeline, and check the **Inspector** window. The controls are the same as you published in Motion 5. Compare the controls in *Figure 17.25* against the originals in *Figure 17.1*.

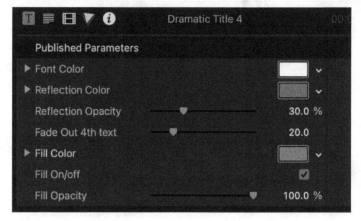

Figure 17.26 – The options in the new title

The **Dramatic** title is a default title supplied with Final Cut Pro; now, let's look at modifying third-party plug-ins in the next section.

Modifying third-party plug-ins

There are free and purchasable third-party plug-ins. They can be just as modifiable as the default plug-ins, with the minor difference that they can be changed directly and overwritten without making a copy, as is the case with the default plug-ins. You may also find that some plug-ins that you purchase will be locked by the developer, so you aren't able to modify them or even make a copy. You can see when you right-click on a third-party plug-in and select **Open in Motion** whether it can be modified or not (see the warning in *Figure 17.26*):

Figure 17.27 – A locked plug-in

If the plug-in is not locked, it will open in the Motion 5 interface without the **could not be opened** warning being displayed.

Figure 17.28 – A third-party plug-in open in Motion 5

After you have made changes to a third-party plug-in, when you try to save the changes, you will be presented with a **Save as Duplicate...** message.

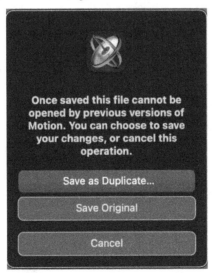

Figure 17.29 – A duplicate warning message

This chapter has spent a lot of time discussing Motion 5 because it is the most significant supporting application for Final Cut Pro. In my mind, Final Cut Pro should at least have the ability to round-trip projects to Motion 5. **Round-tripping** is when an action is sent from Final Cut Pro to Motion 5, where it is modified, and then the modification automatically updates in Final Cut Pro. While Motion 5 is well integrated with Final Cut Pro, so is **Compressor**, another application produced by Apple. The next section looks at how Compressor works with Final Cut Pro.

Compressor

Compressor allows you to create special export modes that are not available by default with Final Cut Pro. Here, we will discuss the integration of Compressor with Final Cut Pro.

The Compressor application is also a separate purchase from Final Cut Pro and greatly assists its export abilities. The principal benefits of Compressor are that it allows better compression than the default Final Cut Pro options, and it allows you to create your own presets that will be displayed in the Final Cut Pro **Share** window.

Accessing Compressor from within Final Cut Pro

The best way to access Compressor from the Final Cut Pro interface is via the **Share** menu. At the bottom of the menu, you can see **Add Destination…**, which will open the Destinations settings window.

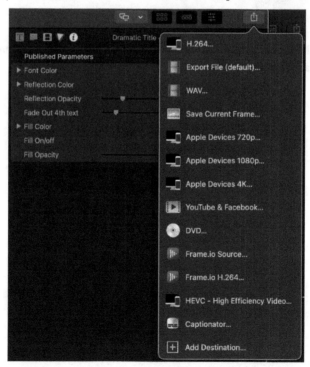

Figure 17.30 – Add Destination… in the Share menu

When the **Destinations** tab is selected in the **Destinations** window, you can drag the **Compressor Settings** icon into the sidebar, which will open Compressor for you to select the Compressor presets, which you can add to the Final Cut Pro **Share** window.

Figure 17.31 – Dragging Compressor Settings into the sidebar

You will be given the choice of **Built-in** presets as well as any that you created yourself in the **Custom** option.

Figure 17.32 – Selecting optional presets

After selecting a Compressor preset, it will appear in the Final Cut Pro settings sidebar, with the **Compressor** icon next to the new setting.

Figure 17.33 – The new preset appears in the Final Cut Pro settings

Once the **Compressor** option is set in **Destinations**, you can access it any time you select the **Share** menu, giving you access to any of the Compressor presets.

Figure 17.34 – The Compressor options in the Share menu

Selecting the **Compressor** option in the **Share** menu will open the **Export** window, allowing you to access the **Settings** button and then the **Change…** button, which will direct you to the presets that have been set in the Compressor application.

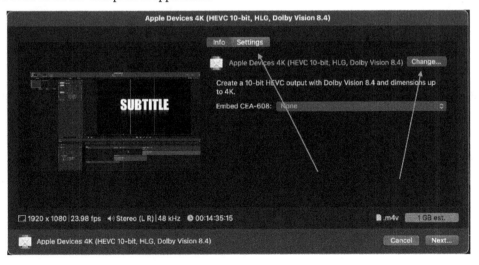

Figure 17.35 – After selecting Settings in the Export window, you can change the export settings

On accessing the Compressor presets, you will only be able to choose the default presets; you are not able to modify the Compressor settings. This is a real pity, as it means you have to open Compressor directly to make any modifications.

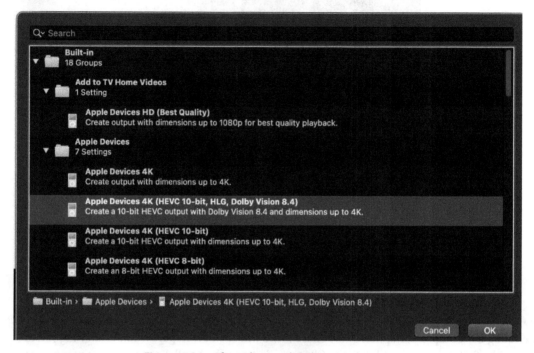

Figure 17.36 – After selecting the Change… button

Opening Compressor directly

When you open Compressor directly, you will be able to modify the presets and add your own custom presets for use with Final Cut Pro. The best way to create your own presets is to choose a default preset and change it to suit your requirements. The workflow in Compressor makes this safe for you, as the default presets only allow you to open a copy, which means the originals are always intact and only the copy is customized.

The Compressor interface has three tabs at the top – **Current**, **Active**, and **Completed**. When the **Current** tab is displayed, you will see in the left panel the settings for the presets discussed in the previous section, about Final Cut Pro access. The middle panel has the **Add File** option and will show any added video that needs to be compressed. The right panel will show the details of the compression of the video when it is added.

If you select any of the presets in the left panel, their details will be displayed in the right-hand panel, known as the **inspector** (if the **Inspector** panel is not visible in the right-hand panel, then click on the **Inspector** button located in the top-right corner), which has three tabs – one showing the summary of that preset known as **General**, and two other tabs called **Video** and **Audio**, which display specific details about the video and audio files, respectively.

Figure 17.37 – The Compressor details of the ProRes 422 preset in the right-hand panel

Drag the video you want to compress into the middle panel, and drag a preset on top of the video in the middle panel; the details will be shown in the **Inspector** panel and can be modified to suit the type of compression you wish to undertake. In my example, the video is 720p, so the **Automatic** frame size shown in *Figure 17.36* is the same as the original video. I have changed the frame size from **1280 x 720** to **1920 x 1080**. The frame size now shows as **1920 x 1080**. I will also change the frame rate to 29.97 fps. Of course, you can change any other setting as well. I am just showing the frame size as an example.

Figure 17.38 – The frame rate and frame size changed in the Inspector panel

Once you have changed the settings in the **Inspector** panel, close it by clicking the blue button at the top right of the window. Irrespective of whether the **Inspector** panel is open or closed, you will be able to drag the adjusted preset from the middle panel to the custom section in the left panel, making it available in Final Cut Pro as an optional preset in the future. In *Figure 17.38*, the adjusted preset is given a title automatically by Compressor. In this case, Motion 5 has titled it **Special ProRes setting**:

Figure 17.39 – The Inspector window closed, with the Special ProRes setting as a custom preset

When the **Inspector** panel is closed, you will be able to start the compression by clicking the **Start Batch** button at the bottom right.

The file compression progress will be displayed on the **Active** tab, and once compression is complete, the file will appear under **Completed**.

Figure 17.40 – The compressed video in the Completed tab

Compressor is just one of the Apple-supplied applications that are useful to Final Cut Pro editors.

Next, we will look at **QuickTime**, which, as the name implies, allows you to quickly make basic trimming edits without having to open Final Cut Pro. For example, trimming long drone footage can substantially reduce the size of clips stored in the Final Cut Pro library.

QuickTime

QuickTime is supplied with every Mac and is the next most useful application after Apple's Motion 5 and Compressor. As it is free, QuickTime is the go-to utility for trimming and combining video, and it also offers an inspector to quickly tell you the format and size of videos. Let's look at QuickTime trimming.

Trimming clips

Trimming a clip before importing it into Final Cut Pro reduces the amount of hard disk space that Final Cut Pro needs to store clips when only a small proportion of the clip is to be used in the edit. Trimming is extremely useful with drone footage because the drone camera is on for the whole flight, but you will only end up using a few seconds of the video.

Open a video from the **File** menu in QuickTime after you have launched the application, or drag directly on top of the QuickTime icon when it is in the Mac's Dock. Selecting **Trim** from the **Edit** menu will display the trim timeline at the bottom of the video.

Figure 17.41 – The trim timeline with the blue Trim button

Press the play button until you reach the frame want to trim. You can use the *J*, *K*, and *L* keys to move backward and forward, as well as the arrow keys to move one frame at a time. Click the red playhead to display the timecode, which you should memorize before you drag the yellow edges to it. You can trim the other edge of the clip in the same way.

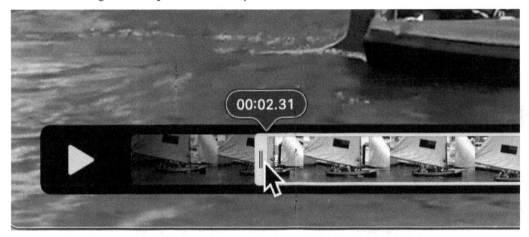

Figure 17.42 – The timecode displayed when you drag the yellow edges

When you press the blue **Trim** button, as shown in *Figure 17.40*, the clip is immediately trimmed.

If you want to cut out a portion in the middle of the clip, select **Show Clips** from the **View** menu. A timeline looks similar to the **Trim** timeline. You can cut the timeline in two places with the **Split Clip** option from the **Edit** menu, deleting the unwanted section.

Once you have split a clip into more than one section, you can double-click any section and trim just that selection. The individual sections created by the **Split Clip** command can be moved around the timeline to change their positions through a simple editing function.

Figure 17.43 – A single clip in the Show Clips timeline can be individually trimmed

The opposite of trimming is combining clips, which we will discuss in the next section.

Combining clips

Select a clip in QuickTime, and then click **Add Clip at End** from the **Edit** menu. This will open a **Finder** window for you to open another video.

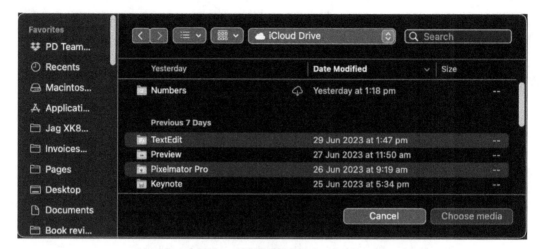

Figure 17.44 – The Finder window

The new clip is added at the end of the timeline, but you can drag it anywhere in the timeline in an already-created split, or to a new split. You can add any number of extra clips and move them around, splitting them or trimming them to produce a basic movie.

Figure 17.45 – The timecode displayed when you drag the yellow edges

You can also use the **Insert Clip After Selection** option to insert a clip from another opened video, by dragging from one video into the split location on another video.

QuickTime is not only a tool for use with already-created videos; it is also a means of recording the screen and recording audio from the computer or an attached microphone, as well as recording from the built-in webcam or any attached camera.

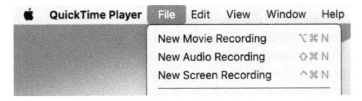

Figure 17.46 – The timecode displayed when you drag the yellow edges

QuickTime is not just useful for recording or a quick cut or edit; it is also useful for providing information about the size and format of a clip. The QuickTime inspector offers an instant way of finding out how a clip is composed.

The QuickTime inspector

Using the QuickTime inspector is an easy way to check the resolution, size, and format of a video file before you open it with Final Cut Pro.

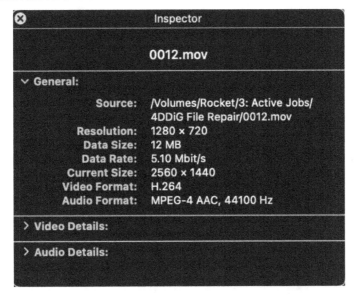

Figure 17.47 – The inspector displaying the resolution, size, and format

The QuickTime application doesn't recognize all types of video formats. You will need to consider another utility for that. If QuickTime does not recognize the format, neither will Final Cut Pro. The *Non-Apple applications* section later in this chapter discusses the **VLC** application, which reads just about every video format you will come across. Combined with **Handbrake**, you will be able to convert just about any format so that it will be recognized by Final Cut Pro. Handbrake is also discussed later in this chapter.

There are several more Apple utility applications that are very useful with Final Cut Pro. QuickTime focuses on video, but the next section is about **Preview**, which is a basic still image editor.

Preview

When it comes to video editing, still images are not always given the attention they deserve. As you know, video is just a batch of still images, and when you only need to display an object that does not move, such as a road sign or a name on the outside of a building, a still image is far clearer than a camera clip. For static signs that you want the viewer to read, it is better not to have a shot with a handheld camera that wobbles. It's far better to either have a still frame or, better yet, a photo of the sign incorporated into the video.

This is where Preview comes in. It is a free option for quickly spicing up a still image, screenshot, or photo. Preview can add shapes and arrows to images, text, signatures, and even freehand drawings. Usefully, Preview can remove some plain backgrounds and, perhaps most importantly, resize images that are too high in resolution for Final Cut Pro.

The highest resolution for still images in Final Cut Pro is 4,000 x 4,000 pixels. As you approach that size, Final Cut Pro slows down significantly. There is no need for a really high-resolution image in the timeline. In fact, too sharp an image will detract from the video around it. To decrease the size of an image in Preview, from the **Tool** menu, select **Adjust size**. Select **pixels** in the Image Dimensions window that opens (*Figure 17.47*). If you are working with a 1,080p Final Cut Pro video, in Preview, set the lowest reading of either **Height** or **Width** to 1920 or 1080, with **Scale proportionally** selected.

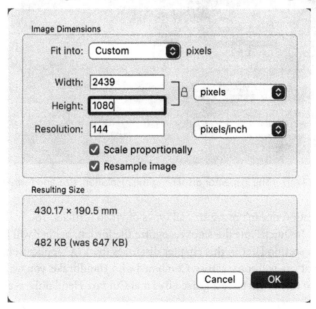

Figure 17.48 – The pixels option selected, with Height at 1080

If you want more room to view the image in Final Cut Pro, set the lowest reading of either **Height** or **Width** in the **Preview** window to double the pixels of the video in the Final Cut Pro timeline.

The key to using Preview is to select the **drawing tools** (accessible from the **A** in a circle icon, as shown in *Figure 17.48*), which opens a second menu bar with a multitude of options, as shown with the red arrows in the following figure:

Figure 17.49 – Preview tools

To remove the background, select the button second from the left on the menu bar and Drag the mouse over the background after selecting the second from left button until as much of the background that you can select of the background has been removed select the second button from the left, then drag the mouse over the background until you have removed as much of it as possible.

Figure 17.50 – The background removed

Preview can be used to quickly adjust still images; it's not as sophisticated as the industry-standard Photoshop, but it's free with your Mac. Later in this chapter, we will discuss **Pixelmator Pro**, which is a lower-priced alternative to Photoshop with some unique video features.

In this section, we saw how Preview supports still image modification for Final Cut Pro. You will see in the next section how another Apple application, **Keynote**, allows you to create slideshow effects that can be exported as videos for use in Final Cut Pro.

Keynote

It's beyond the scope of this book to show you how to create slideshows in Keynote, but it is important to show you how to export a slideshow in a format that you can use in Final Cut Pro.

Once you have created your slideshow, select **Export To | Movie…** from the **File** menu.

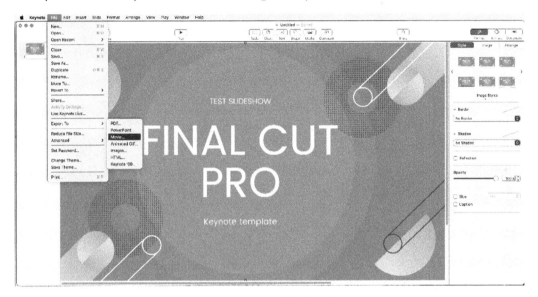

Figure 17.51 – Exporting a slideshow from Keynote

The slideshow can be saved in any format, but if you need transparency in an image, (perhaps you need to see the video behind the slideshow images), you need to select either **HEVC** or **Apple ProRes 4444** and make sure to tick **Export with transparent backgrounds**.

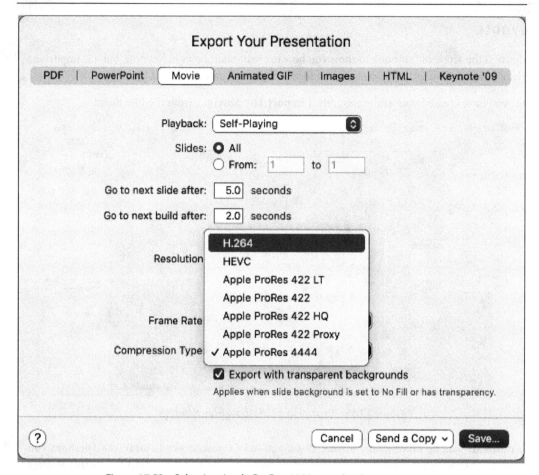

Figure 17.52 – Selecting Apple ProRes 4444 to maintain transparency

The movie can be imported into Final Cut Pro and edited as you would with any other camera clip. The text and objects in the slideshow can't be modified, as they are fixed in the way they were exported from Keynote. If you need to make changes, you will need to do so in Keynote and re-export to Final Cut Pro.

The final two Apple applications, **Photos** and **iTunes Music**, can both be accessed directly in the Final Cut Pro interface, as they are integrated into macOS; we will discuss this integration in the next section.

iTunes and Photos

You can access both iTunes and Photos from the **Clip** browser, by clicking the middle tab with the musical note icon at the top left of the **Final Cut Pro** window.

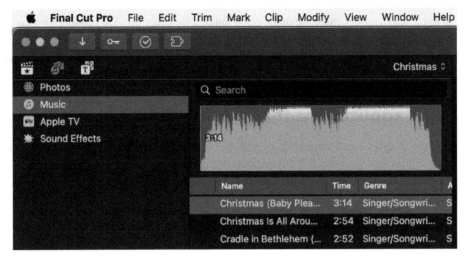

Figure 17.53 – Access to iTunes, Photos and Sound Effects

When you select music and photos, the contents are categorized as you set them in the applications. Drag the music track or photo directly into the project in the Final Cut Pro timeline.

Figure 17.54 – Classifications for the iTunes and Photos apps

Besides the Apple applications, there are many other applications that provide support for Final Cut Pro. The following section features some of those that are the most useful. We'll also mention some others for you to evaluate. Some are specially developed for Final Cut Pro, some are free, and some are purchasable.

Non-Apple applications that support Final Cut Pro

In this part of the chapter, I will focus on listing the important features of the various applications, rather than explaining how they work. We'll start with an application specifically developed for Final Cut Pro, **Final Cut Library Manager**, and then list the other applications, depending on how useful I consider them to be.

Final Cut Library Manager

The purpose of this application is to conveniently organize the contents of all the Final Cut Pro libraries, whether they are on currently attached devices or not. The main objective of Final Cut Library Manager is to reduce the size of the libraries to a minimum, without losing any media that is needed by a Final Cut Pro library. **Optimized** and **proxy** media can be removed by Final Cut Library Manager, providing the **original** media exists. If no original media is available, then Final Cut Library Manager will not remove the optimized media. Final Cut Library Manager always ensures that the Final Cut Pro libraries remain fully editable.

Every Final Cut Pro library that has been opened on any disk that has been connected to the computer previously is displayed, and you can remove disks that are no longer needed from the database. When a disk is ticked at the left of the interface, only the libraries on that disk are shown in the main window on the right. You can choose to tick the options to remove **Optimized** media, **Proxy** media, and **Flow** and **Render** files. The amount of space to be saved is shown under **Potential Space Savings**. As an example, nearly 700 GB could be saved in *Figure 17.54*.

Figure 17.55 – Final Cut Library manager

In the next section, we'll take a look at the **CommandPost** utility, which is also specifically designed for Final Cut Pro and adds hundreds of extra features to it.

CommandPost

CommandPost is application-specific. When Final Cut Pro is active, the options only relate to Final Cut Pro; when the Finder is active, the options change to suit. Perhaps the most important addition is the ability to use control surfaces such as Loupedeck.

The principle behind the free CommandPost application is to ease the mundanity of editing with features such as **Titles to Keywords**, which creates a collection of keywords from clip titles.

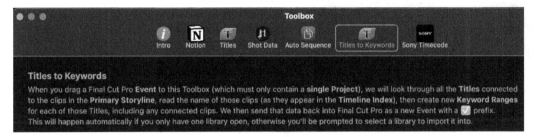

Figure 17.56 – CommandPost Titles to Keywords

Perhaps the most frequently used feature in CommandPost is converting the Final Cut Pro timeline into a scrolling timeline, which scrolls the visible timeline when the playhead reaches the end of the display. The timeline scrolls to continuously keep the playhead in view.

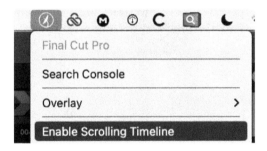

Figure 17.57 – Enabling a scrolling timeline

Social media creators will love the ability to create a `.csv` file from the Final Cut Pro **Index** menu, allowing them to quickly add timestamps to YouTube video descriptions.

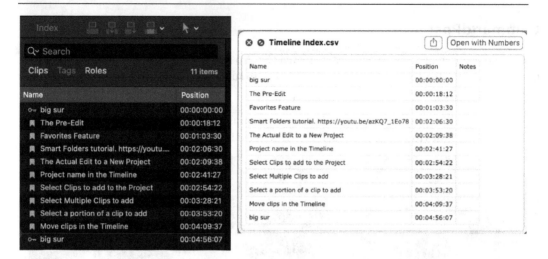

Figure 17.58 – The Final Cut Pro Index menu and a created CSV file

In the *QuickTime* section earlier in the chapter, I mentioned VLC as an application that recognizes and plays just about any video format; let's take a look at this application next.

VLC

The advantage of the free VLC application is that it will recognize and play any video format, converting a file into a suitable format for Final Cut Pro.

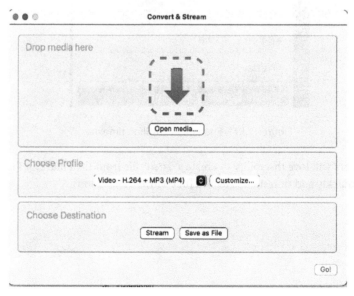

Figure 17.59 – The VLC import window

The next section focuses on an application with more features and an easier-to-navigate interface – **Handbrake**. This is also a free application that converts video formats and compresses files.

Handbrake

Handbrake offers more features for compression and format conversion but does not support all the different formats that VLC does. While Handbrake is easier to use, you will still need VLC for more obscure formats such as Annodex, Matroska (MKV), Raw Audio: DTS, Raw DV, FLAC, FLV (Flash), and MXF.

Figure 17.60 – The Handbrake interface

The utilities discussed so far have concentrated on supporting the video aspect of Final Cut Pro, rather than any specific support for correcting audio. While you could use Logic Pro to sweeten Final Cut Pro's audio, a good deal of your audio correction is covered with the free **Audacity** app.

Audacity

While Final Cut Pro has built-in audio correction facilities, you will find you need to do more than is available with the built-in effects. Audacity has an amazing feature set for a free application.

An example of a feature that is missing within Final Cut Pro is the ability to select a noise, such as a cough or sniff, and extract just that specific frequency range from the audio in a project.

When using Audacity, the workflow from Final Cut Pro involves exporting a WAV file of just the audio from a project and importing it into Audacity. The noise can then be isolated in the Audacity timeline, and then, from the **Effects** menu, select **Noise reduction** and **Get Noise Profile**, as shown in *step 1* in the following figure:

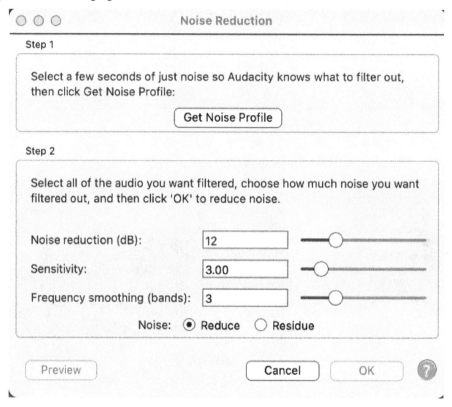

Figure 17.61 – Noise reduction

With the profile recorded, you can extract the saved noise profile by selecting the whole of the Audacity timeline and selecting **Noise reduction** again from the **Effects** menu. Pressing the **OK** button will activate *Step 2* in *Figure 17.60*.

In the *Apple applications that support Final Cut Pro* section of this chapter, you saw how to use Preview to manipulate still images. However, you might find that you will need more than what can quickly be done with Preview. While Photoshop is the powerhouse of image editing, you may not need to go to that extent and avoid the subscription requirements of Photoshop. I suggest that you consider Pixelmator Pro, which is a one-off purchase of around US$40.00 from the Apple store.

Pixelmator Pro

Pixelmator Pro is a Mac-focused app and has many features that are specifically designed with Final Cut Pro in mind, with sophisticated video support. In fact, video can be edited directly in Pixelmator Pro, with layered graphics added and round-tripped to Final Cut Pro so that any changes you decide to make in Pixelmator Pro are automatically applied in Final Cut Pro.

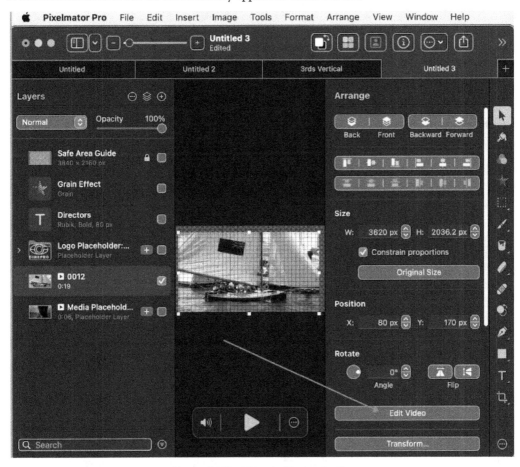

Figure 17.62 – Video in Pixelmator Pro

The applications discussed in this chapter are the main supporting applications for Final Cut Pro. However, there is a multitude of applications that are used for specific needs in Final Cut Pro. Some of these are discussed in the next section.

Miscellaneous applications

There are many other utilities that support Final Cut Pro. I have tried to keep the selections in this chapter relevant to those that offer the most important support.

Make sure you take a look at the free **Sound** app from Crumple Pop. Also, check out **Captionator** from the Apple App Store for simple captions with voice-to-text facilities.

UIti.Media assists Final Cut Pro with clip analysis and an automated way to edit clips to a beat, by dragging a song into **BeatMark**, which will recommend the most effective music cut points. BeatMark will produce an FCP XML file, allowing you to create a new project with the clips cut in time to the music. UIti.Media also has a myriad of other applications, including **Video tags**, which create keywords from media content.

InqScribe is software that transcribes audio to text, a brilliant idea for video interviews where you need to transcribe or take timecoded notes.

You should also check out the offerings from Intelligent Assistance for utilities that integrate with Final Cut Pro. The **XtoCC** utility, also known as **Project X₂7**, uses Final Cut Pro's XML so that a Final Cut Pro project can be imported into Adobe's **Premiere Pro**, **Audition**, and **After Effects**, as well as **Avid Media Composer** and **Pro Tools**. If you want to transfer from Premiere to Final Cut Pro, Intelligent Assistance has an app for that as well, **SendToX**. You can also use SendToX to transfer from the classic Final Cut Pro 7 application to the current Final Cut Pro X. The Intelligent Assistance's **Lumberjack** utility provides live logging and transcription.

After the editing process and when the project has been archived, there is an application that can keep track of the archived libraries on unattached disks. **NeoFinder** is discussed in detail in the next chapter.

Summary

In this chapter, you learned about the applications that integrate with and assist Final Cut Pro. The first section discussed Apple applications that directly integrate via macOS, and the second section discussed applications from non-Apple developers.

In the first section, you learned how to access Final Cut Pro plug-ins to modify them in Motion 5, with detailed instructions about its use. You were also shown details of how to add a myriad of export presets to Final Cut Pro by linking Compressor to the **Share** menu. You were shown how to modify the presets in Compressor and how they can be saved as custom presets, made available in Final Cut Pro.

Also, in the first section, you learned about the Apple applications that are part of every Mac and how the QuickTime, Preview, and Keynote applications can create content that is useful in Final Cut Pro. You also saw how to access Photos and iTunes music directly within the Final Cut Pro interface.

The second section told you about non-Apple-developed applications, such as Final Cut Library Manager, which recovers disk space from your storage devices. We also discussed in detail CommandPost, which adds Swiss-army-knife features to Final Cut Pro.

You saw how VLC and Handbrake can recognize infrequently used formats and convert or compress them for use with Final Cut Pro. You also saw how audio can be sweetened externally from Final Cut Pro with the Audacity application.

Finally, you learned a little about the video options in the image-editing application Pixelmator Pro.

The next chapter covers troubleshooting problems in Final Cut Pro.

18

Troubleshooting Final Cut Pro

In this chapter, you will discover the correct way to go about troubleshooting – that is, by doing the simple things first and then progressing to the more complex things.

The chapter covers deleting render files and resetting your Final Cut Pro preferences, as well as copying the content of one project into another new and clean project.

You will find out how to fix issues caused by faulty plug-ins and how to remove bad plug-ins from your Mac system.

The chapter shows you how to locate corruptions and render issues that cause export errors when you are presented with frame error and render error messages.

You will learn how to resolve issues where libraries won't open by trying another user's account or even another computer. If the issues are not rectified, you will be shown how to reinstall Final Cut Pro as well as how to enter recovery mode.

Finally, you will be shown how to relink missing media, and you will see what happens when Final Cut Pro quits unexpectedly.

The main topics in this chapter are as follows:

- Updating macOS and Final Cut Pro
- The easy fixes
- The harder fixes
- Relinking missing media

By the end of this chapter, you will feel confident in your ability to resolve Final Cut Pro operational errors as well as your ability to export errors and system issues with macOS.

We will cover all the steps in the process of solving issues, starting with the quick and easy solutions first. If your issues are more complex, you will find detailed instructions on how to get around those trickier obstacles. The very first step is to ensure your macOS and Final Cut Pro are working well together, as you will see in the following section.

Updating macOS and Final Cut Pro

There is synergy between your Mac computer and Final Cut Pro. It goes without saying that you need to understand some macOS functionality to be able to successfully diagnose issues that occur when using Final Cut Pro.

It's imperative that you have a good understanding of how files and folders work in macOS and how Final Cut Pro stores its files in the **Users** folder of your system disk. See *Chapter 1, It's All about the Media*, where we located plug-ins in the **Motion templates** folder. Out-of-date and faulty plug-ins are the most likely cause of problems in Final Cut Pro, as you will see when you start to diagnose the issues that Final Cut Pro throws up.

But before anything else, the most important first step is to make sure that your Final Cut Pro application and your macOS are both up to date. Many features of Final Cut Pro require certain versions of macOS to be able to work.

Rule number one: have matching macOS and Final Cut Pro versions, and don't update either until the other is proven stable.

Stable means that the system and the Final Cut Pro version have been well tested before you update. This is particularly important for full-version updates.

As you will be aware, software is updated with full-point and minor-point updates. So, as an example, if you have Final Cut Pro 10.6.6 and there is an update to 10.6.7, that would be referred to as a minor-point update and, in most cases, will not have major changes that could cause issues or affect the use of Final Cut Pro plug-ins. However, if it were an update from 10.6.7 to 10.7, which is a full-point change, you should assume that there could be major disruption.

I stress that you can only *assume* the preceding scenarios. A case in point is that the actual update from 10.6.5 to 10.6.6 *did* have major changes that were required to tie the desktop version of Final Cut Pro with the then-recently-released iPad version. This minor-point update required old Final Cut Pro libraries to be updated.

If a library has been updated with a newer version of Final Cut Pro, that will mean that older versions of Final Cut Pro will not open the updated library. You will see an error message when you try to open an older library, as shown in *Figure 18.1*.

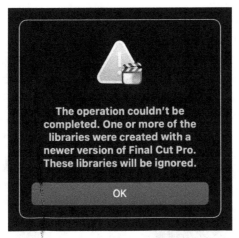

Figure 18.1 – An error message saying that a library was created by a newer version of Final Cut Pro

> **Warning**
>
> If you are working with other editors, make sure everyone updates at the same time; otherwise, editors still using a previous version of Final Cut Pro will not be able to open up-to-date libraries.

When it comes to the decision to update, the main thing for you to be aware of is to be completely sure there are no issues with the new versions of both macOS and Final Cut Pro. The best way to stay up to date on these issues is to join Apple-sponsored Final Cut Pro forums or Facebook groups.

Otherwise, the simple rule when there is a full-point update is to wait until the next minor-point update before committing yourself to anything. For example, if 10.7 is the update, wait until 10.7.1 before you update. As you saw in the preceding example, you also need to check that minor-point updates are safe as well.

You can check your version of Final Cut Pro from the **Final Cut Pro** menu by selecting **About Final Cut Pro**. The flash screen will then appear, giving you the version number.

Figure 18.2 – The Final Cut Pro version number

If you want to be completely safe, you can retain a copy of the old version of Final Cut Pro before updating. You can do that by right-clicking and duplicating the application in **Finder** and then compressing the copy.

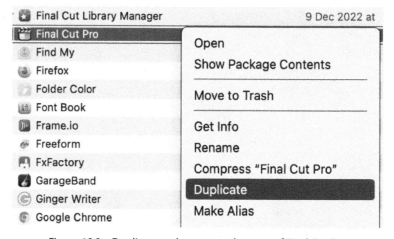

Figure 18.3 – Duplicate and compress the copy of Final Cut Pro

With a compressed copy, you will be able to revert to an older version if you are having issues after an update.

> **Note**
>
> If you are working in a collaborative environment, then wait until the lead editor tells you to update.

You are less likely to have any problems providing you stick to the rule of matching the OS version and the Final Cut Pro versions and not updating until it's safe.

However, that's not a guarantee that there won't be issues that test your patience and cause problems, such as crashing and export errors. There is an indicator that will help you to tell when there are issues: the **spinning beach ball**, which is discussed in the next section.

The spinning beach ball

The spinning beach ball will generally mean that Final Cut Pro is struggling to get enough bandwidth from your disk. Of course, you need to have your media and Final Cut Pro library on an SSD. Anything else will incur the spinning beach ball.

It's not only slow disks that will bring out the spinning beach ball. It can also be an indication of a slow computer or too many applications being open at the same time; even a slow internet connection could be the issue. If you regularly see the spinning beach ball, I suggest you quit all other applications that don't need to be open when you are editing with Final Cut Pro.

Simple fixes for a slower computer are to create optimized media, or even proxy media for even more flexibility with 4k or 8k footage. The spinning beach ball won't be the cause of export errors. If you are unable to export, then you should follow the steps in the next section.

Fixing problems

The secret to fixing problems with Final Cut Pro is to follow the recognized order of trying the simple fixes and progressing through to the more complex ones. It stands to reason that if you can fix an issue with a simple fix, you will save yourself time and effort. After all, video editing is time consuming enough without spending time looking for difficult fixes that can be solved with a couple of mouse clicks.

The order of fixes in the list is important as it relates to the amount of downtime that the fixes are likely to cause. The further down the list you need to progress, the more downtime there will be.

You could be confronted with the dreaded red warning message or an obscure *can't export* error message.

Figure 18.4 – A red warning refers to a missing effect or plug-in

You could see frame or render error messages, which can be even more of a worry – what does it all mean?

Figure 18.5 – Typical error messages

Final Cut Pro can crash with a warning message similar to this:

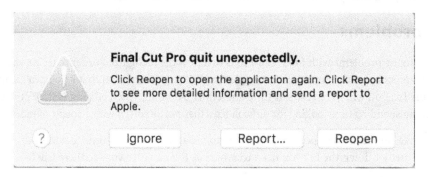

Figure 18.6 – Final Cut Pro quitting unexpectedly

All of these messages will be covered in this chapter, along with the issues that you know are false, as well as issues that stop you from exporting.

If you feel that an issue is more of a global problem with your computer, then it may pay to jump straight to the *Booting into recovery mode* section.

> **Warning**
>
> Other than not being able to export, if you think there is an error that needs fixing, be sure that it's a real error and not just some setting that you have accidentally misconfigured. If you are unfamiliar with Final Cut Pro, I suggest you check the manual or ask on a forum. There is no point in trying to correct an issue that is not an error.

Since we have had rule number one, let's call this rule number two: don't get frustrated or depressed. There is always a solution, and you will find it much quicker by not getting exasperated. Follow troubleshooting tips in this chapter in order and resolution will occur. It's very unlikely to be unfixable; I have encountered no such case in my more than 20 years of experience.

The easy fixes

In most cases, these fixes require only one or two mouse clicks. The rule of thumb is that the easy fixes are most likely to solve the problem.

Quitting Final Cut Pro and restarting the computer

It is surprising how many issues can be resolved by simply restarting the computer. My go-to choice is to quit Final Cut Pro, shut down, and then reboot the computer after a minute or so.

Deleting the render files

Things don't come much simpler than this. Select the library in the **Browser** sidebar. From the **File** menu, select **Delete Generated Library Files...**.

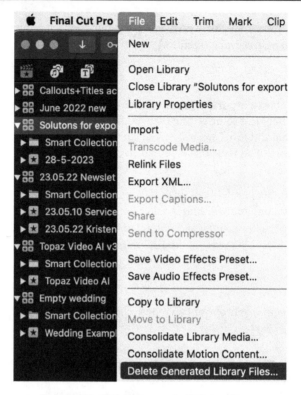

Figure 18.7 – Delete Generated Library Files…

You will be presented with a window with options. The one thing I need to reassure you of at this point is that you cannot lose any original media or any of your work in projects by following this process – it is completely safe. In fact, Final Cut Pro never, in any circumstances, deletes original media from your disk.

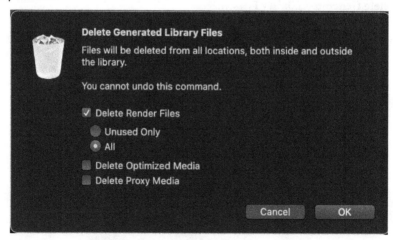

Figure 18.8 – Delete Generated Library Files

Render files are created by Final Cut Pro to make the editing process smoother and for quicker export. The edit will still continue without them and Final Cut Pro will recreate them, as it needs them to be able to export.

There are two things to know about render files: they take up space on the computer, and they can become corrupted. If they are needed again, Final Cut Pro recreates them.

You could just delete only the unused render files; however, since there could be issues with *any* of the render files, I would select all of them. One part of the rationale is that since render files are needed for export, if you delete them all, you will need to wait for them to be recreated.

If you have optimized or proxy media, delete that as well.

If you were having issues with exports, try again. If you have no success, then quit Final Cut Pro and restart the computer before trying again. As I said earlier, macOS and Final Cut Pro are closely linked, so restarting will ensure they are both reset.

It will be valuable for you to understand more about rendering, which is covered in the next section.

Background rendering

Background rendering is a process that can help with rendering by automatically creating render files while Final Cut Pro is not busy (while you are on the phone or having a coffee, for example!). There are advantages to having **Background render** turned on, but there are also downsides.

> Tip
> The background process can be monitored by pressing *Command + 9* to open the **Background Task** window.

You have seen that when render files are created, the export process is made quicker by not having to wait for rendering to complete at export time. Rendered clips also play easier in the timeline, so slower computers can benefit significantly if clips are rendered.

The downsides are that rendered clips take up extra space on your computer and there is a slight processor hit while clips are being rendered, even if you have set rendering in the background.

You can control background rendering in **Settings…** under the **Final Cut Pro** menu.

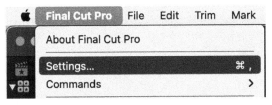

Figure 18.9 – Settings… in the Final Cut Pro menu

A window will open with five tabs. Select the **Playback** tab. The **Start after** option should be increased to a few seconds, as the default setting has **Background render** coming on after only one second of inactivity. This means that Final Cut Pro would be continually turning background rendering on and off. It's best to have it only come on after a longer period of inactivity.

Figure 18.10 – Background render controls

My suggestion for those with a new computer is to have **Background render** unticked. The choice is yours, and you should try out both options to see what suits you best. As for the extra space that render files take up on your computer, you should always delete the files once the library is ready to be archived. Even if you have **Background render** turned off, you will find that render files are automatically created for processes such as **Optical Flow** and **Multicam**.

If your export still does not proceed with the render files deleted, the next step is to reset your Final Cut Pro preferences, as detailed in the following section.

Resetting your Final Cut Pro preferences

The reset process is easier to action than the deletion of render files. The process also deletes temporary files associated with Final Cut Pro but this time with a destructive effect, in that any preference settings you changed in Final Cut Pro will be removed and reset back to the factory defaults.

The things that usually end up being reset to the factory defaults are the window's position on the screen, the position of the audio meters, snapping (which is turned back on), the skimmer, and background rendering (which is turned back on). Most importantly, you will also lose the **Recently Opened** list of libraries, so make sure you know where your libraries are located on your disks. Assume that any settings in the preference settings that you saw in the preceding section about **Background render** will be reset to their factory defaults.

To action the reset, you need to quit Final Cut Pro and then hold the *Command* and *Option* keys as you launch Final Cut Pro. You will see a warning window:

Figure 18.11 – The delete preferences warning

If you delete the preferences, you will see the **What's New in Final Cut Pro** splash screen that showed when you first launched Final Cut Pro.

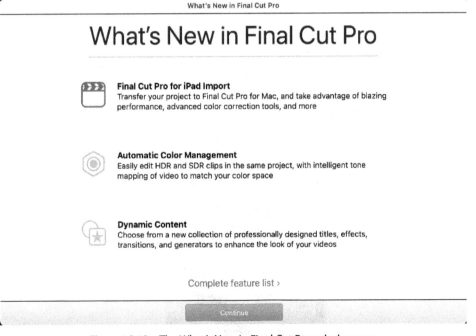

Figure 18.12 – The What's New in Final Cut Pro splash screen

It pays to keep copies of your preference settings, or at least to remember what settings you like, so that you can easily change them back after the factory defaults are reset.

You could take screenshots of all the preference settings before doing the reset, or you could try the free preference manager software from Digital Rebellion: `https://www.digitalrebellion.com/prefman/`.

A quick and easy option, once you have a good set of preferences, is to make a copy of the Final Cut Pro settings file in the following location: `/Users/username/Library/Preferences/com.apple.FinalCut.plist`.

Then, when you need to reset your preferences in the future, you can paste the preferences you have saved back to the location you copied from.

Also, you can use that same process if you want to configure the same settings on other computers.

Now, try to export, or otherwise check that the issues you are trying to fix have been resolved. Any issues that don't appear to be fixed will very likely be a setting that has been accidentally changed; it's likely that Final Cut Pro is working correctly. Time to refer to the manual again.

Copying to a new project

This is also a simple solution that frequently fixes errors that cause exports to fail and does not change any editing that has already been processed.

Right-click on the project that fails to export and click on **Snapshot Project**.

Figure 18.13 – Snapshot the faulty project

Rename the snapshot – it's a good idea to use a prefix such as `Fix Error` before the original name so you know which was the original project.

Try to export the **Fix Error** project. If it doesn't export, then create a new project, copy all the contents from the **Fix Error** project, and paste them into the new project.

If copying to the new project doesn't work, use the XML export and re-import to a new library.

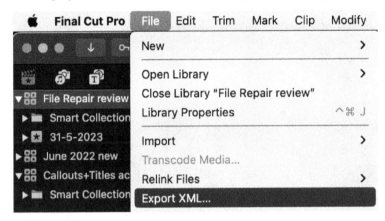

Figure 18.14 – Export XML to a new library

Try to export the project from the new library. If you are still unable to export, then you will need to try the harder solutions in the next section, where the likely culprit is an out-of-date or bad plug-in. However, that's not always the case, so you may need to follow the processes that we cover later on how to find corrupted clips, reinstall the application, or even evaluate possible system issues with macOS.

Once you have completed the easy fixes, you will need to spend much more time on the following fixes.

The harder fixes

These fixes will take time to resolve and are more complex than what you have tried so far. The main consideration is to follow the steps logically and not become frustrated with the process.

These steps will resolve your issues by finding faulty plug-ins, removing them from your project, and ultimately deleting them from the system. If you have resolved any possible plug-in issues and you still cannot export, you need to look for corruptions in your clips.

If you have error messages about render files and frame errors, it's best to jump to the section later in this chapter that covers that: *Locating a corruption*. If you are still having issues other than exporting, then there are further steps you can take.

Fixing a faulty effect, transition, or title

This section will show you how to locate a plug-in that is causing issues. It may be just a matter of a simple check to find a red message in the viewer:

Figure 18.15 – The red plug-in showing on the timeline clip also shows in the viewer

Then you can remove the plug-in with the *Delete* key or disable the plug-in in the timeline with the *Control + V* key shortcut.

Figure 18.16 – The same plug-in disabled with the Control + V shortcut

It's more difficult to find which plug-in is faulty when it does not show as red. Rather than looking at the whole timeline, just select a little at a time using the range tool (the *R* key) and then try to export. Start from the beginning or the end and work through the whole timeline, narrowing down the selection until you find the section that doesn't export. I would suggest deleting the plug-in, but you could just disable it by pressing the *V* key and then trying to export.

Now that you have found the plug-in, you have two things to consider. You could contact the developer to get an update, or if there is no update available, you need to delete the plug-in from your system. You will see in the next section how to remove plug-ins from your system.

Deleting plug-ins from your computer

You saw in *Chapter 1, It's All about the Media*, how to locate the plug-ins folder on your system disk.

As a quick reminder, the path to the **Titles** plug-ins folder is as follows:

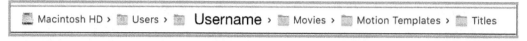

Figure 18.17 – The path for the Titles plug-ins folder

Replace **Username** in *Figure 18.17* with your username. To access **Effects**, **Transitions**, or **Generators**, substitute them for **Titles** in the path.

As an example, to remove the **New Template** title shown in the following figure, just drag it to the trash:

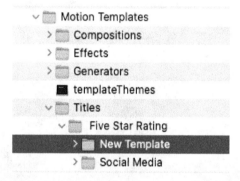

Figure 18.18 – Drag the title to be removed to the trash

> **Warning**
> The **New Template** title will still be visible in the titles browser until you quit Final Cut Pro.

Once you have ruled out a plug-in being the reason for not being able to export, you'll need to locate a corruption in the project.

Locating a corruption

Corruptions can be caused by any number of different circumstances. The first things to check are whether you have used the **Flow** transition, slowed down a clip in the timeline with **Optical Flow**, or even used the **Stabilization** command.

Try **Optical Flow** and the **Flow** transition first as they can fail an export. Open the index of the project in the timeline, make sure the **Clip** tab is selected, and type f low:

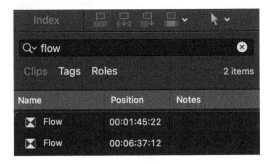

Figure 18.19 – Search the index for Flow

You could remove all the **Flow** transitions or just remove them one at a time, and then try to export. I find that just selecting the **Flow** transitions in the timeline will start activating the **Flow** transition again and possibly fix the issue itself.

Finding the clips with **Optical Flow** and **Stabilization** is much more complex. It is quite common for Final Cut Pro to show a **Stabilization** warning on export. There is no other solution than to check those clips that you think have the added **Optical Flow** and **Stabilization**. If you are not sure whether you have used either of them, there is a way to test the whole project.

Checking for Optical Flow

To check for **Optical Flow**, click in the timeline and press *Command + A*. This will create a yellow outline around all clips. You need to check for clips that have been slowed down by pressing *Command + R*, which will show green for normal-speed clips and orange for clips that have been slowed down:

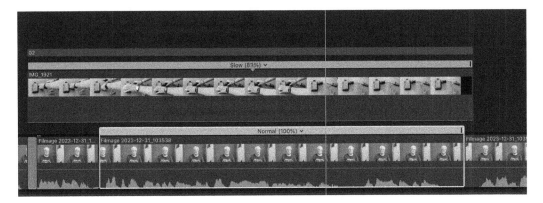

Figure 18.20 – Command + R shows the speed layer

Select each of the orange clips and check for **Video Quality | Optical Flow:**

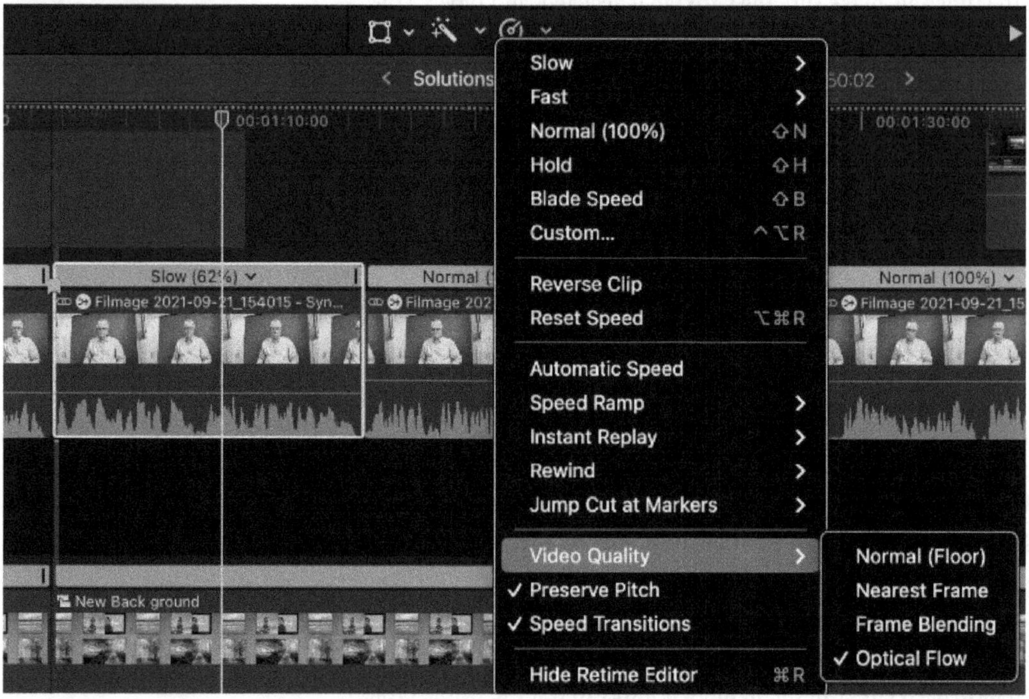

Figure 18.21 – Check for Video Quality | Optical Flow

In a worst-case scenario, you could try **Frame Blending**, but I have found that simply selecting the clip with **Optical Flow** activated will restart any delayed render for **Optical Flow** in the same way as it does for the **Flow** transition.

Checking for Stabilization

The inspector will show whether any video clip has **Stabilization** selected. You need to group all video clips, while avoiding all **Still** images and titles/generators/transitions. Select a group of video clips only, and in the inspector, select the **Filmstrip** tab and scroll down to see **Stabilization**. If any clips have been stabilized, the checkbox will show a dash.

Figure 18.22 – At least one clip in the selection has Stabilization selected

You can remove multiple instances of **Optical Flow** and **Stabilization** by selecting the clips that you suspect contain both **Optical Flow** and **Stabilization** and, from the **Edit** menu, selecting **Remove Attributes**. Make sure only **Compositing** and **Retiming** are ticked, and click **Remove**.

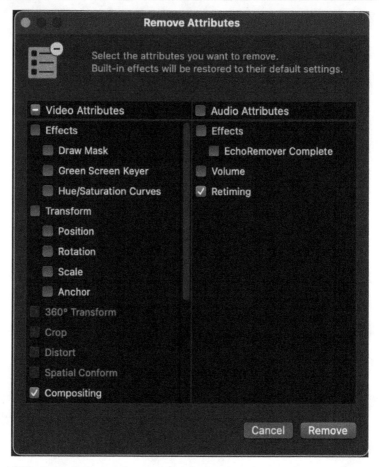

Figure 18.23 – Remove Optical Flow and Stabilization by ticking Compositing and Retiming

Another scenario that you may encounter when a project does not export is when you receive an error message. The following section shows how to find error codes that are shown in warning messages.

Clearing export error messages

Export error messages will show different error codes and what appear to be obscure messages. This section will help you decipher those codes.

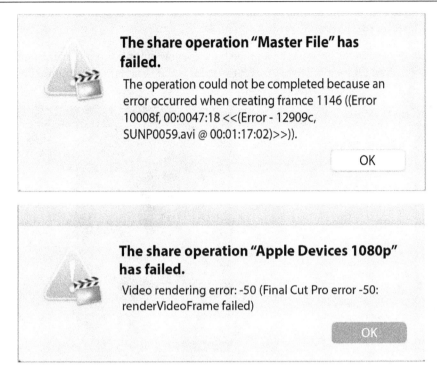

Figure 18.24 – Two examples of error messages with error codes

Since there are many different error codes, there is no point in trying to remember them all. Fortunately, errors occur so infrequently that it's better to have a workflow that will help clear all errors.

There are two distinct types of error messages. You could receive an error such as **Render frame error failed**, which means it's to do with a render file that Final Cut has created previously. The second type of error shows a frame number. In that case, it's a corrupt frame in the timeline. The processes are similar, so let's look at the first workflow.

Render frame error message

This is a similar process to what you saw at the beginning of this chapter when you selected **Delete Generated Library Files**. If you have already deleted the library render files, skip this section and go directly to the *Reinstalling Final Cut Pro* section later in this chapter.

If you haven't deleted the library render files, select the project in your browser and, from the **File** menu, select **Delete Generated Project Files…** | **All Render files**, and then press **OK** and try the export again. If you get the same error message, then quit Final Cut Pro and restart the computer.

If you have already actioned all of the steps previously shown in this chapter, you should create a new library and copy the project from the old library into the new library.

Copying the project to a new library

Select the faulty project in the browser; it will then have a yellow outline. From the **File** menu, select either **Copy Project to Library** or **Move Project to Library**, and then select **New Library…**:

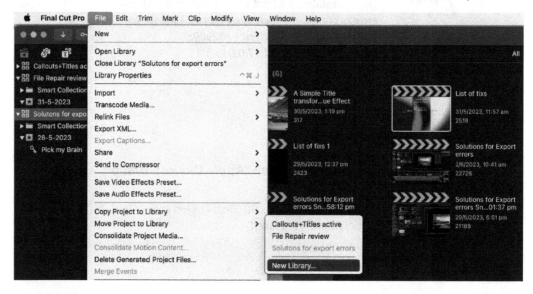

Figure 18.25 – Copy or move the project to a new library

If you still can't export, then the issue may be with Final Cut Pro, so your next step would be to try another user account or a new computer, as shown later in this chapter.

Render errors are one of the two types of export error message; the other is a **Frame error** message, which is discussed in the next section.

Frame number error message

If there is a frame number mentioned in the error message, go to the Final Cut Pro settings, and in the **General** tab, change **Time Display** to **Frames**.

Figure 18.26 – Change Time Display to Frames

You need to navigate in the timeline to the frame number in the error message. The best way to do this is to type the number at the timecode position between the viewer and the timeline.

As an example, in the following error message, the frame number is **1146**:

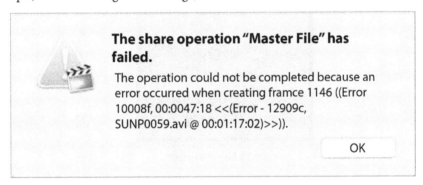

Figure 18.27 – The error frame number here is 1146

Type the error frame number into the number field, press *Return*, and the playhead will jump to that video frame in the timeline:

Figure 18.28 – The error frame number

The process of replacing a clip in the timeline

Make sure the clip is selected in the timeline with a yellow outline and press *Shift + F*:

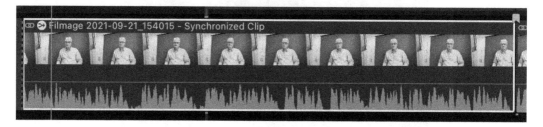

Figure 18.29 – The playhead at frame 1146

You will now see the clip in the browser with a yellow outline. If it's a long clip, you may need to increase the zoom level in the browser so you can see where those yellow outlines are.

As you hover between the yellow outlines in the browser clip, a hand icon will appear as in the following figure:

Figure 18.30 – Hand icon

Drag that inside the clip in the timeline and select the **Replace from Start** option:

Figure 18.31 – Replace from Start

This will replace the corrupt clip in the timeline with, hopefully, a good version from the browser. Try to export the updated project. One of three things will happen: it will export, it will come back with the same frame error, or it will come back with a different frame error.

Before I cover what to do about the new error messages, I'll mention how to retain any effects in the clip that have just been replaced.

Retaining effects in the clip to be replaced

If you need to retain any effects in the clip that is about to be replaced in the timeline, select the timeline clip before you replace it, copy it using *Command + C*, drag the clip inside the clip you want to replace in the timeline, and select **Replace from Start** from the drop-down menu.

Then, select that replaced clip in the timeline and choose **Paste Effects** from the **Edit** menu, which you can do by using *Command + Option + V*. Any effects that were applied to the original clip will be returned to the clip in the timeline. Now, try and export again.

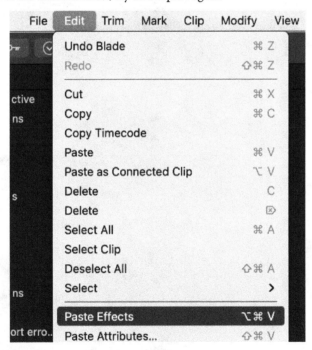

Figure 18.32 – Paste Effects

Now, we return to what to do if the project still doesn't export. If you get the same frame error, then the browser clip was also corrupted; if you get a different frame error, the browser clip has more than one corrupted frame. Your next step would be to import the clip again from the camera card, if you still have it.

> **Tip**
> I would suggest, if it's not critical, that you replace the whole clip in the timeline with another clip.

However, if you do decide to delete the frames, you need to zoom into the timeline so that you can see a single frame. For this, I suggest you duplicate the project first and work on the copy.

Type the frame number where you did before, between the viewer and the timeline, and press *Return*. The playhead will be at the beginning of the frame in the timeline. If you have zoomed in far enough, the frame number will show next to the playhead. The actual frame is the dark gray section; you need to look very closely at *Figure 18.33* to see the gray frame, as it is almost the same color as the black background. The more you zoom in, the bigger that gray section becomes, but it's still just one frame.

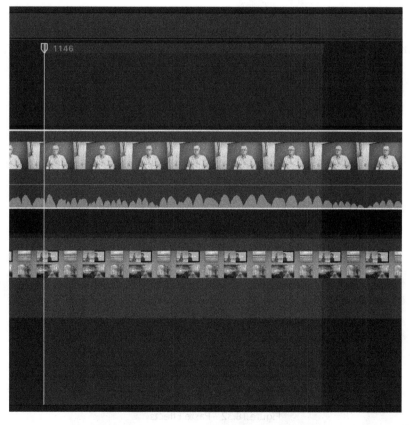

Figure 18.33 – Frame 1146 showing in dark gray

It's a matter of cutting out the frame by pressing *Command + B* and then moving the playhead one frame to the right with the keyboard's right arrow key and pressing *Command + B* again. You can then delete the corrupt frame. Repeat this for each corrupt frame. You can see why I suggested replacing the whole clip if it's practical.

> **Note**
>
> Don't forget to return the **Time Display** setting back from **Frames** to **HH:MM:SS:FF**.

Export issues are not the only problems that can occur in Final Cut Pro. A reasonably common issue is when a library does not open when double-clicked; the next section has an easy solution.

A Final Cut Pro library won't open

You may find that when you try to open a library, nothing happens. This is a reasonably common condition and can easily be fixed by right-clicking on the purple library icon in **Finder** and selecting **Show Package Contents**:

0012.mov
File Repair one
File Repair review
New Illusion trimmed.mov
Open
Open With
Show Package Contents
Move to Trash

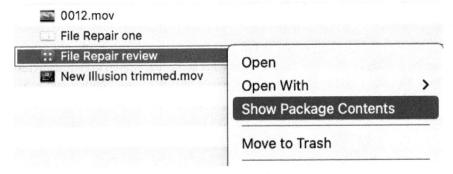

Figure 18.34 – Right-click on the library icon

It's safe to trash **CurrentVersion.flexolibrary** and **Settings.plist**; after you've done that, try to open the library again. This fix almost always works.

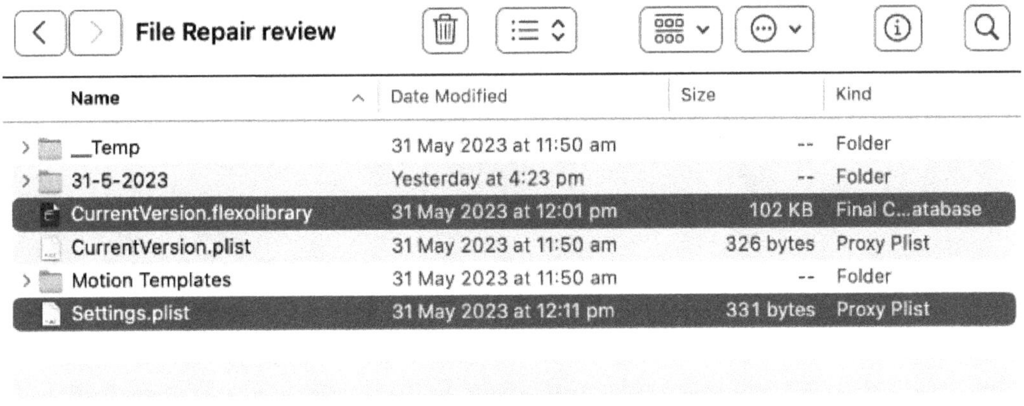

File Repair review
Name
Date Modified
Size
Kind
__Temp
31 May 2023 at 11:50 am
--
Folder
31-5-2023
Yesterday at 4:23 pm
--
Folder
CurrentVersion.flexolibrary
31 May 2023 at 12:01 pm
102 KB
Final C...atabase
CurrentVersion.plist
31 May 2023 at 11:50 am
326 bytes
Proxy Plist
Motion Templates
31 May 2023 at 11:50 am
--
Folder
Settings.plist
31 May 2023 at 12:11 pm
331 bytes
Proxy Plist

Figure 18.35 – Trash CurrentVersion.flexolibrary and Settings.plist

When you open the library again, the following message will be displayed:

Figure 18.36 – Loading the updated library

The next section covers trying the problematic library using another user account on your computer.

Trying another user account

If you are still having problems with Final Cut Pro crashing or behaving erratically, it may be time to consider running it using another user account or another computer, or even to consider reinstalling the application. You could use the guest user, but it would be better to use another user account on your Mac. If you don't have one, create another from the **System Settings…** menu to see whether the problem still persists:

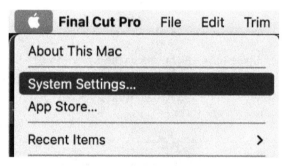

Figure 18.37 – System Settings…

Use **Guest User** or create another user from the **Users & Groups** window in the settings menu:

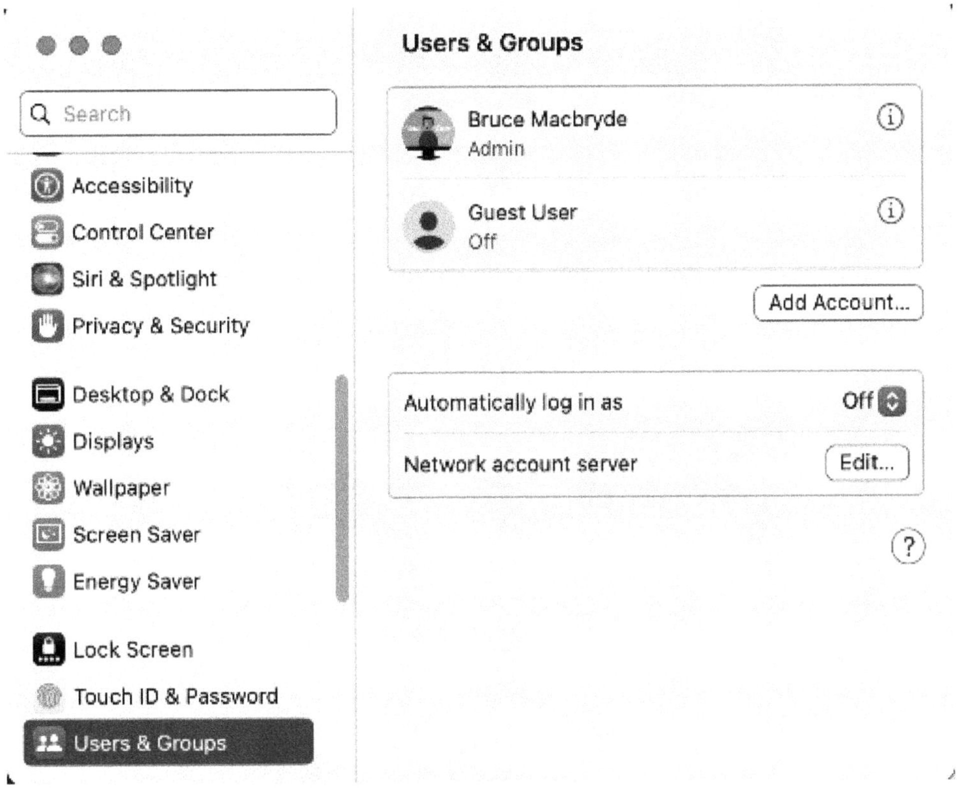

Figure 18.38 – The Users & Groups settings

Before you switch users, make sure that Final Cut Pro has been exited from the current user account and that the library you wish to test is on an external disk, as you will not have access to the system disk once you switch users.

If the library runs without issues, and even successfully exports, then there is an issue with your main user account. If the library still has issues, then try it on another computer.

Trying the library on another computer

You should make sure that all the media is stored using the **In Library** option. Before moving the library, open it on the first computer, select it in the browser sidebar, and from the **File** menu, select **Consolidate Library Media**, as shown previously.

Copy the library to a disk that you can attach to the new computer. If the issues are resolved on another Mac, it could be that your copy of Final Cut Pro is corrupt. The next section shows how to reinstall Final Cut Pro from the Apple App Store.

Reinstalling Final Cut Pro

This is not as drastic a solution as it sounds, but don't rush into it without thought. You won't lose any projects or any footage on your disks. The biggest downside is the time you will spend offline waiting for the app to download, depending on your internet speed.

Before you do anything, quit Final Cut Pro and reset the Final Cut Pro preferences as described earlier in this chapter. There is no point in keeping the old preferences after the new copy of Final Cut Pro has been reinstalled.

The next step, just as a safety measure, is to zip the current copy of Final Cut Pro. This is not necessary but is worth doing for peace of mind.

Go to the `Applications` folder on your system disk, select **Final Cut Pro**, and right-click to compress the application:

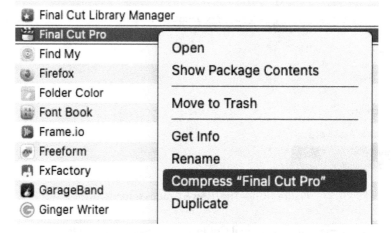

Figure 18.39 – Compress "Final Cut Pro"

Trash the full version of Final Cut Pro and keep the ZIP file.

Now, open the App Store and type in final cut pro x; it will give you **INSTALL** and **OPEN** options.

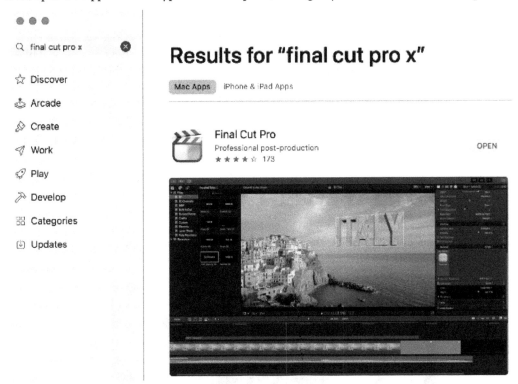

Figure 18.40 – Final Cut Pro in the Apple App Store

You will find the reinstalled version in the `Applications` folder. If you had the icon in your dock previously, it can still be launched from there or double-clicked in the `Applications` folder.

Figure 18.41 – Launch from the dock

You will be able to open all your projects. Check that everything is running correctly, and then you can trash the Final Cut Pro ZIP file from the `Applications` folder.

If things didn't go as expected, you will still have the zipped copy of your previous version of Final Cut Pro. Quit Final Cut Pro if it is open, trash the newly downloaded copy, and open the ZIP file. You will be back to the same copy of Final Cut Pro as you had prior to going to the Apple App Store.

If the reinstall did not solve the issue, then the problem is possibly with macOS. The next section discusses how to check macOS and reinstall the OS by booting into recovery mode.

Booting into recovery mode

There are different methods of entering recovery mode, depending on whether you have an Intel or a Silicon M-series Mac.

For Intel, restart the computer while holding *Command + R* until the white bar comes across the screen; when a window appears, follow the prompts. For Silicon M-series Macs, press and hold the power button until you see the HDD and gear images. Select the gear and click **Continue**.

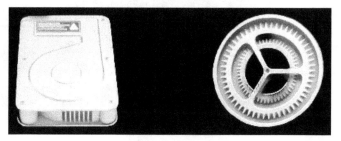

Figure 18.42 – Select the gear option

You will be asked to select an admin user and enter a password. In the next window, select **Disk Utility** and run **First Aid** on both instances of **Macintosh HD**. Depending on the OS you are running, there can be either one or two **Macintosh HD** instances. Run **First Aid** on both if there are two on your system:

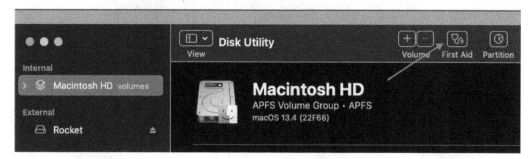

Figure 18.43 – Running First Aid

After **First Aid** has run, reboot the computer. If the issues are not fixed, you will need to speak with Apple support.

There are other troubleshooting issues with Final Cut Pro that you will infrequently encounter. The next section looks at relinking missing media, and the final section discusses what happens when Final Cut Pro unexpectedly quits.

Relinking missing media

Generally, Final Cut Pro is very good at keeping track of where media is located on your disks, even when you move libraries and original footage to different folders. What it can't do is keep track of media that has been trashed or is on a disk that is no longer attached to the computer. This is particularly an issue when you are linked to files that are in cloud storage and the internet goes offline.

You will find that if you attach a missing disk, Final Cut Pro will find most of the files, but for some reason, not all the files will be found, even when the internet is back online.

There are occasions when files will be missing in the browser and hence also in any projects that they have been used in. It is a fairly familiar sight for the red warning to show in the viewer. You will be less likely to have the issue if you store your media using the **In Library** option rather than the **Leave Files in Place** option.

I recommend that you store your media using the **In Library** option and that you use the **Consolidate** option from the **File** menu before you finish with a library. When you use **Consolidate**, any files that are spread around your computer will be added to the library, which means you will be less likely to see the **Missing File** message. (For more on this, see the next section of this chapter.) Obviously, there is no point in consolidating if your workflow uses the **Leave Files in Place** option.

Figure 18.44 – The Missing File message in the viewer

When confronted with the red **Missing File** message, the first thing to know is that it is not as big an issue as it first appears. Final Cut Pro is good at relinking files once you give it a bit of assistance as to where to files are located. You could go to the trouble of having Siri search your whole disk, but that can be time-consuming if the disks have not been recently indexed. You will most likely have some idea of where the missing files are, so it's best to point Final Cut Pro in that general direction, and it will find them for you.

Once it has found one file, it will be able to relink others at that location, so I suggest that rather than selecting too many files at a time to relink, you should just try one or two first.

Figure 18.45 – Missing files in the browser being relinked to originals

The process is to select the missing media in the browser, and then from the **File** menu, select **Relink Files | Original Media...**.

The window that opens allows you to just relink the missing media or all the files, whether the media is missing or not. The second option of selecting **All** means that you can connect to different copies of media at different locations than the currently linked media was originally selected. The files must have exactly the same file content; it's just the location that is different. If you have only selected media that is missing in the browser, then select either the **Missing** or **All** option and click on **Locate All...**:

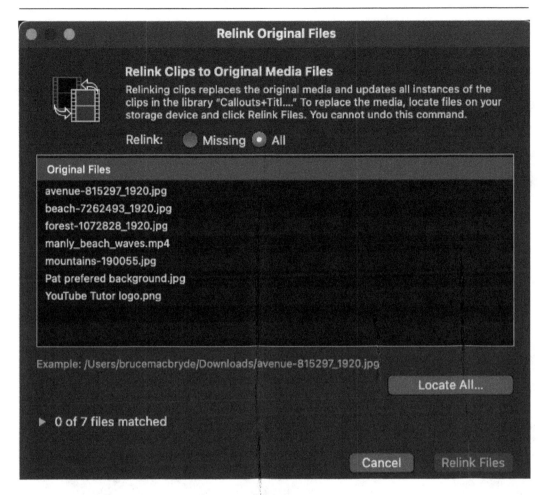

Figure 18.46 – A list of files to be relinked

You can search a part of your disk where you think the missing media might be; you don't need to navigate to the actual missing file, but don't set the search too wide. There's no point in trying to relink by selecting the top level of a multi-terabyte disk; it will probably find the file, but the search could take time.

When Final Cut Pro has located the missing files, they will be removed from the list and you will see the number of files that have been matched. In the following figure, you can see that 7 out of 7 files matched:

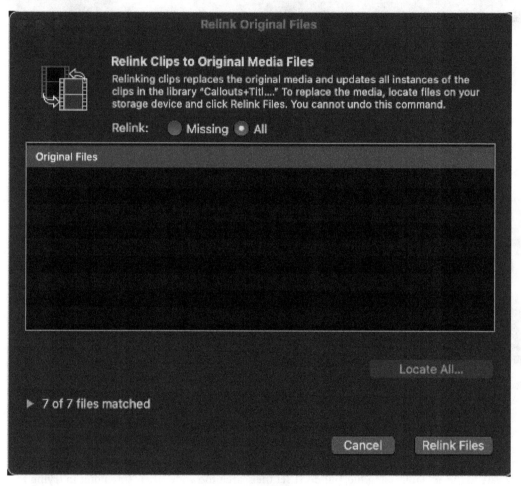

Figure 18.47 – 7 of 7 files matched

Simply click **Relink Files** and they will show in the browser with no red warning messages:

Figure 18.48 – The originals show in the browser and are no longer red warning messages

When you first see the red missing message, it does incur that "heart in your mouth" feeling! Just trust relinking to find the files if they are still on your disks. Consolidating media after you finish with a library will certainly help avoid the missing file message, as you will see in the next section.

Consolidating media

Consolidation is important if your import settings workflow involves using the **In Library** option. Using **In Library** will increase the size of your library on your storage disk to accommodate the size of the media files, but the advantage is that the library is completely portable and can be moved as one entity with everything contained inside.

After you have completed work on a library, even at the end of each session, you should consolidate by selecting the library in the browser sidebar and, from the **File** menu, selecting **Consolidate Library Media…**. Choose whether you want **Original**, **Optimized**, or **Proxy** media. My suggestion if you are archiving is to only select **Original** media, as the other two can be created later if needed, but once the original has gone, you will see the red missing file message.

Figure 18.49 – Consolidate Library Media...

Click on **Consolidate Library Media...** again until you see **There are no files to consolidate:**

Figure 18.50 – All chosen files are now stored in the library

Now, you can rest assured that when you move the library to your archive disk, all the files will be contained inside.

The final issue that you will see while working with Final Cut Pro is Final Cut Pro quitting unexpectedly. The next section explains what actually happens here and what follows after the application has quit.

Final Cut Pro quitting unexpectedly

Unexpected quitting is commonly known as a crash, and even though it can be frustrating, you are well protected by the way that an unexpected quit takes place. It is normal for your software to instantly save every action you take so that if there is a crash, all your work is saved, including the action that caused the crash (but not any actions that may have happened immediately after that).

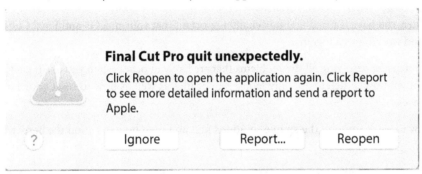

Figure 18.51 – The Final Cut Pro quit unexpectedly message

If you are so inclined, you could check what caused the crash, as Final Cut Pro produces a report with the technical details as well as the state of the Mac system at the time. The report can be sent to Apple for their research by selecting **Reopen**. Be reassured that no personal information is included in the report.

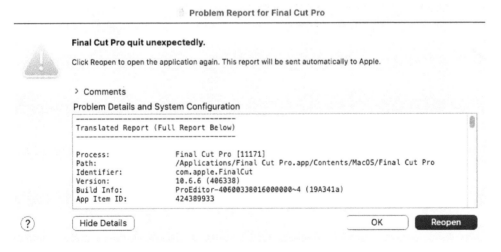

Figure 18.52 – Click Reopen to send a report to Apple

You have the choice of sending the report or simply pressing **OK** to relaunch Final Cut Pro in the exact condition it was in when it crashed. The same libraries will be open, even with the playhead at the exact location in the timeline that it was in previously.

> **Tip**
> The usual cause of a crash is a disk accidentally becoming disconnected.

Summary

In this chapter, you have learned that it is vitally important that your macOS and Final Cut Pro are up to date and working well together.

You saw the steps for resolving all the problems that are likely to occur when you use Final Cut Pro. You were shown how to delete possibly faulty render files as well as how to reset your Final Cut Pro preferences.

You saw how to work through the simple solutions first and then how to action the harder fixes in more detail.

You were shown the solutions for fixing export errors for frame errors and render errors. Also, there were solutions provided to try to resolve a corrupt library by running the library on another user account and then another computer to help decide whether Final Cut Pro needs reinstallation.

Finally, you looked at methods for relinking missing media and reasons for Final Cut Pro unexpectedly quitting.

The next chapter is the last in the book and covers the different methods of archiving Final Cut Pro libraries, as well as the reasons why you need to archive your media.

19
Backing Up and Archiving Libraries

Similar to the saying, *"The task isn't considered finished until all the necessary paperwork is done,"* once the editing process is concluded, there are established protocols for both backing up and archiving libraries, as well as preserving the original footage.

In this chapter, we will gain an understanding of the **Consolidate** media command, which gathers all the footage used in a library and consolidates it in a location of your choice so that no footage is lost when you open an archived library in the future.

Later in this chapter, we will see how media can show as missing after consolidation and how to recover missing files with the **Relink Files** command.

We will learn where Final Cut Pro automatically backs up libraries and how to manage backups. We will see how automatic backups are designed for project recovery while the edit is still in progress as opposed to archiving after the video is exported.

We will also go through the method for removing unneeded render files to save hard disk space with the **Delete Generated Files** command.

The chapter discusses the setup procedures for archiving libraries, keeping them available even years after completion, as well as the maintenance necessary to ensure the storage devices are in working order.

We will be covering the following sections in this chapter:

- Final Cut Pro backups
- Preparing to archive a library
- Consolidating library media
- Relinking missing files
- Deleting render data

- Archiving

- Indexing archives

- Maintaining storage devices

By the end of this chapter, you will have a comprehensive knowledge of the workflows needed to secure the integrity of a Final Cut library, while reducing the size of the library so it takes up less space on your archive devices.

You will understand the implications of different archiving procedures and how to index the locations of the original footage and libraries so they can be accessed indefinitely in the future.

You will see options for ensuring that the devices you archive to are kept up to date and in a condition for you to be able to quickly access the archived libraries.

The sequence of actions outlined in this chapter corresponds to a chronological order you should adhere to once your projects within a Final Cut Pro library are finished. One constant aspect of Final Cut Pro, called **Final Cut Pro backups**, evolves throughout your editing process, and we will delve into this topic in the next section.

Working with Final Cut Pro backups

Backups are automatic in Final Cut Pro. You should understand the difference in terminology between backing up and archiving. Backing up is a temporary and ongoing process that happens while you are editing. Archiving is the process of securing a library's projects in an optimized working state so that they can be opened at a later date without the dreaded red **Missing File** warning:

Figure 19.1 – The dreaded red Missing File warning

The automatic backups that Final Cut Pro activates every few minutes are stored in the **Users** folder on the Mac's system disk. The backups do not take up much space on the disk because they do not include media. The backup library simply points to where the media is stored. This is a good thing – because of the small footprint – but is inherently dangerous due to the media needing to stay available for the backup library to be of any value. If the media is moved, the backup library will only show the **Missing File** warning (*Figure 19.1*) for appropriate clips in the library clips.

The **Final Cut Backups** folder is located in the **Movies** folder, which is inside the **Users** folder of your system disk. All available backups for each library that has been opened in Final Cut Pro will be contained in this folder.

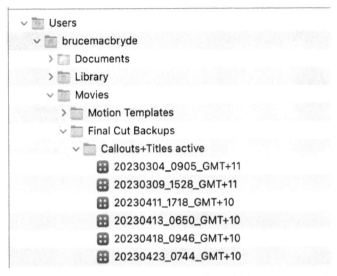

Figure 19.2 – Final Cut Backups folder

Even though automatic backups are small, over time, the storage space can significantly increase if the backups are not managed carefully. I recently checked my **Final Cut Backups** folder, and it contained 368 backups, using 78 GB of storage space.

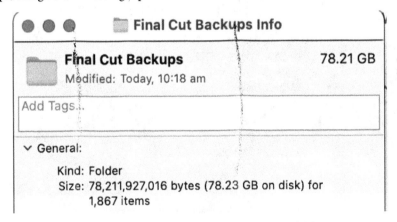

Figure 19.3 – Checking the.Final Cut Backups folder

I deleted backups from 3 months prior and saved 40 GB of space on my system disk.

You can double-click a backup in the **Final Cut Backups** folder and it will open in Final Cut Pro; however, the better method is to open it from **File | Open Library | From Backup...** in Final Cut Pro when you have the current version of the library open:

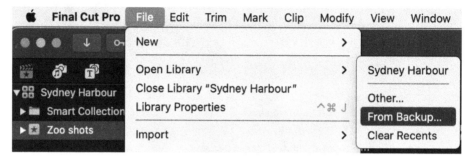

Figure 19.4 – Open library from backup

You will be presented with a list of the available backups for that library showing the dates that the backups were saved in a recognizable date format.

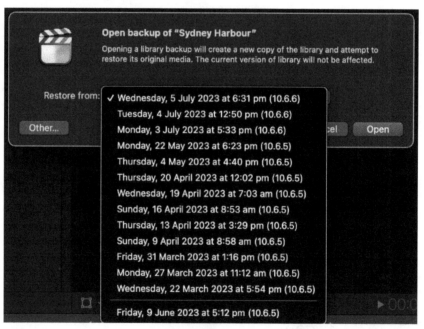

Figure 19.5 – List of available backups

When you view the list of backups in the **Finder** window (see *Figure 19.2*), you will see each library's folder with the dates in a coded format. The format for the dates is four digits for the year, two digits for the month, and two digits for the date, with time in +/- GMT format. When the backup library is opened in the browser sidebar of Final Cut Pro, it shows the same coded format.

Figure 19.6 – Date coded format

When you open a backup library, Final Cut Pro will back up that backed-up library in a folder with the original name including the date code:

Figure 19.7 – Library name changed automatically

So that you don't get confused, I suggest, if you intend to continue to use the backed-up version of the library with the date format, that you change the name in the browser sidebar as soon as you can so that when it is backed up, it will automatically have a meaningful name – such as **Version 2 recovered from Backup**.

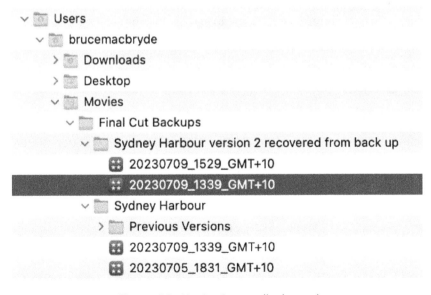

Figure 19.8 – Version 2 manually changed

The automatic backups are for recovery purposes and are not intended to be used for archiving completed projects for posterity. The process to instigate the archiving procedure after a video is exported when the library is no longer currently active is covered in the next section.

Preparing to archive a library

To ensure a library is optimized for archiving, preserving all footage while minimizing its size to save disk space, specific procedures should be adhered to. The first thing is to locate all the media spread across all your disks and consolidate the media in a preferred location for the archived library to be able to access the media in the future.

Then you should check for Motion 5 content, followed by checking the cache location. Let's start with the consolidation process in the next section.

Consolidation

The ingestion of media into Final Cut Pro is controlled in **Settings** (previously **Preferences**). In *Chapter 2*, *Organizing Media*, we saw that the **Settings** instructions control whether the media is stored as **Copy to Library** or whether the media is set to **Leave in place**. Even if the media is set to **Copy to Library**, some files may still not make it to the library if you change the setting after the library is originally created.

The value of consolidation is that you can ensure all the media required for the projects are in one location that can be transferred to the archive. Consolidation will let you store everything as **Copy to Library** or have the media in another folder outside the library.

Some editors prefer to have the media set as **Leave in place** so that the library does not grow too big, while others prefer to have the media set as **Copy to Library**. It doesn't matter which you choose, when you archive, it's necessary to store the original media required for a project somewhere. In my mind, at least for archiving purposes, I prefer to have all media set to **Copy to Library**. In that way everything is in one place, so that when you move a library, all the media moves with it.

With the explanation out of the way, the actual consolidation action is very straightforward.

Select the library you intend to archive, then open the inspector to see where the storage locations are currently set. In *Figure 19.9*, **Media** has been directed to **Copy to Library** storage. **Motion Content** has been directed to **Motion Templates folder**. I'll explain this later in this section, along with **Cache**, which should also be directed to **Copy to Library**. **Backups** are directed to the **Final Cut Backups** folder, as you saw earlier in this chapter. Finally, you will see that the library has been stored on a disk called **Rocket**, taking up 6.6 GB for **Original** content with no **Optimized** or **Proxy** media.

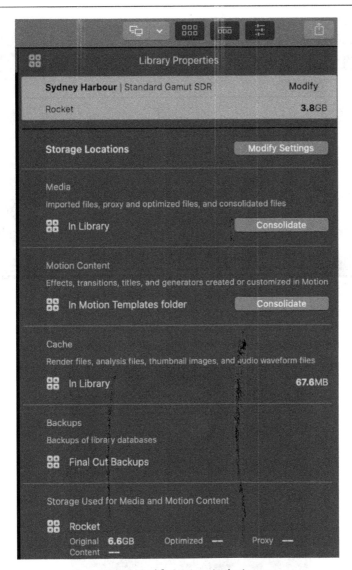

Figure 19.9 – Modify Settings in the inspector

If you want to change these settings, you can click the **Modify Settings** button, then change the media storage location to a folder of your choice, as well as other setting changes if you wish. For this exercise, though, I intend to leave the media storage as **Copy to Library** and click the **Consolidate** button to find any files that are spread out anywhere on the computer or attached disks and move them into the library. Once you click on **Consolidate**, you will be presented with a window to choose **Original Media**, **Optimized Media**, or **Proxy Media**. For archive purposes, the requirement is to reduce the size of the archive as much as possible, which means you should select **Original Media**.

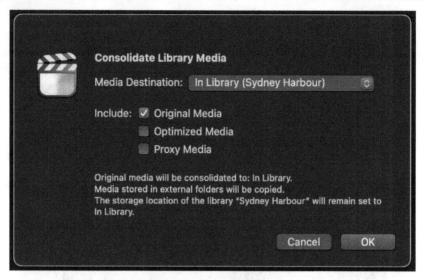

Figure 19.10 – Consolidate only Original Media

Once you do that, hopefully, you will see the **There are no files to consolidate** message. If you don't see a message, click the **Consolidate** button in the inspector again until you see the following:

Figure 19.11 – No files to consolidate

Alternatively, you may see the **Original media does not exist for some clips** message, which means that some media imported into your library can't be located on any disks currently connected to your computer.

Figure 19.12 – Missing files warning

There are several reasons why a file may be unavailable:

- The file may be on a disk that was disconnected after the file was imported
- The media file may have been deleted

If the file had simply been moved to another location on your computer, Final Cut Pro would most likely have been able to keep track of the file.

There is no built-in way of knowing whether the file is on a disconnected disk other than you remembering.

Don't be too worried at this stage, as you may be able to recover the missing files with the **Relink Files** command in the **File** menu. Relinking files is covered later in this chapter under the *Relinking* section.

You also have the option to consolidate libraries by selecting **Consolidate Library Media...** from the **File** menu if you prefer to do so.

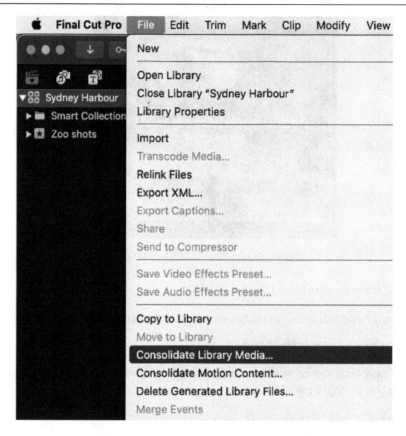

Figure 19.13 – Consolidate Library Media… in the File menu

> **Note**
>
> Whether the clips are copied or moved will depend on how you consolidate. If you consolidate files into a library from a location outside of a library, the files will be copied, which means they remain in the external location as well as in the library.

Although the process occurs invisibly, when you consolidate, all necessary media from various connected disks is copied or moved to the location you specified in the settings shown in *Figure 19.9*.

Figure 19.9 also shows the locations set for **Motion Content** and **Cache**, both of which are explained in the next sections.

Motion Content

As you saw in *Chapter 17, Supporting Software Applications for Final Cut Pro*, **Motion** is a software application associated with Final Cut Pro where all of Final Cut Pro's plug-ins are created. This means that media and other content that has been used by Motion to create plug-ins needs to be available for Final Cut Pro to access in the **Motion Templates** folder. That content is best stored in a central location that can be easily located by any Final Cut Pro library – the **Motion Templates** folder is contained in the **Users** folder, as discussed in *Chapter 1, It's All about the Media*.

Cache

Cache is a term for a stockpile of data that is routinely used by applications. Final Cut Pro requires a cache location for data that is frequently used. Final Cut Pro's cache is best stored as **Copy to Library** unless the library is being shared by several editors, in which case, the cache should be in a location that is readily available to all those sharing the library, as would be the case if the library was located in the cloud for collaborative editing, as discussed in *Chapter 16, Your Job Role – Collaboration* .

You have seen that media can be missing after you consolidate, in which case, it will be necessary to try to relink the missing media, as is discussed in the next section.

Relinking

The **relink** term comes from the situation where **Original** media or **Optimized/Proxy** files are not set to **Copy to Library**, then Final Cut Pro relies on a link to where the actual media is located. When that link is broken, Final Cut Pro displays the red **Missing File** warning message.

One of the main advantages of setting **Original** media to be stored as **Copy to Library** is that when the media is in the library, it's always on hand. If the media is set to be outside of the library and the disk where the media is stored is unmounted, or if you send a file to the trash by mistake, the link will be broken, and you will see the **Missing File** warning.

You can use the **Relink Files** command, provided the disk containing the file is still attached and the file has not been deleted.

You can relink a file by selecting any category heading in the browser sidebar – library, event, smart collection, folder, or keyword collection. You can even relink individual files in the browser.

When you have selected the clip or the category, from the **File** menu, select **Relink Files | Original Media…**:

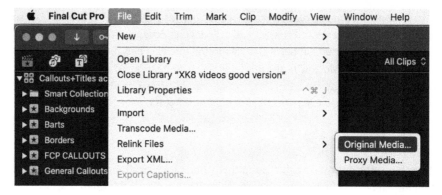

Figure 19.14 – Relink Original Media

The relink window (*Figure 19.15*) allows you to search for just missing media or for all of the original media. There is a significant difference between these two options. If you are only looking to find the missing media, then select the **Missing** button. When you select the **All** button, you will replace all the media with new connections, including clips that are correctly linked. The **All** option is good for replacing corrupt media in a project with good versions of the same media.

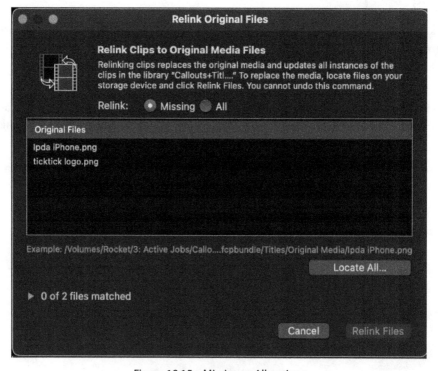

Figure 19.15 – Missing or All options

In the preceding figure, the bottom-right button indicates **Locate All…**, but if you select individual files in the list, the button will change to **Locate Selected…**. When you click the button, you will be able to navigate to folders on your connected disks where you think the files may be located. It pays to be as accurate as possible in selecting folders where the clips are likely to be. If you are not sure where the files may be, you could select the root level of a disk, but it would take some considerable time to find the missing file.

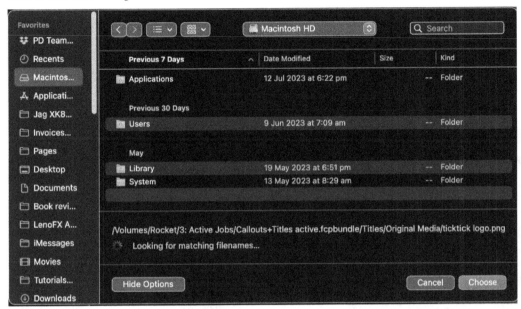

Figure 19.16 – Searching a root location takes time

If you have no idea where the missing file is located, it will be quicker to use the Mac's **Spotlight** to search for the files as Spotlight indexes all your connected disks behind the scenes, so the search is likely to be quicker.

To use the Spotlight option, before you relink the files, in the browser, copy the name of the missing file:

Figure 19.17 – Copy the filename in the browser

Then paste the name into Spotlight, which is accessed by clicking the magnifying glass icon at the top right in the menu bar.

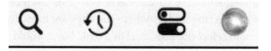

Figure 19.18 – Spotlight is the magnifying glass icon on the left

When Spotlight shows the location of the missing file, you will then be able to narrow down the search with the location that Spotlight has found when you use the **Relink Files** command.

After you have actioned **Relink Files**, you will be shown the files that the relink command has located. Click **Choose** to confirm the selection.

Figure 19.19 – Relink matched two of two files that were searched for

Once you confirm your selection, the number of matched files is shown again and, as you will notice in *Figure 19.20*, they are removed from the search list. If any files are not found, they will remain in the list and the number of matched files will show the number missing. Now, when you click the **Relink Files** button, the red **Missing File** thumbnail in the Final Cut Pro browser will be replaced with the **Matched files** thumbnail.

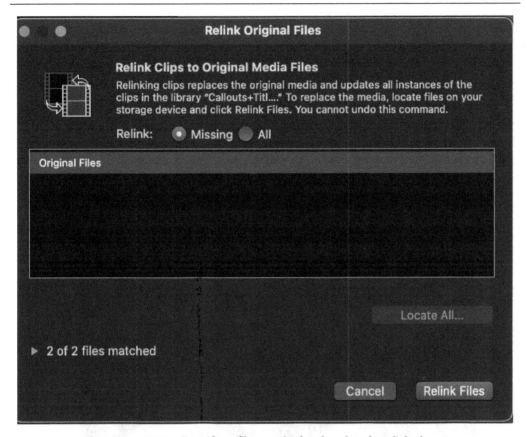

Figure 19.20 – Two of two files matched and ready to be relinked

When all the files have been relinked, don't forget to consolidate again so that the missing files are correctly stored, ready for archiving.

There is one more step before you can archive the library, and that is to ensure that the size of the archived library is as small as possible. The next section discusses how to delete render files to reduce the library size.

Deleting render data

To make the editing and export process as smooth as possible, Final Cut Pro uses rendering techniques to produce temporary files to help smooth the editing process, but that has the downside of adding to the size of the library.

Chapter 1, It's All about the Media discussed how render options can be set up in the **Settings/Preferences** menu. Render files are just some of the generated files produced behind the scenes by Final Cut Pro that also add to the size of the library. These generated files are useful but not absolutely necessary for Final Cut Pro to operate. You don't need to be concerned as generated files can be removed, and Final Cut Pro will regenerate them if needed.

To remove the generated files, select a library in the browser sidebar, and from the **File** menu, select **Delete Generated Library Files**. The window shown in *Figure 19.21* gives a number of options. You have the choice of deleting **Unused Only** or **All** render files.

For the purpose of archiving, you should select **All**. The **Unused Only** option is for when you are in the middle of the editing process and want to reduce the library size without affecting the smooth editing that render files provide. You will also want to select both the **Delete Optimized Media** and **Delete Proxy Media** options for archiving purposes.

Figure 19.21 – Delete Generated Library Files

Once you have completed the operation, with the library selected in the browser sidebar, you can check in the inspector to see the size of the library, as well as the disk it is stored on and the amount of **Optimized** and **Proxy** media, which in this case show as empty. The library size is shown when the library is selected in the browser and the inspector will show library properties. At the bottom, you will see **Storage Used for Media and Motion Content**.

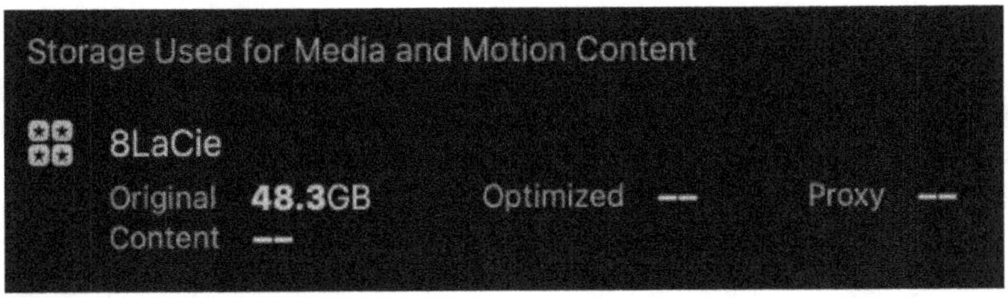

Figure 19.22 – Storage information at the bottom of the inspector

After **Consolidate** and **Delete Generated File** actions are completed, there is a method shown in the next section to be able to reduce the library size even more.

Further reducing the library size

If the size of libraries is a significant concern for you, and you have the available time, there is a method to further decrease the library size. However, it's essential to weigh this against the fact that storage is relatively inexpensive nowadays, and the time investment required to further reduce the library size might not be cost-effective. Nonetheless, if you find it necessary, here's the method.

When the Final Cut Pro project is completed, not all media will have been used in the project. When you archive the library, all the media that you imported will be included, whether you have used it in the project or not. Also, any long clips that have only had a few seconds of them used in the project will go in their entirety into the archive.

The fix for the long clips needs to be done before they are imported. It's impractical to trim them once they have been imported. If you need to know how to cut a clip before you import it, the method was demonstrated in *Chapter 17, Supporting Software Applications for Final Cut Pro*, using the **Trim** feature in the QuickTime App and trimming portions of a long clip.

Removing the unused media is quite simple and only involves moving the project to a new library:

1. Select the project or projects in the browser, and from the **File** menu, select **Move** (or **Copy**) **Project to Library** | **New Library….**

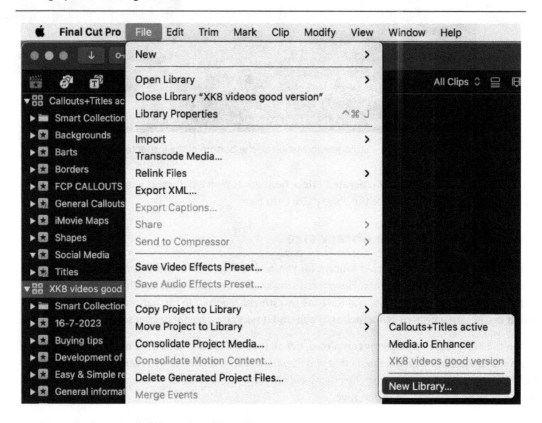

Figure 19.23 – Copy or move to new library

2.   Select **Original media** as shown in *Figure 19.24*. You can also modify the settings as discussed in the *Consolidation* section earlier in this chapter.

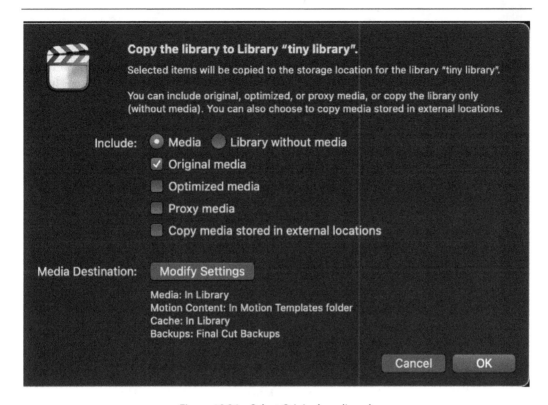

Figure 19.24 – Select Original media only

For me, I copied a project from **XK8 videos good version** to a new library called **tiny library** and the file size was reduced from 49.76 GB to 1.22 GB.

| XK8 videos good version | Today at 8:53 am | 5 Oct 2022 at 1:06 pm | 49.76 GB |
| tiny library | Today at 12:39 pm | Today at 12:39 pm | 1.22 GB |

Figure 19.25 – File size reduced with a new library

When the consolidation and file size reduction is completed, it's time to archive the library, and we will see how to do that in the next section.

Archiving the library

The process of archiving is the simplest of all the operations. Just copy the library to a disk or tape device that you intend to use as the vault for archived libraries. Remember that when you copy from one device to another, the original remains on the first disk so you have two copies. Once the copy is completed, it is wise to check that the copied file is the same size as the original before deleting the original from the first disk. This check is easily done using the Finder **Get info** command. Select both libraries in the Finder, right-click, and select **Get info**. There can be a small difference in size depending on the type of device that the libraries are stored on – as long as they are almost the same, it's OK.

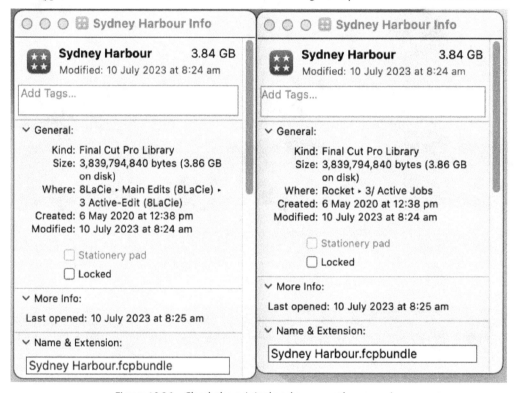

Figure 19.26 – Check the original and copy are the same size

Copying the library to an archive device is not the end of the story; you need to be able to quickly locate the library when you want to restore it from the archive device.

Chances are you will have a number of different devices where your archives are stored. You need to know which disk the library is on without having to mount each disk to search for the library you want to restore.

To avoid having to mount each device, it is useful to be able to index those different devices to quickly locate the library you want to recover. There are software options that will keep an index of the devices. You have seen one of the software options already, called **Final Cut Library Manager**, in *Chapter 17, Supporting Software Applications for Final Cut Pro*. The software that I prefer to use is called **NeoFinder** – both options are discussed in the next section.

Indexing archives

One method of indexing external devices that you are using for archiving is the **Final Cut Library Manager** software utility.

Final Cut Library Manager

This software is purchasable software that is mainly used for reducing the size of libraries, but it will also retain information about any library that has been on any disk, whether it is currently mounted or not.

In the sidebar of **Final Cut Library Manager**, any disk can be selected and the Final Cut Pro libraries that were on that disk the last time it was indexed will be recorded:

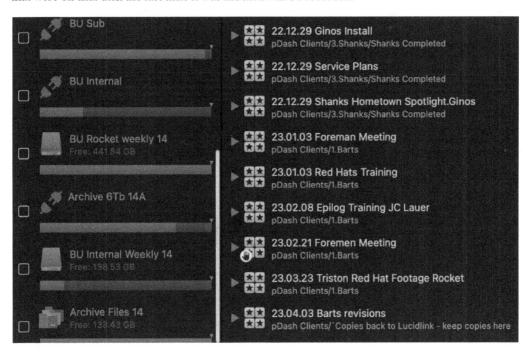

Figure 19.27 – Any disk previously mounted shows in Final Cut Library Manager

NeoFinder

My personal option for indexing is to use **NeoFinder**, which is a $40.00 software utility that keeps an integrated database of storage devices. Download the 7.8.1 version – if you have fewer than 10 devices, the demo license can be used indefinitely for free: `https://www.cdfinder.de/download.html`.

NeoFinder indexes every file while a device is mounted, and the index can be searched when the device is unmounted.

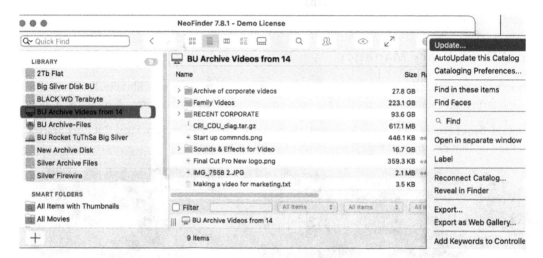

Figure 19.28 – NeoFinder index

To add a new device to the database, click the plus icon at the bottom left. To index the contents of the selected device while it is mounted, click the gear icon at the top right and select **Update**. There are also options to view thumbnails of images so that you can see the contents and not just the filename, without having to mount the device.

Indexing is not the last thing you need to do with your archive devices; they need to be maintained, as discussed in the next section.

Maintaining archive devices

All archive disks need to be backed up just as you do working disks. Archive devices are usually spinning disks so are susceptible to failure over time if frequently used, and are even more likely to fail if they are not used for long periods of time.

Because archive devices are left inactive for long periods of time, they need to be spun up occasionally. I spin my archive devices at the end of every year as part of my housecleaning activities over the festive holiday period.

Summary

In this chapter, we saw the preparation procedures required for archiving libraries as well as storing the original footage.

You learned about the **Consolidate** command, which gathers all the footage used in a library and consolidates it to a location of your choice so that no footage is lost when you open an archived library in the future.

You were shown where Final Cut Pro automatically backs up libraries and how to manage the backups. Automatic backups are designed for project recovery while the editing is still in progress, as opposed to archiving after the video is exported.

You also learned how to recover missing media files with the **Relink Files** command.

You saw the way to remove unneeded render files to save hard disk space using the **Delete Generated Files** command.

You were introduced to software utilities that index libraries stored on unmounted devices so they can be accessed indefinitely in the future.

You now understand the options for ensuring that the devices you archive to are kept up to date and in a condition for you to be able to quickly access the archived libraries.

This was the last chapter of the book, and by now you will be much more proficient in using Final Cut Pro than before you started. Even so, you will always keep learning new techniques and workflows. In my case, while researching this book, I learned many more things than I could have imagined.

Good luck with your editing, and remember: if you don't use it, you will lose it!

Index

A

add action 140
additive colors 438
administrator 533
Advanced LucidLink license 531
Advanced Video Coding High
    Definition (AVCHD) 21
All Curves 493, 494
analogous colors 451-454
Andy's Elastic Aspect 380, 381
Andy's plug-ins
    download link 381
angles 217
animated titles 191
    drop zones 191-194
Apple applications for Final Cut Pro 552
    compressor 570
    iTunes and Photos 586-588
    Keynote 585, 586
    Motion 5 552
    preview 582-584
    QuickTime 578
Apple Motion 5 552
archive devices
    maintaining 658
artificial intelligence (AI) 317

aspect ratio 7
assembler 511
assistant editor 511
Audacity 591, 592
Audio Analysis 317
    Hum Removal 319
    Loudness 318
    Noise Removal 319
    on import 317, 318
audio correction methods
    audio meters, settings 178, 179
    high and low frequencies, removing 180, 181
    loop playback 179
    low volume, increasing methods 179
    male and female voices, enhancing 181, 182
    music, reducing 183
    room noise, removing 180
Audio Enhancements 316
    Equalization options 316
    Voice Isolation 316, 317
audio-focused videos
    assembling 129
audio formats 30
Audio inspector 315, 316
    Audio Configuration 320, 321
    Effects 320

Pan 319
Save Audio Effects Preset 321, 322
audio, in timeline 162, 163
audio filters 165, 166
expanded audio 166-170
sub-frame audio fine-tuning 163, 164
audio issues
fixing, tips and tricks 186-188
modifying, tips and tricks 186-188
audio keyframing 416-419
audio levels
adjusting, in browser 158-161
audio meters
reading 161, 162
audio-only roles
exporting with 185, 186
audio synchronization 216
audio sync, interviews 255-257
Audio Video Interleave (AVI) 21
audio vocal problems, fixing 170
ambient background noise 171, 172
distorted voices 177
echoes 176
fillers 177
voices with variable volume levels 172
wind noise 175, 176
audition feature
using, to replace clips 142-144
Automated Dialog Replacement (ADR) 170
automatic color correction controls 468
Balance Color 469, 470
Match Color 470

B

background rendering 605, 606
BeatMark Pro 272
bins 115

bit depth 8
bit rate/data rate 8
bits per second (bit/s) 8
Blip 545, 546, 548, 549
reference link 549
Boris FX CrumplePop Complete package 400, 401
ClipRemover 402
EchoRemover 401, 402
WindRemover 403, 404
BretFX Power Tools Lite 381
download link 383
Emboss effect 382, 383
PT Border effect 382
Brightness color grading control 468
Broadcast Safe effect 279
B roll 246
browser 103
audio levels, adjusting 158-161
sorting 64-69
browser filters 63
Build In 351
Build Out 351
built-in effects
color-affiliated effects 362
Color Grading Presets 365, 366
non-color-affiliated effects 362, 366
using 362
built-in generators
Elements category 356
Solids category 359-361
using 356
built-in plug-ins 341
creating 377
built-in titles
Bumper/Openers, using 353
Dynamic Titles, using 353
informational titles 342, 343

left lower third, using 349-353
lower thirds, using 348
using 341
built-in transitions
Dissolve category 373
using 373
Wipes category 375-377
Bumper/Openers
Point title 354-356
using 353
bundle 9

C

Cache 647
callouts 99
Canva calculator
URL 457
Captionator 97, 406, 407
categories
media, removing from 63
centralized local server
VPN access to 533
Channel Mixer 440
clip information
exploring 74
method, of exploring 75, 76
ClipRemover 402
clips
adding, to project 116
categorizing 109
grading 109-114
logging 42
replacing, with audition feature 142-144
codec 19
collaboration software 535
Frame.io 543-545
PostLab 535-543

collections 50
color-accurate monitor 458
color-affiliated effects 362
Basics effects category 362, 363
Light effects categories 363, 364
Looks effects category 364, 365
Color Board 309, 310, 446
Color tab 311, 312, 448, 449
Exposure tab 310, 447, 448
Saturation tab 311, 448
color-calibrated monitor 458
color cast 487
color classification 437
cool colors 442
primary colors 438, 439
secondary colors 439, 440
tertiary colors 441
warm colors 441, 442
color correction 461
color curves 473, 489
All color curves 493, 494
eyedropper 494-496
Luma curve 489-493
colored lines, on browser clips 59
analyzing, for people 60
markers 61, 62
color grading 461
Color Grading Presets 365, 366
color harmony 451
Color inspector 307-309
color mask 502-504
color palette
selection 462
colors
reference link 458
color schemes 451
analogous colors 453, 454
complementary colors 452, 453

for non-designers 456, 457
monochromatic colors 452
tetradic colors 455
triadic colors 454
color scopes 473
color spaces
reference link 458
color theory 436, 437
color values 435, 443
color wheels 313, 314, 435, 443-446, 449, 450
Global 314
Highlights 314
Hue 314
Midtones 314
Mix 314
Shadows 314
Temperature 314
Tint 314
CommandPost 589, 590
commercials editors 513
commercial videos
versus entertainment videos 86
complementary colors 451-453
compressor 570
accessing 570-574
opening 574-577
Compressor filter
side effects, fixing 174
using 172-174
conferences and seminars 257
one long event 257, 258
short, independent videos 258, 259
connected clips 116-118
consolidation 642-646
container 19
context-sensitive behavior 295

continuity editing, full-length movies and documentaries
eye-line matching 266
match cutting 265
cool colors 438, 442
corporate video editing 512
corruption
Optical Flow, checking 613, 614
Stabilization, checking 614, 615
cuts, matching to beat
methods 272-274
cutting methods, interviews 241-243
cutting tools 152
Cyan, Magenta, Yellow, and Black (CMYK) 27, 435, 438, 463

D

deinterlacing 26
Delta E 458
Digital Rebellion
reference link 608
director 510
director of photography (DOP) 510
disks
storage 35
types 33, 34
Dissolve category of Transitions 373
Cross Dissolve 374
Fade to Black 374
Flow 374, 375
documentary editing 513
documentary videos 91
dots per inch (DPI) 14
dragging tools 153
drama stories 85
drawing tools 583

Dropbox

collaborating on 525

Final Cut Pro libraries 526

indicators 527

Online only and available offline 527, 528

Dropbox Standard

reference link 528

drop zones 189, 191-194, 339-341

dynamic range 483

Dynamic Titles

using 353

E

EchoRemover 401, 402

effects 189, 199-201, 338

types 201

Elements category generators 356

Counting generator, using 356, 357

Shapes generator, using 357

Timecode generator, using 358, 359

elements, generators

counting 197

placeholders 197

shapes 198

timecode 198

entertainment videos

versus commercial videos 86

Eric Lenz 404

Professionals' Suite of effects 405

events 38-41

export error messages

clearing 616, 617

frame number error message 618, 619

render frame error message 617

extend/shorten clips

reference link 148

external disk

using, reasons for libraries 9-12

eyedropper 494-496

eye-line matching 266

F

family holiday movies 268-271

favorite method

adding to 44

rating as 42, 43

Favorites 38, 42, 239

usage 44

Filespace 529

fillers 177

filming, suggestions to suit multicam editing 210

2-minute rule 211

audio 211

color balance 211

filters 64

Final Cut Library Manager 588, 657

Final Cut Pro

easy fixes 603

hard fixes 609

problem fixing 601-603

SNS EVO, using with 533, 534

unexpected quitting 635, 636

updating 598-601

Final Cut Pro backups

working with 638-642

Final Cut Pro, easy fixes

app, quitting 603

computer restart 603

preferences, resetting 606-608

project, copying 608, 609

render files, deleting 603-605

Final Cut Pro generators 131

Final Cut Pro, hard fixes
corruption, locating 612, 613
export error messages, clearing 616, 617
faulty effect, fixing 610, 611
faulty title, fixing 610, 611
faulty transition, fixing 610, 611
library, opening 623
library, using 625
plug-ins, deleting 612
recovery mode, booting 628
reinstalling 626, 627
user account, using 624, 625
Final Cut Pro libraries
direct transfer 545-549
external disk, using reasons 9-12
storing 9
**Final Cut Pro libraries, storing
and locating media**
camera footage 12, 13
music 14, 15
photos/stills 13, 14
Final Cut Pro User Guide for Mac
reference link 344
Finder 3
media folders, setting up 104-107
template, creating 259-261
fixed playhead 120-122
Flash formats 22
Flow transition 247-249
focus 125
folders 52
Frame.io 543-545
Frame.io free trial option
reference link 549
frame number error message 618, 619
clip effect, replacing 621, 622
clip, replacing 620, 621

frame rates
24 FPS 7
25/30 FPS 7
50/60 FPS 7
120 FPS and above 7
frames per second (FPS) 7
freelance editor 511, 512
freelancer 514
financial reward 515
intensity of work 515
risk/comfort factor 515
schedule 515
time, balancing 515
workload, from client 514
work type, selecting 515
free plug-ins 380
Andy's plug-ins 380
BretFX Power Tools Lite 381
full-length movies and documentaries 264
continuity editing 265
J and L cuts 266, 267
pacing 264
parallel editing (cross-cutting) 266

G

Generator inspector 333, 334
Generators 189, 196
backgrounds 196
elements 197
elements category 131
solids 199
textures 199
Green Screen Keyer effect
reference link 371
group of pictures (GOP) 20

H

H.264/H.265 27, 28
Handbrake 591
  URL 28
HDR format 25
Hide Rejected 64
High-Efficiency Video Coding (HEVC) 27
Highlights wheel 450
histogram 479
hook 88, 268
hue 461
  adjusting 461
hue and saturation curves 496-498
  HUE vs HUE 498
  HUE vs LUMA 500
  HUE vs SAT 499
  LUMA vs SAT 500, 501
  ORANGE vs SAT 501
  SAT vs SAT 501
Hue color grading slider 468
Hue, Saturation, and Lightness
    (HSL) 436, 467, 468
human stories 86

I

image-focused videos
  assembling 129
indexing archives 657
  Final Cut Library Manager 657
  NeoFinder 658
industry groups, requiring video editors
  commercials 513
  corporate 512
  documentary 513
  exploring 512
  movies and TV 513
    social media 512
    trailers 514
informational titles 342, 343
  3D text, using 344-346
  Drop Shadow, using 347, 348
  Face settings, using 346, 347
  Glow, using 347, 348
  Outline, using 347, 348
Information inspector 323-325
  export information 327
  library information 326
  project information 325
initial assembly 101, 103, 127-129, 264
  over-edit, avoiding 129
InqScribe 594
inspector
  keyframing in 419
Institute of Radio Engineers (IRE) 25
instructional videos 98-100
intensity 435
interlaced video 26
interviews 91, 238
  audio sync 255-257
  conducting, with one camera 92
  conducting, with two cameras 92-94
  cutting methods 241-243
  fillers, removing 252-255
  jump cuts, hiding 246
  pre-editing 238-241
  removed clips, restoring 243-246
Intra-frame (I-frame) 20, 21
iTunes 586

J

jam syncing 208
J-cuts 168, 266, 267

job roles
in video production 509
jump cuts 373
jump cuts, hiding in interviews 246
4K footage, using in 1080p timeline 249-252
B roll used 246
Flow transition used 247-249

K

Kelvin (K) 461
Ken Burns on steroids 430-433
Keyer effect 199
keyframes 413-415
adding 425
conventions 420-425
linear/smooth curves, selecting 426, 427
keyframing
in inspector 419
in viewer 425
video animation 429, 430
Keynote 585, 586
Keyper 388, 389
Keyword 103
Keyword Collections 38, 45
creating 45-47
shortcuts, adding to 47-49
keywording 45

L

L-cuts 168, 266, 267
LenoFX Grids 394, 395
LenoFX YouTube Booster 395, 396
letterbox 380
libraries 15-17, 38-41
archiving 656, 657

library information
exploring 74
library size
reducing 653-655
Lock & Load Stabilize plug-in 383-385
LOG footage
manual correction 484, 485
logging 37, 38, 108
Log (logarithmic) profile 408
LOG video 22-24
**lookup tables (LUTs) 22, 70,
408, 409, 484, 516**
lossless compression formats 19
lossy audio formats 30
lossy compression formats 19
lower third titles 342
left lower third, using 348-353
using 348
LucidLink
collaborating with 528, 529
setting up 529-531
URL 533
users, adding 531-533
Luma curve 489-493

M

macOS
updating 598-601
magnetic timeline 123
manual multicam synchronization 216
markers 245
Match Color 470
match cutting 265
Matroska Multimedia Container (MKV) 22
media
importing, directly 107, 108
ingesting 104

removing, from categories 63

transcoding 72-74

media actions

shortcuts for 71, 72

media folders

setting up, in Finder 104-107

media well 339, 355

megabits per second (mbit/s) 8

miscellaneous applications 594

missing media

consolidating 633

relinking 629-633, 647-651

monitor

selecting, considerations 30

monitor calibration 458

hardware calibration 459

online calibration 459

software calibration 459, 460

monitoring angle 217, 224

monochromatic colors 452

Motion 5 552

default plug-ins, modifying 553-568

third-party plug-ins, managing 568-570

Motion 5, panels

library and inspector 555

project 555

timeline 555

timing 555

viewer 555

Motion Content 647

MotionVFX 397

movie editor 513

MPEG-4 Part 14 (MP4) 21

multicam 206

synchronizing 208-210

using, events 206

multicam angle timeline 224

adjustments 217-219

audio levels 225

audio synchronization 224

color matching 226

global adjustments 225

multicam clip

creating 215, 216

multicam editing 211

angle viewer, adjusting 220-224

audio and video mismatches, fixing 219, 220

media, importing and categorizing 211-214

multicam project

angles, correcting 230-232

angles, setting up 228, 229

angles, switching 230

audio issues, fixing 234

editing 226-228

stabilization 232, 233

multicam shoot

simulating, from one camera's
    footage 234, 235

multicam, used for events

concerts 207

conferences 207

feature movies 207

interviews 207

seminars 207

stadium sporting 207

wedding videos 207

N

Neat Video noise reduction 389-392

NeoFinder 658

download link 658

Network-Attached Storage (NAS) 34

Noise Gate 180

noise reduction 390

Nomad software 533

non-Apple applications for
    Final Cut Pro 588
  Audacity 592
  CommandPost 589, 590
  Final Cut Library Manager 588
  Handbrake 591
  miscellaneous applications 594
  Pixelmator Pro 593
  VLC application 590
non-color-affiliated effects 366
  Green Screen Keyer effect 368-371
  Mask effect 371-373
  Scene Removal Mask effect 367, 368
Non-Linear Editors (NLEs) 48, 115, 203

O

online color calculators 457
Open Clip function
  using 70, 71
Open Clip view 69, 70
openers 191
optimized media 72
original media 72
output level 160

P

pacing 151
  conventions, considering 151, 152
pacing, tools 152
  cutting tools 152
  dragging tools 153
  speed controls 153-155
  trimming (clipping) action 153
PaintX 386, 387
Pantone color bridge 464, 465
Pantone color system 464-466

parallel editing style 87
Photos 586
Photoshop 14
Picture Lock 101, 139, 140, 156
picture-locked version 264
pillarbox 380
Pixelmator 14
Pixelmator Pro 584, 593
pixels per inch (PPI) 31
placeholders 90, 131
  alternatives, to adding 132
plots
  types 86, 87
plug-in 189, 203, 339-341
  issues with 203, 204
  media well 342
  terminology 337-339
plug-in folders 17-19
PostLab 535-543
PostLab free trial
  reference link 543
postproduction editing team 511
  assembler 511
  assistant editor 511
  freelance editor 511, 512
  senior video editor 511
pre-editing methods, interviews 238-241
PremiumVFX InfoBars 392-394
preparation procedures, for
    archiving libraries 642
  Cache 647
  consolidation 642-646
  library size, reducing 653-655
  Motion Content 647
  relinking 647-651
  render data, deleting 651-653
presets 281
Preview 14, 582-584

primary colors 438, 439

production team 510

   director 510

   director of photography (DOP) 510

   producer 510

Professionals' Suite for Final Cut Pro X 404

Professionals' Suite of effects 405

projects 115, 116

   clips, adding to 116

   duplicating 133, 134

Project X$_2$7 594

ProRes 26, 27

ProRes Proxy/Proxy 73

ProRes RAW 26

proxy media 35, 72

purchasable plug-ins 383

   Audio correction plug-ins 400

   Captionator 406, 407

   Eric Lenz 404

   Keyper 388, 389

   Lock & Load Stabilize 383-385

   Neat Video noise reduction 389-392

   PaintX 386, 387

   Titles plug-ins 392

Q

QuickTime 578

   clip, combining 580

   clip, trimming 578, 579

   inspector 581

R

RAW video 25

Rec. 709 22

Rec. 2020 25

rectangle tetradic colors 455, 456

Red, Green, and Blue (RGB) 27, 435, 438

redundancy 34

Rejected clips 64

remote video editors

   collaborating, at same premises 523-525

   collaborating, on Dropbox 525

   collaborating, with LucidLink 528, 529

   collaboration between 516

   collaboration software 535

   proxy files, sending 517-523

   SNS EVO, using with Final Cut Pro 533, 534

   VPN access to centralized local server 533

   XML files, sending 517, 518, 522, 523

remove action 140

render data

   deleting 651-653

render frame error message 617

   library project, copying 618

replace action 140

resolution 8

restoring methods, interviews 243-246

RGB Parade 473

ripple edits 146-148

roles 72, 122, 123, 243

   advantages 125, 126

roll edits 149

   reference link 149

root in LucidLink 531

rough cut 101, 103, 130

   projects, duplicating 133, 134

   scratch music, adding 130, 131

round-tripping 570

S

safe zones 280

Saturation color grading slider 468

scopes workflow, in Final Cut Pro 482
   color balance 487-489
   exposure correction 482-484
   manual correction of LOG footage 484, 485
   saturation control 485-487
scratch music
   adding 130, 131
Search functionality
   filtering methods 55-59
   using 54, 55
secondary colors 439
   uses 440
second monitor 30, 31
   using 32, 33
senior video editor 511
sequences 115
Settings/Preferences
   exploring 76-81
shape mask 502-504
ShareBrowser 533, 534
ShareBrowser workflow
   reference link 535
ShareBrowser workflow extension 534
skimmer 120-122, 243
skin tone line 478
slide edit 150
slip edit 150
Smart Collection 38, 49, 50, 103, 240
   adding 50-52
Smart Objects 50
smoothing 305
SNS EVO
   reference link 535
   using, with Final Cut Pro 533, 534
social media editing 512
social media videos 94-98, 267
   key elements 268
Solids category generator 359-361

solid-state drive (SSD) 4
source level 160
speed controls 153-155
spinning beach ball 601
spot cameras 211
Spotlight 649
square tetradic colors 455
Standard Dynamic Range (SDR) 25
standard user 533
stories
   as journey 84
   classifying, reason 85
   drama stories 85
   entertainment versus commercial videos 86
   human stories 86
   literal type 84
   popular type 84
   types 84, 85
storyboards
   creating 90
storyboardthat
   URL 90
Studio Network Solutions (SNS) 533
subframes 77
subtractive model, of color mixing 463

T

tabs, of inspector 296-298
target audience 86
   edit, planning with 89
   understanding 87-89
techniques, complementing editing process
   adjustment layers, adding 279, 280
   angles, cutting with green screen 275-278
   callouts, storing 281, 282
   clips, collapsing into connected
      storylines 288-290

titles and corporate intros, storing 282-285
workspaces, using 285-288
temperature 461
adjusting 461
templates 53
creating 53, 54
tertiary colors 441
tetradic colors 455
rectangle tetradic colors 455, 456
square tetradic colors 455
TextEdit app 339
Text inspector 329, 330
Face checkbox 332, 333
Position division 331
text division 330, 331
third-party plug-ins
uninstalling 410
uninstalling, manually 410, 411
three-point editing 118
timecode 122
accessing 122
timeline 103, 118-120, 189
timeline index 123
timeline view tools 145, 146
ripple edits 146-148
roll edits 149
slide edit 150
slip edit 150
tint 461
adjusting 461
titles 189-191
animated titles 191
text, adding to 194, 195
Titles inspector 327, 328
Titles plug-ins 392
LenoFX Grids 394, 395
LenoFX YouTube Booster 395, 396
MotionVFX 397

PremiumVFX InfoBars 392-394
TOOLFARM 398
to-do marker
using 140-142
TOOLFARM 398
URL 385, 393
Yanobox Motype 2 398-400
Total Running Time (TRT)/picture lock 156
trailer editing 514
Transition inspector 334
transitions 189, 202
categories 202
triadic colors 454
trimming (clipping) action 153
Trim tool 248
TV editors 513

U

unrating 63
Used Media Ranges 60
Users folder 4-6

V

vectorscope 478, 479
video animation
keyframing 429, 430
video codec 19
video file
aspect ratio 7
bit depth 8
bit rate 8
definition 7
resolution 8
video format 19-22
H.264/H.265 27, 28
HDR format 25

interlaced video 26
LOG video 22-24
ProRes 26, 27
RAW video 25
strengths, for different applications 29
Video inspector 299
Crop 302, 303
Distort 302, 303
Effects 299, 300
Rolling Shutter 304-306
Spatial Conform 306, 307
Stabilization 304-306
Transform 301
video post-production
editor/specialists role 103
steps 102, 103
video production
job roles 509
video scopes
displaying 474-476
histogram 479
menu 481
vectorscope 478, 479
Waveformmonitor 476, 477
videos, types
documentary videos 91
instructional video 98-100
interviews 91
planning 91
social media videos 94-98
viewer
keyframing 425
viewer keyframe controls 428
virtual private network (VPN) 545
VLC application 590
Voice Isolation 171

voices, with variable volume levels 172
Compressor filter, using 172-174
side effects of Compressor filter, fixing 174
VPN access
to centralized local server 533

W

warm colors 437, 441, 442
Waveformmonitor 476, 477
weddings 259
cameras, synchronizing 263, 264
media, organizing 259
pre-set keyword collections,
    creating 262, 263
template, creating in Finder 259-261
Windows Media Viewer (WMV) 21
WindRemover 403, 404
Wipes category of Transitions 375-377
workflow extensions 407, 408
workspaces 285

X

XML files
using 184

Y

Yanobox Motype 2 398-400

Packtpub.com

Subscribe to our online digital library for full access to over 7,000 books and videos, as well as industry leading tools to help you plan your personal development and advance your career. For more information, please visit our website.

Why subscribe?

- Spend less time learning and more time coding with practical eBooks and Videos from over 4,000 industry professionals

- Improve your learning with Skill Plans built especially for you

- Get a free eBook or video every month

- Fully searchable for easy access to vital information

- Copy and paste, print, and bookmark content

Did you know that Packt offers eBook versions of every book published, with PDF and ePub files available? You can upgrade to the eBook version at packtpub.com and as a print book customer, you are entitled to a discount on the eBook copy. Get in touch with us at customercare@packtpub.com for more details.

At www.packtpub.com, you can also read a collection of free technical articles, sign up for a range of free newsletters, and receive exclusive discounts and offers on Packt books and eBooks.

Other Books You May Enjoy

If you enjoyed this book, you may be interested in these other books by Packt:

Filmora Efficient Editing

Alexander Zacharias

ISBN: 978-1-80181-420-1

- Navigate Filmora's interface with ease.
- Add and manipulate audio using audio tracks.
- Create high-quality professional videos with advanced features in Filmora.
- Use split screens and Chroma keys to create movie magic.
- Create a gaming video and add humor to it.
- Understand career prospects in the world of video editing.

Video Editing Made Easy with DaVinci Resolve 18

Lance Phillips

ISBN: 978-1-80107-525-1

- Explore how to edit, add effects, and post to social media using the new Cut page.

- Deliver video projects swiftly to a variety of social media formats using the Cut page.

- Fix problems with videos, such as stabilizing footage and syncing audio.

- Enhance the quality of your videos through color correction and other visual effects techniques.

- Discover how to use the Neural Engine AI in the Studio Version of DaVinci Resolve to speed up your work.

Packt is searching for authors like you

If you're interested in becoming an author for Packt, please visit authors.packtpub.com and apply today. We have worked with thousands of developers and tech professionals, just like you, to help them share their insight with the global tech community. You can make a general application, apply for a specific hot topic that we are recruiting an author for, or submit your own idea.

Hi!

I am Bruce G. Macbryde author of *Edit without Tears with Final Cut Pro*. I really hope you enjoyed reading this book and found it useful for increasing your productivity and efficiency using Final Cut Pro.

It would really help me (and other potential readers!) if you could leave a review on Amazon sharing your thoughts on this book.

Go to the link below or scan the QR code to leave your review:

`https://packt.link/r/1804614920`

Your review will help me to understand what's worked well in this book, and what could be improved upon for future editions, so it really is appreciated.

Best Wishes,

Bruce G. Macbryde

Download a free PDF copy of this book

Thanks for purchasing this book!

Do you like to read on the go but are unable to carry your print books everywhere?

Is your eBook purchase not compatible with the device of your choice?

Don't worry, now with every Packt book you get a DRM-free PDF version of that book at no cost.

Read anywhere, any place, on any device. Search, copy, and paste code from your favorite technical books directly into your application.

The perks don't stop there, you can get exclusive access to discounts, newsletters, and great free content in your inbox daily

Follow these simple steps to get the benefits:

1. Scan the QR code or visit the link below

https://packt.link/free-ebook/978-1-80461-492-1

2. Submit your proof of purchase
3. That's it! We'll send your free PDF and other benefits to your email directly

www.ingramcontent.com/pod-product-compliance
Lightning Source LLC
Chambersburg PA
CBHW060633060326
40690CB00020B/4385